The International Missile Bazaar

The International Missile Bazaar

The New Suppliers' Network

EDITED BY
William C. Potter
and Harlan W. Jencks

Routledge
Taylor & Francis Group
LONDON AND NEW YORK

First published 1994 by Westview Press, Inc.

Published 2019 by Routledge
52 Vanderbilt Avenue, New York, NY 10017
2 Park Square, Milton Park, Abingdon, Oxon OX14 4RN

Routledge is an imprint of the Taylor & Francis Group, an informa business

Copyright © 1994 Taylor & Francis

All rights reserved. No part of this book may be reprinted or reproduced or utilised in any form or by any electronic, mechanical, or other means, now known or hereafter invented, including photocopying and recording, or in any information storage or retrieval system, without permission in writing from the publishers.

Notice:
Product or corporate names may be trademarks or registered trademarks, and are used only for identification and explanation without intent to infringe.

Library of Congress Cataloging-in-Publication Data
The International missile bazaar : the new suppliers' network / edited by William C. Potter and Harlan W. Jencks.
p. cm.
Includes bibliographical references and index.
ISBN 0-8133-8796-5
1. Guided missile industries. 2. Arms transfers. I. Potter, William C. II. Jencks, Harlan W.
HD9744.P732I57 1994
338.4'76234519—dc20 93-29533
CIP

ISBN 13: 978-0-367-29318-5 (hbk)

ISBN 13: 978-0-367-30864-3 (pbk)

Dedicated to
Anna and Cheryl

Contents

Introduction

William C. Potter

The end of the Cold War and the greatly diminished threat of superpower conflict has dramatically altered international politics. Although the positive effects of this transformation are easily recognizable, the war in the Persian Gulf and the savage fighting in what was formerly Yugoslavia are grim reminders of the persistence and growth of other very real threats to global peace and security. One poorly understood but increasingly significant danger involves the proliferation of ballistic missiles.

The number of states capable of selling ballistic missile technology, missile components, and the missiles themselves on the international market is large and growing. Argentina, Brazil, India, Iran, Iraq, Israel, North Korea, Pakistan, China, and South Korea are among the countries often noted as actual or potential emerging suppliers.

Many nonproliferation specialists are concerned that the emergence of new missile suppliers not bound by existing international agreements poses a major threat to the nonproliferation regime. Concern regarding the issue of ballistic missile proliferation, however, has not been matched by systematic data collection and analysis, especially that of a comparative nature. There is little agreement, for example, on the nature or magnitude of the problem, the motivations and disincentives for emerging suppliers to enter the international market, the extent to which the new suppliers have departed from the export practices of the more established supplier states, or the processes by which technology is transferred. There is even less agreement about appropriate means to cope with the perceived problem. The purpose of this book, a companion volume to an earlier study on the emerging nuclear suppliers, is to remedy, at least in part, this deficiency.[1]

This study is a product of an ongoing research project at the Monterey Institute of International Studies on International Missile Proliferation (IMP). The first phase of the project entailed development of a conceptual framework for analyzing the emerging missile suppliers. That framework identifies four basic categories of information relevant to understanding the behavior of missile suppliers: transactions, domestic structure, capabilities, and norms. Data on these missile supplier attributes are collected and recorded in machine readable form. This data collection, the product of the second phase of the IMP project, is now accessible on-line and contains thousands of entries from dozens of publications.

The third phase of the project entailed the preparation of a series of comparative case studies of the emerging missile suppliers. These studies, and the management strategies derived from them, constitute the following chapters.

In order to sharpen the volume's focus and to enhance the generalizability of the findings, each of the country case study authors was asked to address the same set of research questions. These questions were grouped under the headings "Transactions," "Capabilities," "Structure," and "Norms."

Questions Pertaining to Transactions

1. What motivates the missile supplier to enter the international market (e.g., hard currency, prestige, political influence, foothold in markets, subsidies for domestic space program, barter arrangements for coveted items, etc.)?
2. What are the major disincentives (economic and otherwise) for entering the international missile market?
3. What have been the major missile transactions involving missile technology, equipment, components, and services?
4. What has been the nature of the most important missile trade agreements (e.g., countertrade, offsets, coproduction agreements)?
5. Does the country serve as a transshipper (i.e., middleman) for missile transactions? If so, for what items and for what countries?
6. What revenues have been derived from missile exports and what revenues are projected?
7. Have there been instances when the country has been approached for the sale of missiles or missile-related items and services but declined? What were the items and states involved?
8. To what extent has the state been engaged in joint venture activities regarding missile trade?
9. What instances, if any, can you discern of illegal/blackmarket activity?
10. What is your overall assessment of the state's missile export activity (i.e., prudent, reckless)?
11. What restrictions or guarantees does the state require as a condition of export?
12. To what extent has the country's export behavior changed over time? If it has changed, why?

Questions Pertaining to Capabilities

1. What is the present and planned capability of the country to produce missile technology, components, and entire missiles?
2. What is the present and planned space launch capability?
3. What are the major bottlenecks/obstacles in acquiring a missile production capability?

Questions Pertaining to Structure

1. What are the relevant export licensing regulations and procedures? What new regulations, if any are planned?
2. What are the relevant governmental agency actors in the export licensing process? What is their relevant weight?
3. What role is played by the private sector, quasigovernmental actors, and multinationals in decisions regarding missile exports?
4. What are the country's major firms engaged in commerce in missiles and missile-related services?

Questions Pertaining to Norms

1. What are the country's declaratory policies regarding missile exports?
2. What is the country's attitude toward the Missile Technology Control Regime (MTCR)?
3. To what extent are prevailing views on missile exports shared by the different parties and political actors?
4. What explains the norms that are discerned?
5. What are the prevailing public attitudes toward missile exports?
6. Is there much linkage in governmental policy between nuclear and missile exports or in declaratory policy toward the Nuclear Nonproliferation Treaty (NPT) and the MTCR?
7. What changes in attitude regarding missile exports and the MTCR can one discern over time? Are any developments likely to lead to a change in attitudes in the short term?

This volume would not have been possible without the efforts of a large number of individuals. The enthusiasm, energy, and insights of the IMP Project staff were a continual source of inspiration. The contributions of IMP analysts Tim McCarthy and Deborah Ozga merit special thanks. Cheryl Jencks and Pat Levac also provided invaluable assistance in preparing the manuscript for publication.

The IMP Project and this volume were made possible by generous grants from the Carnegie Corporation, the Rockefeller Brothers Fund, the

Rockefeller Family & Associates, the Rockefeller Foundation, and the W. Alton Jones Foundation.

Notes

1. See William C. Potter, ed. *International Nuclear Trade and Nonproliferation: The Challenge of the Emerging Suppliers*. Lexington Books, 1990.

About the Contributors

Joseph S. Bermudez, Jr. is an author, analyst and lecturer on ballistic missile developments in the Third World as well as North Korean military and intelligence affairs. His analysis has appeared in such diverse locations as *The Daily Yomiuri, The Financial Times, Jane's Defence Weekly, Jane's Intelligence Review, Japan Military Review, The Korea Times, Marine Corps Gazette, The New York Times, Sekai Nippo, Voice of America, The Washington Post, The Washington Times,* and others. His works are consulted by the United States and other governments. He is currently a consultant to *Jane's Intelligence Review.*

Cameron Binkley, a former army intelligence analyst, is a graduate of the University of Denver and the Monterey Institute of International Studies. From 1990 to 1992, he served as the first manager of MIIS's International Missile Proliferation Project.

Péricles Gasparini Alves is currently completing his Ph.D. at the Graduate Institute of International Studies and the University of Geneva, Switzerland. He is the author of *The Interest of Nonpossessor Nations in the Draft Chemical Weapons Convention: a Brazilian Case Study.* His most recent publication, *Access to Outer Space Technologies: Implications for International Security,* was published by the United Nations Institute for Disarmament Research, at which he holds a position of Research Associate. He is currently working on a publication on Transparency and the Transfer of Sensitive Technology Relating to Outer Space.

Peter Hayes is currently Senior Researcher at Nautilus Pacific Research, in Berkeley California. He writes widely on security affairs in the Asia-Pacific region and is the author of *Pacific Powderkeg: American Nuclear Dilemmas in Korea* (Free Press, 1990), *International Missile Trade in the Two Koreas* (PNS, 1993), and co-author of *American Lake: Nuclear Peril in the Pacific* (Penguin, 1987), among other works. He holds his doctorate from the Energy and Resources Group at the University of California at Berkeley.

Hua Di is a Research Associate at the Center for International Security and Arms Control at Stanford University, and formerly Director of CITIC Research International in Beijing, PRC. He received an engineering degree from Moscow Aviation Institute in the 1950s, and worked in China's ICBM programs from 1960 to 1984, earning a national prize in 1978. Between 1984 and 1986, he studied strategic issues in the Institute of American Studies, Chinese Academy of Social Sciences. He has written widely on space technology, nuclear strategy, international relations, and arms control.

Harlan W. Jencks is Senior Research Associate of the International Missile Proliferation Project at the Monterey Institute of International Studies, and a Research Associate of the Center for Chinese Studies at the University of California, Berkeley. He is the author of *Some Political and Military Implications of Soviet Warplane Sales to the PRC* (1991) and *From Muskets to Missiles: Politics and Professionalism in the Chinese Army, 1945–1981* (1982). He has published extensively on international security affairs in Asia, especially concerning China.

Mark H. Kagan is a consultant and journalist in the areas of defense, chemical and biological warfare, arms control, technology transfer, and the Middle East. Formerly, he was director of the Project on Chemical and Biological Arms Control at the non-profit Committee for National Security. He has been a correspondent for *MidEast Markets* and Jane's Information Group. From 1981 to 1985, he was a Middle East analyst for the National Security Agency and taught at the National Cryptologic School. He then worked at the Defense Intelligence Agency covering the international arms trade in the Middle East. He has studied in Israel and Egypt.

Aaron Karp is a researcher for the Stiftung Wissenschaft und Politik (the German RAND Corporation) in Ebenhausen, Germany, and the Stockholm International Peace Research Institute. A specialist on regional security, he began working on missile proliferation as an analyst for the US Arms Control and Disarmament Agency in the late 1970s. He is the author of numerous articles and monographs on the subject, including the 1990 *Report of the United Nations Secretary-General on South Africa's Ballistic Missile Capability.*

Timothy V. McCarthy is Senior Research Associate at the Program for Nonproliferation Studies at the Monterey Institute of International Studies. He is the author of *A Chronology of PRC Missile Trade and Developments* (1992), and several studies and articles dealing with missile proliferation issues.

Janne E. Nolan, Senior Fellow at the Brookings Institution, is the author of *Trappings of Power: Ballistic Missiles in the Third World* (1991) and *Guardians of the Arsenal: The Politics of Nuclear Strategy* (1989). She previously served as a Senior Designee to the Senate Armed Services Committee, a Senior Consultant at Science Applications International Corporation, and as an official of the US Arms Control and Disarmament Agency during the Carter Administration.

William C. Potter is Professor and Director of the Center for Russian and Eurasian Studies at the Monterey Institute of International Studies. He also directs the MIIS Program for Nonproliferation Studies. He is the author of *Nuclear Power and Nonproliferation: An Interdisciplinary Perspective*

(1982), and *Nuclear Profiles of the Soviet Successor States* (1993); editor of *Verification and SALT: The Challenge of Strategic Deception* (1980), *Verification and Arms Control* (1985), and *International Nuclear Trade and Nonproliferation* (1990); and the co-editor of *Soviet Decisionmaking for National Security* (1984), *The Nuclear Suppliers and Nonproliferation* (1985), and *Continuity and Change in Soviet-East European Relations* (1989). He also has contributed to numerous scholarly books and journals. He has served as a consultant to Lawrence Livermore National Laboratory, the RAND Corporation, and the Jet Propulsion Laboratory.

Gerald M. Steinberg is Senior Lecturer, Department of Political Studies and Director, Center for Strategic Studies, Bar Ilan University in Ramat Gan, Israel. His research focuses on military strategy and technology, arms control, and the impact of new technology on international relations. His publications include "Arms Control in the Middle East" in the *Encyclopedia of Arms Control and Disarmament; Deterrence, Defense or Arms Control: Israeli Perceptions and Responses for the 1990s*; and *Lost in Space: The Domestic Politics of the Strategic Defense Initiative.*

Scott D. Tollefson is Assistant Professor of Comparative Politics and Latin American Studies in the Department of National Security Affairs at the Naval Postgraduate School, Monterey, California. He is the author of *Brazilian Arms Transfers, Ballistic Missiles, and Foreign Policy: The Search for Autonomy* (Ph.D. dissertation, The Johns Hopkins University, 1991) and various articles on Brazilian politics and foreign policy.

1

The Maturation of Ballistic Missile Proliferation

Aaron Karp

It is hard to recall, but as recently as the mid-1980s the threat of missile proliferation seemed remote if not fanciful. A few well publicized launches had raised Western awareness of regional interest in long-range rocketry. But any such concerns were trifling compared to the overwhelming dangers of superpower nuclear confrontation. While no one, to my knowledge, disputed the importance of the issue, only a handful of officials and analysts were prepared to take it seriously.

This situation changed suddenly only five years ago. In 1987–88, missile proliferation became a topic for discussion at the highest levels of government, at international summits, in the press and at academic meetings. A rapid series of revelations forced the issue upon the international agenda. First came the disclosure of the Argentine-Egyptian-Iraqi *Condor II* intermediate range missile program, then the dramatic use of hundreds of ballistic missiles in the War of the Cities between Iran and Iraq. Soon long-range rocket projects were discovered in virtually every region of the world.

In the eyes of many, missile proliferation is a symbol of the anarchy prevailing after the Cold War. The problem appeared just as the superpower confrontation was receding. Not since the world learned of the atomic bomb in August 1945 has a major threat to international security appeared so abruptly. The discovery that dozens of regional actors possessed or were experimenting with large rockets was uniquely chilling. Potentially armed with anything from conventional explosives to thermonuclear warheads, these new weapons threaten to recreate the balance of terror from which the world has just escaped.

Today, five years after the issue rose to the top of the international agenda, is an especially appropriate moment for reflection on the nature of missile proliferation. What have we learned and what more can be done to reduce its dangers? Perhaps most surprising is the apparent maturity of the issue; while surprises undoubtedly await us at every turn, the basic form and substance of the issue seems increasingly complete. The most important implication of this swift maturity is the ability to draw general conclusions about the nature of the problem and the best responses.

To be sure, there are limits to such generalizations. In this as in other proliferation issues every country is unique and ultimately must be dealt with individually. But policy and analysis rely upon a general consensus, a prevailing wisdom. Although we cannot afford to become relaxed about the threat or conceited about our assessments, we can speak with growing confidence about many aspects of the problem such as the actors involved, their motives, the forces regulating their programs, and the best ways to deal with the challenges they create.

The Meaning of a Mature Issue

Contrary to the commonplace view that security problems only become more elusive over time, a growing consensus has emerged about the nature of missile proliferation. In this sense, missile proliferation can be described as a mature policy issue. A mature policy issue is characterized by a narrowing of the discussion, reflecting a consensus over intellectual and policy approaches. Although serious, often acrimonious debates remain, these are increasingly constrained by shared assumptions and goals. While plenty of room remains for mistakes and surprises, in a mature field these tend to concern matters of fact, not basic assumptions.

Mature issues in international politics are distinguished by the following characteristics:

- an accepted foundation of descriptive information, a consensus on the basic facts, covering the most important aspects of the problem and forming a basis for discussion;
- the articulation of a wide range of views, establishing a spectrum of positions on the issue;
- a shared vision unites most leading actors, who agree on which goals to pursue and how best to achieve them;
- basic institutions are established and widely (but not universally) accepted, including national bureaucracies and international organizations such as alliances or groups.

These characteristics do not approach the degree of consensus required to proclaim an international regime.[1] While regimes emerge very rarely among international security issues, the less demanding characteristics of maturity more accurately fit security issues where there is substantial consensus and cooperation, even if it is far from complete. Unlike an international regime, a mature issue may remain highly contentious.

The maturity of an issue, rather, reflects the narrowing of debate. With a consensus on basic principles established and growing, debates become less frequent and tend to focus on increasingly particular issues. One group, whose ranks include most—but not necessarily all—major actors, dominates treatment of the issue, insuring that when disputes erupt they will increasingly tend to be treated the same way. Individual countries or small groups may actively oppose the dominant coalition, but their voices are in the minority and become isolated. Serious and sometimes alarming disputes regarding the issue still may cleave the international community, but the solidification of positions makes debate increasingly formal and predictable.

By giving structure and purpose to both inquiry and policy, maturity is synonymous to the idea of a scientific paradigm, although it applies to much more specific issues than Thomas Kuhn had in mind.[2] A closer analogy can be drawn to an epistemic community or a group of experts sharing basic assumptions and goals. While such communities are usually associated with broad international cooperation, they also can be an important part of smaller multi-national alliances or groups.[3] Like most issues of international security, missile proliferation remains far too controversial between nations to constitute an international regime, with sharp divisions still separating controllers and proliferators. But the rapid intellectual development of the subject makes it a mature one.

A mature policy issue is not without debate, but among most leading actors disagreements are not over basic facts, causal relationships, or long term objectives. Instead disputes focus on tailoring means to achieve widely accepted goals. Nor does the maturity of a policy issue have to do with its age. Many of the oldest issues of international security remain among the least mature, including the causes of war, the arms trade, and the relationship between economics and security. Despite its extreme youth, missile proliferation already joins a smaller group of issues in international security, issues distinguished by the narrowing of debate.

Prominent among mature issues in international security are nuclear deterrence and arms control and nuclear proliferation. Other examples include confidence building, crisis management, sanctions, surprise attack and weapons collaboration. The maturity of nuclear deterrence took almost

30 years after the concept was articulated by Bernard Brodie in 1946. Widespread advocacy of nuclear war fighting in the West yielded to acceptance of deterrence by the mid-1960s. But maturity did not arrive until the race for strategic superiority was abandoned in the early 1970s and deterrence was codified through arms control.[4] Subsequent debates—over targeting policy, extended deterrence, new weapons and ABM treaty interpretation—did not focus on the importance of deterrence itself. Instead, in the style of a mature issue, later debates stressed applied questions of how best to strengthen deterrence and crisis stability. War fighting advocates remain, as do arms control skeptics, but their views have become increasingly marginal.

The debate over nuclear proliferation took even longer to mature. The positions of advocates and opponents of nuclear weapons were clear within a year of the July 1945 Trinity test. Yet the basic arguments of proliferation advocates were incomplete before the early 1980s, when the strongest arguments in favor of widespread acquisition appeared.[5] The center of the spectrum was not filled until the early 1980s when analysts began examining the problem of how to manage the consequences of proliferation when it could not be stopped.[6] In a political sense maturity came even later; even a document as fundamental as the 1968 NPT did not win the support of the leading powers until 1992, when China and France finally joined. Several countries still keep the nuclear option open, but they are more and more isolated.

The rapid maturation of missile proliferation is due largely to the pioneering work in nuclear deterrence and nuclear proliferation. This provided much of the intellectual foundation for understanding the new issue. A second factor was the nature of missile technology itself, which dictates a narrow path of development with few options for its acquisition. This made it possible to make sense of national programs almost as quickly as they were identified. Finally, when the issue began to be widely recognized there already was a vast amount of raw information, further aiding understanding and consensus. In a sense, we knew how to deal with the issue even before it was identified. This undoubtedly will prove true for other new proliferation issues that emerge in the future.

Trends and Capabilities

The discovery of missile proliferation in the late 1980s was such a shock for many observers that it led to exaggeration of the problem. Press reports contributed to the alarm and confusion by revealing dozens of previously obscure regional rocket projects, typically implying these had only recently started and were close to establishing complete regional strategic forces. Public officials in America and elsewhere wove these tales into a lurid picture of rockets out of control. The hype made it easy to overlook the fact that most regional rocket projects had started years or decades ago and few showed signs of rapid progress.

The intervening years have helped separate the wheat from the chaff. There can be no doubt that missile proliferation poses a grave threat to international peace and stability. But it is misleading to view it as a uniform threat; the challenge of missile proliferation varies significantly from country to country. Missile proliferators can be divided into three categories, depending mostly on their technical capabilities: those with substantial indigenous technical resources capable of creating their own strategic missile forces, those with sufficient resources to conduct rocketry development but only with large-scale foreign help, and those dependent on foreign suppliers for entire missile systems.

The first category of missile proliferators, those capable of indigenously developing a complete strategic missile force, is very exclusive. Of all regional powers, only Israel both has developed and deployed its own long-range missile forces. Israel has invested in rocketry R&D systematically since the early 1960s, culminating in the current *Jericho II-Shavit* series, which appears to be fully integrated into its strategic forces. Israel relied extensively on foreign technology—mostly from France—in the early years. Today it has the only truly indigenous regional rocket program among all emerging powers, with little need for foreign assistance.

The only other regional power with comparable technical capabilities is India. The Indian research program is as old as Israel's and considerably larger in scale, although it has not demonstrated equal coherence. With resources divided among several competing civilian and military projects, India has been unable to bring any but the smallest to completion.[7] Nor has New Delhi made strategic decisions establishing clear goals for these projects. Instead, India's rocketry programs exhibit the symptoms of a vague experiment. Despite several test launches of large civilian and military rockets since 1980, little has been accomplished beyond showing long-run potential. Such demonstrations are not without impact; with the launch of the PSLV booster scheduled for 1993, India will mark the ability to develop ICBMs.

North Korea is the other nation known to be developing a strategic rocket force on its own.[8] Although its capabilities are more limited, North Korea stands out for its goals, as much economic as military. Work started in the early 1970s, but there was little progress until the early 1980s when the program was wedded exclusively to SCUD technology. By 1987, SCUD copies were in series production and sold to Iran. An extended-range version was transferred to Syria and Libya in 1992 and assembly arranged for Iran and possibly Egypt. With a 1000 km version under development, North Korea has reached the limits of SCUD technology and seems unlikely to make further advances unless a new source of technology can be found.

After these countries follow a second class that has experimented with large-scale rocket technology but, for one reason or another, has not been able to extend this work beyond the prototype stage. All relied extensively on foreign assistance and have had great difficulty since it became difficult to acquire in the late-1980s. Several dropped their programs before the metal-cutting stage where expenses swiftly rise. Others probably were never committed to the idea of full scale development and abandoned it after some initial experiments, as appears to have been the case in Indonesia, South Korea and Taiwan. A few like Argentina, Brazil, Egypt and South Africa downgraded their programs as regional tensions eased and to avoid antagonizing outside powers, especially the United States. Others like Iran, Libya, and Pakistan found it infinitely easier to rely on missiles purchased from China or North Korea. And one country—Iraq—was forced to stop by the military intervention of UN forces. With their own programs moribund, several of these countries now fall to the third tier.

The overwhelming question in these moribund cases is what technology and what interest remain? Can they still develop long range rockets within a decade or so? Or must they start virtually from scratch? One of the most daunting questions in assessing quiescent missile programs is determining whether a project is over permanently, if technical resources have been shelved for future applications, or if design and development work actually continue. In countries where the armed forces and other agencies have substantial autonomy it is entirely possible for relevant work to continue in extreme secrecy, even without the knowledge or consent of the central government.[9]

A third and final group includes those countries relying entirely on foreign supplied missiles. These countries are both the most susceptible to control and the most volatile; in lieu of foreign help there is little they can accomplish, but one shipment can give strategic clout overnight. The most extreme example is Iraq, which relied on foreign suppliers for all the ballistic missiles it deployed—its 15-year R&D program failed to generate a single usable missile up to the moment that the UN Special Commission began to take it apart. In unique cases, Afghanistan received more than 2,000 SCUDs from Moscow while China furnished Saudi Arabia with DF-3 IRBMs. But these cases appear to be exceptional. Ordinary recipients got only token numbers during the Cold War; from this perspective the small missile forces of countries like Algeria, Cuba and Yemen appear to be historical accidents, not harbingers of future trends. But Libya, Pakistan and Syria have shown how post-Cold War diplomacy offers opportunities to buy from new suppliers if one is willing to endure the financial and diplomatic cost.

The threat these various countries pose to international security varies greatly, as does their susceptibility to international control. A few countries more may be able to build and deploy large rockets on their own in the long run. Their progress, however, tends to be so deliberate it is readily monitored and scrutinized. Consequently they can be countered one way or another long before they become seriously de stabilizing, leaving time for regional arms control and outside reactions. The most immediate danger arises from short range weapons like the ubiquitous SCUD which still can be purchased from foreign suppliers. Unlike long range rockets, which are extremely difficult to buy abroad and equally difficult to improvise, short range missiles can be bought quickly in large numbers, instantly creating grave and permanent threats.

Missile Capabilities

Measuring a nation's weapons almost always has proven easier than determining what it can do with them, much less what it will do. The problem is an old one in international security, far older than missile proliferation. It reflects the inherent unpredictability of war itself. As Clausewitz made clear, war follows rules and principles, but it always is unique in its manifestations.[10] In the end the effect of ballistic missiles in combat depends on too many variables for prediction to be easy.

Only nuclear warheads make long range rockets universally decisive weapons. Although aircraft usually can deliver nuclear weapons effectively, missiles remain the delivery system of choice, especially when they have longer range, because of their suddenness and extreme difficulty to intercept. But very few regional powers can acquire nuclear warheads today, possibly just Israel, Pakistan and India. The missiles of other regional powers only carry conventional explosives or possibly chemical munitions. The question of how effective ballistic or cruise missiles can be under such circumstances is highly controversial.

History offers several examples of the use of conventionally armed missiles in armed conflict, each with different effects and implications:

- The effect of the 4300 V-2s Hitler fired operationally starting in September 1944 is confused by the simultaneous use of four times as many V-1 cruise missiles. Attacks by these notoriously unreliable and inaccurate weapons were dispersed among too many targets to make best use of their conventional armament. Nonetheless, the effect on Britain was sufficient to prompt Eisenhower to write that earlier use could have prevented the D-Day invasion.[11]

- The Egyptian and Syrian attacks during the 1973 war were too small and inaccurate to have much military effect, while Israel minimized the impact on the public by censoring reports.[12]
- On 16 April 1986 Libya responded to the American bombing of Tripoli by firing two SCUD missiles at a US Coast Guard station on Lampedusea. The missiles fell short but had a cautionary effect on some Mediterranean governments.
- After six years of intermittent missile attacks, Iran publicized the roughly 190 Iraqi missile strikes on Tehran during the 1988 War of the Cities in an attempt to win international sympathy. This only helped terrorize its demoralized people, contributing to Iran's defeat.[13] Iraq revealed little about the roughly 90 missile strikes on Baghdad and rode them out with little effect.
- In Afghanistan between November 1988 and the war's end in May 1992, the Soviet Union and the Kabul government fired over 2,000 SCUD at rebel targets, in much the same way the US used B-52 strikes in the terminal stages of the Vietnam war. The attacks occasionally caused serious destruction, inhibiting the insurgents from concentrating their forces.[14] It is feasible that this helped the Kabul government survive temporarily.
- Finally, Iraq's SCUD attacks on Israel in 1991 with at least 38 missiles caused widespread destruction but only one direct death. Even so, Israeli public life came to a virtual halt and its strategic priorities were permanently altered. As Allied countermeasures took effect, and greatly feared chemically armed missiles failed to materialize, these anxieties diminished.[15] The effects of a like number of SCUD attacks on Saudi Arabia were far less dramatic, due to geographic considerations and the better performance of *Patriots* there. Even so, SCUD suppression tied up over 15% of the enormous Allied air war.

The clearest theme running through these cases is the limited effect of conventionally armed missiles. With high explosives, missile attacks seldom are decisive in and of themselves. Their impact is mitigated by their unreliability and inaccuracy, by targeting choices, geography, numbers, an opponent's morale and ability to take countermeasures. Chemical or biological weapons may change this, but only nuclear warheads make ballistic missiles decisive weapons with certainty.[16] Consequently there is a natural and justifiable tendency to view missile proliferation as a handmaiden of nuclear proliferation, to believe that missile proliferation does not matter as much if the nuclear proliferation problem is dealt with first.[17]

The significance of ballistic missiles in and of themselves is the subject of vigorous debate. One side, stressing the importance of their symbolic as well as their military effects, maintains that even small numbers of conventionally armed missiles can be highly significant politically. Symbolic attacks in war can be of great importance—one only need recall the 1942 Doolittle raid on Japan, or the Allied raid on Dieppe.[18] At a minimum, such actions prove that the enemy is not invulnerable and that one's own cause is not lost. In greater numbers, even conventionally armed missiles can play havoc against large targets like cities, air fields, or infantry concentrations. Conventionally armed missiles, moreover, may be a sign of a country's intent to deploy its missiles later with chemical or nuclear warheads.[19]

The other side has pointed out that in most circumstances manned aircraft are more effective delivery systems, carrying greater conventional payloads with greater accuracy through all but the most hermetic air defenses. Regional ballistic missiles forces tend to be too small and too inaccurate to seriously threaten countries within the region, let alone countries further away. Their military threat is minimal and can be dismissed in all but the most particular circumstances.[20] From this perspective regional ballistic missiles are, like the horse cavalry or the battleship after World War One, weapons receiving far more attention than they deserve.[21]

Unfortunately, the debate clouds our understanding of missile proliferation more than it illuminates. It has been needlessly polarized by interest groups re-fighting the Cold War, recapitulating earlier debates over the H-bomb, ABM, MX basing, INF or the SDI. Now, as in those ritualized debates, one side typically exaggerates the threat and urges military confrontation, stressing the seriousness of the dangers to Western security and the need for rapid acquisition of new weapons in response. The other side minimizes the adversary's capabilities and urges political accommodation, arguing that the threat is not so serious and that technical responses will not work anyway.[22]

In the current debate over missile proliferation the positions and arguments are virtually the same as in those Cold War debates, only the names of the countries and weapons have changed. The debate is not really about missile proliferation at all, rather it centers on the politics of SDI versus arms control. The SDI community has exaggerated the threat from ballistic missile proliferation, trying to justify variants of schemes originally devised to counter Soviet missiles. Critiques from the arms control community tend to deride the missile proliferation threat in order to fight SDI-permutations and to assure the sanctity of the 1972 ABM Treaty. In reality it is hard to believe that future security will be based on either a massive defensive scheme or a treaty written to manage Soviet-U.S. relations during the Cold War.

Both perspectives make valid points: the symbolic salience of ballistic missiles is peerless among modern weapons, especially as an instrument of terror and political tool in peacetime; but in wartime other weapons like manned aircraft must be taken no less seriously. On balance, conventionally armed missiles are mostly political weapons, but their military effects cannot be disregarded. National leaders must deal with both aspects of the problem.

Balanced appreciation of the capabilities of ballistic missiles must consider the specific forces and countries involved. Where large quantities of short-range missiles can reach major targets, even with conventional armament they can be militarily significant. But longer-range missiles are too costly to be deployed in such quantities. They are unlikely to be militarily effective without nuclear—or possibly chemical—warheads, although they may have great symbolic clout regardless. More specific assessments of regional capabilities must consider not just the characteristics of regional missile forces and geography, but the operational doctrine of the armed forces, government policy, the resolve of national leaders, and the morale of their people.

The Market and Foreign Technology Transactions

The mechanisms of missile proliferation range from sales of complete rockets to transfers of arcane bits of equipment. Uniting almost all missile proliferators, however, is reliance on foreign technology. No regional actor has deployed operational ballistic missiles or space launch systems without relying on foreign technology. A few of the most advanced regional powers—the first group above—have accumulated enough foreign assistance to become largely autonomous. Yet control over the transfer of technology remains the most effective instrument in efforts to control the spread of missiles, especially over the short run. Deprived of foreign technical assistance, the vast majority of regional missile projects have come to a halt. Even in the most advanced regional powers the rate of progress slows significantly.

The trade in rocket technology has narrowed over the years. By 1992, only North Korea still is known to export missiles with ranges over 300 km. With sources of large missile systems drying up, transfers of short-range missiles, components, and manufacturing technologies have become the most important aspect of the trade. In these areas as well, most potential exporters have become increasingly restrictive. By 1992, the missile technology trade had shrunk to a fraction of its dimensions five years earlier. What remained were alarming exceptions, proof that vigilance never can be relaxed.

The only countries that continue to license major exports of ballistic missiles or related technology do so almost exclusively for economic motives. Income from such transactions tends to go directly to the agency making the sale, be it the armed forces or civilian space agency, subsidizing their own undertakings. The temptations can be great; for supplying DF-3 IRBMs to Saudi Arabia, the Chinese Army earned an estimated $2.5–3.5 billion, North Korea's sale of some 100 SCUDs to Iran in 1987 was the largest part of a $500 million deal, while Russia hoped to earn $250 million in the early 1990s furnishing India with space launch engines.

Among countries adhering to the MTCR, exports of *actual missiles* are increasingly rare. The biggest problem is the transfer of *dual-use technology*. Some of this, like engine nozzle fabrication equipment and fuel processing facilities, have few other likely uses. But a vast array of equipment is required to develop a ballistic missile and much of this, like super computers and testing equipment, has numerous other applications. The growing trade in dual-use technology during the 1980s was not accidental; not only were would-be proliferators designing better procurement programs, but supplier policy often favored such exports.[23] The only way to cope with the dual-use problem is to change export policy, making restrictions as comprehensive as possible.

Extreme restrictiveness is not without cost. The market for dual-use technology is potentially large and stands to benefit industries of strategic importance to supplier nations. The total investment for completion of the Argentine-Egyptian-Iraqi *Condor II*, for example, has been estimated at $4–5 billion, mostly for foreign equipment and support. Unlike most arms deals or defense related transactions, moreover, this is pure income, undiminished by countertrade or offset requirements. To demand that military contractors abandon these opportunities in a time of declining defense spending at home requires a vigorous national consensus.

As transfers to aid foreign rocketry programs became more sensitive, suppliers went to great lengths to maintain discretion, sometimes concealing their activity through special subsidiaries and foreign brokers. Until the late 1980s, however, transactions usually could be kept entirely legal. Indeed, even after the numerous revelations of European and North American firms in regional missile projects, prosecutions have been rare. Discretion was necessary, rather, to minimize other kinds of risks, as illustrated by the attempted murder in 1988 of the European head of the *Condor II* and the assassination in 1990 of Gerald Bull, designer of Iraq's superguns and *Al Abed* long-range rocket. In both cases, the work skirted the law but remained legal, as illustrated by Britain's unsuccessful supergun prosecutions.

Perhaps most surprising is the small role played by espionage and the black market. Both certainly have been present, as shown by American prosecutions of the Egyptian spy Abdelkader Helmy in 1989 and the American businessman James Guerin in 1990. Despite their notoriety, the role of such rascals is marginal. Regional powers seldom depend on the small bits and pieces that the illegal trade can provide. Rocket programs are enormous undertakings, involving the coordinated acquisition of vast arrays of designs, equipment and facilities. They usually require continuous foreign assistance of the sort available only from major contractors, firms with independent financial strength and the protection that only comes with government approval. The black market is more romantic than significant, forever on the fringes of the incomparably more lucrative and secure legal activity. The black market can, at great expense, risk, and delay, provide particular pieces of technology. But it cannot form the basis of a serious rocket program.

Of greater significance is the pooling of technology among missile proliferators. This is a long-standing trend previously noted in other fields.[24] Commonly and mistakenly seen as a reaction against the rise of the MTCR, the trade among regional powers in missile technology dates at least to the late 1970s, when Egypt exported SCUDs to North Korea. Cooperation on the *Condor II* was fully organized between Argentina, Egypt and Iraq a year before the MTCR went into limited effect. Later Israeli support became crucial to the South African rocket program, while Iran received SCUDs from Libya and Iraq got technical help from Brazil.

The pooling of missile technology is potentially of great significance, enabling countries to circumvent multinational export restrictions. In practice it faces technical and political limits. Few regional powers have been able to go beyond SCUD technology independently, and cooperation among themselves cannot overcome this natural limit; the levels of financing, expertise, and foreign technology required for sophisticated rockets differ by orders of magnitude. Few regional actors have sufficient resources even if pooled. Although there may be technical benefits in the short run, in the long term such cooperation tends to combine weaknesses. Emerging exporters, moreover, must balance the diplomatic costs of their activity. In practice, many have abandoned the trade when pressed by outside powers. Having started with the SCUD, regional cooperation rarely can move beyond it.

The Limits of Indigenous Technology

The ability of emerging powers to continue procurement of ballistic missiles without outside assistance varies greatly. Countries in the third rank, having relied entirely on foreign suppliers for complete missiles, cannot acquire additional weapons. Their existing arsenals, moreover, will deteriorate without foreign servicing and oversight, with the readiness of more complex, longer range weapons deteriorating fastest. Such weapons are complex and delicate; liquid fueled IRBMs can become permanently unusable after a few weeks without care. Middle Eastern SCUD operators can be expected to perform routine maintenance to keep their missiles serviceable for as long as several years. But without spares and regular overhauls even these relatively simple systems will become highly unreliable. Five years after a complete cut-off, only unguided, solid fuel weapons like the FROG would be fully operational.

Second rank countries, lacking full indigenous capabilities, also would be stuck with the missiles on hand, unable to continue production of whole rockets or development of new types. Their limited capabilities may be sufficient, however, to maintain their existing missiles more effectively and even perform some modification. Iraq, for example, apparently was able to continue extending the range of its SCUD inventory by itself, but dropped its most ambitious variants (the 900 km *al Abbas* and 2,000 km *Tamuz-al Abed*) when help was cut off. Without outside support, their forces will deteriorate over time, but not as rapidly as in less developed countries.

Only the most advanced emerging missile powers can continue manufacturing large rockets and make technical progress without direct foreign help. Even their progress will slow down. More ambitious projects must be dropped in favor of gradual development of existing technology. As Israel has shown, over time this strategy can lead to highly capable systems. But even a country like India would have to make major concessions in its space launch plans and concentrate its resources on its least demanding projects to assure progress.

Without outside help, missile proliferators must contend alone with the technical hurdles that have impeded development of large rockets everywhere. Unless a country can replicate an enormous array of R&D work, invest tens of billions of dollars, and wait over a decade, foreign help is essential. This must cover such diverse elements as missile aerodynamics, high energy fuels, engine design, guidance and control systems, stage separation, reentry vehicles, fuzing and armament, systems integration, testing, and support. No emerging power has tried to undertake such an effort alone.[25]

The MTCR and the Structure of Proliferation

The importance of outside technical assistance creates tremendous opportunities for export controls to slow or even halt the proliferation process. But the uncoordinated efforts of dozens of potential exporters would not amount to much; left to themselves, as was the case before the mid-1980s, the market for missile technology would attract exporters convinced that "if I don't, someone else will." By establishing even standards for export controls, the Missile Technology Control Regime provided an alternative to this kind of competition.

Like older export groups such as CoCom, the London Nuclear Suppliers Group, and the Australian Group on chemicals, the MTCR does not have the power of a treaty. Its commitments are formalized by trading diplomatic notes. The regime establishes "a strong presumption to deny," exports of rockets and cruise missiles capable of delivering a 500 kg warhead 300 km. Exports of major missile components such as engines and guidance sets are denied except under "binding government-to-government assurances," while facilities for their production "will not be authorized." Transfers of dual-use manufacturing technologies are permitted only with assurances that they will not contribute to long range missiles.[26]

If missile proliferation can be said to symbolize the dangers of the post-Cold War world, the MTCR is typical of the international community's shaky response. Crafted in secret by middle level officials with only a hazy image of the problem (most of its provisions were completed in 1985, before missile proliferation was well understood) it is a modest instrument at best. But by focusing on the weakest link in missile proliferation it was an unusually easy multi-lateral agreement to negotiate and surprisingly effective. It played an instrumental role slowing large rocket projects in Argentina, Brazil, Egypt, South Africa and Pakistan, projects that were subsequently dropped or set aside. Even with the better insulated programs of India and North Korea it has slowed rocketry progress.

The MTCR has become more effective over time through wider membership, better enforcement and tighter restrictions. The growth of membership is most visible. Since it was made public in 1987 the MTCR has seen its formal membership grow from 7 countries to 25 [*see Appendix A—ed.*]. A few of the most important exporters have agreed to adhere to its restrictions unilaterally. China is among the latter but, with international confidence in Beijing low, it remains on virtual diplomatic probation.[27] Only a few countries of any consequence remain to be brought within its framework. North Korea is the most conspicuous exception, the only country still exporting ballistic missiles beyond the MTCR thresholds. Other potential exporters like Brazil, South Africa, Eastern European countries and the Ukraine seem more likely to join in rapid order.

During its first few years, the MTCR was weakened by the low priority of the issue and the unwillingness of many members to enforce it rigorously. Lacking an institutional home, the MTCR has no enforcement agency or mechanism. Its members meet twice a year, share intelligence and conduct a lively diplomatic dialogue. Enforcement, however, is the responsibility of individual members. At first France and Germany were noticeably hesitant to carry out their obligations; the French offer of *Ariane* engine technology to Brazil in 1989 and Bonn's continuing willingness to license exports of dual-use technology to India and Iraq led to major controversies. In practice, participants had to learn through experience. By 1989–90, enforcement had become more efficient and consistent, but lingering domestic disputes seem likely to insure that controversies over missile technology exports will flair up in the future.

Three types of domestic disputes make it difficult for leading supplier countries to resolve their missile export issues once and for all. First, export control issues inevitably involve numerous government agencies and legislative factions. Such disputes are fueled by rival interpretations of the national interest, in which trade needs are sometimes subordinated and sometimes superior to security requirements. Moreover, the national interest itself changes over time, as yesterday's adversaries requiring strict controls become today's allies calling for free trade, inviting further strife.

A final set of problems for the MTCR are the limits of its restrictions. The original Technology Annex represented a series of compromises between the desirable and the feasible. The participants agreed that it would be too difficult to control short range missiles, a belief reenforced by their initial emphasis on missiles as nuclear delivery vehicles. The threshold for 500 kg payload, 300 km range missiles leaves out many of the conventional or chemically armed ballistic weapons of greatest concern today, such as the Russian SS-21 and the Chinese M-11. The performance levels for dual-use technology also were set relatively high in order to permit established export trade. The lessons of Iraq and experience with India and other countries have shown that these limits must be tightened.

The Iraqi experience catalyzed support for the first major revision of the MTCR, released on 4 November 1991. The expanded and tightened Technology Annex is a great improvement, applying the lessons of dozens of controversies.[28] Previously limited to missiles able to carry nuclear warheads, it now covers chemical and biologically armed missiles also. The revisions tighten controls on dual-use technology as well. There has been greater resistance among some members to proposals to reduce the missile range thresholds to 150 or 90 km, as has been widely suggested. Some influential members argue that the technology is too easily available for such measures to be effective. But there clearly will have to be motion in this direction if the MTCR is to continue responding to the problems of greatest current concern.

The Normative Basis for Control

The MTCR will remain the foundation of efforts to stop ballistic missile proliferation for many years to come, continuing to gain support and effectiveness. Despite its strengths, however, the MTCR will never be able to create an image of fairness. Although it is a regime in the legal sense, its basis in adversarial delineations makes it more like an alliance politically. From the perspective of key regional spokesmen, of which India is the most vocal, the whole approach discriminates against the sovereign rights of regional governments to arm themselves as they see fit, to acquire a weapon accepted among other countries. The critique is important because it casts doubt on the legitimacy of North-South export controls in general.

This challenge ultimately is a question of world order. Will future international security affairs be dominated by the pursuit of distinct national interests organized only through us-against-them alliances, or will it give a greater role to collective security organizations based on universal principles? Most missile suppliers are divided on such issues, willing to sacrifice some self-interests, but not if it means providing potential adversaries with weapons like long range ballistic missiles.

The normative issue in this instance focuses largely on regional space launch projects. India and Israel have reached important milestones toward creation of reliable domestic space launch capabilities. Other countries including Brazil and some East Asian countries are interested in doing the same. Although such projects make little sense commercially, they are of great importance as prestige symbols. Given the dual-use nature of long range rocket technology, however, their direct military applications cannot be overlooked. The MTCR originally endorsed such endeavors, but official opinion clearly has grown less tolerant over time.

The revelation in April 1992 that Russia had previously agreed to provide engine technology for Indian space launchers showed that this question is not an abstraction. This deal, worth an estimated $100–250 million, was harshly criticized in Europe and North America. Although clearly intended to serve civilian objectives, it also will give India new military potential. The MTCR is not very helpful on this issue, since it permits members (which Russia is not) to transfer such technology with proper assurances. The dispute points to the need to resolve the larger issue of aid to civil space launch projects if the MTCR is to be fully consistent.

The impact of regional criticism of the discriminatory nature of the MTCR has not been great otherwise. Western leaders may feel some regret, but not enough to reconsider their policies. Contrary to the statements of regional spokesmen, there is no evidence of any country accelerating its rocket projects simply to spite the outside powers trying to slow them down; large rockets are too costly to pursue so frivolously. Indeed, erstwhile adversaries in Latin American and East Asia increasingly support the regime. Even in India there is growing awareness of the advantages of joining.[29]

Conclusion: Beyond Export Control

The maturity of ballistic missile proliferation suggests that our image of the issue is basically complete. There is widespread appreciation of the dangers, of the processes, and the need to address them. The MTCR is the most important element of this mature consensus. Yet it clearly is not the whole solution. In some cases it may be possible to overcome regional resistance and bring additional countries into the regime, as was accomplished with Argentina and Israel. But stopping missile proliferation and dealing with its consequences where that is not possible will require other approaches. Future discussions seem likely to be dominated by the following five:

Incentives for non-proliferation. To make the loss of the missile option more palatable, it has been suggested that regional powers be offered compensation, either security guarantees or civilian space launch services.[30] While there is obvious merit in such proposals, they do not promise a general answer to missile proliferation. It is not clear that outside powers are able or willing to assume the costs and dangers of assuring regional stability sufficiently to reduce the demand for missiles. Nor are new space launch services likely to assuage regional aspirations for prestige symbols. Incentives may be more valuable in specific situations, rather, when a government is searching for a way to halt a controversial rocket project gracefully.

Regional initiatives seem more promising, especially if they involve confidence building measures or arms control agreements. Unfortunately there is not much outside powers can do in this regard except offer encouragement. The key to such arrangements, as demonstrated by the experiences of the superpowers, in Europe and Argentina-Brazil, appears to lie in the resolution of regional political disputes. As often happens in post-Cold War discussions of specific regional peace and security issues, this leads to the conclusion that the key to regional solutions lies not in the specifics of controlling ballistic missiles, but in the generalities of regional conflict resolution.[31]

Active defenses clearly will have a greater role to play. The controversy over *Patriot*'s performance defending cities against Iraqi SCUDs cast doubt on the overall potential of defenses.[32] But regional governments appear to see a growing role for systems like *Patriot* for the less demanding task of defending military installations. Specially designed interceptors like THAADS and *Arrow* will be better suited to defence of cities against limited attacks.It is less clear whether SDI technology should be applied to defence of North America and Europe. Modest versions, relying on a few hundred ground based interceptors, seem more likely to be deployed than the extensive space-based systems envisioned by SDI advocates.

A *ballistic missile test ban* is one way to ameliorate not only competitive pressures for regional missile acquisition but also their prestige. Such proposals have been around since the Eisenhower administration, but they won little support so long as ballistic missiles played a major role in great power forces.[33] Now that the United States and Russia agreed at the June 1992

Washington Summit to eliminate all but a few hundred ground-based ICBMs, the prospects for a test ban are much better. Unlike nuclear weapons, ballistic missiles cannot be developed without extensive testing nor can operational missiles be kept reliable. Many serious problems would have to be resolved first, including differentiating allowable space launchers and the status of sea-launched missiles, but these do not seem insurmountable.

The most straightforward and extreme answer to missile proliferation would be an outright *comprehensive ballistic missile ban*. Previously students of missile proliferation have gone no further than to advocate a global INF treaty, banning the missiles of greatest danger in most regions. But this does not satisfy regional demands for equal treatment since it would leave great power ICBMs and SLBMs.[34] The Bush-Yeltsin Washington Summit, however, made the universal elimination of ballistic missiles seem feasible for the first time. The biggest obstacles are the independent nuclear forces. Tailoring a proposal to permit some SLBMs would meet the objections of Britain and France, but Chinese and Israeli resistance may be harder to overcome.[35] While a ballistic missile ban remains distant, it no longer can be dismissed as fanciful.

The experience of the last few years has shown that missile proliferation remains a serious challenge. It also has shown that missile proliferation is far from inevitable. To the contrary, the 1987 INF treaty, subsequent Russo-American agreements and the fate of the *Condor II* all show that the proliferation of long range missiles can be reversed. It may be true that the battle against missile proliferation cannot be won in an absolute sense, for there will always be future threats, but nor need the battle be permanently lost.

Notes

1. The same point is made on a similar topic by Michael Brzoska, "Is the Nuclear Non-Proliferation system a regime? A comment on Trevor McMorris Tate," *Journal of Peace Research*, May 1992, pp. 215–220. On the scarcity of security regimes in general, Robert Jervis, "Security regimes," *International Organization*, Spring 1982, pp. 357–378.

2. *The Structure of Scientific Revolutions*, 2nd ed. (Chicago: University of Chicago Press, 1970). Paradigms embrace entire fields of science, while maturity describes specific policy issues.

3. Peter M. Haas, "Knowledge, power, and international policy coordination," *International Organization*, Winter 1992, pp. 1–36.

4. Emanuel Adler, "Arms control, disarmament, and national security: a thirty year retrospective," *Daedalus*, Winter 1991, pp. 1–20; and Adler, "The emergence of cooperation: national epistemic communities and the international evolution of the idea of nuclear arms control," *International Organization*, Winter 1992, pp. 101–46.

5. Although voices in favor of proliferation were heard in the 1960s and '70s, such as Pierre Galois and Ashok Kapur, the basic argument remained vague until

the publication of Kenneth N. Waltz, *The Spread of Nuclear Weapons: More may be Better*, Adelphi Paper 171 (London: IISS, Autumn 1981) and K. Subrahmanyam, ed., *Nuclear Myths and Realities* (New Delhi: ABC Publishing, 1981).

6. Especially influential were John Kerry King, ed., *International Political Effects of the Spread of Nuclear Weapons* (Washington, D.C.: Central Intelligence Agency, 1979); Albert Wohlstetter, et al., *Swords from Plowshares* (Chicago: University of Chicago Press, 1979); and Rodney W. Jones, ed., *Small Nuclear Forces and U.S. Security Policy* (Lexington: Lexington Books, 1984).

7. Current Indian projects include three space launchers, the ASLV, PSLV and the GSLV, and two ballistic missiles, the *Agni* and *Prithvi*, as well as many other smaller missiles. The largest system actually approaching deployment is the *Prithvi*, a tactical missile for the Indian Army and the technically least ambitious of all Indian rocketry projects. Based on the a propulsion system borrowed from the Soviet SA-2 Guideline SAM, it comes in 150 km and 240 km versions and could be fully operational in the mid-1990s.

8. A comprehensive list of countries capable of developing ballistic missiles would have to include more distant possibilities, starting with Japan, whose M-series space launchers could be adapted as IRBMs within a few months, although high-performance guidance and reentry vehicles would require a few years for full development. Japan's liquid fuel N- and H-series launchers could be adapted into ICBMs, but with greater difficulty. Britain, Canada, Germany and Italy have industries capable of developing large rockets within as little as five years, while Australia, Belgium, Netherlands, Spain, Sweden and Switzerland could do so in roughly 10 years.

9. An extreme example of this ambiguity is the Argentine *Condor II*, which the Menem government declared at an end in April 1990. The decision prompted a tug of war with the Argentine Air Force which kept the project alive covertly, a dispute which also had to do with the question of who controls the Argentine military. After many conflicting announcements, in February 1992 the remnants of the project were formally transferred to a civilian agency. The saga seems doomed to continue so long as Argentina still has some rocket technology left to fight over.

10. The relevance of Clausewitz's comment was brought to my attention by Martin Navias.

11. The best general works are Walter Dornberger, *V-2: Der Schuss ins Weltall* (Esslingen: Bechte Verlag, 1952); and Heinz Dieter Hilsken, *Die V-Waffen* (Stuttgart: Deutsche Verlags-Anstalt, 1984). Dwight D. Eisenhower recalls his impressions in his memoir *Crusade in Europe* (Garden City: Doubleday, 1953) pp. 250, 258.

12. Joseph S. Bermudez, Jr., "Ballistic Missiles in the Third World—Egypt and the 1973 Arab-Israeli War," *Jane's Intelligence Review*, December 1991, pp. 531–37.

13. Accounts vary. A book sympathetic to Iran, Dilip Hiro, *The Longest War: the Iran-Iraq Military Conflict* (London: Paladin, 1990), attributes virtually no effects to the missiles.

14. David C. Isby, "Soviet arms deliveries and aid to Afghanistan 1989–91," *Jane's Intelligence Review*, August 1991, pp. 348–54.

15. Martin Navias, *Saddam's Scud War and Ballistic Missile Proliferation*, London Defence Studies 6 (London: Centre for Defence Studies, 1991).

16. Steven Fetter, "Ballistic missiles and weapons of mass destruction," *International Security*, Summer 1991; and Aaron Karp, Ballistic missiles in the Third World," *ibid.*, Winter 1984/85.

17. In earlier articles I advocated this position, but I now believe it to be seriously misleading. For example see Aaron Karp, "Space technology in the Third World," *Space Policy*, May 1986.

18. Even an authority normally as skeptical (and dismissive of the V-2) as B. H. Liddell Hart accepts the significance of the Doolittle raid. See his *History of the Second World War* (New York: G. P. Putnam, 1970) pp. 344–46.

19. Kathleen C. Bailey, *Doomsday Weapons in the Hands of Many: the Arms Control Challenge of the '90s*. (Champaign: University of Illinois, 1991) pp. 5–6, 103–107. A more refined and nuanced statement is made by W. Seth Carus, *Ballistic Missiles in Modern Conflict* (New York: Praeger, 1991) chapter 3.

20. John Barker, Michael Elleman, John Harvey and Uzi Rubin, *Assessing Ballistic Missile Proliferation and its Control* (Stanford: Center for International Security and Arms Control, Stanford University, November 1991), chaps. 2 and 5; and John Pike and Eric Stambler, "Constraints on the R&D and Transfer of Ballistic Missile Defence Technology," in Hans Günter Brauch, et al., eds., *Controlling the Development and Spread of Military Technology* (Amsterdam: VU University Press, 1992) chapter 5.

21. On the interwar fascination with the battleship, see Robert L. O'Connell, *Sacred Vessels: the Cult of the Battleship and the Rise of the U.S. Navy* (Boulder: Westview, 1991).

22. The repetitiveness of these debates is a theme in Gregg Herken, *Counsels of War* (New York: Knopf, 1985).

23. An example is the American tilt toward Iraq in 1983, which made possible large sales of dual use technology for Iraq's ballistic missile projects. Kenneth R. Timmerman, *The Death Lobby: How the West Armed Iraq* (London: Fourth Estate, 1992), chapter 12.

24. William C. Potter, *International Nuclear Trade and Nonproliferation: the Challenge of the Emerging Suppliers* (Lexington: Lexington Books, 1990).

25. Even Britain, with extensive American help, was unable to complete its *Blue Streak* IRBM at an acceptable cost and schedule, abandoning it in 1960.

26. *Statement by the Assistant to the President for Press Relations* (Santa Barbara: The White House, 16 April 1987), and *Missile Technology Control Regime: Fact Sheet to Accompany Public Announcement, ibid.*

27. The original members were Britain, Canada, France, F.R. Germany, Italy, Japan and the United States. They have been joined by Australia, Austria, Belgium, Denmark, Finland, Greece, Luxembourg, Netherlands, New Zealand, Norway, Portugal, Spain, Sweden, Switzerland, Argentina, Iceland, and Hungary. Governments that have diplomatically pledged to adhere but have not formally joined include China, Israel, Russia, Brazil, and Romania.

28. The numerous changes in the revised *Technology Annex* can be read as a kind of catalogue of previous disputes among the MTCR members.

29. Gautam Adhikari, "Requiem for non-alignment," *Times of India* (New Delhi), 26 May 1992; Dilip Mukerjee, "The nuclear option: ambiguity difficult to maintain," *ibid.*, 9 June 1992.

30. Janne E. Nolan, *Trappings of Power: Ballistic Missiles in the Third World* (Washington, D.C.: Brookings, 1991) pp. 164–66.

31. The author makes this point more thoroughly in "Controlling ballistic missile proliferation," *Survival*, November/December 1991, esp. pp. 525–29.

32. Theodore A. Postal, "Lessons from the Gulf War experience," *International Security*, Winter 1991/92; and the refutation by Robert M. Stein, *Patriot ATBM experience in the Gulf War* (Lexington: Raytheon, 1991).

33. The Eisenhower administration's consideration of a missile test ban was brought to my attention by George Rathjens. The only full-length study in print is by peace researcher Udo Schelb, *Raketenzielgenauigkeit und Raketenteststopp* (Marburg: Interdisziplinaeren Arbeitsgruppe Friedens- und Abrüstungsforschung, Universität Marburg, 1988) who examines the idea as a way of stopping the MX ICBM. Also see Robert Sherman, "Deterrence through a ballistic missile flight test ban," *Arms Control Today*, December 1987, pp. 8–13, with a rejoinder by Walter B. Slocombe.

34. Bailey, *Doomsday Weapons*, pp. 107, 127.

35. Jasit Singh, director of the Institute for Defence Studies and Analyses in New Delhi, has suggested that India might agree to a global missile ban, but only if it also prohibited sea- and air-launched cruise missiles.

2

Egypt's Missile Development

Joseph S. Bermudez, Jr.

Introduction

Although Egypt became the first "Third World" nation to develop a serious interest in ballistic missiles, less is known concerning its missile programs than any other country in the Middle East.

Beginning during the 1950s and extending through the mid-1960s, the Egyptian military sponsored a missile program staffed by German engineers and scientists to develop ballistic missiles and a satellite launch vehicle based upon experience gained with World War II German missiles. The available evidence suggests that the Egyptians intended to manufacture up to 900 missiles of three models by 1970. Although President Gamal Nasser boasted that missiles were in quantity production, none reached operational service due to insurmountable guidance system troubles and gross mismanagement of the project. By the time of the June 1967 "Six-Day War" the indigenous missile program was at a standstill.

Immediately following its defeat in the "Six-Day War," Egypt turned to the Soviet Union not only for massive conventional military assistance, but also for tactical missiles. The Soviet Union agreed to provide Egypt with the *Luna M* (known in the West as the FROG-7A), to be delivered during 1968-69. These were supplemented by a unit of Soviet-supplied SCUD-B missiles during early 1973. During the October 1973 Arab-Israeli War, Egypt launched approximately 200 FROG-7A, *al-Kahir,* and *al-Zafir* missiles; along with three SCUD-Bs; at Israeli military targets. Although these missiles had only a minimal effect upon the course of the war, the Egyptians (as well as the Israelis and Syrians) came away from that conflict with the belief that ballistic missiles would play an increasingly significant role in any future conflict in the region, at both the tactical and strategic levels.

During the late 1970s, Egyptian interest in tactical ballistic missiles was revived, initially to maintain and upgrade its existing missile inventory, but subsequently in response both to the Iran-Iraq war and as a reaction to Israeli missile developments. As a result, during the early 1980s Egypt initiated a program (partially in cooperation with the Democratic People's Republic of Korea) to develop an improved version of the SCUD-B. This program has continued, in one form or another, until today, although Egypt is not known to have either manufactured or deployed any improved SCUD-B missiles. The SCUD-B program was supplemented by three programs during the early 1980s:

- *Sakr-80*, a program to design and manufacture a FROG-7A replacement with a range of 80 km. This project was a joint venture between the Egyptian companies of the Sakr Factory for Developed Industries, the Abu Zaabal Company for Specialty Chemicals, and the French company SNPE-CE.
- RS-120, a program to initially design and manufacture a 120 km tactical ballistic missile, possibly to be followed by a longer range missile. The primary design contract for this project was with the CONSEN Group firm of IFAT, which contracted with the German firm Messerschmitt-Boelkow-Blohm (MBB) to provide Egypt with technical assistance and equipment.
- *Condor II/Vector/Badr-2000*, a program to produce a 800-1,000 km range ballistic missile in cooperation with Argentina, the CONSEN Group, and Iraq. This missile is known in Argentina as *Condor II*, in Egypt as *Vector* and in Iraq as *Badr-2000*.

By the late-1980s, all three of these programs had succumbed to a lack of Egyptian funding and/or international pressure. Egypt currently has only one known active ballistic missile program—the improved SCUD-B. The resources that had been allocated to the *Condor II* and other missile programs are believed to have been redistributed to the improved SCUD-B project. The current status of this program is obscure. It is, however, currently believed to be proceeding at an advanced stage. Given the proper political climate and financial resources Egypt could quickly produce a SCUD-B equivalent missile.

Two critical factors have strongly influenced missile development in Egypt. First, Egypt simply doesn't possess the economic resources to pursue a missile production program of any significance with indigenous assets alone. Second, Egypt's military industries have repeatedly demonstrated an inability to carry through major development projects. There have been notable exceptions to this when Egyptian companies have been closely aligned with Western counterparts.

The Early Years

During the early 1950s, Egypt initiated a program to develop ballistic missiles. Not possessing the skilled personnel to staff such an ambitious project, Egypt hired large numbers of German engineers and scientists who had gained experience in the World War II German *Wasserfall* and A4 (V2) missile programs. These German engineers and scientists would eventually develop, and partially test, three distinct surface-to-surface missile systems: the single stage *al-Zafir* (*Victor*) with a projected range of 370 km; the single stage *al-Kahir* (*Conqueror*)—projected range of 600 km; and the two stage *Ar-Ra'id (Pioneer)*—projected range of 1,500 km. Each of these missiles was armed with a high explosive warhead of 500–800 kg.

Compounding Egypt's early personnel problems was the fact that it had only the most rudimentary of aviation industries at the time. To address this situation, it committed significant resources to the development of an indigenous missile industry. Primary among the industrial facilities established during this period was Factory 333 (also known as the Sakr Factory). This facility would serve as the production and research center for all rocket and missile design, development and production within the country.[1] Factory 333 was headed by the German engineer, Eugen Saenger, and was organized into three main departments: rocket engine, guidance and airframe.[2] At least two additional facilities are believed to have been involved with the early Egyptian missile program. The Kader factory, located in Heliopolis, is believed to have been responsible for the development of the guidance system, while a second facility handled the production of the various rocket fuels and warhead explosives.

Despite a significant commitment to indigenous infrastructure development, many of the components required for the early missile projects had to be covertly obtained abroad. To facilitate this, the services of at least three European "front" companies were utilized.

By 1961 many of the details surrounding Factory 333 had become known to the Israelis, who had initiated both political and covert programs to halt the German assistance. Israeli efforts to disrupt the Egyptian missile program dramatically increased in size and scope to include bombings, kidnappings and assassinations. By 1964 the Israeli efforts had resulted in the mass exodus of German scientists and engineers, although a few would remain in Egypt for some time.

Despite ambitious plans to produce 900 missiles (400 *al-Zafir* and 500 *al-Kahir*) and outward appearances of great success and significant capabilities, Egypt's missile program was a distinct failure.[3] There were multiple reasons for this state of affairs. The primary technical reasons for this failure were the inability to develop a reliable guidance system and consistently manufacture reliable rocket engines. In essence, the Egyptian missiles were World War II vintage designs, taking little, if any, advantage of post-war developments, simply because the scientists and technicians were not skilled in these areas. Additionally, the elitist attitudes of these scientists and technicians precluded the training of, or transfer of skills to, Egyptian personnel. This had a distinct effect upon the program as the foreign scientists and technicians rapidly left the program during 1963–65. This situation was exacerbated by the scarcity of qualified skilled and semiskilled Egyptian factory workers. On top of this, a majority of the components required for missile production, especially in the areas of guidance and fuel systems, had to be imported covertly and at great expense.

Since the Soviets had no desire to help the Egyptians develop a missile force, the Egyptians were left to their own devices. Despite continued Egyptian claims of progress with their missile program (e.g., in July 1966 Egyptian scientists claimed that they had developed a viable guidance system) the program quickly stalled.[4] The program's position was even more untenable given the severe monetary crisis then being experienced by Egypt. Thus the missile program was secretly suspended. For both propaganda and deception purposes, however, the missiles were still discussed publicly.[5] Threats to use these missiles were a cornerstone of anti-Israel Egyptian propaganda until the 1967 "Six-Day War."

In the aftermath of the 1967 war, Egypt turned to the Soviet Union not only for massive conventional military assistance but also for tactical missiles. The Soviet Union agreed to provide Egypt with a brigade of 36 *Luna M* TELs, known in the West as the FROG-7A, to be delivered during 1968–69.[6] More significantly, the indigenous missile program was finally canceled and those military industries involved in the program were restructured and assigned new responsibilities. The Sakr Factory (Factory 333) moved into the production of Soviet weapons and spares, both with and without licenses from the Soviets. By the time of the 1973 October War, it was producing a wide variety of rocket-related systems, including RPG-2/-7 antitank grenades, 57mm and 80mm air-to-surface rockets, aircraft bombs, smoke-screen rockets, and 132 mm artillery rockets. By 1973, the Kader Factory was producing the *Gomhouria* primary training aircraft as well as the *Walid* armored personnel carrier and an anti-runway "dibber" bomb.

Although a significant portion of the work performed by these companies in the post-war years was not what they had originally been established or trained for, it did serve useful purposes. They provided products that were in demand by the Egyptian Armed Forces, retained a significant number of trained people, and, in some cases, provided additional training in diverse fields. The result was that during the mid-1970s Egypt possessed a military industries infrastructure that was skilled and poised for a rapid expansion.

Prelude to War

During the early 1970s, detailed plans were formulated for a new war against Israel and the recapture of the Sinai Peninsula. Egyptian Chief-of-Staff, Lt. Gen. Saad el-Shazli, sought to provide his army with all possible firepower. To this end he ordered that the *al-Zafir* and *al-Kahir* missiles be taken out of storage and test fired. The initial test launches occurred on 23 September 1971. The results were disappointing, with both missiles proving to be quite primitive. The *al-Kahir*'s range and direction could be controlled only by the elevation and azimuth of its launching rail (it was now being fired as a large artillery rocket without the inertial guidance system originally developed for it). Its maximum usable range in this mode was approximately 8 km (as opposed to its publicly reported range of 600 km)! Its accuracy was equally appalling. Even with successive firings on the same elevation and azimuth, it exhibited a CEP of 1,600 meters at 8 km! Its only merit was the destructiveness of its warhead. The resulting impact craters were impressive. They were typically 27 meters wide and 10 meters deep. Lt. Gen. Shazli would later state that "...apart from the destructive power of its warhead, *al-Kahir* was medieval." The *al-Zafir* had an even shorter range (as opposed to its publicly reported range of 370 km), and was only marginally more accurate than *al-Kahir*. Additionally, it had to be used with caution, since they had developed a TEL to fire four at once. Further tests of the *al-Kahir* and *al-Zafir* missiles were conducted in 1972 and 1973, with similar results.[7]

Lt. Gen. Shazli directed that "...anything was better than nothing," and ordered both systems deployed for the upcoming war, with some restrictions. These missiles could be employed against Israeli positions farther than 2.5 km from Egyptian lines and only during the initial artillery bombardment. Additionally, to maintain operational security Shazli ordered that both systems be renamed. The *al-Zafir* became the *al-Zeitun* (*Olive*), and the *al-Kahir* became the *al-Tin* (*Fig*).[8]

Concurrent with the efforts to resurrect the *al-Kahir* and *al-Zafir*, Egypt sought to expand its missile capabilities. This was done in the belief that an expanded missile force, especially if it had the capability to strike at Israeli populated areas, would act as a strategic deterrent, and prevent another disaster like 1967. Additionally, it would assist in redressing the imbalance of Israeli air supremacy.[9] As noted above, efforts in this area had begun during 1968 when Egypt obtained the FROG-7A. It subsequently requested the more modern and longer ranged R-17E, known in the West as the SCUD-B, but was refused. The Soviets refused because the SCUD-B would provide Egypt the capability of striking at Tel Aviv from west of the Suez Canal, and would be interpreted as a gross escalation of the Middle East arms race.

During May 1972 Lt. Gen. Shazli traveled to Iraq, where he requested Hawker *Hunter* attack aircraft and SCUD-B missiles.[10] Although President Husayn would later claim that Iraqi SCUDs were delivered to Egypt during 1973, no evidence has become available to support this. It is possible, however, since one Hawker *Hunter* squadron did arrive during March 1973. The real importance of Shazli's request for missiles and Husayn's positive reply is that it was apparently the final factor that convinced the Soviets to provide SCUD-Bs directly to Egypt.

Ten months later, the Soviet Union agreed to provide Egypt with an additional 150 FROG-7As, and the equipment and training required to deploy two SCUD-B brigades of 12 TELs each. With the arrival of these TELs also came a small number of Soviet advisors and technicians to assist in the formation of the 65th Artillery Brigade (SCUD-B). These were soon supplemented, during July and August 1973, by an additional 63 Soviet advisors. By August, progress in the formation of the 65th Artillery Brigade had advanced to the point that the unit was able to participate in an army-wide operational exercise.[11] The arrival of the SCUDs is believed to have been the final factor in President Sadat's decision to go to war in October.[12]

The October 1973 War[13]

The 1973 Arab-Israeli War was the first post-World War II conflict to witness use of a wide range of modern rocket/missile systems. Egyptian and Syrian use of such systems has been studied by most Third World nations as they have developed their own ballistic missile inventories and capabilities. The war also planted the seeds of today's Egyptian and Syrian ballistic missile cooperation with other Third World nations.

Counting the 150 newly arrived FROG-7As and approximately 36 already in inventory, the Egyptian Army possessed, at the time of the War, 180-190 FROG-7As. This figure would allow for one and a half times the number of "units of fire" required, according to Soviet doctrine of the period, for conducting an attack against a prepared defender. In addition, the 65th Artillery Brigade had been formed and equipped with 9 TELs, for which the Soviets are believed to have provided approximately 18 SCUD-B missiles.[14]

Of the approximately 300 surface-to-surface missiles available to the Egyptians at the start of the war, they launched 200-220. Despite this large number, the effectiveness and actual damage caused was not overly significant.[15] In fact, there is no record of a successful hit on an Israeli fortification by any of the approximately 100 of these rockets fired at them! The FROG-7As did achieve some limited success in suppressing or damaging Israeli targets. Years later, Israeli sources still recalled with concern the Egyptian FROG-7A strikes upon the Bir Gifgafa airfields.[16]

Although the Egyptians claim to have hit the Israeli bridges across the Suez Canal with FROG-7As, there were no such direct hits.[17] There were, however, several near misses that did result in Israeli casualties. Israeli anti-aircraft artillery was able to shoot down, or detonate before impact, several of the FROG-7As heading towards the bridgehead.[18]

On 16 October, with Israeli forces rapidly expanding their bridgehead within Egyptian territory, President Anwar Sadat gave a speech to the Egyptian People's Assembly. Therein he threatened to employ ballistic missiles against Israeli cities if they continued their penetration. Although Sadat stated that the missile to be employed for any such attack was the *al-Zafir*, it was, in fact, the SCUD-B.[19] Although President Sadat would never carry out his threat to attack Israeli cities, on 22 October, a few minutes before the U.N. cease-fire came into effect, he ordered the launch of three SCUD-B missiles at the Israeli bridges across the Suez Canal.[20] The actual aiming and launching of these SCUDs was carried out by the Soviet instructors attached to the brigade. All three missiles failed to hit the Israeli bridges, and fell harmlessly in the desert.[21] In fact, the Israelis were only able to confirm the firings after they found a crater made by the SCUDs.

Post-War Assessment

The 1973 War witnessed the first combat use of the Soviet SCUD-B and the FROG-7A. It was also the first and only operational use of the indigenous Egyptian *al-Tin* and *al-Zeitun* missiles. While the *al-Tin* and *al-Zeitun* were distinct military failures, the FROG-7A enjoyed moderate military success. The SCUD-B can't be said to have been either a military success or failure in the war. It was, however, a distinct diplomatic success as far as President Sadat was concerned. It provided him with a viable means of threatening Israel and drew the world's attention to the Arab-Israeli situation. This is especially true when it is understood that both the United States, and in response the Soviet Union, went on world-wide alert on October 24-25 when it was believed that the Soviets had shipped nuclear warheads for the SCUDs to Egypt.

The Egyptian post-war military assessment of their use of surface-to-surface missiles was that while they succeeded in causing only minor physical damage, they were more successful in causing a disruption of Israeli command and control during the first critical hours of the war.[22] They further believed that ballistic missiles would play an increasingly significant role in any future conflict, at both the tactical and strategic levels.[23]

Rebirth of an Indigenous Missile Program

During the months immediately following the war the Soviet Union provided significant quantities of replacement arms and ammunition to re-equip the Egyptian armed forces. Included were additional FROG-7A and SCUD-B TELs, bringing the totals to approximately 18 and 24, respectively.[24]

During 1974, however, these arms deliveries slowed as President Sadat displayed a willingness to pursue a pro-West attitude to the resolution to the Arab-Israeli problem, as opposed to a Soviet solution. This reduction in arms and spare parts deliveries led to open Egyptian criticism of the Soviet Union, which in turn resulted in a further decline in Egyptian-Soviet relations. In 1975 Egyptian Armed Forces Chief-of-Staff Lieutenant General Mohammed Ali Fahmy stressed the increasing tactical and strategic importance of ballistic missiles on the modern battlefield, and confirmed that Egypt was committed to a multiple source policy on future weapons procurement. Egypt would never again be dependent upon a single source of supply. Additionally, the acquisition of Western technology was now to be actively pursued.

To achieve these objectives, the Arab Organization for Industrialization (AOI) was established that year with its headquarters in Cairo.[25] The AOI is a multinational activity formed by the Government of Egypt and the Gulf Cooperation Council (GCC) to obtain Western technology and establish an industrial base within the Arab world to produce modern weapons.[26] Egypt provided the industrial facilities and the majority of the personnel, while the GCC provided the financial backing. Among the facilities utilized to form AOI were those which had been involved with the earlier German-assisted missile and aircraft programs, including: the Sakr Factory for Developed Industries, Aircraft Factory 36, Aircraft Engine Factory 135, and the Kader Factory for Developed Industries.[27] The AOI, although nominally a multinational corporation, was actually subordinated to the office of the Egyptian Minister of Defense and Defense Production, through the Ministry of State for Military Production.

Since it would take several years for the AOI to fulfill Egypt's requirements for critically needed spare parts and replacement weapons, it sought the immediate assistance of the PRC and Democratic People's Republic of Korea (DPRK). Both countries responded favorably and within a year spare parts and replacement weapons began to be received.[28] On 14 March 1976, Egypt unilaterally abrogated the 1971 Soviet-Egyptian Treaty of Friendship and Cooperation on the grounds that the Soviets had failed their obligations by not providing spare parts. The following month Egypt signed military agreements with both the PRC and DPRK, thus formalizing the supply of spare parts and replacement weapons.

In a historic move, on 28 March 1979, President Sadat and President Menachem Begin signed a peace treaty between Egypt and Israel in Washington, D.C., thus ending the state of war that had existed between the two countries since 1948. By the end of the following month, all Arab countries except Sudan, Oman and Somalia had severed diplomatic relations with Egypt. Additionally, the GCC withdrew from the AOI. President Anwar al-Sadat's decision to sign the peace treaty was also unpopular among a number of radical factions within Egypt itself, most notably the Muslim Brotherhood, and on 6 October 1981 he was assassinated. President Sadat was succeeded by his Vice-President Hosni Mubarak.

During late 1980, Iraq invaded Iran, thus beginning an eight-year-long war. Because of their fear of radical Islamic fundamentalism, a majority of the Arab countries, including Egypt, sided with Iraq. Because of the AOI's military production capabilities, Egyptian cooperation with Iraq was close from the beginning of the Iran-Iraq conflict.[29] As a result of Egypt's vigorous support for Iraq and President Mubarak's political efforts, the GCC decided to reactivate the AOI during late 1982.[30] Three years later, in June 1985, a cooperation agreement was signed between Egypt and Iraq. Egyptian military-industrial cooperation with the GCC as well as AOI cooperation with Western countries increased significantly from late 1987 onwards.[31]

It was against the above background that Egypt, during the mid- to late 1970s, initiated a modest program to maintain and upgrade its inventory of FROG-7A and SCUD-B missile systems. This program appears to have been limited to maintaining systems operability by replacing Soviet parts with indigenously produced, or foreign purchased, components. By the early 1980s this modest program had evolved into a program to develop a product-improved SCUD and had been supplemented by at least three additional projects:

- *Sakr-80.*
- RS-120.
- *Condor II/Vector.*

Because these programs overlap in time, resources, and personnel, it is often difficult to distinguish exactly what was occurring in a specific program at a specific time, or if a specific effort was intended to benefit a specific program.

Before these programs are discussed on an individual basis, it is important to note two critical factors that have strongly influenced missile development in Egypt. The first is that Egypt is a poor country with a high foreign debt and few natural resources. Had it not been for substantial foreign assistance over the years Egypt would be essentially bankrupt. The second factor is the organizational weakness of Egypt's military industries, which have repeatedly demonstrated an inability to efficiently conceive, implement and conclude major development projects. There have been notable exceptions to this, however, when Egyptian companies have been closely aligned with Western counterparts.

The SCUD-B Program

During the past ten years, Egypt has demonstrated an unwavering commitment to the acquisition of both SCUD-B and SCUD-B related technologies. The initial program is believed to have been limited to developing the capability to maintain the FROG-7A and SCUD-B systems in the Egyptian inventory. In order to accomplish this Egypt apparently began replacing, on a selective basis, Soviet parts with indigenously produced, or foreign purchased, components. This program is believed to have been managed primarily by the Sakr Factory for Developed Industries.

By the early 1980s, Egypt apparently made the decision to expand beyond the simple maintenance stage and into the development of product-improved versions of both the FROG-7A and SCUD-B. To this end, Egypt approached the PRC and DPRK seeking cooperation and assistance. Since neither country operated the SCUD-B, or a missile in its class, they were unable to directly assist Egypt. The DPRK, however, did provide a viable alternative. The most efficient and economical way was to reverse engineer the SCUD-B as an interim step to the future production of an indigenously designed tactical ballistic missile with greater range and accuracy. Since the ballistic missile interests of both the DPRK and Egypt coincided, the two countries are believed to have agreed to the exchange of missile information and technicians sometime during 1979–80. More significantly, during the early 1980s Egypt, in violation of its agreement with the Soviet Union, transferred a small number of SCUD-B missiles to the DPRK. On 21 August 1981 the Egyptian and DPRK Governments signed an agreement in Pyongyang covering cooperation in, and exchange of, scientific technology between the two countries for 1981–1983.[32] It is conceivable that portions of this agreement covered missile technology. To complement the Egyptian delivery, the DPRK apparently requested, and received, PRC technical assistance in the areas of rocket engine design/ production, metallurgy, and airframe technology.

With the transfer of SCUD-B missiles, and the decision to cooperate with Egypt, the DPRK reorganized its indigenous missile efforts into a multifaceted missile research and development program. Its goal was to produce both a reverse-engineered and an extended-range variant of the SCUD-B known as the SCUD Mod. B and the SCUD Mod. C, respectively. In return for the transfer of the SCUD-B missiles, Egypt apparently was allowed wide access to both the DPRK SCUD Mod. B program and technology. Despite an ambitious start, the DPRK's SCUD Mod. B program proceeded slowly due both to technical difficulties and the DPRK's severe budgetary crisis.

Shortly after the Egyptian missile transfer to the DPRK, Iran approached both the DPRK and PRC seeking missile technology and tactical ballistic missiles in the SCUD-B class.[33] The PRC didn't have a missile in this class, but the DPRK was working on its SCUD Mod. B. It is believed that during their October 1983 visit to P'yongyang, Iranian Prime Minister Musavi and Defense Minister Colonel Mohammad Salimi discussed the acquisition of SCUD Mod. B technology and missiles.[34] As a result of Musavi's visit, Iran agreed to a bilateral exchange of missile technology, and to provide long term financing for the DPRK's SCUD Mod. B program, in exchange for an option to purchase DPRK manufactured SCUD Mod. Bs when they became available in several years. The Iranian interest and funding allowed the SCUD Mod. B program to make rapid progress.

During 4–5 April 1983, Egyptian President Hosni Mubarak paid an official visit to the DPRK to discuss arms acquisitions and trade.[35] He also renewed the 1981 scientific technology agreement.[36] Six months later, during 5–10 September 1983, Egyptian Minister of Defense Field Marshal Abdel Halim Abu Ghazala, led a high-level military delegation to the DPRK.[37] In April 1984, the DPRK test launched its first SCUD Mod. B missiles.[38] This was followed by a second test in September, which brought the total number of missiles test fired to three.[39]

DPRK progress with its SCUD Mod. B continued at a steady pace and the missile entered production during early 1987. By the end of that year the first DPRK SCUD Mod. B missiles were delivered to Iran. These were subsequently employed by Iran during the "War of the Cities" (29 February–21 April 1988). It is somewhat ironic that at the same time that Egypt was cooperating with the DPRK in developing its SCUD Mod. B, they were also cooperating with the Iraqis in their *al-Husayn*, *al-Abbas* and *Condor II* programs. At present there is no evidence of any transfers between the DPRK and Iraq through Egypt.[40]

With the SCUD Mod. B's attainment of production status during 1987, published reports began to surface that the DPRK was assisting Egypt with an improved SCUD-B program.[41] These accounts were followed by additional reports during 1988 and 1989 that the DPRK was directly involved in assisting with the establishment of an improved SCUD production facility in Egypt.[42] The extent to which these reports are correct is currently unknown. It is currently believed that the DPRK provided Egypt with liberal access to its SCUD Mod. B program, including the technical documentation and engineering drawings for the missiles. In May 1991, U.S. intelligence officials are reported to have stated that Egypt was negotiating with the DPRK to purchase the SCUD Mod. C.[43] This was followed in September 1991 by Israeli reports that "...Egypt soon will start local production of enhanced SCUD-C missiles..."[44] To date there is no confirmed evidence that Egypt has either produced an improved SCUD-B based upon DPRK technology, or purchased DPRK produced SCUD Mod. Bs or Mod. Cs.

The ballistic missile related cooperation between Egypt and the DPRK is, no doubt, significant, and is unquestionably beneficial to both countries.[45] It is likely to continue at its present level for the foreseeable future, as is indicated by the continued exchange of high level political and military delegations. It is probable that Egypt will gain access to the DPRK's 600 km SCUD Mod. C and 1,000 km SCUD Mod. D programs.

Although the DPRK may have occupied a leading role in Egypt's improved SCUD-B program, it is by no means the only player. Egypt has pursued technology for its improved SCUD-B program through a number of other countries, for example the U.K. and U.S. During the mid-1980s, Egypt conducted an ambitious covert program to acquire missile-related technology and components in the U.S. to support the *Condor II* project (see below). These operations were coordinated through Abdel Kader Helmy, a naturalized U.S. citizen. Included among the items Helmy and his co-conspirators either exported or intended to export were a number specifically related to the SCUD-B program (identified by Helmy as the "...SCUD B-100...").[46] The extent to which these acquisitions have assisted the SCUD-B program is unknown.

In the first week of June 1990, the PRC and Egypt reportedly concluded an agreement which called for the PRC to update Egypt's Sakr Factory for Developed Industries to allow it to produce "...newer versions of Soviet anti-aircraft missiles, the surface-to-surface SCUD-B and Silkworm..."[47]

During early 1991, it was discovered that Arab British Dynamics (ABD) was planning to produce SCUD components for the Egyptian Armed Forces. ABD is an AOI company located in Heliopolis, Egypt, of which British Aerospace (BAe) owns 30%. Later that year, the U.K. Government brought pressure on BAe to halt the production of SCUD components by ABD. As of early 1992, the Egyptian Government had resisted these actions.[48] BAe withdrew from ABD in September 1992.[49]

The current status of the Egyptian SCUD-B program is obscure. However, the program is believed to be proceeding at an advanced stage. Given the proper political climate and financial resources, Egypt could quickly produce a SCUD-B equivalent missile.

The *Sakr-80* Program[50]

By the early 1980s, Egypt's FROG-7A maintenance program had evolved into a program to design and manufacture a FROG-7A replacement, known as the *Sakr-80* (*Eagle-80*). Primary contractor and systems integrator for this project was the Sakr Factory for Developed Industries. The Abu Zaabal Company for Specialty Chemicals was responsible for the rocket motor and propellant.

During 1983, Sakr was able to secure the services of the French company, Societe Nationale des Poudrers et Explosifs–Division Chimie Expansion (SNPE-CE) to assist it in a number of its projects. This collaboration is believed to have centered upon two projects: development of the *Sakr-30* artillery rocket, a longer-ranged version of the *Sakr-18*, and the *Sakr-80*. SNPE-CE's primary responsibility was to provide experience and technology in designing and developing the propulsion sub-assemblies (especially the propellant grains and ignition trains). Sakr was responsible for the airframe, warhead, guidance, fire-control, launchers and system integration. Provision was also made for the transfer of technology from SNPE-CE to Abu Zaabal Company for Specialty Chemicals. Sakr and SNPE-CE jointly shared the *Sakr-80* research and development costs, which were reported in 1988 to have totaled approximately $100 million. Egypt, however, retained all rights to the *Sakr-80*.

It was hoped that the *Sakr-80* would attract interest in a number of countries that also employed the FROG-7A, or who were interested in an inexpensive long-range area suppression weapon (e.g., a "poor-man's" MLRS). Development, apparently, proceeded well, and during the 1987 Cairo Defense Exhibition, it was announced that the *Sakr-80* firing trials were well under way. These tests confirmed the validity of the *Sakr-80* and its ability to serve as an enhanced FROG-7A replacement. Sakr has stated that it could begin mass production of the missile within a year of a procurement contract being signed. At present, however, no procurement orders are known to have been received.

The *Sakr-80* is a spin-stabilized ballistic missile, which is 310 mm in diameter, 6.5 m in length, and has a total weight of 660 kg of which 200 kg is warhead. Its maximum velocity is 1,200 m/s and time of flight to the maximum range of 80 km is 160 seconds. The maximum altitude, which depends on the launch angle, is 29,000 m. Three warheads were developed, High-explosive, anti-personnel/anti-vehicle cluster (950 bomblets), and anti-tank cluster (65 anti-tank minelets). Publicly, Sakr has stated that no chemical munitions are planned. The *Sakr-80* can be launched from the existing FROG-7A launcher, or from two new Egyptian platforms. These new TELs are a 8x8 ZIL-135 truck, carrying three missiles on launch rails; and a T-54 tank chassis carrying four missiles in launch-containers. Neither of these TELs is known to have proceeded beyond the design stage.

The RS-120 Program[51]

Very little is presently known concerning the Egyptian RS-120 missile program. Sometime during 1986–1987, Egypt approached the CONSEN Group firm of IFAT (located in Zug, Switzerland) seeking assistance in a project known as RS-120. The initial goal of this project was to develop a missile with a range of 120 km. There are, however, indications that the ultimate goal is a much longer-ranged missile. This, however, remains to be confirmed.

IFAT contracted with the German firm of Messerschmitt-Boelkow-Blohm (MBB) to provide Egypt with technical assistance and equipment. So as to not violate West German export regulations, MBB agreed to undertake only part of the work. The balance was contracted out to the Italian firm of SNIA, a subsidiary of the Fiat Corporation.[52] By December 1987, growing international concerns over ballistic missile proliferation in the Middle East (especially the Argentina-Egypt-Iraq *Condor II* program) resulted in West German security authorities advising MBB to discontinue their involvement in the RS-120 project. This was accompanied by concerns that the U.S. might "blacklist" the company if it continued its involvement. As a result, during early 1988, MBB withdrew from RS-120 project, whose fate is now unknown. It probably continued for awhile after the withdrawal of MBB. Also unknown is the extent of SNIA's involvement, and any accomplishments that the project may have achieved.

The *Condor II/Vector* Program[53]

During the 1980s, Egypt was involved in a program to produce a 800–1,000 km range ballistic missile in cooperation with Argentina, the CONSEN Group, and Iraq. This missile is known in Argentina as *Condor II*, in Egypt as *Vector* and in Iraq as *Badr-2000*.[54] The more popular name *Condor II* will be used to ease readability. Egypt's efforts to acquire a 1,000 km range ballistic missile at this time are believed to have been prompted by several factors:

- Egypt's long-term desire to acquire a ballistic missile for both political prestige and practical military use (i.e., the SCUD-B lacks sufficient range to be targeted against Israel from launching sites west of the Suez Canal, or many targets in Libya).
- Egypt's realization, in light of the 1973 War, that ballistic missiles would play an important part in any future Middle East war.
- Israel's deployment of its nuclear capable *Jericho II* missile, with a reported range of 1,000–1,500 km.
- Libya's continued efforts to both acquire ballistic missiles and develop an indigenous capability to produce them.

In 1992, the precise details of the *Condor II* project are still incomplete, as are the substance of Egypt's involvement in the project.

The *Condor II* is a direct descendant of an earlier Argentine project known as the *Condor I*, which was begun by the Argentine Air Force during 1977–78 as a sounding rocket (see the chapter on Argentina by Scott Tollefson). Argentina realized that such an endeavor was beyond its limited indigenous capabilities, so the assistance of MBB was secured. This assistance, which was funneled in part through the CONSEN Group, successfully developed the *Condor I* sounding rocket.[55] The Italian firm of SNIA-BPD was also involved in the project, providing quantities of solid rocket fuel.[56] The *Condor I* was a single-stage, solid-fuel, sounding rocket capable of lifting a 400 kg payload to an altitude of 70,000m. Although the *Condor I* project was publicly described as non-military, it had obvious military utility.[57]

The *Condor I* project hadn't reached its test stage when, in late 1982, the decision was made to produce an even more capable system, known as the *Condor II*, which was clearly a ballistic missile. The *Condor II* was designed as a two-stage, solid-propellant missile having a range of 800–1,000 km, with a payload of approximately 500 kg, which would be carried by a wheeled TEL. To expedite development, CONSEN also arranged for a number of well established European firms to provide key components for the *Condor II* project, including:[58]

- MAN of West Germany: the wheeled TEL.
- MBB of West Germany: guidance systems and general missile technology.
- Sagem of France: the inertial navigation systems.
- SNIA-BPD of Italy: rocket motors and solid fuel technology.
- Additional *Condor* contractors reportedly included the Swedish firm Bofors and the West Germany firm Wegmann.

As world concerns regarding the transfer of ballistic missile technology to Third World nations continued to grow, the role of the CONSEN Group became even more critical. It performed pivotal roles on *Condor II*; including in the Egyptian and Iraqi parts of the project; and in Iraq's missile chemical and nuclear programs.[59]

At this time Egypt's interests in developing a ballistic missile coincided with Argentina's. During late 1982 or early 1983, a memorandum of understanding was signed between the two countries calling for cooperation in the development of the *Condor II*. This relationship was reinforced on 15 February 1984, when the Egyptian Ministry of Defense, through the offices of Ballistic Missile Egypt (BME) signed an agreement with IFAT for the joint development of the *Condor II*. By the end of 1984, Egypt, Argentina, Iraq, and the CONSEN Group had entered into additional agreements that solidified Iraqi funding for the project.[60] Egypt's primary contribution would be technical expertise.

The initial plans are believed to have called for Argentina to complete the construction and testing of 10 missile. Five of these were to be delivered to Egypt and five delivered to Iraq. One source estimates that, eventually, each of the three countries would procure 200 missiles.[61] Both the Egyptians and Iraqis anticipated that they would then begin production of additional *Condor II* missiles in their respective countries by the end of the 1980s. In Egypt the construction of *Condor II* facilities was known by the code name DOS, in Iraq they were known as DOT, and in Argentina they were called DAT.[62] The Egyptian DOS facilities are believed to have included missile fuel and test areas at Abu Zaabal, northeast of Cairo, and a missile production facility at Helwan (believed to be designated Factory 17).[63] The Abu Zaabal Company for Specialty Chemicals was probably responsible for the missile fuel facility, while the Sakr Factory for Developed Industries was responsible for systems integration, missile production and testing.

The two CONSEN Group companies most heavily involved with Egypt's participation in *Condor II* were the IFAT Corp., ltd., located in Zug, Switzerland (responsible for the financial aspects) and CONSEN S.A.M., located in Monaco (responsible for contracting). With other CONSEN Group companies (e.g., Transtecno, Delta Consult, etc.) playing smaller roles.[64]

Egypt's *Condor II* program was controlled through BME, which was under the direct control of Defense Minister Field Marshal Ghazala. BME was in turn headed by General Abdel El-Gohary, a member of Defense Minister Ghazala's staff. The chief engineer for the project was Colonel Fuad al-Gamal. To coordinate the development of the *Condor II* project with IFAT and CONSEN, Colonel Ahmed Hussam El-din Yossef Khairat was selected to established an office in Salzburg, Austria. This office was co-located with those of IFAT and CONSEN.

It was Colonel Khairat, through the services of Abdel Kader Helmy, a naturalized U.S. citizen, who conducted an ambitious program to acquire missile related technology and components in the U.S., not only to support the *Condor II* program, but also Egypt's other missile projects. Between 1983 and 1988, Helmy and his co-conspiritors either exported, or intended to export, the following U.S. missile related technology and components;

- A test stand for analyzing the thrust of rocket motors up to 20 tons. This test stand was apparently to be installed at the Sakr Factory for Developed Industries.
- Strap-down inertial guidance systems.
- During 1984, the Egyptian Ministry of Defense attempted to acquire U.S. fuel-air explosive bombs and technology, reportedly for use in clearing minefields. It was, however, intended for use in developing a *Condor II* warhead. This initial effort was blocked by the U.S. State Department and Customs Service because they were on the Munitions Control List. The following year, through the services of Helmy, they attempted to obtain these items again.

- Software for inertial guidance and warhead trajectory optimization modules. This aspect of the Egyptian acquisition program was handled through TRANSTECNO, U.K., another CONSEN Group company.
- Carbon-carbon and ceramic-ceramic composite materials for nose cones.
- Various chemicals required for the manufacture of composite solid propellant rocket fuels and motors, including:
  1. 18,000 pounds of military grade aluminum powder.
  2. 425 pounds of the anti-oxidant Cyanox
  3. 11,000 pounds of the synthetic rubber compound HTPB (hydroxyl-terminated polybutadine).
  4. 500 pounds of EPON from the Miller-Stephenson Company. EPON is used for gluing composite fabrics to surfaces in the aerospace industry.
  5. Veramide 125 and Versamide 140 from the Hemkel Co. These two chemicals are epoxy hardeners used in conjunction with EPON.
  6. 40 pounds of MAPO (tris-2-methyl aziridinyl phophine oxide), a rocket propellant component, from Arsynco Co.
  7. HMDI (hexamethylene diisocyanate), a curing agent for HTPB in solid rocket fuels.
- 21,200 pounds of maraging steel, intended for the motor casing of the first stage of the *Condor II*, and for making the connection between the casement sections and the head and the nozzle of the rocket.
- 185 yards of Rayon-based ablative carbon fabric from the HITCO Co. This was required for a heat shield for *Condor II* payload covers.
- 436 pounds of MX-4926, an ablative carbon phenolic fabric from the Fiberite Co., an essential material for manufacturing the flexible nozzles that would maneuver the *Condor II*.
- Microwave rocket telemetry antennas from Vega Precision Laboratories.

Due to poor operational security and inexperience, the majority of these efforts failed. In June 1988 Helmy and a number of his co-conspiritors were arrested.[65] The scope and quantity of the items desired was considerable, indicating the slow progress being made with the *Condor II* project and Egyptian missile development in general. The loss of the U.S. conduit for missile-related technology and components was a staggering blow to the *Condor II* project.[66]

By mid-1988, as a direct result of U.S. political pressure arising from the arrest of Helmy and his co-conspiritors, Egypt officially withdrew from the *Condor II* project.[67] This was marked by the contract between the Egyptian

Ministry of Defense (i.e., BME) and IFAT being formally canceled on 11 July 1988.

This Egyptian withdrawal was accompanied by Iraq withdrawing its financial support for the project. There appears to have been a long-standing Iraqi concern with Egypt's technical capabilities and management practices. Iraq apparently believed that, in numerous instances, it was being charged twice for development work on *Condor II*; first, by contract European engineers and scientists, and second by Egypt. Additionally, workmanship at the DOS *Condor II* facilities in Egypt is believed to have been significantly inferior to that in Iraq, and there was concern that an explosion of missile fuel would occur at the Abu Zaabal facility.[68] These Iraqi concerns came to a head during 1988, with the arrest of Helmy.

A direct result of the collapse of the *Condor II* project was the reorganization of the Egyptian component of the program. This witnessed the sideways promotion of its principal backer, the former defense minister, Field Marshal Abdel Halim Abu Ghazala in April 1989 and the replacement of a number of key personnel.[69] In mid-1989, the project was probably headed by a General Mustafa, assisted by a Dr. Toufik, while a Col. Essam Ayoub was responsible for the DOS construction program.[70] It is currently believed that sometime during 1989–90, Egypt re-examined the status of its various missile programs and made the decision to cancel all internal development of the *Condor II*.[71] The resources that were allocated to the *Condor II* project were probably then redistributed to the SCUD-B program, which was being pursued with DPRK assistance (see above).[72] It is conceivable that the *Condor II* production facilities at Helwan and the fuel fabrication facility at Abu Zaabal, which were never completed, have been reassigned to the SCUD-B program.

Three of the more unusual aspects of the Egyptian involvement in the *Condor II* project concern reports of an Egyptian test launch; the delivery of *Condor II* components from Argentina to Egypt, and Egypt to Iraq; and the Egyptian acquisition of uranium. During 1987, at least one report suggested that Egypt conducted a test firing of a *Condor II* missile.[73] If this is correct, the missile must have been constructed in Argentina and delivered to Egypt for testing.

Few sources mention any transfers of missiles by Argentina to Egypt or Iraq, or Egyptian missile transfers to Iraq, and those few sources provide confusing details. One report suggests that 5 *Condor II* airframes were delivered to Egypt.[74] A second source, however, indicates that Argentina provided Egypt with 12 to 30 airframes between September 1988 and March 1989.[75] A third source states that Egypt provided Iraq with 3 missile "kits," including a prototype *Condor II* during 1987. This was followed by a further shipment of 16 prototype *Condor IIs* during the first half of 1988.[76] At present there is insufficient evidence to substantiate any of these reports.

In addition to the pressure the U.S. focused upon Egypt concerning *Condor II*, it also applied considerable pressure to Argentina (see Tollefson). During April 1992 the remnants of the *Condor II* program were transferred to CNAE, which reported directly to President Menem.[77]

The final casualty of the *Condor II* project was the CONSEN Group itself. As a result of the negative publicity it received, the CONSEN Group suffered financial disaster. By the end of 1990, the CONSEN Corp. and IFAT Corp., Ltd. (both in Zug, Switzerland) and Delta Consult and Delta System (both in Salzburg, Austria) had been liquidated. The remaining companies were either on the verge of liquidation or had been restructured and were attempting to acquire new businesses in the civilian engineering market.[78]

Although the cancellation of the *Condor II* project was a significant blow to Egyptian ballistic missile development, it wasn't a complete loss. The project provided Egypt with practical experience in a number of areas and resulted in the transfer of a large body of missile-related technology to Egypt. These benefits are apparently now being applied to the improved SCUD-B program.

Notes

1. The Sakr factory was established during 1953 in Heliopolis, an eastern suburb of Cairo. It included not only the factory complex itself, but also a small rocket and missile test site. It is unclear as to whether this factory was identified as the Sakr factory when it was established. The term Sakr factory will be used to facilitate readability. Robert R. Ropelewski, "Improvisation Key to Egyptian Growth," *Aviation Week & Space Technology*, November 13, 1978, pp. 38–47.

2. These three departments are believed to have been initially headed by Wolfgang Pilz (rocket engine), Paul Goercke (guidance) and Walter Schuran (airframe). It appears that Hans Kleinwachter was also a leader within the missile project, but his exact role is unclear. It is probable that he was somehow involved in the development of testing and control telemetry.

3. Bar-Zohar, p. 216.

4. *Washington Post*, July 14, 1966, p. A21.

5. Lieutenant General Saad el-Shazly. "The Crossing of the Suez," *American Mideast Research*, 1980, pp. 78–80; and Edwards H. Kolcum. "Soviets Shifting Mideast Balance," *Aviation Week & Space Technology*, May 11, 1970, pp. 21.

6. Edgar O'Ballance. *The Electronic War in the Middle East*, Archon Books, 1974, pp. 39. O'Ballance mistakenly identifies these as *Luna* 2s (FROG-3). The Soviet designator for the rocket itself is 3R-11. For a description of the *Luna M* system see: *Soviet Tanks and Combat Vehicles: 1946 to Present*, pp. 130–139 & 153.

7. Shazly, pp. 78–80, and 309.

8. Ibid.; and Lieutenant General (Ret.) Saad el-Shazly. Letters to Joseph S. Bermudez, Jr., dated 10 July 1988 and 19 June 1989.

9. There is some debate as to whether this Egyptian strategy was effective. Some believe that the Egyptian possession of Scud-Bs during the war had no impact on

the Israeli decision not to bomb Egypt strategically. Others believe the SCUDS played a significant role in the decision not to bomb Egypt strategically. See: Jon Glassman. *Arms for the Arabs,* The John Hopkins University Press, 1975, footnote no. 40, p. 226

10. Shazly, pp. 145–147.

11. Hanoch Bartov. *Dado: 48 Years and 20 Days,* Ma'ariv Book Guild, 1981, p. 232; Glassman, pp. 101–102; and Col. Dr. Yehudia Wallach, Dr. Moshe Lissak,. and Arieh Itzchaki. *Carter's Atlas to the History of the State of Israel: The Third Decade 1971–1981,* Carter , Jerusalem, 1983, p. 44.

12. Major General Chaim Herzog. *The War Of Atonement: October 1973,* Little, Brown & Company, 1975, pp. 24–25; and Glassman, pp. 101–102.

13. An earlier version of this section appeared as: Joseph S. Bermudez, Jr. "Egypt: Ballistic Missiles in the Third World, *Jane's Intelligence Review,* Vol. 3, No. 12, December 1991, pp. 531–537.

14. By the end of 1973 Egypt had established two SCUD brigades. One brigade (the 65th) had been semi-operational since before the war. The equipment for the second brigade had arrived in Egypt by December 1973. Personnel for this second brigade are believed to have completed their training in the Soviet Union during the later part of December 1973. The actual formation of this second brigade apparently took several weeks, so that it wasn't until the first quarter of 1974 that this brigade became operational.

15. Shazly, pp. 78–80.

16. Drew Middleton. "Influx of Arms Caused by War Worries Israel", *The New York Times,* November 2, 1980, p. 21.

17. Badri, p. 106.

18. Herzog, p. 229.

19. Robert Hotz. "Israeli Aircraft, Arab SAMs in Key Battle," *Aviation Week & Space Technology,* October 22, 1973, p. 14.

20. Shazly, p. 268; and Herzog, p. 245.

21. Cecil Brownlow. "Soviets Poise Three-Front Global Drive," *Aviation Week & Space Technology,* November 5, 1973, pp. 12–13.

22. Badri, p. 94.

23. *Ibid.*; and Robert Hotz. "Battlefield Equation Changes Seen," *Aviation Week & Space Technology,* July 14, 1975, p. 15.

24. Williams, p. 188; and "Egypt," *Military Powers,* Volume 2, February 1987, p. 38.

25. Ropelewski, November 6, 1978, pp. 16–18; and Ropelewski, November 13, 1978, pp. 38–47.

26. The GCC includes Bahrain, Kuwait, Oman, Qatar, Saudi Arabia, and the United Arab Emirates.

27. AOI assumed responsibility for a total of nine key production facilities: Aircraft Factory 36 at Helwan; Aircraft Engine Factory 135 at Helwan; Kader Factory for Developed Industries at Heliopolis; Electronics Factory within the Kader Factory; Sakr Factory for Developed Industries; Arab British Helicopters Company; Arab British Engines Company; Arab British Dynamics; and the Arab American Vehicles Company. *Military Powers: The League of Arab States,* pp. 99–100.

28. "International News: Mubarak," *United Press International*, April 2, 1983; "Egypt, An Air Power in Transition," *AIR International*, Volume 22, Number 4, April 1982, pp. 168 & 197; "China," *AIR International*, Volume 14, Number 1, January 1978, pp. 3–4; "Egypt," *AIR International*, Volume 10, Number 5, May 1976, p. 210; and Drew Middleton. "Soviet Arms to Cairo Reported Continuing," *The New York Times*, February 2, 1977, p. 7.

29. "Egypt's Role in Gulf War, Arms Manufacture Assessed," *Al-Hawadith*, 15 January 1988, pp. 26–27, as cited in *JPRS-NEA*-88-014, 7 March 1988, pp. 2–3.

30. For a detailed overview of the Egyptian aerospace industry and the capabilities of the AOI at the time, see the special report "Middle East Aerospace," *Aviation Week & Space Technology*, August 15, 1983, pp. 129–65.

31. "AOI Courted by Western Aircraft Manufacturers for Joint Projects," *Jane's Defence Weekly*, 21 November 1987, pp. 1172–1173; Thalif Deen,. "Egypt Set to Head Arab Arms Bid," *Jane's Defence Weekly*, 9 April 1988, pp. 681–685; and Robert Bailey. "Building an Arab Armaments Industry," *Middle East Economic Digest*, 5 March 1988, pp. 6–7.

32. "Events in September, 1981," *Vantage Point*, Vol. IV, No. 9, p. 28.

33. Typical of these reports is, "Iran Goes Shopping," *Foreign Report*, July 19, 1984, p. 6.

34. "Iranian Prime Minister Arrives in North Korea," *Reuters*, October 24, 1983.

35. "International News: Mubarak," *UPI*, April 2, 1983.

36. "Events in April, 1983," *Vantage Point*, Vol. VI, No. 5, p. 22.

37. This delegation also visited the PRC. "International News: Foreign Briefs," *UPI*, September 2, 1983; and "Events in September, 1983," *Vantage Point*, Vol. VI, No. 10, p. 24–25.

38. During the same year, both countries signed a contract calling for DPRK technical assistance with the Egyptian program to develop a variant of the SA-2b Mod. 1 surface-to-air missile, the *Ta'ir al-Sabah (Morning Bird)*. This agreement may have been concluded during DPRK Defense Minister Oh Jin-u's 12-day visit to Egypt in November 1984. "Egyptian Military Delegation Visits Pyongyang," *North Korea News*, No. 467, March 20, 1989, pp. 3–4.

39. Yu Yin-taek. "North's Military Reorganization, Mobilization Analyzed," *Pukan*, No. 6, June 1985, pp. 132–141; as cited in *JPRS-KAR*-85-070, 31 October 1985, pp. 1–9.

40. There are numerous reports which state that the DPRK was instrumental in the development of the Iraqi *al-Husayn* and *al-Abbas* missiles. These reports, however, show many internal inconsistencies and factual errors. There is presently no reliable evidence of any Iraq-DPRK cooperation in the field of ballistic missiles. Bill Gertz. "Cuba, North Korea Getting Cozy, U.S. Fears," *The Washington Times*, November 29, 1991, p. A5; "Britain-Iraq," *The Associated Press*, September 5, 1989; "Soviets Say Missiles Given to Baghdad Unable to Hit Iran," *The Washington Times*, March 10, 1988, p. A10; and Ed Blance. "Iran-Iraq," *The Associated Press*, March 4, 1988.

41. Tony Walker, Andrew Gowers, and David Buchan. "Egypt And Argentina In Long-Range Missile Plan," *Financial Times*, December 21, 1987, p. 28.

42. "Korea Helps Egypt Build SCUD-B," *Flight International*, 16 July 1988, p. 19; and Nicolas B. Tatro. "Israel-Missiles," *The Associated Press*, December 29, 1989.

43. Bill Gertz. "U.S.: Iran Fired Ballistic Missile," *The Washington Times*, May 24, 1991, p. A5.

44. "Egypt to Build Scuds," *Defense News*, September 2, 1991, p. 2.

45. Tony Walker, Andrew Gowers, and and Anthony McDermott. "A Deadly Race Out of Control," *Financial Times*, June 8, 1988, p. 20.

46. United States District Court for the Eastern District of California. United States of America, Plaintiff v. Abdel Kader Helmy, et. al., Defendants, Cr. No. S-88-201-RAR [corrected to read S-89-201-RAR], November 17, 1989.

47. Adel Darwish. "China to Update Egypt's Missiles," *The Independent*, June 14, 1990.

48. Alan George. "BAe Told to Stop Scud Work," *Flight International*, 29 January 1992, p. 7; and "British Company Helps Chile, Egypt Build Rockets," *Reuter*, June 24, 1991.

49. *Janes Defense Weekly*, September 5, 1992, p. 31.

50. Christopher F. Foss."Egypt's Winning Formula," *Jane's Defence Weekly*, December 14, 1991, p. 1181; Gerard Turbe. "Egyptian rockets and the French connection Sakr and SNPE," *International Defense Review*, February 1, 1988, p. 202; "Weapon Systems and Equipment—Egypt Moving to More Co-operation," *International Defense Review*, June 1, 1989, p. 858; Brian Wanstall. "Egyptian Arms Industry and Forces Update: The Legacy of Camp David," *Interavia Aerospace Review*, May 1, 1988, p. 469; Gerard Turbe. "Egypt Arms Manufacturing Base for the Arab World?," *International Defense Review*, January 1, 1988, p. 73; "More Details of the Egyptian Sakr 80 Rocket System," *Jane's Defence Weekly*, March 12, 1988, p. 462; and "Sakr Rocket Under Development," *Jane's Defence Weekly*, November 28, 1987, p. 1254.

51. Alan George. "Saddam's Secret Weapons," The Middle East, June 1989, p. 21; Alan George and Herben Lansinger. "Rocket Merry-Go-Round," *Profil*, 20 March 1989, pp. 36–38, as cited in *JPRS-TND-89-009*, 5 May 1989, pp. 31–34; and Alan George and Herben Lansinger. "Death Through DOT," *Profil*, 24 April 1989, pp. 38–42, as cited in JPRS-TND-89-009, 5 May 1989, pp. 34–36.

52. For an excellent study of Fiat's efforts in assisting ballistic missile development in the Third World see: Allen Freidman. "All In the Family," September 1988, pp. 220–234.

53. Among the more significant documents available concerning Egypt's involvement in the *Condor II* project are, United States District Court for the Eastern District of California. United States of America, Plaintiff v. Abdel Kader Helmy, et al., Defendants, Cr. No. S-88-201-RAR [corrected to read S-89-201-RAR], November 17, 1989; and Affidavit of David E. Burns, Customs Investigator, dated June 24, 1988. These documents were used throughout the preparation of this section. To ease readability, however, they will be cited only this once. Other supporting sources will be cited as required.

54. "Secret Egypt-Iraq Accord Collapses," *Financial Times*, June 12, 1989. The code name *Badr-2000* is sometimes erroneously applied to the Egyptian version of the *Condor II*. The Egyptian version is variously reported as either *"Vector"* or *"Delta."* It is conceivable that *"Vector"* and *"Delta"* are actually two different projects, but insufficient information is currently available to determine this.

55. For an overview of the CONSEN Group see: Alan Friedman. "The Flight of the Condor," *Financial Times*, November 21, 1989, p. 10.

56. Kenneth R. Timmerman. *The Death Lobby*, Houghton Mifflin Co., Boston, 1991, pp. 53–54, and 152.

57. "Condor Project to Continue," *DYN*, 5 October 1989, as cited in *JPRS-TND-89-020*, 26 October 1989, p. 21.

58. "The Flight of the Condor," p. 10; Robert Gillette. "3rd World Missiles Linked to German, Italian Firms," *The Los Angeles Times*, February 8, 1989, p. 1; and Robert Gillette. "CIA Chief Cites Firms' Weapons Aid to 3rd World," *The Los Angeles Times*, February 10, 1989, p. 13.

59. "Saddam's Secret Weapons," p. 21; "Rocket Merry-Go-Round," pp. 36–38; and "Death Through DOT," pp. 38–42.

60. Karl Gunther Barth and Lambrecht. "How German Scientists Developed a New Medium-Range Missile for Egypt and Argentina Which Can Carry Nuclear Warheads," *Stern*, August 25, 1988; "In Search of the Forbidden Missile," *Corriere Della Sera*, September 1, 1988; and *U.S. News & World Report*, July 25, 1988, p. 38. There are some indications that the Saudi Government may have also provided some initial funding for the Egyptians in the project.

61. "In Search of the Forbidden Missile," *Corriere Della Sera*, September 1, 1988.

62. "MidEast Markets: Iraq Goes it Alone on Condor II," *Financial Times*, May 15, 1989. It appears that there were also Condor II facilities in Romania where they were identified as DET. The extent of the Romanian connection is currently unknown.

63. *Ibid.*, and "The Flight of the Condor," p. 10.

64. "Saddam's Secret Weapons," p. 21; "Rocket Merry-Go-Round," pp. 36–38; and "Death Through DOT," pp. 38–42.

65 John. Howard. "Five Charged With Plotting to Export Rocket Parts," *The Associated Press*, June 24, 1988; Philip Shenon. "U.S. Accuses 2 Egyptian Colonels In Plot to Smuggle Missile Material," *The New York Times*, June 25, 1988, p. 1; and Ruth Marcus and David B. Ottaway. "Egyptian Officer Tied to Smuggling Effort," *The Washington Post*, June 25, 1988, p. A1.

66. United States District Court for the Eastern District of California. United States of America, Plaintiff v. Abdel Kader Helmy, et. al., Defendants, Cr. No. S-88-201-RAR [corrected to read S-89-201-RAR], November 17, 1989, Attachment #2.

67. Tatro, December 29, 1989; and , David B. Ottaway. "Egypt Drops Out of Missile Project; State Department Official Offers No Details on Iraqi Program." *The Washington Post*, September 20, 1989, p. A32. President Mubarak subsequently stated that the U.S. did not intervene in any Egyptian decisions concerning *Condor II*, see: "Mubarak Addresses Missiles in Interview With Qatari Papers," *MENA*, 27 December 1989, as cited in *JPRS-TND-90-002*, 17 January 1990, pp. 13–14.

68. "Secret Egypt-Iraq Accord Collapses," *Financial Times*, June 12, 1989. Ironically, on 17 August a explosion ripped through an Iraqi production facility at al-Hillah. "Britain-Iraq," *The Associated Press*, September 5, 1989; and Victor Mallet and Tony Walker. "Egyptians Confirm Explosion in Iraq," *Financial Times*, September 7, 1989, p. 4.

69. Alan Cowell. "Cairo Aide's Ouster Tied to Effort to Get Missile Parts in U.S.," *The New York Times*, April 18, 1989, p. A8.

70. "MidEast Markets: Iraq Goes it Alone on Condor II," *Financial Times*, May 15, 1989; and Secret Egypt-Iraq Accord Collapses," *Financial Times*, June 12, 1989.

71. For example see: "Egypt 'Has Pulled Out of Condor Program'," *Jane's Defence Weekly*, 30 September 1989, p. 630.

72. Tatro, December 29, 1989.

73. Walker, et. al., December 21, 1987, p. 28. Argentina is known to have conducted tests of the *Condor II* missile as late as July 1989 from the Chamical Airspace Base. "Defense Minister Denies Missile Pact With Iraq," p. 29

74. "We Have Power in the Tank," *Der Spiegel*, 25 February 1991, pp. 112-115, as cited in *JPRS-TND*-91-005, 28 March 1991, pp. 32–35.

75. "Iraq's Involvement in Condor II Project Viewed," *SOMOS*, 28 January 1991, pp. 1–4; as cited in *JPRS-TND*-91-003, 25 February 1991, p. 13.

76. Adel Darwish and Gregory Alexander. *Unholy Babylon*, St. Martin's Press, 1991, pp. 87–89. This same source suggests that during 1987 Iraq purchased "...over 120 Badr-2000 missiles from Egypt, subsequently using them..." during the 1988 "War of the Cities." This statement is extremely suspect and casts some doubt on the validity of the statements concerning *Condor II* transfers.

77. "Argentine Missile Developments Placed Under Civilian Control," *International Defense Review*, 9/1991, pp. 908–909; Jimmy Burns and Alan Friedman. "US Concern Over Argentine Missile Links to Baghdad," *Financial Times*, March 9, 1992, p. 3; and John Barham. "Argentina Yields to US Over Missile," *Financial Times*, February 11, 1992, p. 4.

78. "Take-Off Delayed," *The Middle East*, January 1991, p. 16.

3

Iran's Missile Development

Joseph S. Bermudez, Jr.

Introduction

At the time of the fundamentalist revolution in 1979, Iran had no long-range artillery rocket or ballistic missile capabilities to speak of. This situation remained essentially unchanged through the following year when Iraq launched its invasion. The continued Iraqi use of FROG-7A artillery rockets against Iranian cities led to Iran's interest in artillery rockets and ballistic missiles. Thus began a see-saw race with Iraq for superiority in these weapons which would last throughout the eight-year-long war, plus the evolution of a strategic concept concerning the military and political importance of ballistic missiles. Unfortunately for Iran, it lost both the ballistic missile race and the war. This, however, only reinforced their desire to possess and produce ballistic missiles.

The development of ballistic missiles in Iran has been influenced by several interrelated factors:

- The short range to Iraqi strategic targets.
- The quantity and quality of missiles and missile related technology acquired.
- The size and experience of the indigenous missile related manpower pool.
- The capabilities of the Iranian military-industrial infrastructure.

It remains to be seen exactly what influence "Operation Desert Storm" had upon Iranian thinking. Preliminary estimates are that it has only reinforced the need for larger numbers of more modern missiles, and possibly the need to pursue cruise missile technology.

From a proliferation standpoint Iran currently presents a number of problems. Primary among these are:

- The continued willingness of the Democratic People's Republic of Korea (DPRK) and the People's Republic of China (PRC) to provide Iran with both missiles and missile related technology that at the very least exceed the intentions of the Missile Technology Control Regime (MTCR). This has been complemented, to a lesser extent, by the willingness of Libya and Syria to also provide Iran with ballistic missiles.
- The ongoing ability and willingness of Iran to fund the development of missiles and missile related technology in other countries (e.g., the DPRK and Syria).
- Both development of an indigenous missile design and production capability and the evolution of a strategic doctrine that foresees Iran as a "center" for other Third World nations seeking missile capabilities.

"Project Flower"[1]

The origins of the Iranian missile program can tenuously be said to date back to the late 1970s, during the last years that the Shah Mohammed Reza Pahlavi ruled Iran, and the joint Israeli-Iranian "Project Flower." This project was concerned with the development of a longer ranged (150–200 km) and more heavily armed version of the Israeli *Gabriel* anti-ship missile (not, as sometimes reported, with the development of a ballistic missile based upon Israeli *Jericho* surface-to-surface missile—SSM).

In 1978 Iran made a down payment for "Project Flower" by providing Israel with $280 million worth of oil. To support this project, a team of Iranian experts began construction of a missile assembly facility near Sirjan, in south central Iran, and a missile test range near Rafsanjan. During February 1979, the Imperial Iranian regime collapsed, and along with it died "Project Flower."

The *Oghab* Program

Early Development

The first two years of the Iran-Iraq war were chaotic for Iran. By the end of 1982, however, continued Iraqi usage of FROG-7As, their initiation of SCUD-B attacks, and the Iranian inability to respond in kind, resulted in a resurgence of Iranian interest in battlefield support rockets and ballistic missiles.

Iraq had begun the war with an inventory of approximately 24 FROG-7A and 12 SCUD-B transporter-erector-launchers (TELs). Only the FROG-

7As, however, were employed against Iranian targets, with the SCUD-Bs being held as strategic reserves. By October 1982 Iraq had launched at least 67 FROG-7As at Iranian cities, primarily Dezful and Ahvez. On 27 October 1982, the war entered a new phase as Iraq launched its first SCUD-B missile at Dezful, killing 21 and wounding 107.[2] This was followed two months later by another SCUD attack. On the night of 19 December, two missiles killed 62 and wounded 287.[3] Although it appears that the Iranians had initiated an indigenous artillery rocket and missile program earlier in 1982, these two SCUD-B attacks, with their high casualty rates, probably convinced them of the correctness of their decision and stressed its urgency.

The details of the early Iranian program, as well as its immediate objectives, are unknown.[4] By the end of 1982, the program appears to have consisted of three major components—acquisition of SCUD-B missiles, indigenous design and production of an artillery rocket comparable to the FROG-7A, and development of a capability to produce tactical ballistic missiles. The greatest obstacle to developing any indigenous capabilities was the status of the Defense Industries Organization (DIO), and later Islamic Revolution Guard Corps (IRGC) Construction Jihad, industrial infrastructure. The DIO had been severely handicapped by the withdrawal of foreign advisers and technicians during 1979. As the artillery rocket component developed over the years it would actually consist of a series of concurrent programs pursued semi-independently by the Air Force, DIO and the IRGC Construction Jihad. This often resulted in competition, the dilution of effort, and abortive programs.

One facet of this program begun in 1982 resulted in the development of the *Oghab* (Persian for Eagle) artillery rocket.[5] The *Oghab* proceeded slowly and with numerous complications. According to one report, several people, including one of the designers, were killed during a 1983 test launching.[6] Possibly as a result of the slow progress, Iran looked towards its suppliers for assistance. It is believed that the PRC was instrumental in providing Iran with critical artillery rocket technology and manufacturing equipment that resulted in the *Oghab*.[7] How much of the *Oghab*'s design and components are indigenous is unclear. Even with the PRC's assistance the *Oghab* still proceeded slowly and it wasn't until late 1986 that it entered production and subsequently became operational. This long development cycle for a simple system was most probably a result of the low technical capabilities of Iranian military industries. Although the Iranians frequently call the *Oghab* a missile, it is actually a 230 mm unguided artillery rocket, with a range of 45 km, and a warhead of 70 kg.[8] It has been suggested that with the *Oghab*, the Iranians had failed, since they had not produced a system in the same class as the FROG-7A. Technically this may be correct, since the FROG-7A has both greater range (70 km) and a larger warhead (450 kg). Operationally, however, the *Oghab* would prove to be of strategic and political importance. In most armies, a short range artillery rocket such as the *Oghab* would only be of value as a tactical weapon because of its range. In the Iran-Iraq War the *Oghab* was employed as a strategic system because important Iraqi cities and towns were close to the Iranian border.

Operational Employment

On the morning of 7 December 1986, the *Oghab* made its operational debut as three *Oghabs* were launched at the southern Iraqi city of Basra by "Missile Units of the Iranian Ground Forces." Unlike the SCUD-Bs (see below), which were assigned to the IRGC Air Force the *Oghabs* were assigned to the regular army. Apparently, this was because the design and development for the *Oghab* were initiated by the military and conducted through the DIO. Thus it was an army system.

Although the DIO began initial production of the *Oghab* during late 1986, it is obvious from the numbers fired that production rates remained quite low through most of 1987. By the last quarter of 1987, however, *Oghab* production appears to have achieved a satisfactory rate. By the end of 1987 approximately 70 *Oghabs* had been fired (9 in 1986 and 61 in 1987) during two distinct periods. From 6 December 1986 until 15 February 1987, 53 *Oghabs* were fired, primarily at Basra and Khanaqin. Then on 17 September 1987 17 *Oghabs* were launched against Basra.

Between 29 February and 21 April 1988, Iran and Iraq engaged in what has become known as the Second "War of the Cities" (see below). During the 52 days of this battle, Iran brought the total number of *Oghabs* fired during the entire war to approximately 365.

Air-Launched Variant

Development of the *Oghab* continued through 1987 and 1988. According to U.S. Navy sources, by early 1988 an air-launched version of the *Oghab* had been developed that could be carried by F-4 and F-14 fighters.[9] An air-launched *Oghab* has obvious weaknesses, since its lack of guidance makes accuracy problematic. The large size of the warhead, however, would ensure a devastating impact. Adapting a weapon like the *Oghab* to an air-launched role requires considerable technical skill. Designers must compensate for the aerodynamic affect of the weapon on the aircraft, provide for an interface to control launch, and ensure that the weapon separates from the aircraft on launch without endangering it. The ability of the Iranians to make these adjustments demonstrates that, in at least some areas, the military industries were gaining technical skill.

The status of the *Oghab* program is unknown. The ground-launched *Oghab* probably will be superseded by systems such as the *Fajr-3*, which has an identical range. The air-launched variant will probably be replaced by modern Soviet/CIS precision guided munitions.[10]

The SCUD Program

By late 1982, Iran initiated the indigenous development of battlefield support rockets. This was complemented in early 1983 by efforts to acquire SCUD-B ballistic missiles, which were, however, limited by the available sources. The Soviet Union was then supplying Iraq with the missile, and those countries to which the Soviets had sold SCUD-Bs were under contract not to transfer them to third parties. Additionally, the majority of the states that had SCUD-Bs where siding with Iraq. Of the nations with whom Iran had relations, only two were likely to run the risk selling it SCUD-Bs: Libya and Syria. Negotiations with both countries are believed to have opened during early 1983.

In 1983, Syria provided multiple rocket launchers (MRL) and other military assistance, while Libya provided a small number of SAMs. Sometime during 1984, Iran successfully concluded a secret agreement with Libya for the purchase of SCUD-B TELs and missiles.

The DPRK Connection

During this period Iran also approached both the DPRK and PRC seeking missile technology and tactical ballistic missiles in the SCUD-B class.[11] The DPRK had earlier acquired a small number of SCUD-Bs (the R-17E variant) from Egypt and was pursuing a multifaceted missile research and development program.[12] The goal was to produce both a reverse engineered version and an extended range variant of the SCUD-B known as the SCUD Mod. B and the SCUD Mod. C, respectively. Despite an ambitious start, the DPRK's SCUD Mod. B program proceeded slowly due both to technical difficulties and its severe budgetary crisis. It is probable that the DPRK's SCUD Mod. B program was a major topic of discussion during the October 1983 visit to Pyongyang by Iranian Prime Minister Musavi and Defense Minister Colonel Mohammad Salimi.[13] It is believed that as a result of Musavi's visit, Iran agreed to a bilateral exchange of missile technology and to provide long term financing for the DPRK's SCUD Mod. B program in exchange for an option to purchase DPRK manufactured SCUD Mod. Bs when they became available. The Iranian interest and funding allowed significant progress, and during April and September 1984, the DPRK test launched its first three SCUD Mod. B missiles.[14] Apart from the Egyptian transfers of SCUD-Bs, Iranian financing has proved to be the single most important factor contributing to the DPRK's indigenous tactical ballistic missile production development.

The First "War of the Cities," March–June 1985

As a result of the 1984 agreement with Libya, approximately two SCUD-B TELs and 20 missiles are believed to have reached Iran during January or February 1985.[15] Upon arrival, the missiles were assigned to a newly created missile unit of the IRGC Air Force, whose personnel had received preliminary training in both Libya and Syria. Syria reportedly provided special advisers to complete the training and to assist in operating the SCUD-Bs.[16]

On 12 March 1985 Iran conducted its first missile attack against Iraq, when Iranian troops launched a Libyan-supplied SCUD-B at Kirkuk. This was followed two days later by an early morning attack on Baghdad.[17]

During the next three months both sides conducted a small-scale "war of the cities," with Iran launching missiles at Baghdad and Iraq countering with SCUD-B attacks upon a number of Iranian cities. As a result of a cease-fire agreement this "war of the cities" came to a halt in mid-June. Neither side is known to have launched any missiles for the remainder of the year.

Aside from depleting the missile arsenals of both sides, the "war of the cities" had a significant impact on both sides. For Iran it was a propaganda and morale-building victory to be able to repeatedly attack the Iraqi capital with relative impunity. However, Iraqi missile attacks on Iranian cities caused hundreds of casualties. Thus, both the value of a viable ballistic missile force and their own vulnerability to missile attacks were impressed upon the Iranians. Iraq was extremely frustrated at not possessing missiles with the range to strike at Tehran (approximately 450 km from the Iraqi border). It appears likely that the subsequent Iraqi *Al-Husayn/Al-Abbas* missile program was motivated by this inability to strike Tehran.[18]

One of the more curious aspects of this first Iranian use of SCUD-Bs was a report that suggested that Iranian missiles were a modified version of the SCUD-B. An Iraqi official went further and stated that the size of the explosions in Baghdad indicated a much smaller weapon, carrying 120–200 kg of TNT, as opposed to the standard 1,000 kg SCUD-B warhead. The Iranians were extremely fortunate in simply acquiring and successfully employing their few SCUD-Bs. It is extremely unlikely that they had modified them.[19]

As with the earlier Egyptian transfer to the DPRK, the Libyan sale to Iran was in contravention of an arms agreement with the USSR. Within two weeks of the first Iranian SCUD-B attack, Iraqi Foreign Minister Tariq Aziz and Minister of State for Military Affairs Abdul-Jabber Shanshel made an unscheduled visit to Moscow to enlist its support in stopping future Libyan SCUD-B deliveries.[20] Within a month, the Soviets slowed down the aid flow to Libya.[21] The effect of the Soviet pressure upon Libya was relatively quick and typically Libyan—they asked Iran to return the SCUDs saying that it "had only lent" them to Iran.[22] More significantly, the Libyans declined to provide additional SCUD-Bs, although they would continue the low-level supply of other military assistance to Iran.[23]

Turning Point, 1985

For a number of reasons, 1985 would prove to be a turning point in the political and technical development of Iran's missile capabilities. At the height of the March-June "war of the cities," Speaker of the Iranian Parliament Hashemi-Rafsanjani publicly stated that the acquisition of a ballistic missile force had become a national priority and that Iran would soon become "...a missile power second only to the superpowers."[24]

The week after the cease-fire Hashemi-Rafsanjani led a high-level Iranian delegation to Libya and Syria seeking to secure additional SCUD-Bs.[25] The following week he visited the PRC and DPRK. These two trips apparently laid the foundation for future deliveries of missiles and missile-related technology to Iran. Sometime in 1986, Syria reportedly provided Iran with a small number of SCUD-B missiles for $15 million.[26]

The visits to the PRC and DPRK were also successful, and although all parties publicly stated that no military assistance agreements were signed, circumstantial evidence suggests that while this may have been technically correct, the reality was otherwise. It is believed that Hashemi-Rafsanjani secured both increased military assistance and agreement to sell Iran missiles and engage in bilateral missile technology exchanges. Specifically, during the visit to the PRC, Hashemi-Rafsanjani apparently secured PRC agreement in the following missile related areas:

- The delivery of HY-2 SILKWORM coastal defense missiles beginning in 1986 and assistance in establishing an assembly facility for these missiles.
- The continued delivery of HN-5A and HQ-2 SAMs.[27]
- Technology transfer and long-term assistance in the development of Iranian SSMs and artillery rockets.

The visit to the DPRK was equally fruitful, apparently securing DPRK assistance in:

- The delivery of HN-5A SAMs and assistance in establishing an assembly facility for these and the HQ-2 SAMs.
- Long term assistance in the establishment of factories to manufacture the HN-5A and HQ-2.
- Technology transfer for new Iranian missiles and artillery rockets.
- Assistance in the establishment of a factory to assemble the DPRK SCUD Mod. B equivalent missile.

Also agreed upon was the continued presence of DPRK military advisors within the Iranian armed forces and military industries. These advisers were then believed to exercise a crucial supervisory and technical role in Iran's SAM production. During early 1986, a DPRK colonel was reported to be assisting an Iranian plant manager supervise production and engineering at a large SAM facility in Sadhzi, near Esfahan. His technical staff included 48 DPRK military personnel, 18 East Germans, two Yugoslavs, and a Pakistani.[28]

Additionally, as a result of recent DPRK progress in reverse engineering the SCUD-B, the Iranians apparently agreed to provide continued financing for the DPRK's SCUD Mod. B program in exchange for an option to purchase the first production quality SCUD Mod. Bs.[29]

Between June 1985 and June 1986, neither Iran nor Iraq launched any missile attacks, as each side was occupied with the ground war and with developing missile production infrastructure. Beginning in June 1986, possibly as a result of receiving Syrian SCUD-Bs, Iran began to conduct isolated SCUD-B attacks against Baghdad and Kirkuk. By the end of 1986, Iran had launched and additional 8 missiles, bringing its total of SCUD-Bs fired at Iraq to 22.

Acquisition of DPRK SCUD Mod. Bs

By early 1987 the DPRK had initiated production of its SCUD Mod. B. This probably came as a tremendous relief to the Iranians who were running out of SCUD-Bs provided by Libya and Syria. There was little hope of obtaining more from either of them because of Soviet pressure. Even without Soviet pressure, it is unlikely that either country could provide additional missiles, in the quantities that Iran desired, without severely hampering their own military capabilities. Iraq was also acquiring large quantities of SCUD-Bs from the Soviet Union and making significant progress on it indigenous long-range variant the *Al-Husayn*.

Sometime during June 1987, Iran concluded an estimated $500 million arms agreement with the DPRK, which included the supply of SCUD Mod. B missiles, TELs and HY-2 SILKWORM coastal defense missiles. The exact details of the agreement are unknown, but it is estimated to have consisted of 90-100 missiles and at least 12 TELs. Most sources suggest that these missiles arrived by sea between August 1987 and February 1988.[30]

These transactions have been widely mis-reported in the Western press. Contrary to many accounts, the Iranians have obtained no SCUD-B missiles from either the Soviet Union or the PRC.[31] The missiles provided earlier by Libya and Syria were manufactured in the Soviet Union, while those obtained from the DPRK were produced in the DPRK. Upon arrival in Iran, the DPRK SCUD Mod. Bs were assigned to the "Missile Unit of the IRGC

Air Force," which has been responsible for all SCUD operations against Iraq.

Indigenous Assembly and Production

Following Hashemi-Rafsanjani's June 1985 trip to the DPRK, Iran established an indigenous SCUD program. Though little is known concerning this program, it appears that its initial goal was the establishment of a DIO facility to assemble the DPRK SCUD Mod. B, as soon as it completed its development program. The probable long term goal was the indigenous manufacture of this missile. The first public reports of this program began to appear in mid-1987.[32] These reports indicated that Iran was establishing production lines for a reverse-engineered SCUD-B. Although discounted by Western observers, these reports were essentially correct.[33] Iran was not only serious about its SCUD program, but was also devoting significant resources to it. Progress of the program was relatively steady.

During early 1988 Iranian officials claimed that the SCUD-B had entered production. On 11 April 1988, Brigadier General Mohammad Jalali stated "...two missiles with ranges of 130 kms and above are manufactured by Defense Industries Organization."[34] It is known that the first of these was the *Mushak* (see below). That the second was the DPRK SCUD Mod. B is evident in a statement, three days later, by Colonel Rahimi, First Deputy Minister of Defense: "...We have also succeeded in manufacturing missiles with a range of 320 kms."[35] This 320 km range is the range of the DPRK produced SCUD Mod. B, and is slightly greater then that of the standard Soviet produced SCUD-B, which is 280 km. It is unlikely that the Iranians manufactured these missiles. Rather, they were assembled from components provided by the DPRK.

During 1987, the Iranians fired an additional 18 SCUD-B missiles, increasing to 40 the total number launched against Iraq. This probably expended all of the missiles obtained from Libya and Syria. However, published reports suggest that in late 1987 the Libyans may have supplied 12 additional SCUD-B missiles in return for a supply of chemical munitions.[36]

The Second "War of the Cities," 29 February–21 April 1988

On 29 February, Iran launched three SCUD Mod. Bs against Baghdad in response to an air attack on an oil refinery in Tehran two days earlier. Iraq responded that afternoon, launching five of its new long-range *Al-Husayn* missiles against Tehran. Thus began the second "war of the cities," which would last for 52 days and would witness the launching of approximately 532 rockets and missiles by both sides.

Iran's ability to conduct these attacks was primarily the result of two factors. First was the experience gained in missile operations during the previous three years, especially by the missile units of the IRGC Air Force. Second, it had enlarged its SCUD and *Oghab* inventory during 1987, with DPRK SCUD Mod. Bs and indigenous production. During the first week Iran launched 10 *Oghabs* and 26 SCUD Mod. Bs. At first the Iranians believed they not only were matching the Iraqi missile efforts but were also inflicting greater damage then they were receiving.[37]

However, Iraq soon outpaced Iran in the intensity of missile attacks, in the amount of physical damage caused and, most importantly, in the psychological damage inflicted. By the end of March it was becoming apparent that the Iranians were aware of the limitations of their missile forces compared with Iraq's.[38]

By 1 April, Iran had fired a total of 258, but only 61 were SCUD Mod. Bs, against 129 Iraqi *Al-Husayn* missiles. From then on, Iran quickly depleted its inventory. This was accompanied by further morale problems and the continuing civilian evacuation of Tehran. For a variety of reasons, Iraq declared a unilateral cease-fire on 21 April 1988. The Iranians tacitly agreed and the "war of the cities" was over.

Ultimately, the Iranian ability to respond to Iraqi missile attacks appears to have been limited by the size of its inventory. As indicated by the declining rate at which SCUD Mod. B missiles were launched during the "war of the cities," the Iranians were running out. It is unlikely that they totally depleted their inventories before they stopped launching missiles, but they probably ended up with no more than 10-20 SCUD Mod. Bs. If reports concerning Iran's development of chemical warheads for its SCUD Mod. Bs are correct, it is conceivable that these remaining SCUD Mod. Bs were so equipped; held in reserve as weapons of last resort, or to retaliate for a chemical attack on Tehran by Iraqi *Al-Husayns*.[39] There can be little doubt that Iran had the capability to produce chemical weapons, for on 22 August 1988 Hashemi-Rafsanjani publicly declared that Iran had the "...capacity for mass production..." of chemical weapons.[40]

One report, of uncertain reliability, suggests that the Iranians had considerable problems with their SCUD Mod. B missiles during the "war of the cities." According to this account, eight of the missiles exploded on launch, inflicting numerous casualties among the launch crews. As a result, on 17 March 1988, the Syrians sent a delegation of military advisers to provide assistance.[41]

Within four months of the end of the second "war of the cities," and following a continuing string of Iraqi ground victories (most notably on the Fao Peninsula), Iran sued for peace. On 8 August 1988, after eight years of bitter fighting and tens of thousands of casualties, the Iran-Iraq war formally ended. Iran had been defeated not only on the battlefield but also, more significantly, at home. Its economy was depleted, its civilian industry was near collapse, and its population was simply exhausted from the war.

Reorganization of the SCUD Program

Currently, Iran is pursuing a multifaceted medium-range ballistic missile program, with the assistance of both the PRC and DPRK.[42] There are conflicting indications as to the level of coordination and integration of this assistance within Iran. Some sources suggest that it is very close. During July 1991, PRC Premier Li Peng visited Iran. Traveling to Esfahan, he reportedly visited, "...the military complexes in the North and west of the city where PRC and North Korean workers and experts are working side-by-side with the Iranians on projects to produce ballistic missiles and advanced surface-to-surface and surface-to-air missiles."[43]

Other sources suggest that while Iran is receiving assistance from both the PRC and DPRK with its SCUD program, the two countries are working independently, but in coordination. In addition to the PRC and DPRK, there have been reports that Iran's post-war SCUD program has been aided by the acquisition of production hardware and non-restricted components from eastern European countries. This has not yet been verified.[44]

There is evidence that during the last year of the war the Iranian SCUD program actually developed into two distinct components. The first, described above, began with the establishment of a factory to assemble the DPRK SCUD Mod. B, and was intended to develop into an indigenous capability to manufacture the missile. The second component appears to have developed out of the PRC's transfer to Iran of missile technology and its assistance in the various Iranian missile and artillery rocket programs. Sometime during 1988, it is believed, the PRC agreed to help Iran establish a factory to manufacture "M-class" SSMs.[45] The earlier press reports suggesting that Iran was manufacturing the PRC versions of the FROG or SCUD-B are clearly incorrect.[46]

The SCUD Mod. B/C Program

During late 1988 and early 1989, Iran and the DPRK reportedly established two joint commissions. The first was to promote economic, scientific and technological cooperation, and the second to facilitate military collaboration. One of the primary responsibilities of the latter commission is believed to be continued cooperation in the missile field. During their May 1989 visit to the DPRK, Minister of Construction Foruzesh and President Khamene'i probably reached an agreement for the supply of additional SCUD Mod. Bs and continued Iranian funding of the DPRK's SCUD program. Sometime during early 1990, Iran reportedly received an additional 20 DPRK SCUD Mod. B missiles.[47]

In November 1990, Minister of the Korean People's Armed Forces Oh Jin-u led a military delegation to Tehran.[48] It is believed that this trip resulted in a second series of military agreements. Iran would purchase

DPRK-produced SCUD Mod. Cs and the DPRK would help convert a missile maintenance facility in eastern Iran to assemble and then to manufacture the SCUD Mod. C. By early 1991, DPRK military technical advisers arrived in Iran and commenced the conversion work. Concurrently, Iranian military personnel traveled to the DPRK to receive training in the manufacture and operation of the new missiles.[49]

It was probably emotionally satisfying when, during "Operation Desert Shield/Desert Storm," Iraq reportedly approached Iran with a request to buy, among other items, approximately 100 SCUD Mod. B missiles.[50] Iran, however, did not provide any military assistance to Iraq.

Beginning in January 1991, shipments of SCUD Mod. Cs and related equipment were tracked being flown from the DPRK capital of Pyongyang to Iran by Iranian Boeing 747 aircraft. The exact number of missiles acquired by the Iranians is not known, but U.S. officials believe that as many as 100 SCUD Mod. Cs may have been purchased.[51] That month, the Iranian Ministry of Defense and Armed Forces Logistics announced that, in February, it would begin mass producing "...powerful long-range surface-to-surface missiles..."[52]

In May 1991, Iran test-fired a medium-range ballistic missile from a mobile TEL which traveled more than 500 km. U.S. intelligence agencies identified it as a DPRK SCUD Mod. C.[53] Four months later, reports surfaced that Iran and Syria had agreed to jointly produce the DPRK SCUD Mod. C. Apparently, Iran will finance the construction of a missile factory in Syria that will be built by the DPRK.[54]

Tondar-68 and *Iran-700*

An accurate assessment of post-war ballistic missile related activities between Iran and the PRC is difficult. There have been numerous reports concerning the direct transfer of DF-15/M-9 and M-11 missiles, but there is no hard evidence to support them.[55] Even the U.S. State Department says, "...there is no evidence that intermediate range ballistic missiles built in China have been sent to any country besides Saudi Arabia, either directly or indirectly."[56]

At present, the best estimate is that, as a result of agreements signed during 1988, the PRC agreed to provide Iran with the following:

- "M-class" missile technology required to produce ballistic missiles with range comparable to the Iraqi *Al-Husayn* (600 km) and *Al-Abbas* (900 km). This included the training of Iranian engineers and technicians and the provision of PRC advisers.
- Equipment and technical assistance in developing the infrastructure required to indigenously design, test and produce such missiles (e.g., manufacturing equipment, test range instrumentation, etc.).

It appears that infrastructure development progressed rapidly. During March 1989 it was reported that the PRC was helping Iran establish a facility, located in northeastern Iran, to manufacture an 800 km SSM.[57] By the end of 1990, launch range and test facilities are believed to have been completed near the city of Semnan, 175 km east of Tehran.[58] During May 1991, reports indicated that the PRC was assisting Iran with production facilities for HY-2 SILKWORM anti-ship and M-class missiles at Esfahan.[59] By March 1991, Iran is reported to have tested at least two new ballistic missiles at the Semnan facility, one with a range of 700+ km, and a second with a range of 1,000+ km.[60] Since the range of the DPRK SCUD Mod. C is 600–650 km, these missiles are probably the products of the Iranian-PRC program. In February 1992, *Jane's Defense Weekly* reported that, "China and North Korea have been indispensable in developing Iran's missile production capabilities. Projects underway include a new variant of the Chinese M-11, possibly under the Iranian designation Tondar-68, with a range of 1,000 km."[61]

Until the Iranians associate a name with the 1,000 km missile, this provisional *Tondar-68* designation will be used to identify and differentiate it from other missiles. Likewise, the 700+ km missile will be identified as the *Iran-700*. No additional information has come to light concerning either the *Tondar-68* or the *Iran-700*. These are provisional names and are only used for convenience until the actual Iranian names become available.

The HY-2 SILKWORM

Initial Acquisition and Deployment

Sometime during mid-1986 Iran took delivery of its first battery of HY-2 SILKWORM coastal defense cruise missiles from the PRC.[62] These missiles were deployed with IRGC Navy units at sites in the northern end of the Persian Gulf, on the Al-Fao peninsula, and in the Straits of Hormuz, near Bandar-e Abbas and Kuhestak. The units apparently became operational in early 1987, conducting several test launches in February.[63]

Under strong international pressure, primarily from the U.S., the PRC in mid-1987 agreed not to supply any further HY-2 SILKWORMs.[64] Iran, however, continued to receive SILKWORMs. This resulted in growing concerns that in spite of the PRC's statements to the contrary, they were still providing SILKWORMs either directly from the PRC or transshipped through a third country (e.g., the DPRK).[65] During June 1987, Iran concluded an estimated $500 million arms agreement with the DPRK, which not only included the supply of SCUD Mod. B missiles and TELs, but also SILKWORMs.[66] All SILKWORM sales for the remainder of the war were DPRK-produced.

Despite this assured supply of SILKWORMs, by the end of 1987 the IRGC had, with PRC assistance, initiated a program to first assemble and then manufacture the missile indigenously. In April 1988, Iran's Ambassador to the PRC claimed that Iran was manufacturing its own SILKWORM missiles, copying the design from examples captured from Iraq.[67] Although the reference to captured Iraqi SILKWORMs and the suggestion that Iran was manufacturing SILKWORMs were not true, this was the first public mention of an Iranian program.

Post-War Deployment

In November 1988, IRGC Minister Mohsen Rafiqdust said, "...with regard to surface-to-air and surface-to-sea missiles, we are busy copying these. Mass production of these will begin in the near future.[68] During 1989, Iran continued to receive HY-2 SILKWORMs from the DPRK and probably the PRC. By early 1990, the supply of completed SILKWORMs was apparently phased out and replaced by components that were assembled in Iran. Sometime during 1990 or early 1991, Iran is believed to have initiated the indigenous production of the SILKWORM at a PRC supervised factory in Esfahan.[69]

The *Mushak* Family of Missiles

Mushak-120/-160

On 1 December 1987, Tehran radio stated that a new series of SSMs was to be "...placed at the disposal of the battlefronts in the next few days..."[70] This statement was premature as indicated by later Iranian statements. The first solid information on the new missile appeared in an interview given by Hashemi-Rafsanjani at the end of March 1988. He said that, "...mass production of Iranian-made missiles will shortly enable Iran to fire as many as 20 missiles a day into Baghdad.... The missiles, slated to be mass produced, have a range of 130 km. ...the Iranian missiles are not imitations of the SCUD-B's or other missiles."[71] A week later, Iran's Defense Minister, Brigadier General Mohammad-Hoseyn Jalali, said, "...a missile with a range of over 130 km and constructed by the defense industries of our country was recently tested. It has completed its final testing stages and will go into mass production at the end of the current month [month ends 20 April]. ...two missiles with ranges of 130 kms and above are manufactured by Defense Industries Organization (DIO)."[72]

It was not until mid-August 1988 that Hashemi-Rafsanjani revealed that among the weapons being built by Iran was the "...Mushak missile which we have recently been manufactured [sic] by the Guards Corps, the Army, and also by the Reconstruction Jihad."[73] It appears that the *Mushak* is not a single missile, but rather a family of designs, design of which is believed to have begun during late 1985 or early 1986. At least two different versions of the *Mushak* were identified and discussed by Iranian officials during the war. The first had a design range of 130 kilometers, but achieved a range of only 120 kilometers. The second model was test fired in July 1988, and was reported to have a range of 160 kilometers. To differentiate these models, the first will be called the *Mushak-120* and the second the *Mushak-160*. Iranian officials have indicated that the *Mushak-120* has not performed as expected.[74] The reasons for the failure of the *Mushak-120* to reach its design range are unclear. It probably was overweight and the rocket motor did not achieve its designed thrust levels. Design and production of solid rocket propellants is difficult. Additionally, limited or non-available advanced components, such as ammonium perchlorate, would be a difficult problem to overcome. It appears that the failure of the *Mushak-120* led to the transfer of effort to a new version of the missile with a range of 160 kilometers.[75]

Operational Employment

Despite its technical shortcomings the *Mushak-120* apparently entered limited production during early 1988 and made its combat debut in mid-March 1988, during the "war of the cities." It appears that the *Mushak-160* didn't complete developmental testing until just after the war ended and that initial production was scheduled for 1989. On 4 September 1988, IRGC Minister Rafiqdust announced plans to inaugurate two large munitions and casting factories, and for the mass production of the *Mushak-160* and American-designed TOW anti-tank missiles the following year.[76]

The high cost of obtaining systems from abroad, and the difficulties of circumventing the arms embargo, had impressed upon the Iranians the importance of indigenously designed and manufactured systems. It appears that the *Mushak-120* and the *Mushak-160* are new weapons not currently operational elsewhere. Although the Iranians claim that they were designed locally, there is reason to believe that expertise was provided by the PRC, DPRK, and possibly from elsewhere.

No technical descriptions of either the *Mushak-120* or the *Mushak-160* are currently available, but certain surmises can be made. In order to manufacture and fire a missile of this type in large numbers, it must be simple to build and maintain. These missiles have sufficient range to require some kind of guidance, and the need for simplicity and low cost implies that they rely upon a simple inertial system. This inertial package was probably based on components intended for civilian applications and available on the open market. Although it was unlikely to be highly accurate, for Iran's purposes at the time this was not a liability.

Mushak-200

At the end of the Iran-Iraq War, Iran was pursuing at least five missile programs.[77] We believe we know the identities of four of these five missiles. Until early 1989, however, the identify of the fifth was unknown, though it was assumed to be within the *Mushak* family. In April 1989, a new 200 kilometer missile was announced. Although no name was given to this new missile, and in light of the fact that it was manufactured by the DIO—which manufactured the *Mushak-120/-160*—this missile is believed to be a new development within the *Mushak* family. Until a name is associated with this new system, and to differentiate from the earlier *Mushak* models, it will be identified here as the *Mushak-200*. No additional information has come to light concerning the *Mushak-200*. Since it is a development of the earlier *Mushaks* it is probably propelled by a solid-fuel rocket, and has a simple inertial guidance system. Due to the 200 km range it is possible that the rocket motor utilizes an improved propellant (possibly including ammonium perchlorate). If the *Mushak-200* proves to be successful, it would probably supplant the earlier versions of the *Mushak* family on the production lines and in the Iranian Armed Forces. During September 1989, the Ministry of Construction Jihad announced that, "...the production of a particular surface-to-surface missile made in Iran has started...." [78]

There are, however, some doubts concerning the production status of the *Mushak-200*. Iran's acquisition and production of the 8610 during 1990 (see below), has been interpreted by some analysts as an indication that Iran is still having considerable difficulty with its *Mushak* family of solid-propellant missiles. Otherwise, why would Iran purchase a foreign missile of the same category? The current status of the *Mushak-200* and the *Mushak* family is unknown, but development is believed to be continuing.

New Rockets—*Nazeat, Ran, Shahin-1/-2* and *Fajr-3*

In November 1988, Iran held a huge military exhibition in Tehran. Displayed for the first time were a number of Iranian short-range surface-to-surface rockets, including some previously unknown types. These were identified as the *Oghab*, "*Shahin 333*" and the "*Ran*."[79] At that time nothing was known about the latter two types.[80]

Three months later, during February 1989, an Iranian defense industry delegation displayed some of its products at the SECARM arms exhibition in Libreville, Gabon. In May, the Iranians attended the IDEA '89 defense exposition in Ankara, Turkey.[81] Included in the displays at these exhibitions were examples of the *Oghab*, *Nazeat*, *Shahin-2*, and a fourth unnamed system. For the first time, details were also provided on the first three (see Table 3.1). Also mention during these arms exhibitions was the *Shahin-1*, though no details were provided. Additionally, Iranian representatives

TABLE 3.1 Iranian Artillery Rockets and Missiles

	Nazeat	*Oghab (Eagle)*	*Shahin-2 (Falcon 2)*
Caliber (mm)	355	230	333
Length (m)	5,900	4,820	3,870
Total weight (kg)	950	360	580
Warhead (kg)	150	70	—
Number of nozzles	1	1	7
Thrust (kN)	110	75	220
Propellant weight (kg)	400	138	175
Burning time (secs)	10	3.6	1.8
Maximum range (km)	90	45	20
Storage temperature	-30°/+60° C	-30°/+60° C	+60° C

Source: "Baghdad and Ankara Draw Out New Exhibitors," *International Defense Review*, June 1989, pp. 857–859; and "Iran Moves Into Marketing," *International Defense Review*, June 1989, p. 846.

made several significant claims concerning the capabilities of their military industries, including production of ammonium perchlorate and "...the production of thermal nonconductors for missile nozzles." That suggested that they could manufacture advanced ceramic components and piping by the flow-forming method.

Other than the physical characteristics provided by the Iranians at the arms exhibitions little is known concerning these systems. All except the *Oghab* were probably either in the development stage or limited production in 1989. The *Oghab* and *Shahin*-1/-2 are reported to be manufactured by the DIO, and thus are likely to have developed out of the same program that produced the *Oghab*.[82] The "*Ran*" has not been publicly discussed since the Tehran exhibition. The *Nazeat* bears several similarities to the PRC WS-1 artillery rocket, but there is currently no evidence connecting the two.[83] There are no indications, at present, that any of these systems are operational with the Iranian armed forces. All the systems that were on display were of crude and relatively unsophisticated construction. The *Shahin*-2 relies upon clusters of small rockets, rather than a single large rocket motor. These rocket motors most likely were originally intended for use with smaller weapons. For example, during 1987, the IRGC initiated manufacture of several small short-range artillery rockets. These were identified as "*Katyusha*," "*Nakhudsha*," or "*mini-Katyusha*" rockets.[84] Before the overthrow of the Shah in 1978, the Iranians reportedly initiated efforts to reverse-engineer the rockets for the Soviet BM-21 122 mm multiple rocket launcher. The Iranians have probably utilized clusters of small motors as an expedient to allow them to field the *Shahin*-2 until they are able to manufacture larger motors in production quantities. The majority of these rockets appear to be able to utilize the same launcher as the *Oghab*, or slightly modified versions of it.

During March 1990, Iranian Defense Minister Akbar Torkan announced that mass production had begun of the *Fajr-3* (Persian for *Dawn*) artillery rocket, with a range of 45 km.[85] Little else is known concerning this new rocket, but there is some speculation that the *Fajr-3* was the unidentified radially folding fin artillery rocket displayed at the SECARM arms exhibition.

There is little information currently available concerning the status of these various artillery rocket systems. Development can safely be assumed to be continuing.

The PRC "8610" Missile

During late March 1990, U.S. intelligence reported indications that the PRC had agreed to provide Iran with at least 50 short-range SSMs called "8610," which the PRC was producing for export.[86] At that time little was publicly known of 8610 except that its range was 120–130 km. Subsequently it has been learned that 8610 is the surface-to-surface version of the PRC's HQ-2 SAM (see the chapter by Hua Di).[87] It appears that the first 8610s reached Iran as early as May 1990, approximately "...48 short-range, surface-to-surface missiles..." were delivered to Iran by a PRC freighter.[88] This, reportedly, was the first time the PRC had sold and delivered missiles to the Middle East since their April 1988 statement that they would suspend missile sales to the region. Little is known concerning any further deliveries of the 8610s or their operational deployment by the Iranian Armed Forces.

By early 1991, it appears that Iran placed the 8610 into production.[89] This would not have been very difficult since Iran had previously established a facility to produce the HQ-2 SAM in Esfahan. Production of the 8610 is believed to be continuing.

Developing Strategic Thoughts

As noted above, in 1985, Hashemi-Rafsanjani established in no uncertain terms that the acquisition of ballistic missiles and the attainment of an indigenous missile capability was a strategic Iranian goal. Iran would become "...a missile power second only to the superpowers."[90] Two years later he expanded upon his earlier statement, "Our military power, that is, our military industries, which we established during the war—which we were forced to establish—was significant, and I have no doubt that in the future, among the Third World countries and its peoples, Iran will be one of the centers for weapons, armaments, and military industries. In the past, this was a monopoly of Eastern and Western arrogance. Today another place has been established which can help people in military techniques, military training, and also in armaments."[91]

Reports during January 1992 suggest that Iran might now be implementing this strategy. At that time, it was reported that during a visit to Sudan, Hashemi-Rafsanjani had concluded an agreement to provide that country with an estimated $20 million worth of arms. Included within this agreement were provisions for the transfer of HY-2 SILKWORMs to Sudan.[92]

The Future

Development of ballistic missiles is an Iranian national priority. In this effort, the Iranians have achieved a number of major accomplishments. They have created the infrastructure to support their effort, reportedly involving 100 different facilities and thousands of people (see Table 3.2). Their factories have produced a number of indigenously designed artillery rockets and short-range ballistic missiles. Iran has also developed the infrastructure required to assemble and produce foreign-designed ballistic missiles (e.g., 8610, DPRK SCUD Mod. B and SCUD Mod. C). It now appears to be in the process of designing and producing, with PRC assistance, ballistic missiles with ranges of 700+ and 1,000+ km (e.g., the *Tondar-68*).

These accomplishments demonstrate the absurdity of the popular notion that Iran is a country run by fanatics who despise science and technology. Actually, the officials responsible for Iran's military forces, and especially men like Hashemi-Rafsanjani, have paid close attention to Iran's technological resources and consider the expansion of the defense industry a major national objective. Moreover, they appear aware of the difficulties involved in such initiatives, and are willing to adopt a methodical, step-by-step approach.

Should Iran's missile industries accomplish the stated objectives, the missile units of the IRGC and regular armed forces will have stockpiles of missiles sufficient to be a major concern to all the countries in South Asia. This ballistic missile capability is of even more concern now that Iran has publicly stated that it has a chemical weapons capability, and is forging ahead with what appears to be a nuclear weapons program.

As noted above, during 1988 and 1989 Iran publicly displayed a number of its then new rocket artillery systems at international arms exhibitions. Also displayed were three indigenously designed and produced remotely piloted-vehicles (RPV)—the *Baz*, *Shahin*, and "22006."[93] While not directly connected with the development of missiles, this RPV capability, if combined with experience gained in the assembly and operation of the HY-2

TABLE 3.2 Reported Iranian Missile-Related Locations[94]

Location	*Activity*
Bakhtaran *(formerly Kermanshah)*	• IRGC base for missile units located along the central Iraqi front. • Syrian advisors were stationed in both the Kermanshah and Dezful regions to assist Iranian missile operations as a result of a secret agreement reached in Tehran during January 1985.[95] • Area from which Iran was launching SCUD-B missiles at Baghdad in 1985.[96]
Bandar-e Abbas	• Main port of entry for ships bringing arms and other supplies into Iran.
Damghan	• The site of a factory that manufactures nerve gas and chemical missile warheads.[97]
Esfahan *(or nearby Mobarakeh)*	• IRGC SCUD-B missile support facility. • Site where missiles are equipped with chemical warheads and prepared for the front.[98] • DIO has established a science and defense industries academy in Esfahan which admitted 700 students in 1989.[99] • During July 1991 PRC Premier Li Peng went to Esfahan to visit the military complexes in the north and west of the city, where PRC and DPRK workers and experts were working side by side with the Iranians on projects to produce ballistic missiles and advanced SSMs and SAMs.[100]
Rafsanjan	• Missile test range under construction in 1977 for use in conjunction with the Iranian-Israeli "Project Flower."[101] • Reportedly a missile launch test site. It has been associated with facilities at Damghan that produce chemical warheads for missiles. • Launch and range facilities, not production facilities.[102]
Semnan	• Missile assembly facility under construction in 1977 for use in conjunction with the Iranian-Israeli "Project Flower."[103]
Sirjan	• IRGC military school and training center (Fajr Air Base); location of IRGC Missile Factory.
Tehran	• The first announced test launching of the Soviet-supplied SA-6 missile took place at the "...Fajr missile base..." The test was conducted by the IRGC.[104]
Qom	• May 1991 site of a test launch of a DPRK SCUD Mod. C. The missile was fired eastward from a mobile transporter-launcher near the Iranian city of Qom. It was tracked on a flight path of more than 500 km to impact in a remote region of the country.[105]

SILKWORM anti-ship cruise missile, could provide Iran with the foundation upon which to develop both harassment drones and long-range cruise missiles.[106]

The danger that Iran will achieve its stated goal of being "...a missile power second only to the superpowers..." and an arsenal for Third World countries has grave implications for missile proliferation throughout the world.

Notes

1. Martin Bailey. "The Blooming of Operation Flower," *The Observer*, 2 February 1986, p. 19; and Elaine Scoliono. "Documents Detail Israeli Missile Deal With the Shah," *The New York Times*, April 1, 1986, p. A17.

2. "Iran Says Iraq Missiles Killed 21," *The New York Times*, October 28, 1982, p. A4; and Drew Middleton. "New Iraqi Strategy Is Seen in War With Iran," *The New York Times*, October 31, 1982, p. 6.

3. "Iran-Iraq," *Xinhua*, 21 December 1982.

4. It is also unknown whether the Iranians utilized any of the personnel or facilities involved with the earlier "Project Flower."

5. Vahe Petrossian. "Iran Stocks Up Its Arsenal," *Middle East Economic Digest*, May 2, 1987, p. 11.

6. "Iran Stocks Up Its Arsenal," p. 11; and James Bruce. "Iran Building Up Its Own Arms Industry," *Jane's Defence Weekly*, 20 June 1987, p. 1302.

7. Many researchers, including this author, originally believed that the *Oghab* was an Iranian produced version of the PRC Type-83 273 mm artillery rocket. This now appears to be somewhat incorrect. It appears, however, that the same PRC technology that produced the Type-83 was transferred to Iran and utilized in the design of the *Oghab*. "Iran Announces Development of Two New Missiles," *The Los Angeles Times*, March 29, 1987, p. 25. The latter source indicates, somewhat incorrectly, that China had helped Iran develop a short-range version of the Soviet FROG-7 with a range of 40 miles. For information on the Type-83, see "Chinese 273 Type 83 Multiple Rocket System," *Jane's Defence Weekly*, 24 January 1987, p. 124.

8. For photographs and a short technical description of the *Oghab* see, Mark Daly. "Display Reveals 'Evidence' of Growing Iranian Defense Industry," *Jane's Defence Weekly*, 31 October 1987, pp. 976–977; "Iranian Rockets Head SECARM Display," *Jane's Defence Weekly*, 11 February 1989, p. 219; and Mark Daly. "Iran Pitches for Arms Market at SECARM," *Jane's Defence Weekly*, 4 February 1989, p. 163; "Baghdad and Ankara Draw Out New Exhibitors," *International Defense Review*, June 1989, pp. 857–859; and "Iran Moves Into Marketing," *International Defense Review*, June 1989, p. 846.

9. Rear Admiral William M. Fogarty. *Investigation Report: Formal Investigation into the Circumstances Surrounding the Downing of Iran Air Flight 655 on 3 July 1988*, July 28, 1988, pp. 40 and 44, indicates that Iranian F-14s were thought to be armed with "modified Eagle" missiles/unguided rockets. Department of Defense sources believe that these are modified versions of the *Oghab* surface-to-surface missile.

10. For an overview of Soviet air-launched weapons see: Nick Cook. "Soviet Air-Launched Weapons—As Smart As They Come," *Jane's Intelligence Review*, Vol. 4, No. 1, January 1992, pp. 16–32.

11. Typical of these reports is, "Iran Goes Shopping," *Foreign Report*, July 19, 1984, p. 6.

12. Interview data. The transfer of the SCUD Bs was a violation of Egypt's agreement with the Soviet Union. Egypt agreed to the transfer as a result of the precipitous decline in Egyptian-Soviet relations at the time, and in return for the DPRK's assistance during the October 1973 War. Egypt also agreed to cooperate with the DPRK in the field of missile development. For a complete discussion of DPRK missile developments see: Joseph S. Bermudez Jr. and W. Seth Carus. "The North Korean 'SCUD B' Programme," *Jane's Soviet Intelligence Review*, Vol. 1, No. 4, April 1989, pp. 177–181; Joseph S. Bermudez Jr. "North Korea's HY-2 'Silkworm' Programme," *Jane's Soviet Intelligence Review*, Vol. 1, No. 5, May 1989, pp. 203–207; and Joseph S. Bermudez Jr. "New Developments in North Korean Missile Programme," *Jane's Soviet Intelligence Review*, Vol. 2, No. 8, July 1990, pp. 343–345.

13. "Iranian Prime Minister Arrives in North Korea," *Reuters*, October 24, 1983.

14. Yu Yin-taek. "North's Military Reorganization, Mobilization Analyzed," *Pukan*, No. 6, June 1985, pp. 132–141; as cited in JPRS-KAR-85-070, 31 October 1985, pp. 1–9.

15. Barry Schweid. "Washington News," *The Associated Press*, January 9, 1986. The exact number of TELs and missiles obtained from the Libyans is uncertain, with estimates ranging from 20 to 50. Given the known numbers fired during the war, it would appear that an estimate of 20–30 is most likely correct.

16. *Foreign Report*, July 18, 1985.

17. "Iran-Iraq," *Xinhua*, 14 March 1985.

18. For a discussion of the early Iraqi program see, W. Seth Carus. and Joseph S. Bermudez, Jr. "Iraq's Al-Husayn Missile Programme, Part I," *Jane's Soviet Intelligence Review*, Vol. 2, No. 5, May 1990, pp. 204–209; W. Seth Carus. and Joseph S. Bermudez Jr. "Iraq's Al-Husayn Missile Programme, Part II," *Jane's Soviet Intelligence Review*, Vol. 2, No. 6, June 1990, pp. 242–248; and Joseph S. Bermudez Jr. "Iraqi Missile Update," *Jane's Soviet Intelligence Review*, Vol. 2, No. 7, July 1990, p. 329.

19. "Iraq Says it Has Pinpointed Iranian Missile Launching Base," March 29, 1985.

20. *Ibid.*

21. "USSR Seen Trying to Block Supply of Scuds to Iran," *KUNA*, 20 May 1985, as cited in *FBIS-NES*, 21 May 1985, p. Q1.

22. Kuwait *KUNA*, June 1, 1987, as cited *FBIS-NES*, June 2, 1987, p. D1.

23. Arie Egozi. "Libya's Gadhafi Indicates Strong Interest in Chinese Ground-to-Ground Missiles," *Defense News*, June 13, 1988, p. 33.

24. "Hashemi-Rafsanjani's Remarks," NHK Television Network, June 11, 1985, as cited in *FBIS-SA*, June 12, 1985, I1.

25. *Foreign Report*, July 18, 1985.

26. Anthony H. Cordesman. *The Iran-Iraq War and Western Security 1984–87*, Jane's Publishing Co., Ltd., New York, 1987, p. 33.

27. These are PRC manufactured versions of the SA-7 and SA-2 SAMs, respectively. "Reagan Defends Military Shipments to Iran, Restates Desirability of Worldwide Embargo," *Aviation Week & Space Technology*, November 24, 1986.

28. Jack Anderson and Dale Van Atta. "North Korea Aids Iran's War of Terror", *The Washington Post*, February 3, 1986, p. B12.

29. "Majlis Reschedules 'Entirety' of DPRK Debt," *IRNA*, 7 December 1986, as cited in *FBIS-NES*, Vol. VIII, 10 December 1986, p. I5.

30. Interview data; Peyman Pejman. "International News: Iran," *UPI*, September 18, 1987; "Pyongyang Missile Sale to Tehran Reported," *The Washington Times*, June 1, 1988, p. A2; John M. Broder. "Five Key Nations Sold Arms to Iran," *Los Angeles Times*, January 20, 1988, p. 5; and "Al-Musawwar Interviews Ramadan on War," *Al-Musawwar*, 20 May, 1988, pp. 20–21, as cited in *FBIS-NES*-88-100, 24 May 1988, p. 18.

31. Typical is the report in *Flight International*, April 25, 1987, p. 13, that Iran bought 200 SS-1 Scud-B missiles from the Soviet Union, or an *AFP*, October 23, 1985, story that Iran was negotiating with the PRC to acquire Scud-A or Scud-B missiles. Peyman Pejman, *UPI*, September 18, 1987, stated that the Bulgarians had sold Scuds as well. It is not possible to confirm these reports.

32. Vahe Petrossian. "Iran Stocks Up Its Arsenal," *Middle East Economic Digest*, May 2, 1987, p. 11; "Scud B Remains Iran's Main Missile Capability," *Jane's Defence Weekly*, 20 June 1987, p. 1289; and James Bruce. "Iran Building Up Its Own Arms Industry," *Jane's Defence Weekly*, 20 June 1987, p. 1302.

33. "Minister on Missile Manufacture, New Submarine," *IRNA*, 8 November 1987, as cited in *FBIS-NES*-87-216, 9 November 1987, p. 61; "IRGC Minister on Military Self-Sufficiency," *IRNA*, 8 November 1987, as cited in *FBIS-NES*-87-222, 18 November 1987, p. 55; and "IRGC Commander, Minister Outline Arms Production," *Keyhan*, 8 November 1987, as cited in *FBIS-NES*-87-219, 13 November 1987, p. 66.

34. "Defense Minister on Manufacturing of Missiles," *IRNA*, 11 April 1988, as cited in *FBIS-NES*-88-070, 12 April 1988, p. 71.

35. "Radio Phone-In Program With Defense Officials," *Tehran Domestic Service*, 14 April 1988, as cited in *FBIS-NES*-88-073, 15 April 1988, pp. 49–51.

36. "Iranians Back Off Claim for Weapons," *The Washington Times*, December 31, 1987, p. 9.

37. "Commander on Damage to Iraq," *Tehran Domestic Service*, 9 March 1988, as cited in *FBIS-NES*-88-046, 9 March 1988, p. 59.

38. "'Most' Iraqi Cities Now Within Missile Range," *IRNA*, 29 March 1988, as cited in *FBIS-NES*-88-061, 30 March 1988, p. 48.

39. Farzad Bazoft and Allan George. "Missiles Armed With Chemical Warheads 'In Sight'," *The Observer*, 13 March 1988, p. 23.

40. "Hashemi-Rafsanjani Addresses Defense Conference," *Tehran Domestic Service*, 11 August 1988, as cited in *FBIS-NES*-88-158, 16 August 1988, pp. 47–53.

41. Since there has been no confirmation of these eight misfires they are not included in the figures cited above. *Al-Watan Al-Arabi*, 15 April 1988, p. 17, as cited in *FBIS-NES* (For Official Use Only Edition), April 20, 1988, p. Annex 1.

42. U.S. Senate. *Hearing of the Senate Governmental Affairs Committee, Subject: Weapons Proliferation in the New World Order*, January 15, 1992.

43. "PRC To Supply Nuclear Technology," *Sawt Al-Kuwayt Al-Duwali*, 11 July 1991, p. 1, as cited in *JPRS-TND*-91-012, 8 August 1991, pp. 19–20.

44. "Reviving the Force of Islam," pp. 1299–1300.

45. John W. Lewis, Hua Di, and Xue Litai. "Beijing's Defense Establishment: Solving the Arms-Export Enigma," *International Security*, Spring 1991, pp. 87–109. David B. Ottaway. "China Sale Report Concerns U.S.," *The Washington Post*, June 23, 1988, p. A33; Michael R. Gordon. "Beijing Avoids New Missile Sales Assurances," *The New York Times*, March 30, 1990, p. A7; and "Weapons Watch," *Bulletin of the Atomic Scientists*, March 1988, p. 55.

46. Numerous sources suggest a PRC connection in the manufacture of Scud-Bs, but none provide details. For example, see: Bazoft, Farzad and George. "Missiles Armed With Chemical Warheads 'In Sight'," *The Observer*, 13 March 1988, p. 23; Dilip Hiro. "Iran: Up in Arms With a Big Hand From the Chinese," *The Wall Street Journal*, June 5, 1987; John M. Broder. "Five Key Nations Sold Arms to Iran Last Year," *The Los Angeles Times*, January 20, 1988, p. 5; and "Iran Announces Development of Two New Missiles," p. 25.

47. Steven Emerson. "The Postwar Scud Boom," *The Wall Street Journal*, July 10, 1991, p. A12.

48. "Events in December, 1990", *Vantage Point*, Vol. XIV, No. 1, January 1991, p. 26.

49. "The Postwar Scud Boom," p. A12.

50. Ruth Sinai. "Gulf-Iraqi Scuds," *The Associated Press*, January 30, 1991; and Knut Royce. "The Gulf War Briefing: Iran's Arsenal Worries Analyst," *Newsday*, January 30, 1991, p. 16.

51. Bill Gertz. "Iran Fired Ballistic Missile," *The Washington Times*, May 24, 1991, p. A5. Other reports suggest that the contract was for 200 Scud-B and -C missiles, see "The Gulf War Briefing: Iran's Arsenal Worries Analyst." Several months later, during October, reports surfaced that indicated that the DPRK had exported 20 Scud missiles to Iran and that some of them already had arrived there and were fully assembled. "DPRK Scuds Said to Arrive in Iran," *KBS-1 Television*, 13 October 1991, as cited in *FBIS-EAS*-91-199, 15 October 1991, pp. 26–27.

52. Ed Blanche. "Gulf-Iran Missiles," *The Associated Press*, January 29, 1991.

53. Bill Gertz. "Iran Fired Ballistic Missile," *The Washington Times*, May 24, 1991, p. A5.

54. "Syria-Iran-Missiles," *The Associated Press*, October 1, 1991; "Syria and Iran Pool SRBM Resources," *Flight International*, 16–22 October 1991, p. 15; and "Iran-Syria," *The Associated Press*, October 1, 1991.

55. Michael R. Gordon. "Syria is Studying New Missile Deal," *The New York Times*, June 22, 1988, p. A6; "China's M-11 is Revealed," *Jane's Defence Weekly*, 9 April 1988, p. 655; "Beijing Avoids New Missile Sales Assurances," *The New York Times*, March 30, 1990, p. A7; and Bill Gertz. "Chinese Build Reactor for Iranian Program," *The Washington Times*, October 16, 1991, p. A3. CPMIEC, the company that markets the M-11, indicates that it utilizes a solid propellant and has a range of 120–150 km. Other sources suggest the range is 290 km when carrying a 800 kg warhead. This longer range is quite plausible, considering that the missile is similar in size to the Scud-B and appears to utilize the standard Scud-B TEL. The M-11 is believed to have entered PRC production sometime during early 1990.

56. U.S. State Department. "Briefing by Charles Redman," February 23, 1989.

57. "The World," *The Los Angeles Times*, March 9, 1989, p. 2; "'Sources' Say PRC Helping To Build Missile Plant," *Kyodo*, 9 March 1989, as cited in *FBIS-NES*-89-045,

9 March 1989, p. 48; and Blanche, Ed. "Gulf-Iran Missiles," *The Associated Press*, January 29, 1991. Available evidence suggests that rather then construct an entirely new factory, the PRC assisted the Iranians in converting an existing facility, possibly one originally intended to produce the DF-15/M-9.

58. Interview data. It is possible that instead of developing an entirely new test range the PRC helped the Iranians update and expand an existing one.

59. Bill Gertz. "China Can't Say No to Arms Buyers," *The Washington Times*, May 28, 1991, p. A1; and Bill Gertz. "Stop Arming the Mideast, Bush Urges Iran Now Top Threat in Region," *The Washington Times*, May 30, 1991, p. A1.

60. Interview data. It is possible that instead of two distinct missile systems, that these two ranges represent different tests of the same system.

61. Tony Banks and James Bruce. "Iran Builds its Strength," *Jane's Defence Weekly*, 1 February 1992, p. 158.

62. For a technical description of the HY-2 Silkworm see: Jim Bussert. "HY-2 'Silkworm' Anti-Ship Missile Detailed," *Jane's Soviet Intelligence Review*, March 1991, p. 120.

63. Numerous sources discuss the early Iranian acquisition and deployment of the HY-2, some of the better ones include: Bernard E. Trainor, "New Iran Missiles Reported at Gulf Entrance," *The New York Times*, March 15, 1986, p. 1; Richard Beeston. "U.S. Sees Iran Escalating 'Tanker War'," *The Washington Times*, April 24, 1987; Jim Bussert. "Iran's Silkworm Threat in the Golf," *Jane's Defence Weekly*, 6 June 1987, p. 1113; John Kinner. "U.S. Knew of Iran Arms, Officials Say," *The New York Times*, June 15, 1987, p. 11; U.S. Senate. *War in the Persian Gulf: The U.S. Takes Sides*, Staff Report to the Committee on Foreign Relation, U.S. Senate, October 1987; and "Armed Forces Install 'Powerful' Antiship Missiles," *IRNA*, 28 April 1987, as cited in *FBIS-NES*, 29 April 1987, p. I3.

64. There are numerous sources that discuss China's agreement to stop supplying HY-2 Silkworms, for example see: Edward A. Gargan, "China Says It Will Stop Arms for Iran," *The New York Times*, November 4, 1987, p. A3; and "China Halts Arms to Iran," *Jane's Defence Weekly*, 28 November 1987, p. 1257.

65. "More Silkworm Missiles From China Unloaded in Iran," *The Washington Times*, January 13, 1988, p. A11; David K. Shipler, "U.S. Says Iran Received More Chinese Missiles," *The New York Times*, January 13, 1988, p. A7; and Richard Beeston. "U.S. Won't Criticize Missile Sale," *The Washington Times*, January 15, 1988, p. A10; and Richard Beeston. "China Pledges No Sale of Silkworms to Iran," *The Washington Times*, March 10, 1988, p. A8.

66. "Pyongyang Missile Sale to Tehran Reported," p. A2; "Five Key Nations Sold Arms to Iran," p. 5.; and "Al-Musawwar Interviews Ramadan on War," p. 18.

67. "Iran Says It Makes Silkworms," *Defense Asia-Pacific*, April 1988, p. 8.

68. "Minister on Missile Manufacture, New Submarine," *IRNA*, 8 November 1987, as cited in *FBIS-NES*-87-216, 9 November 1987, p. 61; "IRGC Minister on Military Self-Sufficiency," *IRNA*, 8 November 1987, as cited in *FBIS-NES*-87-222, 18 November 1987, p. 55; and "IRGC Commander, Minister Outline Arms Production," *Keyhan*, 8 November 1987, as cited in *FBIS-NES*-87-219, 13 November 1987, p. 66.

69. Bill Gertz. "China Can't Say No to Arms Buyers," *The Washington Times*, May 28, 1991, p. A1.

70. "Iran About to Introduce SSM," *Jane's Defence Weekly*, 12 December 1987, p. 1347.

71. "'Most' Iraqi Cities Now Within Missile Range," *IRNA*, 29 March 1988, as cited in *FBIS-NES*-88-061, 30 March 1988, p. 48. A missile with a 130 km range could reach Baghdad from the Iranian border, since the distance is approximately 120 kms. Operationally, it would be very difficult to conduct missile operations so close to an active front.

72. "New Missile Nearly Ready for Production," *Tehran Domestic Service*, 7 April 1988, as cited in *FBIS-NES*-88-068, 8 April 1988, p. 53; and "Defense Minister on Manufacturing of Missiles," *IRNA*, 11 April 1988, as cited in *FBIS-NES*-88-070, 12 April 1988, p. 71.

73. Since *Mushak* is Persian for missile, it is possible that this quote may be a translators error. Regardless, in this account the term *Mushak*, followed by the range in kilometers, will be used to differentiate the various models of indigenous Iranian missiles. It is important to note that these are provisional names and are only used for convenience until the actual Iranian names become available. In earlier articles, co-authored by this writer, the term "Iran-130" was used as a provisional designator for the missile described here as the *Mushak-120*. The term "Iran-130", unfortunately, was picked up by the popular press and used as the actual name of the missile. This is incorrect. "Hashemi-Rafsanjani Delivers Friday Prayer Sermon," *Tehran Domestic Service*, 19 August 1988, as cited in *FBIS-NES*-88-162, 22 August 1988, pp. 49–53.

74. "Radio Phone-In Program With Defense Officials," *Tehran Domestic Service*, 14 April 1988, as cited in *FBIS-NES*-88-073, 15 April 1988, pp. 49–51.

75. "IRGC Minister Rafiqdust on New Missiles," *Tehran Domestic Service*, 31 July 1988, as cited in *FBIS-NES*-88-148, 2 August 1988, p. 52.

76. "Sector-By-Sector: Armaments Industry," *Iran Focus*, October 1988, p. 13.

77. "Interview With Mohsen Rafiqdust," *Tehran Television Service*, 3 June 1988, as cited in *FBIS-NES*-88-107, 6 June 1988, p. 70.

78. "Ministry Announces Production of New Missile," *IRNA*, 13 September 1989, as cited in *FBIS-NES*-89-077, 14 September 1989, p. 48.

79. The *Oghab* has a launcher which comes in at least three versions, two trucks and one towed.

80. Joseph Bermudez and W. Seth Carus. "Show Throws Light on Iran's Arms Industry," *Jane's Defence Weekly*, 19 November 1988, pp. 1252–1253. The title *"Shahin 333"* refers to the 333 mm diameter of the *Shahin-2*.

81. "Iranian Rockets Head SECARM Display," p. 219; "Iran Pitches for Arms Market at SECARM," p. 163; "Baghdad and Ankara Draw Out New Exhibitors," pp. 857–859; "Iran Moves Into Marketing," p. 846; and "Missile Production With PRC Discussed," *Al-Ittihad*, 18 September 1989, p. 1, as cited in *JPRS-TND*-89-020, 26 October 1989, p. 35.

82. "Defense Industries Manufacture New Missile," *IRNA*, 17 April 1989, as cited in *FBIS-NES*-89-073, 18 April 1989, p. 52.

83. For details on the WS-1 see the CPMIEC sales brochure: "WS-1 Non-Guidance Rocket Weapon System."

84. "IRGC Official Views Defense Industry," pp. 48–49.

85. Ed Blanche. "Gulf-Iran Missiles," *The Associated Press*, January 29, 1991.

86. Michael R. Gordon, "Beijing Avoids New Missile Sales Assurances," *The New York Times*, March 30, 1990, p. A7. During the same month there were additional reports which indicated that the PRC was selling Iran M-1B surface-to-surface missiles, which have a range of 80–95 km. It is conceivable that the export designation for the 8610 is M-1B. Daniel Southerland, "China Said to Sell Missiles; Shipment Reported Bound for Middle East," *The Washington Post*, March 29, 1990, p. A1. There was at least one report of Syrian interest in the 8610, see: Dan Raviv and Yossi Melman. "Iraq's Arsenal of Horrors; Baghdad's Growing Menace Alters Israeli Strategy," *The Washington Post*, April 8, 1990, p. B1.

87. Interview data.

88. Bill Gertz. "Photos Show Iraqi Missile Launchers in Mauritania," *The Washington Times*, May 30, 1990, p. A3. There were further reports during December, that the PRC had recently delivered a number of "...CM-5 short-range missiles..." to Iran. Bill Gertz and Rowan Scarborough. "Iraqis Literally Dig in to Fortify Kuwait Defenses," *The Washington Times*, December 17, 1990, p. A8

89. Bill Gertz. "Stop Arming the Mideast, Bush Urges Iran Now Top Threat in Region," *The Washington Times*, May 30, 1991, p. A1.

90. "Hashemi-Rafsanjani's Remarks," *NHK Television Network*, June 11, 1985, as cited in *FBIS-SA*, June 12, 1985, I1.

91. "Hashemi-Rafsanjani Delivers Friday Prayer Sermon," *Tehran Domestic Service*, 19 August 1988, as cited in *FBIS-NES-88-162*, 22 August 1988, pp. 49–53.

92. "Iran Reportedly Intends to Send Chinese Arms to Sudan," *United Press International*, January 13, 1992.

93. "Iranian Rockets Head SECARM Display," p. 219; "Iran Pitches for Arms Market at SECARM," p. 163; "Baghdad and Ankara Draw Out New Exhibitors," pp. 857–859; "Iran Moves Into Marketing," p. 846; and "Missile Production With PRC Discussed," *Al-Ittihad*, 18 September 1989, p. 1, as cited in *JPRS-TND-89-020*, 26 October 1989, p. 35.

94. Press accounts, all of uncertain reliability, have identified a number of locations believed to be associated with Iran's missile program. Most of this information is unconfirmed and should be treated with some caution.

95. *Foreign Report*, July 18, 1985.

96. "Iraq Says it Has Pinpointed Iranian Missile Launching Base," March 29, 1985.

97. Farzad Bazoft and Allan George. "Missiles Armed With Chemical Warheads 'In Sight'," *The Observer*, 13 March 1988, p. 23.

98. *Ibid.*

99. "Defense Industries Manufacture New Missile," *IRNA*, 17 April 1989, as cited in *FBIS-NES-89-073*, 18 April 1989, p. 52.

100. "PRC To Supply Nuclear Technology," *Sawt Al-Kuwayt Al-Duwali*, 11 July 1991, p. 1, as cited in *JPRS-TND-91-012*, 8 August 1991, pp. 19-20.

101. Martin Bailey. "The Blooming of Operation Flower," *The Observer*, 2 February 1986, p. 19; and Elaine Scoliono. "Documents Detail Israeli Missile Deal With the Shah," *The New York Times*, April 1, 1986, p. A17.

102. Interview data.

103. Martin Bailey. "The Blooming of Operation Flower," *The Observer*, 2 February 1986, p. 19; and Elaine Scoliono. "Documents Detail Israeli Missile Deal With the Shah," *The New York Times*, April 1, 1986, p. A17.

104. "Gulf-Iran," *The Associated Press*, December 27, 1990.

105. Bill Gertz. "Iran Fired Ballistic Missile," *The Washington Times*, May 24, 1991, p. A5.

106. For a detailed discussion of cruise missile proliferation in the Third World (including Iran), see W. Seth Carus. *The Prospects for Cruise Missile Proliferation in the 1990s*, CSIS, Washington, D.C., forthcoming.

4

Pakistan's Ballistic Missile Development: The Sword of Islam?

Cameron Binkley[1]

Introduction

The ballistic missile program of the Islamic Republic of Pakistan is less well documented than other countries discussed in this book. However, Pakistan has had three decades of experience in the development of sounding rocket technology.[2] This experience provides a basis for the country to achieve its principal goal: possession of a nuclear-capable missile force with the needed range to hold significant Indian targets at risk.

The firms and national agencies of several Western nations, especially France but including Germany and perhaps the United States, have attempted to assist Pakistan in its efforts to acquire rocket technology. However, one nation clearly stands out: China, with its sale to Pakistan of M-series missiles, components, launchers, and technology. Chinese involvement, which has been evident since the late 1980s, is undoubtedly the single most important factor affecting Pakistan's rate of progress in ballistic missile development.

This chapter will examine the history of Pakistan's existing space- and missile-related capabilities, its acquisition of foreign technology through various types of transactions and techniques, and its future export potential, as well as the motivations driving Pakistani decision makers toward the deployment of strategic and tactical missiles. Finally, the country's susceptibility to nonproliferation measures will briefly be considered.

History

Pakistani efforts in the field of rocketry began as long ago as 1961 with the formation of SUPARCO—Pakistan's Space and Upper Atmosphere Research Commission. Although the missile program itself may well have begun in 1974 under directives issued by Zulfiqar Ali Bhutto,[3] serious interest in developing the infrastructure and expertise necessary to support indigenous space, rocket, and missile-related activities emerged only during the 1980s.

Pakistan's modest intent, announced by SUPARCO Chairman Dr. Salim Mehmud in May 1980, was to develop and launch an indigenously built satellite, the *Badr*. By May 1981, however, following an improvement in U.S.-Pakistani relations, SUPARCO's status was upgraded and its funding greatly increased, due in part to the "personal interest and direction of the President of Pakistan [Gen. Zia al-Haq]."[4] More announcements followed later that year and it became apparent that SUPARCO had embarked upon a serious 10-year space technology acquisition and development program.[5]

By the end of the decade, Pakistan had constructed a satellite (orbited by a Chinese launcher) with foreign assistance, and Mehmud was stating that Pakistan had designed and indigenously manufactured a space launch vehicle (SLV) booster. He claimed that SUPARCO had made "considerable progress in rocket manufacturing and tests" and that all of SUPARCO's programs were making progress.[6]

In February 1988, India announced the first test launch of the *Prithvi*, a short-range tactical missile capable of carrying a nuclear warhead. Three months later, the *New York Times* reported U.S. administration sources apparently confirming that Pakistan had also test-fired "a missile capable of carrying a nuclear weapon."[7] Exactly one year after India's first *Prithvi* test, General Mirza Aslam Beg, Pakistan Army Chief of Staff, announced that Pakistan had tested two 500 kg payload missiles, "one having a range of 80 km and the other 300 km."[8]

In subsequent Congressional testimony, William H. Webster, Director of the CIA, identified Pakistan as one of 15 developing countries that will be making its own ballistic missiles by the year 2000.[9]

Suppliers of Rocket Technology

U.S. and German firms, among others, may have helped Pakistan to achieve a ballistic missile capability. France and China, however, have made the most significant contributions toward that goal (see Table 4.1). In the French case there is no apparent reason to believe that the supply of technology was intended to fulfill a military role, whereas China's involvement clearly stems from a geopolitical interest and the desire to generate income from arms exports.[10]

TABLE 4.1 Selected Suppliers of Rocket Technology to Pakistan

Supplier	*Technology/Items (Sought or Transferred)*	*Notes*
British Commonwealth		
British National Committee of Space Research	Training/Experience; Scientific Cooperation in Sounding Rocket Research (1960s)	Canadian scientist Dr. Gerald Bull may have provided some assistance through a tri-party space effort (Canada, Pakistan, and India).
Canadian Defense Department	Training/Experience (late 1950s?); Other (?)	
Federal Republic of Germany		
Aviatest	Missile Testing Equipment (1989)	Scattered reports implicate OTRAG in attempts to assist Pakistan's development of a military missile capability from the early to mid-1980s. No confirmation of technology transfer.
Lebold-Heraeus Gmbh	Dual-Use Furnace Equipment (mid-1980s)	
OTRAG	Sounding Rocket Technology, Assistance, Components, Production facilities (?) (early 1980s)	
France		
Aerospatiale (Sud-Aviation)	Sounding Rockets, Technology & Experience (1960s & 1970s)	Licensed transfer of French sounding rockets & technology is the basis of both Pakistan's civil and military rocket programs.
CNEA	Cooperation in Sounding Rocket Research (1960s & 1970s)	
People's Republic of China		
Ministry of Aerospace Industries (post-1988)	M-11 Missiles (1991), Components (1991), Guidance Units (1992), Launchers & Dummy Training Frames (1991)	CGWIC has transferred space, and perhaps missile, technology. Many sources have reported M-series technology transfers; it is not clear whether China has provided only M-11s, or M-9 technology as well. Unconfirmed reports suggest China's 4th nuclear bomb design was given to Pakistan.
[Marketed by CPMIEC.; possibly Polytechnologies(?)]	M-9 Missiles/Technology (1990–92?)	
General	Propellant Production Facilities (1987); Development Assistance; Missile Technology; Training (1988–present); Warhead Design (?) (pre-1983?); Space, Defence & Science Cooperation Agreements (1989, 1990)	
United States		
NASA	Training/Experience; Limited Scientific Cooperation in Sounding Rocket Research (1962–1967)	The US imposed trade sanctions on SUPARCO in June 1991 for MTCR violations.

Source: Press and journal accounts compiled by the author.

France: Sounding Rockets

The principal objective of SUPARCO, the Pakistani space agency, is "acquiring and using space science and technology for peaceful applications, primarily aimed at the socio-economic uplift of the people of Pakistan."[11] From the outset, SUPARCO sought foreign assistance to reach this broad goal but also concentrated on developing an indigenous sounding rocket program. Early on, Pakistan achieved limited cooperation in launching imported sounding rockets through collaboration with the National Aeronautics and Space Administration (NASA), the Centre National d'Etudes Spatiales (CNES) of France, and the British National Committee of Space Research.[12] The principal contribution to Pakistan's nascent rocket-manufacturing industry, however, was made by France's Sud-Aviation, a private aerospace firm later incorporated into the state-run Aerospatiale.

Pakistan, of course, was not the only French patron in South Asia. Indian engineers were also provided with the means to build Sud-Aviation *Centaure* sounding rockets under a 1964 agreement.[13] Eventually, France's CNES provided India with access to the type of advanced liquid-fueled rocket motor technology used in the *Ariane* space launcher. Although more is known about Indo-French rocket-related transactions, it appears that France also licensed Pakistan to produce *Stromboli* sounding rocket engines.[14] SUPARCO established Pakistan's first plant for the production of rockets for scientific and meteorological purposes in 1968. At some point thereafter, the country acquired an indigenously based launch capability.[15]

From the late 1960s through the 1970s, French sounding rocket technology provided Pakistan with the basis for its later attempts to develop ballistic missiles.[16] Statements by SUPARCO indirectly admit French assistance in Pakistan's sounding rocket program. However, the most revealing evidence derives from photographic comparisons of Pakistani sounding rockets and *Hatf* missiles with sounding rockets manufactured by Sud-Aviation. Pakistan's *Rehnuma* and *Shahpar* sounding rockets are modeled on Sud-Aviation's *Centaure, Dauphin, Dragon,* and *Eridan* sounding rockets. The *Hatf-1* appears to be a military version of the *Dauphin* or the *Dragon*'s first stage (Pakistan's *Shahpar*) while the *Hatf-2* closely resembles the *Eridan*.[17] There is little question that the *Hatf* missiles directly descend from this French-supplied technology. Pakistan simply acquired the rockets through commercial means, then proceeded to obtain the blueprints and manufacturing technology necessary to replicate its own civil and military versions.[18]

Germany: Nuclear Ties & Commercial Launching

An unknown number of private German enterprises have assisted Pakistan's rocket development. An example is Aviatest, a firm reportedly prepared to provide Pakistan with missile testing equipment in 1989.[19] Other German firms probably became involved while helping to equip Pakistan's nuclear weapons-related facilities through illicit technology transfers. This was true for Leybold AG, a German industrial manufacturer. Formerly Leybold-Heraeus GmbH, Leybold was implicated in Pakistani, and later Iraqi, conspiracies to acquire export-controlled uranium enrichment technology. Some of the sophisticated equipment and materials supplied by Leybold for nuclear weapons programs (for instance, high temperature brazing furnaces) are equally useful in missile development.[20] As other studies have documented, German firms like Leybold were extensively involved, wittingly or unwittingly, in Pakistan's clandestine nuclear procurement schemes. It is probable that related missile development equipment and materials have also found their way to Pakistan through illicit networks.

There are some indications that the private German space launch company Orbital Transport und Raketien AG (OTRAG) was involved in Pakistan's rocket programs. From the late 1970s until the firm ceased operations in 1987, OTRAG sought to develop a small commercial launch vehicle for use by developing countries. The firm conducted its most important and controversial testing in Libya until international pressure and poor relations with the German government forced it out of Africa in 1981. Libya's interest in the program was undoubtedly military; one of the most damaging allegations was that Libyan military officials were directing aspects of the firm's operations.[21] In 1981, Libyan leader Colonel Mu'ammar al-Qadafi reportedly contacted Pakistan to offer OTRAG technology.[22]

Further, but unsubstantiated, allegations based primarily on Indian sources have suggested that Pakistan's army had "a wide-ranging agreement" with OTRAG to receive "a large batch of intermediate-range missiles."[23] This source also claims that a manufacturing facility was established which would allow Pakistan to assemble its own missiles from OTRAG components, the plan eventually being for Pakistan both to manufacture the subsystems and to develop its own missiles based on those supplied by OTRAG. Another Indian writer claims that OTRAG may have assisted Pakistan in the development of its *Rehnuma* and *Shahpar* sounding rockets.[24]

Curiously, OTRAG's alleged interest in assisting Pakistan followed that company's expulsion from Zaire, its problems in Libya, and Pakistan's renewed emphasis on its own space technology program in 1981. OTRAG could indeed have offered some services to Pakistan as another potential client on its list of developing country customers. There would seemingly have been a convergence of interests, in that Pakistan was probably seeking to develop a military capability beneath the cover of a civilian space program while OTRAG was seeking to sell space launch technology to countries whose need for such capabilities was dubious at best. However, as far as is known, Pakistan's civil and military rockets are based entirely on solid propellant motor technology whereas OTRAG was marketing liquid fuel vehicles. SUPARCO did announce efforts to construct an SLV booster in 1989. If this rocket turns out to be liquid-fueled, a major technical leap for Pakistan, then greater credence to the OTRAG connection might be considered. As no liquid fuel rockets have been reported in Pakistan, it is likely that any relationship between OTRAG and Pakistan was limited.

United States: Cooperation & Fraud

From 1962 to 1967, the United States cooperated with Pakistan in the area of space research through an international program established by NASA. This assistance centered on efforts to launch at least two varieties of U.S.-supplied sounding rockets.[25] The first such rocket, an American *Nike-Cajun* known as the *Rehbar-1*, was launched from a range near Karachi in June 1962.[26] U.S. government participation in Pakistan's rocket program was limited to basic scientific research. Later French willingness to transfer rocket technology to Pakistan may have helped Sud-Aviation to supplant U.S. assistance.

The most significant involvement of a U.S. firm in Pakistan's missile development relates to the financial scandal surrounding James Guerin, a former deputy chairman of the major defense manufacturer Ferranti International. Guerin used Ferranti's U.S. subsidiary, International Signal & Control Technologies (ISC Technologies), in a scheme to inflate the value of his company by developing fraudulent agreements. According to U.S. Internal Revenue Service (IRS) testimony, ISC Technologies established five bogus contracts from 1984 to 1989, involving several U.S. and Swiss banks accounts, front companies, and falsified documents.[27] The most important of these deals involved Pakistan and was known as the Khyber-Pass contract. The deal was apparently facilitated through the auspices of the Chilean arms manufacturer, Carlos Cardoen. The scheme also utilized Guerin's contacts in South Africa and the U.S. intelligence community, and implicated a high ranking Pakistani, Gen. Talat Masood, who was formerly in charge of the Pakistan Ordnance Factories.[28] The contract was booked at $460 million and included the construction of an entire missile system and launch facilities. However, both the lawyers representing Ferranti against Guerin and the IRS investigators have stated that Pakistan received no equipment, technology, or services and that no money was received from Pakistan as a result of the deal.[29] Guerin on the other hand, claimed that there was a personal arrangement with General Zia ul-Haq, and that this deal had gone bad when the Pakistani leader was killed in 1988.

The important question regarding Pakistan's relationship with ISC Technologies is whether there ever was an active deal or whether it was a fiction entirely created by Guerin. Pakistan's past involvement in this type of technology procurement chicanery does fit an established pattern of behavior. However, the extent of Pakistan's actual complicity in this particular incident is difficult to gauge. The most revealing fact may simply be that so many supposedly knowledgeable arms merchants were duped—a testament to the strength of perception that links Pakistan to an active interest in acquiring advanced missile technology.

China: Strategic Interests

China's involvement in Pakistan's missile program is a natural extension of an already existing relationship. Although it may not be possible to determine precisely the extent of Chinese missile-related aid, numerous press accounts and government comments, plus China's own remarks and an obvious pattern of behavior, suggest the significance and strong character of that relationship.

China has provided Pakistan with complete missile systems, manufacturing facilities, components, training and technical assistance. In May 1988, Pakistan reportedly test-fired a nuclear-capable missile. Attributing its information to a national with close ties to the Pakistani government, the *New York Times* stated that the missile, able to hit both New Delhi and Bombay, was indigenously built with Chinese assistance. A U.S. government source confirmed China's involvement.[30] In July 1989, a senior State Department official stated that the United States had unconfirmed reports that China was trying to sell its M-9 missile to Libya, Syria, Iran and Pakistan.[31] Other media reports alleged the sale or transfer of M-11 missiles, launchers and training mockups.[32] China is also said to have provided Pakistan guidance technology for both the *Hatf*-2 and M-11 missiles.[33]

In 1987, Prime Minister Mohammad Khan Junejo openly expressed appreciation for a rocket propellant factory that was "a testimony of Chinese cooperation."[34] More importantly, China itself has admitted to the sale of missiles to Pakistan: In June 1991, while denying M-9 sales to Syria, China's U.S. Ambassador Zhu Qizhen, confirmed that China had sent "a tiny number of short-range tactical missiles" to Pakistan. Wu Jianmin, a spokesman for the Chinese Foreign Ministry, later issued a similar comment.[35]

There are two principal factors behind China's missile-related assistance to Pakistan. First, Pakistan has an important geostrategic relationship with China. Former Pakistani leader Mohammed Zia ul-Haq once told a U.S. reporter that his country's relationship with China was the foundation of its foreign policy and that "if ever Pakistan's security was threatened, China would not stand by idly."[36] Zia's belief was based on the peculiarities of geography and history that have inextricably linked Pakistan to China in the long-standing Sino-Indian dispute. The Sino-Pakistani convergence of interests dates to the early sixties and follows the dissolution of China's ties with the Soviet Union. Pakistan consistently spends nearly seven percent of its GNP on defense, a fact that at least complicates Indian defense planning in China's favor.[37] Additionally, China has been able to acquire some sophisticated defense technology by working with Pakistan. This arrangement possibly includes access to uranium centrifuge enrichment techniques and equipment, acquired and developed by Pakistan for its nuclear weapons program.[38]

Second, Pakistan is the most important importer of Chinese nuclear and weapons technology, and is a significant source of hard currency earnings for China.[39] Beyond speculation that China supplied Pakistan with substantial nuclear weapons development assistance, future transfers of nuclear technology, including a 300MW power reactor, could offer sales worth millions of dollars. Moreover, China and Pakistan have major joint development projects in the commercial, defense, and aviation sectors. China has also provided significant aid for the development of Pakistan's indigenously manufactured surface-to-air missile, the *Anza*. Finally, though hard evidence is lacking, China's successful sale to Saudi Arabia of its DF-3 (CSS-2) missiles for $2.5 billion was undoubtedly facilitated by its close association with Pakistan.[40] Presumably, close Sino-Pakistani ties help China's efforts to market weapons to other Mideast Islamic countries, such as Syria and Iran, with whom it has no traditional relationship.

In addition to these factors, Pakistan and China share interests in the area of remote sensing and satellite telecommunications. They signed an extensive space cooperation agreement on December 9, 1991.[41] The relationship supports China's efforts to diversify its client base in the space and launch services export market. Though meager in comparison to Sino-American trade, such cooperation is especially useful in view of recent U.S. sanctions that denied China access to missile-related aerospace technologies and which nearly canceled a number of multi-million dollar satellite launch contracts involving U.S. firms or components.[42]

Arguably, Pakistan's military and economic value is more significant to China than that of any other developing state. This situation hardens Chinese willingness to supply Pakistan with missile technology despite recurrent U.S. opposition.

Space Research and Ballistic Missiles

Like some other developing states, notably Brazil and India, Pakistan has apparently utilized the experience and technological gains of a civilian space program to further its military interests. Such a program can ease a country's access to foreign technology when its use for military purposes might otherwise be denied. Even after adopting MTCR guidelines, supplier states find it more difficult to justify restrictions on aerospace exports when they are destined for civilian programs.[43]

The most direct indication of SUPARCO involvement in Pakistan's missile development program relates to the determination by the U.S. State Department in June 1991 that it had "engaged in missile technology proliferation activities" requiring the application of trade sanctions.[44] These sanctions were applied simultaneously to the China Great Wall Industry Corp., the China Precision Machinery Import-Export Corp., and SUPARCO following numerous reports regarding China's missile sales to Syria and Pakistan. The implication is that SUPARCO had acquired technology relating to M-series missiles from China.[45] Additionally, the *Washington Post* reported that SUPARCO was responsible for the missile test that apparently took place in April 1988.[46]

Several other observations further suggest that Pakistan has acquired missile technology through its space program. First, the country is quite familiar with the use of deliberate subterfuge as a state-sponsored policy for technology transfer. Numerous books and articles have documented the elaborate network of front companies, industrial espionage, technology smuggling and illicit banking transactions that Pakistan has successfully utilized to further its nuclear ambitions. Pakistan's nuclear weapons development began under the auspices of an ostensibly civilian nuclear power project which funneled acquired technology into its military program. SUPARCO was itself established as part of the Pakistan Atomic Energy Commission and would naturally serve a similar dual purpose.

Second, although the space program has many genuine civil applications (e.g., the use of sounding rockets for high-altitude research), it also has had a military orientation. In December 1981, after announcing Pakistan's plan to develop space technology over a ten-year period, SUPARCO Chairman Mehmud expressed concern over falling behind India in the space race. He announced that Pakistan was considering the design of a satellite that "can serve strategic purposes by taking pictures of military installations, army movements and acting as control, command and communication bases."[47]

Indian sources have also alleged that there is a connection between Mehmud and Abdul Qadeer Khan, the scientist responsible for Pakistan's military-directed attempts to enrich uranium for nuclear weapons, and that both individuals are involved in the missile program.[48] Qadeer has apparently boasted about his attempts to persuade President Ghulam Ishaq Khan to permit technicians from the Kahuta enrichment facility to work on the manufacturing of arms and missiles.[49] It is possible that Qadeer is now in charge of the missile program.[50]

Hence, there is ample reason to suppose that Pakistan's drive toward a space launch capability is also motivated by a military intent to acquire ballistic missile technology.

Export Potential and the Indigenization of Arms

Pakistan has a limited ability to provide missile-related training and technical aid to other countries and may have provided some such assistance to Saudi Arabia.[51] According to congressional testimony given in February 1992 by Admiral Edward Sheafer, Director of U.S. Naval Intelligence, Pakistan may be looking to export its *Hatf-1* missile in the near future, but it is uncertain whether the country presently could do so.[52] It appears that lack of progress in its own program has forced Pakistan to seek whole systems and critical subsystems from China.

Nonetheless, Pakistan has a consistent policy of indigenization regarding the defense field and has become self-sufficient in ammunition and artillery.[53] The Pakistan Ordnance Factories claim to export munitions worth $30 million annually with current foreign orders for anti-tank missiles worth $360 million more.[54] This policy is designed to overcome what is termed the "suffocating restrictions" imposed by developed states on the use of their military exports.[55] Another aim, according to Pakistani Minister of State for Defense, Colonel (retired) Ghulam Sarwae Cheema, is to enable Pakistan to provide defense goods to countries which are "culturally and historically" similar to Pakistan, but which have been denied more sophisticated technology from developed states.[56]

Pakistan has long harbored the notion of serving as the arsenal of the Muslim world. Given a reasonable level of quality, many Islamic nations would prefer to buy arms from Pakistan instead of traditional suppliers. For instance, Saudi Arabia appears to have purchased Pakistani laser range-finders comparable to U.S. or European models.[57] Some states, like Iran and Syria, have fewer alternatives. It is thus possible to envision Pakistan one day seeking to supply missile technology, components, and perhaps whole systems to other developing countries whose only potential suppliers today are North Korea and China. Such a policy would also help offset the considerable costs of indigenous ballistic missile development.

Moreover, Pakistan lacks any significant technology export controls or legislation and is actively promoting the privatization of its defense industry.[58] This situation contributes to the probability that future missile-related exports and cooperative arrangements, beyond those already existing for China, will develop.

Pakistan's Missile Capabilities

Pakistan now can manufacture and test basic rocket components. Although progress seems slow, with future efforts likely to depend on foreign assistance, the U.S. Director of Naval Intelligence has testified that Pakistan should be able to deploy its *Hatf-2* missile by 1995.[59] The *Hatf-1* is probably deployed already.

This section outlines Pakistan's major rocket and missile systems, including the Chinese-supplied M-series, and discusses the country's production capabilities and level of technical development.

Indigenous Rocket & Missile Systems

In 1962, SUPARCO began launching its imported sounding rockets from a testing range on the Indian Ocean. Since then it has apparently produced and flown at least three types of two-stage, solid propellant sounding rockets, the "*Rehnuma* I," the "*Shahpar*," and a third, more capable rocket reportedly tested in January 1989.[60]

Pakistan claims the development of three specific ballistic missiles systems, the *Hatf-1* and *Hatf-2* and a third, longer-range missile whose designation is uncertain.[61] In February 1989, General Beg announced that Pakistan had tested two missiles, "one having a range of 80 km and the other 300 km."[62] These missiles, the *Hatf-1* and -2, are both believed capable of lifting 500 kg payloads to at least a portion of their stated maximum ranges, if not the whole distance. Pakistan has released photos of a *Hatf-1* launch.[63] In April 1989, the *Hatf-2* was displayed for the first time during a Pakistan Day Joint Services parade. It was mounted on a mobile launcher which had been converted from a British anti-aircraft gun carriage.[64]

Pakistan claims the *Hatfs* are missiles and not artillery rockets, but this crucial distinction is closely tied to the level of accuracy of a given system. While it is not possible to independently assess accuracy in the absence of test data or technical details, the foreign sounding rocket technology upon which the *Hatfs'* designs are based clearly lacks a guidance and control function.[65] Overcoming the technical obstacles to achieve indigenous manufacture of missile-related guidance technology is quite a challenging task.[66] Hence, it is unlikely that Pakistan, absent the resources of an advanced aerospace industry, could successfully develop the necessary technologies to construct guided missiles without foreign assistance.

Assuming an accuracy little better than one percent of range, meaning an approximate CEP of 1,000 m at a distance of 100 km or 3,000 m at 300 km,[67] the *Hatf-1* and -2 would be unsuitable for most military requirements. Essentially, these "missiles" are poorly guided, solid-propelled, artillery-type short-range rockets. Although their inventory levels are unknown, a 1988 report stated that Pakistan had components sufficient to build 48 presumed *Hatf* missiles.[68] If produced in sufficient volume, the *Hatf-1* and -2 could be suitable for artillery bombardment missions. With greater accuracy derived through foreign assistance, the missiles could fulfill a wider range of conventional missions. In either case, if production rates were low, this would suggest that the missiles are intended for the short-range delivery of nuclear weapons.[69]

In an October 1989 interview with *Jane's Defence Weekly,* General Beg claimed that Pakistan was testing a 600km range missile that "is not so sophisticated in terms of guidance system because we don't have [the] technology."[70] Little is known about this missile.

Finally, Pakistan also claims to be developing an indigenous SLV booster.[71] The country has also been able to produce a small experimental satellite, which was successfully launched by a Chinese *Long March* carrier in July 1990.

Chinese Assistance & M-Series Missiles

By providing Pakistan with access to missiles and technology, China has significantly upped the ante in the South Asian missile race. However, there is a certain amount of confusion regarding which systems and what type of assistance have been supplied.

Allegedly, China has helped to develop Pakistan's indigenous *Hatf* missiles. It is also known that Pakistan has received Chinese M-series technology as well as entire missile systems. Although press reports do not reliably indicate which type, there is little doubt that M-11s have been transferred.

China itself has admitted few specific details regarding this issue. It might be mistaken to assume that only M-11s have been delivered.[72] Curiously, the undesignated 600 km range missile reported by General Beg has the same range as that ascribed to China's M-9.[73] Most accounts assume that Ambassador Zhu Qizhen's and Foreign Ministry spokesman Wu Jianmin's confirmation of Chinese missile deliveries to Pakistan implies M-11 deliveries. However, these comments seem more important for the questions raised than for the information provided. First, the statements reveal no data on quantities. Even "a tiny number" of missiles is very important if those missiles are to be armed with nuclear warheads. One Indian source reported that China transferred 60 M-11s, and that these were now in service as part of a long-range artillery brigade.[74] Second, what China means by "short range" is the subject of academic speculation.[75] The Chinese classify a short-range missile as falling below 1000 km. Thus, they could be referring to either system. A transfer of the longer range M-9, however, would be of greater international concern due to the larger number and significance of Indian targets that would be brought within range.

In either case the strategic importance of Pakistan's possession of a few M-series ballistic missiles cannot be underestimated. By delivering M-11 missiles, launchers, and apparently "dummy" training frames, China may well have provided Pakistan with a credible nuclear-capable missile force.[76] Given possession of real missiles, even the presence of training systems is important as the difficulty in distinguishing between the two types could easily complicate Indian target planning. Furthermore, as operational use during the Gulf conflict demonstrates, it is difficult to destroy deployed mobile missiles. Presumably, this new option would free up some Pakistan Air Force F-16s from their missions as nuclear delivery platforms while presenting India with an increased threat from the same aircraft in their deep strike and air defense roles.

Production Facilities

SUPARCO maintains production facilities for solid propellant sounding rockets.[77] SUPARCO is able to completely fabricate rocket motors from basic raw materials, has a solid composite propellant plant, and maintains an instrument development facility and a rocket testing range. If SUPARCO statements are accurate, Pakistan possessed these basic capabilities from the 1970s onward.

The extent of the country's current military manufacturing ability is more difficult to gauge. However, Pakistan's efforts to build a nuclear explosive production capability, virtually from scratch and in the face of international nuclear technology export controls, hint at its determination and ability to master high-priority defense-related fields. Pakistan has entered several joint defense production agreements with China, including the coproduction of a jet trainer and a main battle tank. The Pakistan Ordnance Factories have acquired considerable experience in producing munitions, a skill related to the production of solid rockets, and as noted above, Prime Minister Mohammad Khan Junejo reportedly opened a rocket propellant factory in March 1987.

It thus appears that Pakistan has or will soon possess sufficient manufacturing abilities to mass produce solid propellant rocket motors for short- to medium-range ballistic missiles. What the country probably lacks, and may continue to lack for some time, is the more sophisticated manufacturing equipment, skills, and techniques necessary to independently produce high quality components and composite materials for guidance, navigation and high temperature applications such as thrust control and heat shielding.

Technical Expertise

Although SUPARCO has enabled Pakistan to acquire some level of technical competence in the fields of rocketry and space science, it has faced serious obstacles. In May 1982, Chairman Mehmud remarked that SUPARCO's most pronounced problem was the non-availability of skilled technical specialists, that space technology-related training facilities were non-existent, that financial limitations constrained the space program, and that technological development was stymied by a limited industrial infrastructure.[78] In the decade since, SUPARCO has tried to improve this situation through university collaboration and the establishment of an

Aerospace Institute designed to turn out 50 space science engineers per year. This institute, however, was still under construction in 1990.[79] Pakistan has also worked with China to improve its aerospace infrastructure, and negotiated the construction of a military aircraft rebuild plant in 1981.[80] However, lacking a substantive aerospace manufacturing industry from which to draw qualified technicians, the missile program is probably still restricted by its relatively small pool of trained and available manpower. This situation could be overcome by hiring foreign experts.

Motives for Missile Proliferation in Pakistan

Although Pakistan's missiles may be intended to fulfill a tactical role as artillery rockets, the main goal is to acquire a nuclear-capable vehicle. The strongest evidence for this relates to Pakistan's known dedication to the acquisition of nuclear arms. Possession of a bomb requires a delivery method; ballistic missiles are the most suitable instrument for this purpose.

Moreover, India's rapid progress in the development of its own space launch and missile capabilities is a compelling motivation for Pakistan. India's short-range tactical missile, the *Prithvi*, has undergone a series of successful test flights and is expected to see deployment in 1993.[81] The country is continuing to develop its intermediate-range missile, the *Agni*, and after two previous failed attempts, is making progress in its satellite launching program with the third semi-successful flight of the Advance Satellite Launch Vehicle. This serious pace of development forces Pakistan to keep up with India in both the scientific and the military arms races. Pakistan's ballistic missiles have tactical and strategic influence. These systems can help place Indian cities under a potential nuclear threat while, as conventional weapons, endangering Indian air bases, staging points, and major industrial targets. In the evolving defense postures of South Asia, missiles have become important guarantors of deterrence while rocketry programs have become symbols of national technical achievement. The very designation *"Hatf,"* for instance, has both religious and nationalist appeal. Although the term is Arabic and means "Deadly"—as in the name given to the prophet's sword—Arabic words are often chosen in Pakistan to denote items of particular religious or cultural value.[82] The name thus appeals to both indigenous and Arabic audiences and highlights Pakistan's desire to establish an identity and capability separate from India.

CIA Director Robert Gates has implied in testimony that Pakistan has the capability to deliver nuclear weapons using its U.S.-supplied F-16s.[83] However, by deploying a credible nuclear-capable missile force Pakistan not only complicates Indian military strategy, but presumably releases these able aircraft for critical non-nuclear operations. At any rate, Pakistan's long-term interest demands an indigenous capability. The

United States has historically shifted its policy too many times for Pakistani leaders willingly to rely on it for the supply of a critical defense element. Pakistan may seek aircraft from other countries, such as France, but it is unquestionably better off not having to rely on whatever it can get. This belief is the cornerstone of the country's present policy of arms indigenization.

The character of Chinese missile-related aid to Pakistan supports this policy. China is a purveyor of technology and production assistance, not merely equipment. To the extent that Pakistan lacks a sophisticated aircraft industry, but can apply its related experience in the fields of artillery and munitions manufacturing to missile development, then again this policy clearly makes sense.

There is also an institutional factor acting upon Pakistan's interest in missile development: the Pakistan Army. The military has had a long involvement in Pakistani politics. Even under civilian rule, the military exercises considerable influence in decision making, especially pertaining to defense manufacturing, an area in which many present and former officers hold key positions. However, Pakistan's military services compete for resources and influence and have failed to cooperate even in war. Possessing aircraft that could be used to carry nuclear weapons, the air service has gained access to a symbol with potent patriotic appeal. In order to counter this situation, the Pakistan Army must possess its own means to deliver nuclear weapons. Hence, there are political as well as military reasons for it to support the missile program.

Pakistan may have one final reason to deploy a missile deterrent—to meet the threat posed by Soviet-supplied SCUD missiles in neighboring Afghanistan. Although India has been and will remain Pakistan's chief security concern, the government has noted the serious menace presented by these missiles to important Pakistani cities and installations.[84] This perceived threat was made more real when the Soviet-backed regime launched a SCUD attack into Pakistan in January 1990.[85] The end of Communist rule may not ease the fear of missile strikes from the north until stability returns to Afghanistan. With the fall of Kabul, radical Mujahideen forces, no longer backed by the Pakistani government, captured a fully operational SCUD base complete with technicians and mobile launchers.[86]

Conclusion

This chapter has sought to examine the development of ballistic missiles in Pakistan. Most importantly, it has found that French technology and the enduring strategic cooperation that Pakistan enjoys with China have proven crucial in helping the country to achieve an indigenous capability. Pakistan also has employed various channels to acquire necessary outside assistance, including the use of its civilian space agency, SUPARCO, to funnel rocket technology into military efforts.

As far as international export controls are concerned, the MTCR has undoubtedly increased the difficulty, time, and costs needed for Pakistan to reach its goals. But restricting technology transfer will not end the perceived security threat that acts as the primary driver behind Pakistan's missile development. If MTCR restrictions lead to greater export returns for states who can successfully acquire and market missile technology that is not available from regime members, then Pakistan, like Argentina and North Korea before it, may even find an economic incentive to overcoming the technical and political barriers of ballistic missile development. Except for Turkey, a NATO member, Pakistan is currently the only Muslim state with the desire and potential for significantly engaging in the weapons export business.

U.S. pressure has had little impact on staying the course of Pakistan's nuclear weapons program. Because the country's missile ventures support not only this effort but provide conventional military utility as well, it is unlikely that U.S. influence will have much effect here either. The United States might be more successful in offering incentives to gain Pakistani restraint should it eventually emerge as a missile technology exporter. This scenario, however, would require a willingness to cooperate, probably by granting aid and assistance, that is politically unpopular considering Pakistan's nuclear posture and the relative decline of its strategic value to the United States following the collapse of the Soviet Union.

Finally, though future Chinese exports of whole missile systems are unlikely, little evidence suggests that U.S. pressure can entirely halt the flow of Chinese aid and technology to Pakistan's missile program. For a variety of reasons, the United States can expect its influence over China to diminish with time. Hence, U.S. interests may better be served by efforts to improve the dialogue between Pakistan and India, and between India and China, than through punitive actions. As it now stands, there is no doubt that Pakistan's missile program is heading toward a full-fledged indigenous manufacturing capability.

Notes

1. The author gratefully acknowledges the helpful comments and assistance provided by Yan Kong, George Harris, Ignace Liu, Tim McCarthy, Nooria Noor, and Glynn Wood during the preparation of this chapter.

2. Sounding rockets are primarily used to carry small scientific and meteorological payloads on sub orbital trajectories high into the Earth's upper atmospheric regions.

3. "Bhutto Welcomes Pakistan Missile Tests," U.S. State Department cable, 2/7/89. Benazir Bhutto made this claim during her speech in February 1988. Bhutto's father, and former prime minister of Pakistan, is widely remembered for his remark that if India were to develop nuclear weapons, Pakistan would be forced to spare no effort and would be willing to "eat grass" to acquire its own bomb.

4. "An Introduction to SUPARCO," Pakistan Space & Upper Atmosphere Research Commission, Lahore: SUPARCO Public Relations Office, 4/82, pp. 5–6; "Space and Upper Atmospheric Research Council Upgraded," *Morning News*, 6/4/81, p. 3.

5. B. Radhakrishna Rao, "Pakistan's Space Ambitions: A Military Option?," *Nature*, 12/10/81, p. 507. "S.R.C. Studying Plan for Development of Space Science Technology," *Pakistan Times*, 9/21/81.

6. "Booster Rocket Developed for Satellite Launcher," AFP (Hong Kong), 3/21/89 in *FBIS, Daily Report: Near East & South Asia*, [hereafter: *FBIS*] 3/22/89, p. 69; "Manufacturing Program Continues," Islamabad Domestic Service, 3/21/89 in *FBIS*, 3/22/89, pp. 69–70; JANG (Lahore), 3/21/89 in *FBIS*, 4/5/89, pp. 56–57.

7. Bernard E. Trainor, "Pakistan Accused of a Nuclear Move: Islamabad is Said to Test Fire Atomic-Capable Missile, *New York Times*, 5/24/88, pp. A1, A9; David B. Ottaway, "U.S. Asks Soviets, Chinese to Cease Ballistic Missile Sales in Middle East," *Washington Post*, 5/26/88, p. A16.

8. "Pakistan in Missile Build Claim," *Jane's Defence Weekly*, 2/18/89, p. 267; "Army Chief: Surface-to-Surface Missiles Tested," Islamabad Domestic Service, 2/5/89 in *FBIS*, 2/6/89, p. 72.

9. That is, projectiles capable of carrying a 500kg payload 300kms or more. Peter Grier, "Nations Seeking Missile Technology Try to Circumvent US Regulations," *Christian Science Monitor*, 3/15/89, pp. 1, 2; Congress, Senate, Committee on Governmental Affairs (Testimony of CIA Director William Webster), *Nuclear and Missile Proliferation*, 5/19/89, p. 12.

10. Beyond the four main states discussed in this section are others who have provided some rocket-related training or scientific cooperation, most notably Britain and Canada.

11. "An Introduction to SUPARCO," p. 5.

12. "An Introduction to SUPARCO," p. 8; John J. Fialka, "Space Research Fuels Arms Proliferation," *Wall Street Journal*, 7/6/89, p. A8; Salim Mehmud, *Glimpses of Space Research in Pakistan* (Karachi: Pakistan Space and Upper Atmosphere Research Commission, Public Relations Office, 12/83), p. 2.

13. "Andrew Lawler, "U.S. Sanctions Imposed; India Deal with Russia Still On," *Space News*, 5/18/92, p. 14; and Congress, House, Committee on Science and Technology, Subcommittee on Space Science and Applications, *World Wide Space Activities* (Congressional Research Service Report), 95th Congress, 9/77, p. 120.

14. Mark Balaschak, et al., "Assessing the Comparability of Dual-Use Technologies for Ballistic Missile Development" (Report prepared for the U.S. Arms Control and Disarmament Agency), (Massachusetts: Center for International Studies, MIT, 6/81), p. 53.

15. Pakistan also claims to have launched the *Rehnuma-1*, a two-stage, solid-propellant rocket in March 1969. A heavier version of this rocket, the *Shahpar*, then

followed, and is claimed capable of reaching a 450 km altitude with a payload of 55 kg. See "An Introduction to SUPARCO,"pp. 23–31; S. M. Fazal, "Future of Space Technology in Pakistan," *Pakistan and Gulf Economist*, 5/15/82, pp. 11–13.

16. See Seth Carus, "Trends and Implications of Missile Proliferation" (Unpublished manuscript: Naval War College, 1990), p.12, fn. 30; *Assessing Ballistic Missile Proliferation and Its Control* (Stanford, Center for International Security & Arms Control, 1991), pp. 74–75; and Aaron Karp, "Ballistic Missile Proliferation," *SIPRI Yearbook*, 1991 (Stockholm International Peace Research Institute, 1991), p. 331.

17. For information and photos regarding Sud-Aviation sounding rockets see John W.R. Taylor, editor, *Jane's All the World's Aircraft*, 1969–70 (London: Jane's Yearbooks, 1969), pp. 620–622; "French Rockets," *McGraw-Hill Encyclopedia of Space* (New York: McGraw-Hill Publishers, 1968), pp. 112–114; and Congress, House, Committee on Science and Technology, pp. 146–148. For information and photos regarding Pakistan's *Hatf* missiles see Roger Frost, "Pakistan's New Defense Minister on Missiles, Self-Reliance and Afghanistan," *International Defense Review*, 4/89, p. 428; and Duncan Lennox, ed., "Hatf," *Jane's Strategic Weapons Systems*, Issue 06. For information and photos regarding Pakistan's sounding rockets see "An Introduction to SUPARCO" (Second edition), Pakistan Space & Upper Atmosphere Research Commission (Karachi: SUPARCO Public Relations Office, 10/88), pp. 36–38.

18. Sud-Aviation provided sounding rocket technology to SUPARCO at a time when there were no international missile-related export guidelines except for CoCOM restrictions governing high technology transfers to Communist countries. Even the U.S. State Department's Munitions List exempted sounding rockets from export restrictions.

19. "Government Said Involved in Technology Transfer," *Der Spiegel* (Hamburg), 6/12/89, pp. 70–86 in JPRS *Nuclear Developments*, 7/14/89, pp. 30–36.

20. Mark Hibbs, "Agencies Trace Some Iraqi URENCO Know-How to Pakistan Re-Export," *Nucleonics Week*, 11/28/91, pp. 1, 7–8.

21. Judith Miller, "West German Concern Ends Libyan Rocket Project," *New York Times*, 12/27/81, p. 7.

22. Radhakrishna Rao, p. 507. This article also suggests that OTRAG could have provided up to 2,000 technicians for Pakistan's program.

23. V. D. Chopra & Rakesh Gupta, *Nuclear Bomb and Pakistan: External and Internal Factors* (New Delhi: Patriot Publishers, 1986), pp. 3–4, 47; See also V. D. Chopra, "Writer Details Evidence of Nuclear Capability," *Patriot*, 11/10/86, p. 4 in *JPRS Worldwide Report*, 1/2/87, pp. 63, 64.

24. "Concern Expressed Over Pakistani Missile Test," *Hindustan Times* (Delhi), 2/28/89, p. 13 in *FBIS*, 3/5/89, pp. 63–65.

25. William R. Corliss, *NASA Sounding Rockets, 1958–1968: A Historical Summary* (Washington D.C.: NASA, Scientific and Technical Information Office, 1971), pp. 48–51, 70–71.

26. *Ibid.*, pp. 90–91.

27. Angela Mackay, "Ex-Ferranti Chief 'Ran $1bn Fraud,'" *Times* (London), 5/16/90, p. 23B.

28. Andy Pasztor, "Investigators Say Chilean Dealer Smuggled U.S. Weapons to Iraq," *Wall Street Journal*, 11/20/91, p. A10.

29. Edward T. Pound, "Shadowy Trail: American Arms Dealer was Amazing Success, or So Ferranti Believed," *Wall Street Journal*, 1/23/90, pp. A1, A6; Mackay, p. 23B.

30. Trainor, pp. A1, A9.

31. Susan F. Rasky, "Kuwaiti to Seek Reversal of Missile Ban," *New York Times*, 7/14/89, p. A3.

32. For instance: David Ellis, "China's Eager Merchants of Death," *Time*, 4/15/91, p. 17; John J. Fialka, "China is Selling Missile to Pakistan, U.S. Aids Believe," *Wall Street Journal*, 4/5/91, p. A2; Leslie H. Gelb, "China Ties About to Snap," *New York Times*, 4/24/91, p. A15; George Leopold, "China Markets Missiles to Middle East Buyers," *Defense News*, 4/8/91, pp. 1, 29; Bruce W. Nelan, "For Sale: Tools of Destruction," *Time*, 4/22/91, p. 44; and R. Jeffrey Smith, "U.S. Reports Chinese Missile Launchers Sighted in Pakistan," *Washington Post*, 4/6/91, p. A17.

33. Mushahid Hussain, "Pakistani Missiles—first Pictures," *Jane's Defence Weekly*, 3/11/89, p. 386; and Elaine Sciolino, "China Said to Sell Parts for Missiles," *New York Times*, 1/31/92, pp. A1, A2.

34. "Junejo Opens Propellant Plant in Havelian," Karachi Domestic Service, 3/7/87 in *FBIS, Daily Report: Middle East & South Asia*, 3/17/87, p. F1.

35. "'Prudent' Arms Trade Attitude," *Xinhua* (Beijing), 6/20/91 in *JPRS, Proliferation Issues*, 7/10/91, p. 1; "In Brief: Chinese Missiles," *Jane's Defence Weekly*, 6/6/91, p. 7; "India," *Hindustan Times* (Delhi), 6/21/91, p. 11 in *JPRS, Proliferation Issues*, 7/24/91, p. 14; "Pakistan," *Milavnews*, 7/91, pp. 20–21.

36. Al Webb, "American Arms to Pakistan: "A Test of U.S. Credibility," *U.S. News & World Report*, 9/21/81, pp. 45–46.

37. U.S. Arms Control and Disarmament Agency, *World Military Expenditures and Arms Transfers 1990* (Washington, D.C.: U.S. Arms Control and Disarmament Agency, 1991), p. 39.

38. For a discussion of this issue and other Sino-Pakistani nuclear ties, see Rodney W. Jones, "Pakistan: Emerging Nuclear Supplier Issues," in William C. Potter, ed., *International Nuclear Trade and Nonproliferation* (Lexington: Lexington Books, 1990), pp. 228–232. China has also been accused of providing Pakistan with a nuclear bomb test design.

39. This statement is reflected by an *International Herald Tribune* survey conducted late in 1991, which also reported U.S. officials as saying that China provided Pakistan with enough weapons grade uranium to produce two nuclear devices and that the country is in possession of a nuclear bomb weighing only 180 kg. See "Incidental Intelligence," *Pacific-Defense Reporter*, 9/91, p. 19. According to figures published by the U.S. Arms Control and Disarmament Agency, in the five year period from 1985 to 1989 Chinese weapons sales to Pakistan were valued at $410 million. These figures were only exceeded by the DF-3 deal with Saudi Arabia ($2.5 billion), and wartime arms sales to Iran ($2.8 billion) and Iraq ($1.6 billion). With the end of both Gulf wars and the loss of Iraq as a client, the consistency of Pakistani weapons purchases should become even more important. See U.S. Arms Control and Disarmament Agency, pp. 131–134.

40. Pakistan's position as a middleman was undoubtedly based on its good relations with both countries and potentially motivated by a desire to provide missile

support services in the wake of the sale. There have been subsequent reports of Pakistani technical assistance provided in relation to these missiles. See "Pakistani Missile Experts for Saudi Arabia," *Defense & Foreign Affairs Weekly*, 4/30/90, p. 3; "Saudi Arabia Wanted to Use CSS-2 MRBMS Against Iraq," *Defense & Foreign Affairs Weekly*, 4/15/91, p. 1; R. R. Subramanian, *India, Pakistan, China: Defense and Nuclear Tangle in South Asia* (New Delhi: ABC Publishing House, 1989), p. 27.

41. Andrew Lawler, "Congress Cautious On Lifting Satellite Ban Against China," *Space News*, 2/10–16/92, pp. 1, 29.

42. Andrew Rosenthal, "Bush Renewing Trade Privileges for China, but Adds Missile Curbs," *New York Times*, 5/27/91, pp. A1–A4; Gerald Seib, "Bush to Renew Favored Status for China Trade," *Wall Street Journal*, 5/28/91, pp. A3, A6; "China," *Milavnews*, 6/91, p. 7.

43. In 1987, France became a charter member of the MTCR. Facing strong pressure from the United States, China also announced that it would adhere to "MTCR guidelines and parameters" in February 1992. The regime specifies that its "guidelines are not designed to impede national space programs or international cooperation in such programs as long as such programs could not contribute to nuclear weapons delivery systems." Furthermore, the MTCR has no standing as an instrument of international law; decisions on technology transfer are understood to remain the "sole and sovereign judgment of the supplying government."

44. "Imposition of Missile Proliferation Sanctions Against Chinese and Pakistani Entities," *Federal Register* (Vol. 56, No. 137), 7/17/91, p. 32601.

45. However, the Bureau of Politico-Military Affairs claims that the listing of these entities together in the *Federal Register* does not necessarily imply their involvement in a mutual transaction.

46. Ottaway, p. A16.

47. Radhakrishna Rao, p. 507.

48. "Concern Expressed Over Pakistani Missile Test," *Hindustan Times* (Delhi), 2/28/89, p. 13 in *FBIS*, 3/5/89, pp. 63–65.

49. "Renowned Scientist Declares Nuclear Capability," *Dawn* (Karachi), 10/22/91, p. 1 in *JPRS, Proliferation Issues*, 11/7/91, pp. 26–25.

50. Were this true it would indicate the degree of priority attached to the development of missiles by Pakistan, not only because of A. Q. Khan's association with the nuclear bomb program, but because of his demonstrated managerial talent as well.

51. See note 40. Limited assistance might also be available from the military contingent Pakistan stations in Saudi Arabia.

52. Congress, House, Armed Services Committee on Intelligence Issues; Seapower, Strategic, and Critical Materials Subcommittee, *Statement of Rear Admiral Edward D. Sheafer, Jr. (Director of Naval Intelligence)*, 2/5/92, p. 75.

53. Geoffrey Kemp, *The Control of the Middle East Arms Race* (New York: Carnegie Endowment for International Peace, 1991), p. 88.

54. "Prime Minister Urges Muslim Weapons Cooperation," *AFP* (Hong Kong), 12/1/91 in *FBIS*, 12/2/91, p. 72; "Nuclear [sic] Exports Sold to Saudi Arabia," *Nawa-I-Waqt* (Lahore), 10/22/91, pp. 6, 8 in *JPRS, Proliferation Issues*, 1/16/92, pp. 21–22.

55. "Prime Minister Urges Muslim Weapons Cooperation," p. 72.

56. Roger Frost, "Pakistan's New Defence Minister on Missiles, Self-Reliance, and Afghanistan," *International Defence Review*, 4/89, pp. 427–428.

57. "Renowned Scientist Declares Nuclear Capability," *Dawn* (Karachi), 10/22/91, p.1 in *JPRS, Nuclear Developments*, 11/7/91, pp. 26–25.

58 Pakistan is neither a party to the Nuclear Proliferation Treaty nor the MTCR, though it has promised to join the former when India agrees likewise.

59. Congress, House, Armed Services Committee on Intelligence Issues, p. 76.

60. "An Introduction to SUPARCO," 4/82, p. 5; Taylor, p. 620; "Indigenous Rocket Launched into 'Deep Space,'" Dehli Domestic Service, 1/29/89 in *FBIS*, 1/30/89, p. 77.

61. Some sources have listed Pakistan as developing a *"Hatf-3,"* though there is currently insufficient information to clearly establish that such a system exists and is so designated by Pakistan. If Pakistan has designated a *Hatf-3* missile, this term could variously refer to an indigenously produced model or, less likely, an M-series unit.

62. He said that the missiles and their guidance systems were locally produced. "Pakistan in Missile Build Claim," *Jane's Defence Weekly*, 2/18/89, p. 267; "Army Chief: Surface-to-Surface Missiles Tested," Islamabad Domestic Service, 2/5/89 in *FBIS, Daily Report: Near East & South Asia*, 2/6/89, p. 72; "Further on Beg Comments," AFP (Hong Kong), 2/5/89 in *FBIS, Daily Report: Near East & South Asia*, 2/6/89, pp. 72–73.

63. Hussain, "Pakistani Missiles—First Pictures," p. 386.

64. *Jane's Defence Weekly*, 4/15/89, p. 635; This development helps demonstrate the country's narrowly defined military-industrial capability. Even relatively simple artillery rockets (the *Hatf* is held to be a more sophisticated system) require that a field-certified TEL at least be mounted on a vehicle with suitable suspension and off-road handling abilities to overcome moderate environmental hazards. The principal utility of a tactical ballistic missile, other than the payload/range characteristics of the missile itself, relates to the system's mobility. Using such means to haul around a delicately instrumented missile, even with solid propellant, does not lend itself to durable and reliable operation, which suggests that the missiles are transported separately from their launchers and mounted on the trailer only for firing, increasing deployment time. It seems that while Pakistan can produce a missile, it cannot manufacture a suitable vehicle on which to carry it.

65. See Taylor, pp. 620–622; and Congress, House, Committee on Science and Technology, pp. 146–148 for the flight characteristics of the sounding rocket series (produced by France's Sud-Aviation) upon which Pakistan's *Hatf-1* and *-2* are apparently based.

66. Other determinants of missile system accuracy include the capabilities to precisely regulate thrust output, termination and vector control, the timing of stage separation, and the aerodynamic affects of high velocity flight on ballistic projectiles. These skills must also be supplemented by the ability to successfully design and integrate a myriad of components and processes into the missile vehicle itself. Lastly, effective intelligence is also crucial for target acquisition and launcher control. The successful indigenous development of long range ballistic missile guidance technology (i.e., inertial navigation) requires a level of national dedication and commitment of scientific and financial resources somewhat comparable to those

necessary for the acquisition of a nuclear explosive device. See Donald MacKenzie, *Inventing Accuracy: A Historical Sociology of Nuclear Missile Guidance* (Cambridge: MIT Press, 1990) for the definitive study on this subject.

67. This analysis is based on the rudimentary technical characteristics of the attitude control equipment used by the French *Eridan* and *Dauphin* sounding rockets as suggested by *Assessing Ballistic Missile Proliferation and Its Control*, p. 75, fn. 52. The actual accuracy of the *Hatf-1* and -2 could be greater, again depending on the nature and degree of outside assistance.

68. Trainor, p. A9.

69. At least one observer believes that the *Hatf* missiles would be incapable of lifting a first generation Pakistani nuclear warhead. See Karp, p. 331. This fact, of course, cannot be precisely known and is undoubtedly influenced by the degree of Chinese engineering assistance, which is strongly suspected.

70. Interview with Gen. Mirza Aslam Beg by Mushahid Hussain, "Pakistan 'Responding to Change,'" *Jane's Defence Weekly*, 10/14/89, p. 779.

71. "Booster Rocket Developed for Satellite Launcher," p. 69; "Manufacturing Program Continues," pp. 69–70; *JANG* (Lahore), pp. 56–57.

72. Bill Gertz, for one, has written that China transferred both M-9s and M-11s. Bill Gertz, "China, N. Korea, Secretly Deliver Missiles to Mideast via Cyprus," *Washington Times*, 7/2/91, p. A4.

73. His comment in October 1989 that this missile was unsophisticated because it lacked suitable guidance may be linked to a later *New York Times* article reporting the transfer of M-11 guidance units to Pakistan in January 1992, although these components might also be intended for the *Hatf-2*. See Hussein, p. 779; Sciolino, p. 1. It is also possible that a relationship exists between the Pakistani space launch booster and China's M-series missiles.

74. "Pakistan," *Milavnews*, 8/91, p. 19.

75. John Lewis, Hua Di, and Xue Litai, "Beijing's Defense Establishment: Solving the Arms Export Enigma," *International Security* (Spring 1991), p. 98, fn. 18.

76. Of course, Pakistan still would need to devise suitable command, control, and targeting procedures, as well as integrate or weaponize such missiles with nuclear warheads.

77. "An Introduction to SUPARCO," 4/82, pp. 23–31; S. M. Fazal, "Future of Space Technology in Pakistan," *Pakistan and Gulf Economist*, 5/15/82, pp. 11–13.

78. S. M. Fazal, pp. 12–13.

79. "Space Research in Pakistan 1990," National Report to XXVIII COSPAR Meeting, June 25–July 6, 1990, (Karachi: SUPARCO, 6/90), p. 43. All of Pakistan's higher academic institutions were founded after the country was separated from India in 1947. Most of these had their origins in the 1960s. This inequity is one of many Pakistan has faced in its attempt to compete with the far greater resources of neighboring India.

80. John E. Fricker, "Chinese Assisting Pakistan Industry," *Aviation Week & Space Technology*, 3/30/81, pp. 58–59.

81. "Parliament Briefed on Missile System Production," Delhi All India Radio Network, 3/26/92 in JPRS, *Proliferation Issues*, 4/8/92, p. 1.

82. Pakistan's civil rockets typically use names derived from Urdu or Persian.

83. Congress, Senate, Governmental Affairs Committee, *Weapons Proliferation in the New World Order* (testimony of CIA Dir. Robert Gates), 102nd Congress, 1/15/92.

84. "Minister Comments on Afghan Missile Threat," Islamabad Domestic Service, 2/23/89 in *FBIS, Daily Report: Near East & South Asia*, 2/23/89, p. 54.

85. "Bhutto Condemns Kabul for Missile Firing," Islamabad Domestic Service, 1/11/90 in *FBIS, Daily Report: Near East & South Asia*, 1/12/90, p. 38.

86. Colin Barraclough, "Afghan Rebels Capture Soviet-Supplied Scuds," *Christian Science Monitor*, 5/12/92, p. 3.

5

Brazilian Missile and Rocket Production and Export

Péricles Gasparini Alves[1]

General Introduction

The search for technological, economic and political progress is a major preoccupation for any country, and in the case of Brazil this led to the growth of an arms industry such that, by the 1980s, war material had become a significant component in the country's exports. The objective of the present chapter is, therefore, to discuss Brazil's production of missiles and rockets which has always been, and continues to be, an important feature of its weapons exports.

Regard is first given to production capacity. Small missiles, particularly air-to-air missiles, and artillery rockets have been technically and financially successful, but the production of long-range missiles has run into various problems. In addition, since many countries regard R&D on space launching vehicles with circumspection, arms analysts often question *whether* and *when* Brazil will reach indigenous ballistic missile manufacturing status, either by developing dedicated ballistic missiles or via a non-dedicated rocketry program. Therefore, this chapter also briefly addresses the common concern that Brazil's sounding rockets could be converted into ballistic missiles and thus boost the country's military and political prestige in and outside Latin America. Another concern, of course, is the possible availability of such missiles for the export market.

Attention is also directed to the legislation governing Brazil's export of war material. Unfortunately, the literature on the subject is both limited and incomplete, mainly because of importers' and/or exporters' wish for secrecy. An appraisal is given of the role of the Brazilian Armed Forces and the Ministry of External Relations in the inspection and control of missile and rocket exports. In addition, international restrictions on the transfer of sensitive technology are examined for their effect on Brazil's production of military- and civil-purpose rockets as well as a possible reduction of export capability.

The chapter concludes with a summary of the status and future of missile and rocket production and their export by Brazilian companies.

Missile and Rocket Production

It is common knowledge that over 90 percent of Brazil's production of war material is exported. This is not entirely accidental but, unlike other major exporters of war material, Brazil has not been motivated by a particular political or security rationale. Although arms exports have—whether intentionally or not—diplomatic, regional and other geopolitical implications, Brazil's approach has been based on the economic requirements of its long-term political and development planning. In strategic terms, the civil and military regimes in the early 1960s brought Brazil to a new level of industrialization, an integral component of which the aim was first, autonomy and, later, self-sufficiency in specialized areas of high technology in a relatively short period. Since this called for ventures of a high-spending nature, these ventures could obviously not be undertaken for the national market alone, and they were thus also directed to the export market to generate foreign currency.

This drive for autonomy encouraged the government to support the development of an industrial park in aerospace, outer space, and the arms industry. Most of the companies concerned are located in the states of Minas Gerais, Rio de Janeiro, and São Paulo and the government has offered them such incentives as special financing arrangements (loans) and tax waivers, especially in respect of war material.[2] Accordingly, the 1960s saw an increase in arms production with significant orders for armored vehicles and tanks being received by the beginning of the 1970s. However, it was not until the end of that decade that missiles and rockets began to be exported.[3] Although over forty Brazilian companies and government entities are technically and financially capable of producing entire weapon systems, only a few have done so, the three major entities being: ORBITA Sistemas Aeroespaciais S.A., AVIBRAS Indústria Aeroespacial S.A., and the Centro Técnico Aeroespacial (CTA).[4]

ORBITA was formed in 1987 to coordinate the production of guided missiles in Brazil. The company was assisted by other Brazilian companies and entities already established in the field of aerospace, missiles, and other war materials, such as: Engenheiros Especializados S.A. (ENGESA), Empresa Brasileira de Aeronautica S.A. (EMBRAER), Engenharia de Sistemas de Controle de Automação (Esca), Indústria de Material Bélico do

TABLE 5.1 Missile/Rocket Technology Development by ORBITA Sistemas Aeroespaciais S.A.

Missile or Rocket	*Type & Function*	*Payload & Propulsion*	*Range (km)*	*Stage of Development*
MB/EE-150	• Missile	• Conventional • Solid	90 to 150	R&D (Cancelled)
MB/EE-350	• Missile	• Conventional • Solid	215 to 300	R&D (Cancelled)
MB/EE-600	• Missile	• Conventional • Solid	370 to 600	Conceptual (Cancelled)
MB/EE-1000	• Missile	• Conventional • Solid	620 to 1000	Conceptual (Cancelled)
MSS-1 *Leo*[a]	• Missile • Anti-tank combat	• Conventional	—	Conceptual (Cancelled)
MSA-1	• Missile • Anti-tank combat	• Conventional	—	Conceptual (Cancelled)
Piranha MAA-1 Mol[a]	• Missile • Anti-tank combat	• Conventional	5	R&D (Cancelled)

[a]Inherited from CTA.

Sources: Adapted from information given in Martin Navias, "Ballistic Missile Proliferation in the Third World," *Adelphi Papers*, 252, Summer 1990, pp. 29–31 (see tables and their sources); Scott D. Tollefson, *Brazilian Arms Transfers, Ballistic Missiles, and Foreign Policy: The Search for Autonomy*, dissertation submitted to The Johns Hopkins University, Baltimore, Maryland, 1991 (unpublished); and others.

Brasil (IMBEL), and Participações e Consultoria (Parcom).[5] In its five years of existence, ORBITA inherited missile projects from its shareholders, the aforementioned companies, and also developed new missile concepts. Of the major missile projects undertaken by ORBITA (see Table 5.1),[6] the MB/EE-150 and MB/EE-300 were the most advanced, although neither of them reached the production stage, nor did the *Piranha* missile, a fairly advanced project inherited from the CTA via ENGESA.[7] However, all of the ORBITA missile projects have now been canceled due to lack of capital.

AVIBRAS Indústria Aeroespacial is the private company that produces most of the missiles and rockets in Brazil (see Table 5.2), as well as manufacturing a variety of products for civil use. Unlike ORBITA, AVIBRAS has been able to place its products in both the domestic and the international market and it is presently the country's largest exporter of missiles and rockets.

One of its best-selling products is the surface-to-surface Artillery Saturation Rocket System (ASTROS) II, which has been in full production since

TABLE 5.2 Missile/Rocket Development by AVIBRAS Indústria Aeroespacial S.A.

Missile or Rocket	*Type & Function*	*Payload & Propulsion*	*Typical Range (km)*	*Stage of Development*
S-20	• Missile • Theater combat	• Conventional	40 to 70	Production & Sales
SS-150	• Missile	• Conventional • Solid	150	R&D (temp. suspended)
SS-300	• Missile	• Conventional • Solid	300	R&D (temp. suspended)
SS-1000	• Missile	• Conventional • Solid	1200	R&D (temp. suspended)
ASTROS II SS-30	• Rocket • Artillery saturation rocket	• 32 tubes of 127mm rockets–high explosive	9 to 30	Production & Sales
ASTROS II SS-40	• Rocket • Artillery saturation rocket	• 16 tubes of 180mm rockets–high explosive	15 to 35	Production & Sales
ASTROS II SS-60	• Rocket • Artillery saturation rocket	• 32 tubes of 127mm rockets–high explosive	20 to 60	Production & Sales
FOG-MPM	• Missile • Multiple-purpose fiber-optic guided missile (anti-tank/ helicopter/ fortifications)	• 180mm diameter, warhead penetration of over 1000mm • Conventional	10	Production & Sales

SS = surface-to-surface ASTROS = Artillery Saturation Rocket System
FOG-MPM = Fiber-Optic-Guided Multiple-Purpose Missile

Sources: AVIBRAS Indústria Aeroespacial S.A. and others

1983. ASTROS is sold as a complete system for battery- and battalion-sized units. These include a 3.9 m rocket of 127 mm (SS-30) fired from a Universal Multiple Launcher (AV-LMU). Other rockets include the SS-40, a 4.2 mlong rocket with a 180 mm caliber. However, the largest of all the ASTROS II rockets is the SS-60, which measures 5.6 m and has a 300 mm caliber.

One of the AVIBRAS missiles is the 1.50 m long FOG-MPM which employs a modern guidance system based on fiber-optic wire. Unlike the ASTROS II, the FOG-MPM has not been sold to the Brazilian military or for export, but it is available on the market.[8] AVIBRAS is also said to have assisted in the prototype development of a SM-70 *Barracuda* missile to equip the Brazilian Navy's corvettes for coastal defense.[9] However, the most controversial AVIBRAS projects are the SS-150, SS-300, and SS-1000 missiles. Because of their range and payload capacity, many analysts expect that the SS-300 and the SS-1000 could be the first short- and mid-range ballistic missiles listed in Brazil's arms export catalogue. Moreover, it is also suspected that the SS-1000 could be nuclear-capable. However, the SS series has been temporarily suspended, reportedly because of lack of finance and confirmed orders.[10] Nevertheless, AVIBRAS demonstrated its interest at the time and may well continue to develop these missiles in the future.[11]

Other Brazilian entities working on missile/rocketry development are the Air Force's Instituto de Atividades Espaciais (IAE)—Institute for Space Activities—and the Instituto Technológico da Aeronautica (ITA)—Technological Institute of Aeronautics, both of which are part of the CTA in São José dos Campos. Among the missiles developed by CTA is the SBAT missile (see Table 5.3) which, although reportedly used in the Iran/Iraq war, is usually considered to be obsolete for contemporary war operations.[12] The technology employed in the *Piranha* air-to-air missile is also considered obsolete and the project was, as discussed above, inherited by ORBITA. However, the cornerstone of Brazilian rocketry technology is the SONDA series, the research of which originated at the AVIBRAS Indústria Aeroespacial in the early 1960s.[13] From 1965 to 1975, SONDA I, SONDA II-B and SONDA II-C reportedly utilized technology and components developed by both AVIBRAS and the Ministry of Aeronautics.[14] As of 1965, the two-stage SONDA I served to develop technology for solid propellants and short-range rockets. Over 200 SONDA I rockets were launched in a twelve-year period. In 1966, development was initiated on the single-stage SONDA II rocket which was then aimed at the delivery of civil loads into space orbit. Over fifty SONDA II rockets have been launched since 1966 for technology innovation such as thermic protection, new propellants, aerodynamic configuration, and electronic components testing.[15]

Work on a two-stage SONDA III rocket to study magnetic anomaly in the South Atlantic began in 1969 and over twenty such rockets have been launched since then. In 1974, however, a bi-stage SONDA IV rocket was developed for the major propulsion components of a future satellite launching vehicle. The development of the Veículo Lançador de Satélites (VLS)—Satellite Launching Vehicle—was officially approved with the creation of the Missão Espacial Completa Brasileira (MECB)—Brazilian Complete Space Mission.[16] The VLS consists of SONDA IV technology using a four-stage, solid-propelled rocket. Different versions of SONDA rockets have been constructed for the VLS. The VLS-R1 failed a test flight in 1987 (reportedly because of gyroscope guidance technology problems), but the VLS-R2 version successfully completed a later test flight. In addition, a two-stage rocket, the VS-40, consisting of a combination of stages from existing sounding rockets, is under construction for propulsion tests in

TABLE 5.3 Missile/Rocket Technology Development by the Centro Técnico Aeroespacial (CTA)

Missile or Rocket	*Type & Function*	*Payload & Propulsion*	*Range (km)*	*Stage of Development*
SBAT	• Missile (unguided) • Air-to-ground combat	• Conventional	—	Production (obsolete)
Carcara MAS-1	• Missile (unguided) • Air-to-surface combat	• Conventional	—	Cancelled
Piranha MAA-1 Mol	• Missile (unguided) • Air-to-air combat	• Conventional	5	Transfered to ENGESA
SONDA I	• Sounding rocket • Technology acquisition—low-orbit launch	• Propellant test • Solid	60 to 75	Production & Launch
SONDA II	• Sounding rocket • Technology acquisition—low-orbit launch	• Civil load • Solid	100 (44 kg max. payload)	Production & Launch
SONDA III	• Sounding rocket • Technology acquisition—low-orbit launch	• Civil load • Solid	500 (50 kg max. payload)[a]	Production & Launch
SONDA IV	• Sounding rocket • Place satellite in low orbit	• Satellite • Solid	600 (500 kg max. payload)	R&D
VS40	• Sounding rocket • Test engine in low orbit—over 60 km (not guided)	• Engine test • Solid	60	R&D
VLS	• Rocket • Place satellite in low orbit	• Satellite • Solid	250 to 1,000 (100 to 200 kg max. payload)	R&D

[a]Basic version: 50 to 80 kg for high altitudes; alternative version: 130 to 160 kg for low altitudes.

Source: Compiled from information given in "Brazilian Space Program," *Centro Técnico Aeroespacial*, Instituto de Atividades Espaciais Brochure, Ministry of Aeronautics, Department of Research and Development, São José dos Campos; and others.

vacuum. The final version of the VLS has now (1992) been fully mounted and is undergoing vibration tests at IAE.

The VLS is a civil launcher program which, with launching site capabilities, is expected by analysts to ensure Brazilian participation in the international satellite launching market before the end of this century, and into the next. The further development of the MECB program will therefore provide Brazil with devices and vehicles for the establishment of an international satellite launching site for low (i.e., circular orbit between 250 and 1,000 km) and geostationary orbits.

However, the VLS program is also the subject of comment in the literature, because of the dual-capability of launchers and ballistic missiles and the possible development of a Brazilian intercontinental ballistic missile.[17] This issue is further complicated by the fact that Brazil has chosen to develop solid-fueled rockets instead of liquid-fueled ones, and some defense analysts from countries possessing ballistic missiles argue that R&D on solid-fueled rockets places Brazil in a more suitable position to convert VLS-type rockets into ballistic missiles in the future. Nevertheless, Brazil's option to develop solid-fueled rockets is often explained by the fact that such rockets are cheaper and simpler to manufacture, and thus more attractive for a *relatively* low-investment space program. In spite of these arguments, one other concern expressed by foreign defense analysts is that the launching leg of the Brazilian space program is being developed by the IAE under the auspices of the Air Force and not, like the satellite leg, by a civil entity.

Nevertheless, the VLS type of R&D arrangement is not unique to Brazil and is in fact quite common in developing countries, particularly in Latin America. For instance, the Ministry of Aeronautics—the Air Force—is not only in charge of outer space matters, but also a number of other activities such as civil aviation, including civil air fields and airports. Moreover, other international concerns related to Brazilian development of VLS type rockets include Brazil's record in the field of arms exports, particularly missiles/rockets and the international market demand for these weapons, which attracts arms manufacturers.

Although the VLS is being developed by a military institute, its conversion to a ballistic missile program would have several political/military, economic, and technological implications.[18] The Brazilian government has not officially stated that it intends to develop ballistic missiles, nor has it formally abstained from the possession of such missiles. A political decision to convert launching rockets into ballistic missiles would therefore have to be part of a specific military policy whereby regional and international security needs would justify such a stance. For example, over and above ballistic missile manufacturing for reasons of power and prestige, arms analysts have often contended that the conversion of SONDA IV or VLS into ballistic missiles would counter-balance a possible development of the Argentine Air Force's *Condor II* missile. However, this contingency is less plausible in the light of Argentine/Brazilian efforts for political/economic *rapprochement* and reports of President Menem's halting of the

Condor II project (including the destruction of about thirty assembled and disassembled missiles).[19] In terms of technology, however, conversion estimates made in 1988 by the then deputy director of the IAE covered a period of between five and ten years, depending on the level of threat perception and government commitment.[20] These estimates probably did not envisage the VLS program's problems concerning funding, access to technology and political resolution on the part of the Brazilian Government. In any event, much has to be done in terms of specific military technology which the IAE does not yet possess for example, while special computers and software for guidance for intermediate- or intercontinental-range missiles can be modified from a space launcher, the major technology problems in conversion of a space launcher to a ballistic missile would concentrate on two different aspects: (a) the re-entry of the rocket or missile nosecone and its control during the re-entry part of the flight, and (b) flight testing.[21]

Last but not least, there are economic considerations. Conversion would require large investment for new installations and test facilities, such as missile guidance and telemetry systems. In addition, the conversion of the VLS to a ballistic missile would require large sums of money which would probably not be justified by the use of conventional payloads. The converted missile would therefore have to be biologically, chemically, or even nuclear loaded. As well as political, military/strategic, and legal constraints to manufacturing and possessing such payloads,[22] there is no doubt that Brazil does not yet possess the technology to manufacture a *miniaturized* nuclear warhead meeting the technical characteristics of a VLS-type rocket.

However, if conversion from VLS to ballistic missile is indeed plausible, it would be more appropriate to think in terms of the private sector, especially companies which are already working in the area of missiles and rockets.[23] Given Brazil's political and economic situation, it is likely that government and military interest in ballistic missiles will be limited in the near future and that the main outlet for such missiles would then be the international market, just as it would probably be for the civil use of the VLS.

Missile and Rocket Export

Government support of companies entering the missile/rocket export market is usually motivated by political and economic factors; the former may range from regional to global security (e.g., military considerations, political prestige).[24] In the case of Brazilian government entities, support for missile/rocket export is apparently seen as a matter of prestige, in that Brazil is able to pursue state-of-the art of technology.[25] This would not be surprising, since this would lead to reduced dependency on developed countries, greater regional political influence, and military and economic autonomy. There is also concern for both economic and security reasons that Brazil should not lag behind Argentina in the R&D of missile technology.

Nevertheless, Brazilian missiles/rockets are exported by commercial companies—not primarily because of Brazil's regional or extra-regional political influence but because overseas buyers wish to purchase them. The companies' interest is economic, but not, in principle, incompatible with that of the government. Thus, these companies have developed a strategy, supported by the government, which enables them to gain a foothold in the export market via the direct sales of these weapons and services, partnership alliances for the development of missile/rocket programs, and bartering or other special arrangements.

Table 5.4 shows the major transactions involving the export of missiles and missile equipment, components, technologies, and services since the 1980s. Given the secrecy surrounding war material exports, it is difficult to evaluate past and future export revenues, or the exact nature of the most important trade agreements, e.g., counter trade, offsets, coproduction, etc. In some cases, secrecy in arms transaction may be due to some exporters' request depending on political and other factors, but it is normally the result of demands on the part of the importers—which in some cases request secrecy about the transaction in clauses of the purchase agreement. Secrecy is therefore one way of avoiding the spread of information about the type of weapons importers possess. It is known that, up to 1990, sales of the most commercialized Brazilian rocket system—the ASTROS II series—totaled over US$1 billion. Purchases by the Brazilian Armed Forces of ASTROS II are said to be only about two percent of the total sales,[26] and this figure may well include a recent order for about US$10 million worth of ASTROS II equipment.[27]

Apart from unconfirmed sales to Japan and Sweden, most of the reported sales of ASTROS II were to countries in the Middle East and North Africa. Iraq is often quoted as the major importer of Brazil's missile/rocket technologies, equipment, components, and services in the 1980s. It has also been reported that Iraq partly funded the ASTROS II.[28] To this must be added the joint venture activities and services supplied to Iraq by Brazilian companies, one example being the adaptation of certain missiles, including, it is said, Soviet missiles, by a São Paulo company called HOP (*Hugo de Oliveira Piva*). However, it now appears that Saudi Arabia will overtake Libya, and even Iraq, to become Brazil's chief importer of war material, particularly for the ASTROS II series.

Nevertheless, negotiations with several other Middle East and African countries have been halted. For example, it has been reported that Libya had intended to fund a family of ORBITA MB/EE missiles, but this proposal appears to have fallen through.[29] Table 5.5 lists the main missile/

TABLE 5.4 Brazilian Commercial Transactions Involving Missiles/Rockets, and Their Equipment, Components, Technologies, and/or Services: Reported Data

Importer	*Year*	*Missile/ Rocket Type*	*Imports*	*Number*	*Comments*
Chile	Late 1980s[b]	ASTROS I	Missile/Rocket	—	ASTROS first version
Iran	—	ASTROS II SS-30	Missile/Rocket	—	
Iraq	1983[a] 1984[b]	ASTROS II SS-30	Missile/Rocket	6[a] 6[b]	
	1983[a] 1988[b]	ASTROS II FCU	Equipment	— 13[b]	Radar Fire Control Unit (FCU)
	1984[a] 1985[b]	ASTROS II SS-30	Missile/Rocket	22[a] 22[b]	
	1985[a] 1988[b]	ASTROS II SS-60	Missile/Rocket	— 20[b]	
	1985[a] 1986[b]	ASTROS II SS-30	Missile/Rocket	38[a] 19[b]	
	1985 to 1990	—	Technology and Services	—	Engineers working on *Al-Husayn*, *Al-Taw-Han*, & SCUD missiles
	1989[a] 1990	*Piranha* technology	Services	—	Development of a short-range air-to-air missile
Libya	1986[a]	ASTROS II SS-40	Missile/Rocket	30[a]	
	1987[a]	ASTROS II SS-40	Missile/Rocket	15[a]	Not confirmed
	1987[a]	ASTROS II SS-60	Missile/Rocket	15[a]	Not confirmed
	1988[a]	MB/EE	Technology	—	Not completed
Japan	1986[a]	ASTROS II	Missile/Rocket	—	Not confirmed
Saudi Arabia	1986[a]	ASTROS II SS-40	Missile/Rocket	30[b]	Not confirmed
	1988[a]	ASTROS II SS-30	Missile/Rocket	10[b]	Fire Control Unit
	1988[a]	ASTROS II FCU	Equipment	4[b]	Delivery initiated
	1990[a]	ASTROS II	Missile/Rocket	—[c]	
Sweden	1986[a]	ASTROS II	Missile/Rocket	—	Not confirmed

[a]Ordered
[b]Delivered/Ended
[c]US$60–70 million

Sources: Adapted from Reiner Pungs, *A Indústria de Armamentos e a Politica Externa Brasileira*, June 1989; "Piva Details Research Activities," *O Estado de São Paulo*, 6 December 1990, p. 11; Tollefson, *Brazilian Arms Transfers...*, 1991 (unpublished); *Global Arms Trade...*, Congress of the U.S., June 1991, pp. 144-45; *SIPRI Yearbooks*, 1970 through 1990; and others.

TABLE 5.5 Missile/Rocket Technology: Cancelled Exports

Importer	*Period*	*Missile/ Rocket*	*Amount Reportedly Involved (US$)*
Libya	• 1983 • 1988	ASTROS II SONDA, MB/EE (technologies)	14 billion 2 billion, including other weapons
Iraq	—	ASTROS II	400 million
Oman, Bahrain, The Arab Emirates, Angola, Nigeria, Venezuela	—	—	—

Sources: Adapted from Tollefson, *Brazilian Arms Transfers...*, 1991, pp. 95-96 (unpublished); "Latin America: Brazil and Libya, Pinochet and Chile," *Defense & Foreign Affairs Weekly*, 5 June 1983, p. 3; Barham, "Brazil Ignores US Protest Over Arms For Libya," *Sunday Times*, 31 January 1988, p. 5.

rocket and technology export cancellations that have been reported in the open literature. Other agreements are also reported to have fallen through since the late 1980s, but this has not been confirmed. The loss of traditional and potential clients has obviously been exacerbated with the end of the Iran-Iraq war, Iraq's inability to honor its purchase orders, and the United Nations arms embargo on Iraq since the end of 1990.

Thus, with bottlenecks in the production of both war material in general and missiles/rockets in particular, the Brazilian missile/rocketry industry faces serious economic and political, as well as technological problems. The economic crisis has resulted in budget constraints on several areas of science and technology, causing delays in the release of established program funding and diminished financing for new programs.[30] Of particular concern to the arms industry is the departure of experts to other sectors of the economy, or to other countries, for higher salaries. This has caused cuts in program developments and delayed testing on weapons as well as rockets and other space-related equipment.

The major enterprises engaged in manufacturing and selling rocketry technology (such as missile/rocket and related services) are undergoing major change, and one, AVIBRAS, was declared bankrupt in early 1990.[31] Another reported bankruptcy was that of ENGESA which, in 1991, had an estimated debt of US$400 million.[32] The situation has so deteriorated that even civilians working for a military entity, under military management, have gone on strike. Restructuring has included extensive personnel layoffs, regrouping of production capabilities, and other drastic measures aimed at narrowing product lines and economy of scale. As of January 1992, the major Brazilian entities and companies working in the aerospace and missile/rocket fields had been affected as shown in Table 5.6.[33]

TABLE 5.6 Economic Distress in the Brazilian Aerospace Industry

Company or Entity	*Strike*	*Restructuring*	*Declaration of Bankruptcy*
AVIBRAS		×	×
EMBRAER		×	
ENGESA			×
IAE (CTA)	×		
INPE	×		
ORBITA		×	

AVIBRAS has been able to redress its economic problems, partly because of its dual-purpose products for civil and military use. In contrast, ORBITA is gradually reducing its activities on missile R&D. Should the international export market and Brazil's economic situation not improve for arms export, ORBITA is expected to have a short life. Efforts are being made to prevent EMBRAER and ENGESA from suffering the same fate. EMBRAER, in which the Brazilian government holds over 95 percent of the voting stock, has been listed among the companies to be privatized in the course of 1992. ENGESA, which is accused of having accumulated strategic planning problems in the last five years, may well be sold to The Royal Ordinance or its mother corporation, British Aerospace.[34] The Brazilian government, which had envisaged investment in the defense sector to redirect some companies to the civil market, now seems to be more interested in preserving the arms industry's laboratory technology.[35] In this connection, some Brazilian arms exporters argue that President Collor de Mello's Government had encouraged a rethinking of the objectives of the arms industry set-up in the 1960s, and this has directly affected the quest for missile/rocketry technologies.[36] Indeed, from the commercial standpoint, the new liberal policy adopted by the Collor Government left little room for government subsidies, and companies have to face economic difficulties on their own.[37]

The assessment of Brazil's missile/rocket export activity cannot but reflect the country's present production of these weapons. While little is known about planned transactions, missile/rocket exports have changed in the past ten years. Loss of R&D capabilities (projects and experts) will have an adverse impact on the production and export of missiles/rockets, including any projected production of ballistic missiles, for several years to come because Brazil's production is largely dependent on the international market. In fact, there is no large-scale production of medium or long-range missiles in Brazil, and only artillery rockets and short-range missiles are being manufactured for specific customers.

Transaction Processes and Government Policy

Brazilian exports of missiles/rockets are controlled in two ways: first, through licensing regulations and legal administrative procedures governing exports (see Table 5.7), and secondly, through a more flexible mechanism whereby export policy is adapted both to the prospective client and to the circumstance of the purchase in the light of the product concerned as well as some other factors.

The overall control of war material exports has been written into the Federal Constitution of Brazil. Article 21, paragraph VI of Chapter II provides the Government with the competence to authorize and oversee the production and commerce of war material.[38] This legal competence originates from a Presidential Decree of July 1934, regulating the establishment of companies intending to produce arms and war munitions for both national use and export.[39] The Decree also assigned the supervision of these regulations to the Ministry of the Army.[40] Present regulations require detailed reporting of an exporting company's production capacity to the Ministry of the Army, including: the total number of buildings, personnel, equipments, location, product formulas of a secret character, storage capability, and all other aspects of production such as transport and commerce. In addition, under a Federal Decree of 28 January 1965, which approved the Regulation for the Supervision of Controlled Products (R-105), any company producing controlled material must also obtain a Certificate of Registry from the Ministry of the Army as a license to operate. The companies concerned include exporting companies, subcontracting companies, and producers of controlled raw material.[41]

Regulations also require exporters of controlled products to comply with the legal norms and regulations of importing countries.[42] Further control is also exercised by the Ministry of External Relations which must legalize all documents in Brazil or through its consulates in importing countries. Other legal restrictions are found in Article 137 which stipulates that the export of controlled products should not affect the supply of controlled products to the Brazilian market.[43] More than 500 controlled items are listed, classified into ten groups of utilization and three categories (1, 2, and 3) of control. The lower the category number, the stricter the control. Missiles (item 475) are part of category 1 and, together with rockets, fuel, oxidants and additives, are classified under the same group and subject to the most stringent supervision.[43]

The export of Brazilian missiles/rockets may involve various entities. The exporter files an application for authorization with the Ministry of

TABLE 5.7 Brazilian Regulations on the Production and Export of Controlled Products (including Missiles/Rockets)

Document	*Date*	*Scope*
Federal Decree No. 24 602	July 1934	Articles 1-14: Authorizes the Ministry of the Army to supervise the follow-up of requirements made by the Federal Government with respect to the production and commerce of war material for both national consumption and export.
Federal Decree No. 1 246-36	11 Dec. 1936	Regulation for the Supervision of Controlled Products (R-105)
Federal Decree No. 55 649	28 Jan. 1965	Approved the new edition of the *Regulamento para a Fiscalização de Produtos Controlados* (R-105), approved by Federal Decree No. 1 246-36, 11 Dec. 1936 Chapter II, Article 10: Establishes the directives for the execution of Federal Decree No. 24 602 Chapter III, Article 11: Export authorization Chapter VII, A, Article 43: Certificate of Registry, detailed information on the company's location, assets, and production capacity Chapter XV, Article 136: Authorization for export Chapter XIX, Articles 157-59: Nature of controlled products and their categories Chapter XXI, Articles 164-65: Classification of missiles, their components and a list of controlled products
Federal Decree No. 88 113	28 Jan. 1983	Amended Federal Decree No. 55 649 of 28 January 1965
Constitution of the Federative Republic of Brazil	5 Oct. 1988	Chapter II, Article 21, para. VI: Provides the Government with the competence to authorize and oversee the production and commerce of war material[a]

[a]The scope of this regulation in the preceding constitution was the same.

Source: Regulamento para a Fiscalização de Produtos Controlados, (R-105), Ministério do Exército, Estado-Maior do Exército, Primeira edição, 1965; *Constituição Federal do Brasil*, 5 Outubro 1988.

External Relations, which analyses the application in the light of its export policies—the Politica Nacional de Exportação de Material de Emprego Militar (PNEMEM)—National Policy for the Export of Material for Military Use. The Ministry of External Relations then forwards the application to the Secretaria de Assuntos Estratégicos da Presidência da República (SAE)—Secretariat of Strategic Affairs of the Presidency of the Republic, for consideration, which consults with the Ministry of the Army. (Further consultations, if needed, may include other Armed Forces Ministers or the Conselho de Defesa Nacional (CDN)—National Defense Council.[45])

Decisions regarding authorization for export are subject to approval by all the entities concerned, including the President of the Republic himself. A favorable response by SAE, to the Ministry of External Affairs, implies Presidential authorization for export and the exporter is given permission to start other administrative procedures. The private sector (e.g., industrialists), other groups such as political parties, the public, and non-governmental, quasi-governmental and multinational entities have little, if any, influence on export authorization.

Brazilian sales of arms, including missiles/rockets and related technologies, have led many analysts to conclude that Brazil's export policy is lenient, and that its exports are often in pursuit of an "oil for arms" policy,[46] because of a need to generate foreign exchange. Other descriptions of Brazil's export policy are: "free-for-all," "no questions asked," "no strings attached", again partly because of the country's declared policies regarding arms exports in general and missiles/rockets in particular. In fact, Brazil limits arms exports to "friendly nations,"[47] but the term is ambiguous and conveys the impression that decisions are made case by case. In principle, however, there are two major factors which influence arms exports: one is the prospective buyer's direct relationship with Brazil and its foreign policy, and the other is the buyer's standing in the international community at the time of purchase. A prospective buyer must not represent a political or military threat to Brazilian security. Secondly, sales normally honor Brazil's commitments in such international action as United Nations arms transfer embargoes.[48] Examples include the embargoes on the transfer of technology and arms to Iraq and South Africa, although here too Brazil's policy is said to have been flexible in the recent past. The United Nations Security Council Resolution 748 imposing, *inter alia*, an embargo on the delivery of arms and related material to Libya places Brazil in a delicate political and economic position. A military embargo on Libya could affect the ability of Brazilian companies to redress their present economic situation, since Libya has been, and is still a potential, customer for ASTROS II missiles and other material.

Nevertheless, there are signs that the Ministry of External Relations has adopted a more stringent attitude towards arms exports so as to change the image of a too-liberal export policy. Public statements by former Minister for External Relations Francisco Rezek have indicated that new restrictions are to be introduced, requiring guarantees of the end use of Brazilian arms.

In addition, legislative changes are also expected following informal discussions on a draft law regulating the import and export of war related material, which was submitted to Congress in February 1992.[49] The proposal is to regulate import/export operations for goods of direct bellicose employment, dual-use, and use in the nuclear area, as well as services directly linked to them. The proposal also contains a disposition to define these goods in import/export lists, which would be periodically updated and published in the *Diário Official da União*. The addition of Article 2, commonly known as the *Piva Law*, aims at closing a legal gap, whereby Brazilian nationals and private companies cannot be legally restrained by the Government from exporting services related to goods under Article 1.

If approved, this law will introduce a Certificado Internacional de Importação (CII)—International Import Certificate, whereby the importer will undertake not to re-export the goods received without previous authorization from the competent Brazilian authorities. It will also introduce a certificate attesting to the entry of the goods in the country—the Certificado de Verificação de Entrega (CVE)—Verification of Delivery Certificate, which will be valid only after confirmation of the recipient destination during customs clearance. Article 7o establishes the need for previous authorization from competent federal organs for the import and export of goods inscribed in the import/export lists, as well as the export of service directly related to the goods in question. In addition, paragraphs 1 and 2 of Section IV establish the right for federal organs to solicit documents of guarantee of destination and end-use to the exporter, issued by competent entities of the importer country, including copies of the contracts.

Another feature of this draft law will be the creation, within the ambit of the Presidency of the Republic, of a Comissão Permanente Interministerial (CPI)—Permanent Interministerial Commission,[50] which will, *inter alia*, establish criteria and procedures for the analysis of import/export operations as well as their authorizations.[51] The Commission will therefore regulate the import/export of missiles/rockets and related services.[52] However, this draft law also proposes that the Executive Branch of the Government should have the power to deny or restrict import/export operations, including the export of services, as a function of the origin, precedence, and destination of the goods and services.

Penalties for non-compliance with the proposed law range from administrative notification to suspension of the right to import/export for a period ranging from six months to five years. Stricter penalties include withdrawal of the export license in the event of repeated non-compliance. Article 14 establishes as a *crime* the import/export of goods and services which would contradict the provisions of the law and its regulation, and establishes the liability of the controller, director, administrator, or manager of the juridical person responsible for the *crime*. They would risk a jail sentence ranging from one to four years.

Analysis of this draft law shows that it gives legitimacy to, and reinforces the present practice of, arms exports. Through the form of a law, it endorses the role played by the Executive Branch in regulating and granting authorization for the import/export of war material. Although the draft law has passed the Congressional commissions with few changes, arms experts also wonder whether Congress should not be given voting power on arms export transactions, an alternative which is attractive from the institutional standpoint since it would represent a revolutionary change in Brazil's arms export policy. Responsibility for decision-making and procedure would move from a restricted policy group to a multiparty congressional commission whose decisions would be made by vote. It would also provide more transparency in arms transactions.

However, the political implications of such a change will have to be carefully studied. One possible compromise presently under discussion is the inclusion of representatives from the Congress in the CPI, although this option has not yet been fully articulated. While it is possible that the draft law will be modified following the debates in Congress, it is expected that its basic features with respect to the scope of import/export operations and penalties for non-compliance will be maintained.

Missile and Rocket Technology Control: Implications for Brazil

The most important barrier to Brazilian import of rocket-related technology is the 1987 Missile Technology Control Regime (MTCR).[53] Brazilian missile/rocket programs would fall within the controls of the MTCR include the SS-300, SS-1000, SONDA III, SONDA IV, and VLS.

Considering the fact that ORBITA's MB/EE-350, MB/EE-600, and MB/EE-1000 missile programs have been canceled, only AVIBRAS and CTA's SONDA-based technology missiles and rockets would eventually fall within MTCR restrictions. Because of the political sensitivity of the dual-capable technologies required for the development of the Brazilian VLS, the space program is most affected by the MTCR, especially the SONDA IV technology on which each stage of the VLS is based.

Brazil's need to purchase certain space equipment, parts, and technologies abroad has been defended on the grounds that its domestic industry is not yet able to produce components with space qualifications.[54] As Table 5.8 shows, some of the technology transfer and service restrictions have affected Brazil's missile/rocketry programs.[55] Restrictions have been applied by most of the MTCR members, but US restrictions are the most stringent of all. For example, one major incident involving US technology service restrictions concerned Brazilian VLS components in 1990. The lack of infrastructure, such as wind tunnels and heat-treatment ovens to produce, harden and test certain types of engines and structures, led the IAE to send seven Brazilian steel rocket casings to Lindberg Engineering of Chicago to be heat-treated for insulation by a special annealing process.[56] At the request of the US Department of Defense (which feared that Brazil might provide Iraq with missile technology during the 1991 Gulf war), the State Department refused to allow the Chicago firm to return the rocket

TABLE 5.8 Unsuccessful Attempts to Acquire Missile/Rocket-Related Technologies

Period	Exporter	Item	Technology Involved
1989–1990	France	Rocket, SONDA program	*Ariane's Viking* engine
1989–1990	United States	Rocket, Launcher program	*Delta* 2 rocket
—		Missile, SS-300	—
1990	France United Kingdom, United States	Rocket, Launcher program	Material and Services
	United States	Rocket, VLS program	Servicing VLS Outer Shells

Sources: Anthony, "The Missile Technology Control Regime," *Arms Export Regulations*, 1991, pp. 226–27; Tollefson, *Brazilian Arms Transfers...*, 1991, pp. 95–96 (unpublished); Bailey, "Can Missile Proliferation be Reversed?," *Orbis*, Winter 1991, pp. 6-7, and others.

casings to Brazil. The casings were released a little over a month later, when the United States received assurances from Brazil that it was not providing assistance to Iraq. However, the hardening of eleven other rocket casings are reportedly aborted.[57]

One of the MTCR's major drawbacks is that it directly links civil R&D effort with the development of dual-capable technology for military use. This affects Brazilian R&D on rocketry and satellites intended for civil use. The Brazilian authorities question not only the MTCR itself, but also the very concept of *ad hoc* and selective restrictions on technology transfers. According to the official Brazilian view, as expressed in a joint statement with Argentina, the main inadequacies of these mechanisms are considered to be their limited scope, discriminatory features, perception of the different needs of the exporting and recipient countries, and inability to ensure international security.

Brazil's non-accessibility to qualified space technology has already resulted in a three-year delay in its space program and additional expenditures running into millions of dollars.[58] Restrictions have also delayed Brazil's entry into the international satellite launching market, as shown in Table 5.9.

Technology transfer restrictions have therefore prompted two types of reaction in Brazil. One is national investment in the production of restricted end-products. In some cases, indigenous production circumvents technology transfer embargoes and therefore limits dependence, as has happened in the case of Brazilian satellite production. In rocket building technology, moreover, construction of a large heat-treatment oven by a Brazilian

TABLE 5.9 Major Effects of Sensitive Technology Restrictions on Brazilian Rocketry Research & Development

- Slows down rocket production and causes R&D to lag behind schedules
- Increases total cost of MECB by provoking a search for autonomous alternatives, such as the development and production of indigenous components and equipment
- Provides ground for friction between Brazil and other countries
- Stimulates a search for alternative partners outside mechanisms aimed at controlling the transfer of sensitive technology

company oriented towards rocket component production is under way to absorb the demand for the VLS and other rocketry programs.

The second reaction is a search for new suppliers of space-based technology, notably China and Russia. With respect to Chinese technology, the China/Brazil CBERS program provides some grounds for reflection.[59] Brazil has already had problems concerning access to Chinese satellite technology in the CBERS program,[60] including problems of an institutional nature. In addition, little is known in the literature on the progress of the idea to develop a joint Brazilian/Chinese rocket for launching satellites from the Brazilian Alcântara Launch Center in the State of Maranhão; or of the Brazilian interest in the Chinese liquid-fuel *Long March* (CZ-3) rocket.[61] As far as Russia is concerned, the Brazilian negotiations with the former Soviet Union to launch SCD-1 on-board a *Kosmos* rocket from the Brazilian Alcântara Launch Center, including the transfer of technology, came under some pressure from certain western governments and private companies.[62] Of major concern was the fear that Brazil could acquire technology which could be used for a Brazilian ballistic missile.

All in all, the search for partners outside the membership of the MTCR has not been so successful. This is true not only because China appears unwilling to supply the space and/or space-related technologies, or because of pressure against the creation of a Brasília-Moscow axis, but also because there are few countries outside the MTCR possessing space technologies and/or producing components with space qualifications of interest to the MECB.

The Brazilian Government is considering other alternatives to avoid MTCR restrictions while also reinforcing the country's international credibility with respect to technology transfers and end-use practices. One step could be the transfer of work being done on space rocketry under the auspices of the Air Force to a civil entity. In this case, INPE, which functions under the Special Secretariat for Science and Technology, stands as the natural heir of the space launcher leg of the MECB.[63] Such a step would certainly be welcomed by MTCR members, particularly if the Brazilian VLS program is undertaken for civil purposes, since Brazilian engineers would become familiar with technologies related to the production of missiles. This is usually argued because the military use of such capability is believed to be more difficult if the rocketry program is directed and controlled by civil entities offering more guaranties in terms of end uses.

Nevertheless, this argument does not stand up when one analyses the experience other countries have had with MTCR restrictions which do not distinguish between civil and military activities. Changing the administrative organization of the launching leg of the Brazilian space program from military to civilian hands is but a marginal aspect of the complicated issue of sensitive technology transfer. The crux of the matter is more likely to be intertwined in and influenced by perceptions and actions related to political/military issues such as the Non-Proliferation Treaty and the development of intermediate/continental-range ballistic missiles, as well as more commercial issues such as the interests of space competent nations in the international satellite launching market.[64] Another measure is the draft law on end-use of dual-use goods discussed above, which is to be debated in Congress before the end of 1992.

At the international level, the Brazilian Government is pursuing a policy which fosters the participation of the international community at large in addressing the issue of export controls. Such a collective measure would not only avert the effect of the MTCR, but would also cut short other *ad hoc* restrictions on technology transfers by a limited number of countries.

The Brazilian delegation to the United Nations Disarmament Commission has proposed, jointly with Argentina, that the international community establish a set of basic rules for the international transfer of sensitive technologies.[65] Based on the principle that dual-purpose sensitive technologies are not inherently harmful, but that it is the intent or purpose underlying their utilization that may have security implications, the proposal aims at ensuring the flow of these technologies for peaceful purposes via the establishment of a mechanism which would be transparent, universal, and effectively controlled through an international system of safeguards. The proposal also contains draft guidelines that could serve as the first step toward the elaboration of such rules, which could conceivably lead to institutional arrangements implementing such norms at the operational level.

Brazil has also taken a clear stand on weapons of mass destruction by embarking on confidence-building measures with some states in South America.[66] For example, with respect to nuclear issues, Brazil has signed a number of declarations and agreements with Argentina and the IAEA in the last twelve years to clarify its nuclear energy policy. Of most relevance here is the agreement between Argentina and Brazil for the Exclusively Peaceful Use of Nuclear Energy, signed in Guadalajara on 18 July 1991, whereby both countries have agreed to abstain from the possession of nuclear weapons.[67] While this agreement endorses Brazil's orientation toward the peaceful uses of nuclear energy,[68] it also prevents Brazil from developing a nuclear-armed missile. This may, in turn, discourage private companies from contemplating, either individually or collectively, the production of intercontinental-range ballistic missiles for domestic supply. It may also even reduce the probability for the production of any such missiles for the export market.

However, perhaps the most important step would consist of Brazilian adhesion to the MTCR, if indeed adhesion would ensure, under specific guaranties, the lifting of restrictions to the transfer of sensitive technology aimed at the development of SONDA rockets for the VLS and equipment of the Alcântar Launch Center. In this connection, reports have appeared in the press indicating that Brazil has considered adhesion to the MTCR and that a delegation of the MTCR visited the Brazilian capital on 24 April 1992.[69] However, the chances of Brazil adhering to the MTCR have apparently decreased since 6 June 1992 when Brazil was placed in the US Department of Commerce list of countries which are not allowed to receive sensitive technology.[70]

Conclusion

Brazil's exports of missiles and rockets at the end of the 1980s and the beginning of the 1990s have decreased in comparison with those of the previous eight or nine years. This trend is expected to continue well into the present decade. This is due, first, to the ending of the Iran/Iraq conflict and, secondly, the United Nations embargoes on military exports to Iraq and Libya, which previously had been Brazil's main customers for missiles and rockets. In addition, the country's prolonged economic crisis, and inadequate strategic planning on the part of certain key manufacturers, have significantly affected the production of war materials.

Economic disincentives, political restraints, and lack of military interest make it very unlikely that Brazil's VLS rocket will be assigned a military use. Moreover, international restrictions, particularly those imposed by the United States, on the transfer of sensitive technology constitute an additional obstacle to the production of long-range missiles and rockets. However, while these restrictions have affected Brazil's capability to manufacture missiles and rockets, they have, concomitantly, forced investment on the part of private companies and other entities in the development of indigenous manufacturing capabilities. The pursuit of these alternatives is expected to provide Brazil with more autonomy in future manufacturing endeavors, although at higher cost.

In addition, the Brazilian Government is considering a number of domestic and international initiatives to regulate the end use of dual-purpose technology and arms export procedures. Beyond the attempt to avoid restrictions on technology transfer, the main objective of such initiatives is to secure Brazil's image as a *responsible* exporter of arms. One of the national initiatives is the draft law on the import/export of war and nuclear materials and directly related services, which is to be discussed by the Brazilian Congress in the course of 1992. Other measures include the recent Argentina/Brazil agreement on the exclusive peaceful use of nuclear energy, which prohibits the manufacture, production, acquisition, testing, and use by any means of any nuclear weapons, and the application of safeguards by a Brazilian-Argentine bilateral agency and the IAEA.

It is true that these prohibitions do not preclude the development of conventionally loaded intermediate-range ballistic missiles either by the Armed Forces or the private sector. Nevertheless, any such production and, particularly *export*, would be subject to control by the Ministry of the Army, government entities, and the President of the Republic himself. Although somewhat unlikely and depending on the outcome of the Congressional debates on the draft law regulating arms exports, missile and rocket exports may eventually be partially or totally controlled by a special Congressional Commission.

However, judging from observations made in international fora, it appears that those who supply sensitive technology are reluctant to accept half-way or *modus vivendis* measures. One cannot, therefore, but ask how far the Brazilian government is prepared to go to rebuild its international reputation without, of course, either compromising its legitimate right to self-defense or endorsing technology control regimes based on the *cliché* of a bi-polar world separating the *have* states from *have nots*.

It seems fitting to conclude that a survey of Brazilian missile and rocket production and export illustrates that it is, at present, more appropriate to discuss Brazilian exports of missiles for tactical operations, rather than ballistic missile capability and possible exports. This viewpoint is sustained by the halting of the SS-1000 and MB/EE-600/1000 missile programs and the development of the FOG-MPM missile.

Notes

1. The views expressed in this article are the responsibility of the author and not of United Nations Institute for Disarmament Research (UNIDIR) or anyone else. The author is indebted to Roberto Lopes, Vasques Pato, and João Evangelista Steiner of São Paulo, and Reiner Pungs of Brasília, Brazil, and S. Chandrashekar of Bangalore, India, for their kind comments.

2. For a discussion see Reiner Pungs, *A Indústria de Armaments e a Politica Externa Brasileira*, unpublished thesis, University of Brasília, Brasília, June 1989, pp. 77–84. Pungs notes that some companies such as ENGESA, AVIBRAS, and EMBRAER received tax waivers on industrialized products—Imposto sobre Produtos

Industrializados (IPI)—when they turned totally to the export market. Other incentives included waiving the payment of import tax on raw material and equipment for the arms industry. For an interesting view on the role of multinational companies in the rapid development of the Brazilian defense industry, see Raul de Gouvea Neto, "The Role of Transnational Companies in the Brazilian Defence Tripod, *Journal of American Studies*, No. 23, 1991, pp. 573–97.

3. Often, the terms *missile* or *rocket* are used interchangeably in the literature on international security as if they were one and the same thing. One definition of a missile is an object, in a rocket form, that is projected by a guiding system or thrown unguided at a target. A missile therefore has a military purpose and carries a payload and may be conceived for different types of trajectory, such as ballistic or cruise. A rocket is usually defined as a vehicle propelled through the air by a thrust powered by solid or liquid fuels. A rocket may have a military payload and not be called a missile, but it may also be used for civil purposes, i.e., to conduct experiments (sounding rockets) or to place objects in a particular orbit in outer space (launchers). The term *missile/rocket* is used in this chapter to accommodate the two definitions of rocket for civil and military purposes.

4. CTA is the Aerospace Technical Center of the Ministry of Aeronautics. Another company that could be cited is Engemissil.

5. Reportedly, the participation of these companies in ORBITA's capital is: ENGESA (40%), EMBRAER (40%), Esca (11%), IMBEL (5%), Parcom (4%). See ORBITA corporate video presentation, São Paulo, November 1988, quoted in *Global Arms Trade: Commerce in Advanced Military Technology and Weapons*, Washington, D.C.: Congress of the United States, Office of Technology Assessment, United States Government Printing Office, June 1991, p. 150.

6. The collection of data on arms production and exports, particularly in developing countries, is generally a long and often unrewarding task and Brazil is no exception. The tables in this chapter were prepared by adapting information from Brazilian companies and entities working in the field of missile/rocketry production as well as from various sources in the academic literature. The fact that the latter have been cited does not necessarily imply that the information is fully accurate.

7. See a discussion in Scott D. Tollefson, *Brazilian Arms Transfers, Ballistic Missiles, and Foreign Policy: The Search for Autonomy*, dissertation submitted to The Johns Hopkins University, Baltimore, Maryland, 1991 (unpublished), pp. 457–58. Other missiles which ORBITA is believed to have worked on include the MSAAV, a surface-to-air missile, and the MAF, an anti-tank missile. See a discussion in Augusto Varas, "The Effects of Military Industrialization in Latin America, *Disarmament*, Volume XV, Number 1, 1992, pp. 100–03. Not all of the Brazilian missile projects are developed solely by national companies. For a discussion on joint ventures or missile production under foreign license agreements (such as the production of the Leo missile reportedly based on Italian Oto Melara technology) see Gouvea Neto, p. 593.

8. Author's interview with AVIBRAS, 6 January 1992.

9. See *Global Arms Trade: Commerce in Advanced Military Technology and Weapons*, pp. 149–50; Varas, p. 102. Varas states that the *Barracuda* program has apparently been resurrected after a program freeze in 1988. The missile, reportedly nuclear-

capable, is expected to be ready in the 1990s, although little is known about the technical characteristics of the Barracuda program.

10. See Aaron Karp, "Ballistic Missile Proliferation," *World Armaments and Disarmament*, SIPRI Yearbook 1990, SIPRI: Oxford University Press, 1990, p. 377 (the lack of funding and suspension of the SS-300 project was confirmed by AVIBRAS in a letter to Aaron Karp).

11. Author's interview with AVIBRAS, 6 January 1992; see also *Ibid*.

12. This is because the SBAT requires proximity to the target for operation, which increases the level of exposure of the fighting aircraft to ground fire.

13. For a discussion of the issues advanced in this paragraph, see *AVIBRAS AEROESPACIAL* Brochure, AVIBRAS: São José dos Campos; "Brazilian Space Program," *Centro Técnico Aeroespacial*, Instituto de Atividades Espaciais Brochure, Ministry of Aeronautics, Department of Research and Development, São José dos Campos; *VLS—Veículo Lançador de Satélite*, Brochure, Centro Técnico Aeroespacial, Ministry of Aeronautics, Department of Research and Development, São José dos Campos.

14. *AVIBRAS Indústria Aeroespacial S.A.* Brochure, p. 3. Over 50 of this first rocket, originally constructed under contract by AVIBRAS and code named DM-6501, were launched until the late 1970s. Launch of this same rocket was continued thereafter under the code name SONDA I by the IAE of the CTA. See Marco Antônio Raupp and Paulo Trombini de Souza Nascimento in "A Evolução das Atividades Espaciais no Brasil," *Revista Brasileira Tecnhologica*, Brasília, v. 18 (4), Julho, 1987, pp. 6–14.

15. "Brazilian Space Program," *Centro Técnico Aeroespacial*, Instituto de Atividades Espaciais Brochure, pp. 2–7.

16. The MECB is a federal government project partly inspired by a search for self-sufficiency and autonomy in the space field. The program is coordinated by the Comissão Brasileira de Atividades Espaciais (COBAE)—Brazilian Commission for Space Activities—which is subordinate to the Presidency of the Republic. The program consists of three entities, two of which are subordinate to the Ministry of Aeronautics with responsibility for developing the launcher and constructing the launch base: the Instituto de Atividades Espaciais (IAE) and the Centro de Lançamento de Alcântara (CLA)—Alcântara Launch Center in the State of Maranhão. The third entity is the Instituto Nacional de Pesquisas Espaciais (INPE)—National Institute for Space Research, which functions under the auspices of the civil Secretaria Especial de Ciência e Technologia—Special Secretariat for Science and Technology. The INPE is responsible for the satellite program and its associated ground segments (Satellite Control Center, Tracking and Command Ground Stations, and a Mission Center). For a brief review on the creation and objectives of the INPE, see Raupp and Souza Nascimento, pp. 6–7. See also *Satélite de Coleta de Dados (SCD-1)—Data Collecting Satellite*, Instituto Nacional de Pesquisas Espaciais, São José dos Campos, June 1991; "Interview with Marcio Barbosa," Director-General of the Brazilian Institute for Space Research, August 1990; A. B. Carleial, *The MECB Satellite Program*, Instituto Nacional de Pesquisas Espaciais, São José dos Campos, paper presented at the *VI Simpósio Nipo-Brasiliero* of Science and Technology, 10–12 August 1988. Brazil has also signed, on 6 July 1988, an agreement with China for a cooperative program to develop two earth resources

satellites. For a discussion see *China-Brazil Earth Resource Satellite—CBERS*, Brochure, Instituto de Pesquisas Espaciais: São José dos Campos; Barbosa, *op. cit.*, p. 3. Also see "A Política Brasileira para o espaçço,", by Fabíola de Oliveira, *Revista Brasileira de Tecnologia*, Brasília, v. 18 (4) Julho, 1987, pp. 35–38; "A contagem Regressiva do Satélite Nacional," Aydano Barreto Carleial, *Revista Brasileira de Tecnologia*, Brasília, v. 18 (4) Julho, 1987, pp. 50–55; and "VLS, O Lançcador Brasileiro de Satélite," *Revista Brasileira de Tecnologia*, Brasília, v. 18 (4) Julho, 1987, pp. 56–60.

17. Dual-capable, dual-purpose and dual-use technology are used in this paper to refer to technology serving both civil and military applications.

18. This has been endorsed by the Director of the IAE, Air Force Colonel Vasques, in his statement that the VLS is a civil program and that the research and investment undertaken since its inception are commensurate to that purpose (interview with the author, IAE, 6 January 1992). For a discussion on the conversion of sounding rockets to ballistic missiles, see Stephen E. Doyle, *Civil Space Systems: Implications for International Security*, UNIDIR, forthcoming 1992.

19. See a discussion by Nathaniel C. Nash, "Argentina Battles Its Air Force Over Plan to Develop Missile," *New York Times*, 13 May 1991, pp. A1, A7. See also a statement by the Brazilian Representative to the Conference on Disarmament, "Statement submitted by Brazil," *Conference on Disarmament*, CD/PV 610, 6 February 1992, pp. 7–8. *Agreement between the Republic of Argentina and the Federative Republic of Brazil for the Exclusively Peaceful Use of Nuclear Energy, Conference on Disarmament*, CD/1117, 22 January 1992; *Agreement between The Republic of Argentina, The Federative Republic of Brazil, The Brazilian-Argentine Agency for the Accounting and Control of Nuclear Materials and the International Atomic Energy Agency for the Application of Safeguards, Conference on Disarmament*, CD/1118, 22 January 1992.

20. See a discussion in Tellefson, p. 450, footnote 115; Malin, Mauro, "U.S. Policy Hinders Satellite Program" (in Portuguese), *Jornal do Brasil*, 6 November 1988, p. 12, translated and reported in *FBIS LAT-88-217 (Annex)*, 9 November 1988, pp. 2–3.

21. The author is indebted to S. Chandrashekar for his relevant suggestions regarding the major technology modifications in this type of conversion.

22. Brazil has ratified the 1972 Biological Convention and the 1925 Geneva Protocol. See a discussion in *The Interest of Nonpossessor Nations in the Draft Chemical Weapons Convention: A Brazilian Case Study*, Péricles Gasparini Alves, Vantage Press, New York, 1990. See also "Letter Dated 7 February 1992 from the Heads of the Delegations of Argentina, Brazil and Chile addressed to the Secretary-General of the Conference on Disarmament Transmitting the Text of the Joint Declaration on the Complete Prohibition of Chemical and Biological Weapons, 'The Mendoza Agreement'", submitted to the *Conference on Disarmament*, CD/1126, 17 February 1992. On nuclear issues, see CD/1117 CD/1118.

23. However, reported discussions by the AVIBRAS spokesman and the Director of ORBITA have emphasized their interest in exporting Brazilian-made *tactical* missiles. See, for example, Tollefson, p. 448.

24. An examination of all of the reasons motivating government support for war material exports is beyond the scope of this paper. See a discussion in Martin Navias, "Ballistic Missile Proliferation in the Third World," *Adelphi Papers*, 252, Summer 1990, pp. 10–11; Pungs; Gouvea Neto; and Tollefson, p. 432. Tollefson

makes a fine analysis of this point, advancing the argument that these motives are not mutually exclusive and that, for example, economic and technological motives overlap considerably, while still falling under the category of "national security." However, "national security" in this case includes national economic and technological development and regional security in the traditional sense.

25. See a discussion in Navias, pp. 10–11; Pungs; and Tollefson, p. 432.

26. Author's interview with an AVIBRAS executive, Sao José dos Campos, 6 January 1992.

27. Tollefson, p. 115.

28. See a short discussion in *Global Arms Trade: Commerce in Advanced Military Technology and Weapons*, p. 50.

29. See "Missiles in the Middle East: A New Threat to Stability", by W. Seth Carus, in *Policy Focus*, No. 6, June 1988; John Barham, "Brazil Ignores US Protest Over Arms For Libya," *Sunday Times*, 31 January 1988, p. 5; "Libya: Brazil to Resume Negotiations with Libya on Arms Sales," *African Defence Journal*, 66, February 1986, pp. 4–5; see also a discussion in Tollefson, pp. 306–7.

30. For more detailed discussion and references, see "Brazilian firm files bankruptcy," *Defense News*, 15 January, 1990, p. 26; Brooke, J., "Peace unhealthy for Brazilian Arms Industry, *New York Times*, 25 February 1990, p. 19; Aaron Karp, "Ballistic Missile Proliferation," *World Armaments and Disarmament*, SIPRI Yearbook 1991, SIPRI: Oxford University Press, 1991, pp. 328, 329; Tollfeson, pp. 439–70.

31. Reports indicate that AVIBRAS has reduced its work force from 6,000 in the mid-1980s to 900 in 1990. See a discussion in Gouvea Neto, p. 578.

32. See a discussion in "Generais Decidem Destino da ENGESA: Indústria Britânica pode Dominar a Produção de Armamentos no Brasil," *Technologia & Defesa*, Ano 7, No. 5, Julho/Agôsto, 1991, pp. 20–22. Gouvea Neto, referring to a *Wall Street Journal* source, quotes the number of ENGESA's employees as dropping from 3,000 in the mid-1980s to about 1,100 in 1990; see Gouvea Neto, pp. 578–79.

33. "Brazilian Firm Files Bankruptcy," *Defense News*, 15 January, 1990, p. 26; Brooke, J., "Peace Unhealthy for Brazilian Arms Industry, *New York Times*, 25 February 1990, p. 19; "Generais Decidem Destino da ENGESA: Indústria Britânica pode Dominar a Produção de Armamentos no Brasil," pp. 20–22.

34. "Generais Decidem Destino da ENGESA: Indústria Britânica pode Dominar a Produção de Armamentos on Brazil," pp. 20–22.

35. This has been argued in the case of ENGESA. See *Ibid.*, p. 22.

36. Author's interview with AVIBRAS executive, Sao José dos Campos, 6 January 1992. Also see a discussion on the privatization of state-owned enterprises and its effect on the arms industry by Gouvea Neto, p. 578.

37. President Collor has often stated that, should companies collapse, their representatives should not "climb the *rampa do Planalto*"—the ramp to the official entrance of the Presidential Palace—to request subsidies, but rather look for other areas to conduct business.

38. *Constitution of the Federal Republic of Brazil*, 5 October 1988, Chapter II, Article 21, VI, p. 31.

39. Decreto No. 24 602—De 6 de Julho de 1934, *Regulamento para a Fiscalização de Produtos Controlados*, Ministério do Exército, Estado-Maior do Exército, 1 edição, 1965.

40. *Ibid.*, pp. 121–24.

41. Federal Decree No. 55 649. See Chapter XIV, Article 132 (production authorization) and Chapter III, Article 11 (export authorization) of *R-105*. However, Article 132, *parágrafo único*, excludes the authorization for exports by the Ministry of the Navy and the Ministry of Aeronautics.

42. This is controlled by requesting a certificate from the importing country in which the sale of the controlled product is acknowledged—see Article 133.

43. Article 137, paragraph 3, of R-105 states that, whenever possible, an exporter shall include documents related to the production and consumption of the product in Brazil to demonstrates that the expected sale would not be prejudicial to the national market. Also see Article 134, *parágrafo único*.

44. See Chapter XIX, Articles 157–65, *R-105*, pp. 59–73.

45. The CDN is a consultative body to the President in matters related to sovereignty and defense. The members of the CDN are the Vice-President of the Republic, the President of the House of Representatives, the President of the Federal Senate, The Minister of Justice, the Ministers of the Armed Forces, the Minister of External Relations, the Minister of Planning.

46. This argument is mainly based on the fact that Brazilian arms exports have been largely directed to Egypt, Iran, Iraq, Libya and Saudi Arabia; and that, in some cases, part of the sale involved either payment in oil or Brazilian purchase of the importer's oil under special arrangements. See, for example, discussions by Allebeck, p. 41; Barham, p. 5. See also a discussion and references in Christian Catrina, *Arms Transfers and Dependence*, United Nations Institute for Disarmament Research, New York: Taylor & Francis, 1988.

47. For a discussion of this issue, see Tollefson, pp. 157–58.

48. For discussions and references, see Allebeck, p. 41, and Tollefson, pp. 157–58.

49. See "Dispõe Sobre as Operações Relativas à Importação e Exportação de Bens de Emprego Bélico, de Uso Duplo e de Uso na Area Nuclear e de Serviços Diretamente Vinculados," Projecto de Lei No. 2.530, de 1992, *Câmara dos Deputados*. Also see, *Diário Official*, 10 de Fevereiro de 1992.

50. The proposed Commission would be composed of representatives from the following: Ministry of the Navy, Ministry of the Army, Ministry of External Relations, Ministry of the Economy, Ministry of Aeronautics, Joint Chief of Staff of the Armed Forces, the Secretariat of Science and Technology of the Presidency of the Republic, and the Secretariat of Strategic Affairs of the Presidency of the Republic; the last-named would function as the executive secretariat.

51. The Commission would also be responsible for drawing up and maintaining the import/export lists, resolving any problems deriving from the applicability of the law, and approving its regulations.

52. This taking into consideration the interests of the Brazilian foreign policy, the effects that import/export operations may have on the national defense and the country's technological capacity, the need to respond first and foremost to the national market, and the interests of the Brazilian foreign trade. Imports of goods and services by the Armed Forces, for their exclusive use in fulfilment of their constitutional duty, would not be subject to authorization.

53. Refer to Appendix A for MTCR members and adherents.

54. Interview of Marcio Barbosa, Director-General of the Brazilian Institute for Space Research, August 1990, p. 5.

55. See, for example, discussions in Tollefson, pp. 462–66; Rik Turner. "Brazil Says Missile Technology Controls Hamper Launch Industry," *Defense News*, 4, No. 30, 24 July 1989, p. 18.

56. For more details see Michael Wines, "U.S. Approves Export of Rocket Parts to Brazil Despite Link to Iraq," *The New York Times*, 7 September 1990, p. A8; Alan Friedman, "Iraq may Gain from US Exports to Brazil," *Financial Times*, 8–9 September, 1990, p. 2; Andrew Lawler, "Brazil Chafes at Missile Curbs," *Space News*, Vol. 2, No. 35, October 14–20, 1991, p. 1, 20; Karp, p. 329.

57. Wines, p. A8.

58. See Lawler, p. 1. With the delay in the production of the VLS, the first Brazilian satellite is expected to be launched by a US *Pegasus* rocket, of Orbial Science Corporation in late 1992, under an additional cost of US$ 12 million.

59. Besides the CBERS programme with China, which is a government-to-government undertaking, the Brazilian AVIBRAS and Chinese Great Wall companies have formed in 1989 a joint venture named *Inscom* designed for the sales of space programmes. See "Collor Quer Usar Programa Espacial Para Projetar o País no Esterior," Roberto Lopes, *Folha de São Paulo*, 14 April 1990, p. A-8.

60. See a discussion in Barbosa, p. 6.

61. See Roberto Lopes, "EMFA Admite Lançar 1o. Satélite Brasileiro em Foguete," *Folha de São Paulo, 12 de Junho de 1988, 2o. caderno, A.29.*

62. Roberto Lopes, "Satélite do INPE Gera Disputas entre EUA e USSR," *Folha de São Paulo*, 10 de Abril de 1991, I-6.

63. Such an increase of INPE's activities would certainly be supported by those who advocate that INPE is likely to play the role of a Brazilian space agency before the end of the decade. (See Barbosa, p. 4.) However there are several obstacles blocking the creation of such an agency, one being the reluctance of the Air Force to hand over its space program, assembly and test sites, and qualified personnel to a civilian entity. Moreover, this move would represent a shift in attempts to restructure the Brazilian space program. In the late 1980s, unsuccessful attempts to join both civil and military directorships of the space program aimed at placing INPE activities under the directorship of the military.

64. This was apparent in 1988 when the United States did not take up the suggestion made by a Brazilian delegation in Washington, which guarantied that the VLS program would be devoted exclusively to peaceful missions and that the US could follow all of its stages, including, its rescue at sea. See José Monserrat Filho, "Foguetes Proibidos," *O Globo*, 24, June 1992, p. 6.

65. "The Role of Science and Technology in the Context of International Security, Disarmament and Other Related Fields," International Transfer of Sensitive Technologies, Working Paper submitted by Argentina and Brazil, *Disarmament Commission*, A/CN.10/145, 25 April 1991. Another complementary proposal involving the establishment of a set of principles guiding international cooperation has been presented by the Brazilian delegation in another UN forum, the COPUOS [Committee on the Peaceful Uses of Outer Space]. See "Statement by the Brazilian Delegation at the 31st Meeting of the Legal Subcommittee of the Committee on the Peaceful Uses of Outer Space," Geneva, 24 March 1992. For a discussion on the legitimate interests and concerns of both supplier and recipient States, see a summary in "Consideration of the Question of International Arms Transfer by the

United Nations," by Alessandro Corradini, *Transparency in International Transfers*, Disarmament Topical Paper 3, United Nations Department for Disarmament Affairs, New York: United Nations Publication, 1990.

66. On peaceful uses of nuclear energy, see: Co-operative Agreement of Buenos Aires, 30 May 1980, Nuclear Policy: Joint Declaration of Foz do Iguaçú, 1985, Joint Declaration of Brasilia, 1986, Joint Declaration of Viedma, 1987, Peaceful Uses of Nuclear Energy: Joint Statement of Buenos Aires, 6 July 1990, Common Nuclear Policy: Declaration of Foz do Iguaçú, 28 November 1990, CD/1117, CD/1118. On biological and chemical weapons, see: CD/1126, 2.

67. CD/1117.

68. CD/PV 610, p. 8. In this connection, the Brazilian Government expects "...that these actions will be matched by clear recognition in practice, as well as in theory, of [its] legitimate right to acquire and develop advanced technologies."

69. See Monserrat Filho, p. 6.

70. See "Expansion of Foreign Policy Controls: Missile Technology Destinations," Rules and Regulations, *Federal Register*, vol. 57, no. 118, 16 June 1992, p. 26774.

6

The Two Koreas and the International Missile Trade

Peter Hayes[1]

Introduction

An increasing number of developing countries are missile-capable due to their independent development of a space booster rocket capability. Many others have a long run missile option in train due to their burgeoning modernization and industrialization. The diffusion of rocket technology is unstoppable in this regard and the world will be forced to turn to mixes of incentives and sanctions to ensure that ploughshares are not beaten into swords.[2]

Divided Korea is a unique example of this set of issues. The situation in Korea (including Korean missile activities) is peculiarly influenced by the continuing division of the Korean nation. No other current or likely missile-making or exporting state exhibits the same degree of political-military volatility nor lethal competition. Conversely, the cultural similarities, common history, and geopolitical contiguity of the two Koreas highlight domestic political-economic and institutional factors which help to explain why the two Koreas' missile strategies have diverged.

This study first examines the missile-related capabilities of both Koreas. It also emphasizes the role of imports or transfers from allies to endow them with initial capacities.

Three major conclusions arise from this study. First, North Korea (the Democratic People's Republic of Korea, DPRK) will continue to be a renegade supplier of missiles in the immediate and medium term. Second, South Korea (the Republic of Korea, ROK) is moving inexorably to obtain a missile/booster rocket capability in the medium term. Therefore, the ROK must join the Missile Technology Control Regime (MTCR). A reunited Korea would end the DPRK's missile activities, but the fusion of DPRK with ROK capabilities would enhance the need to expand the MTCR to include the ROK. Finally, the MTCR is inadequate to the task of curtailing DPRK and/or ROK missile development activities and should be supplemented by other global or regional incentives to forego missile-related exports.

Definitions

In this study, "ballistic missile" is taken to mean a military weapon that uses a projectile to deliver a warhead to range of 50 or more kilometers. To be "ballistic," the missile must arrive by following "gravity's rainbow" rather than under its own power. Multiple rocket launchers are included; long range artillery pieces are not. One exception to the general rule used in this study is that cruise missiles (which are not ballistic) are included.

A second important conceptual issue is "capability." Here, capability is defined to encompass the organizational, learning, and research and development techniques to design, manufacture, and deploy missiles, as well as such physical hardware that might be traded, imported, or exported. Thus, an important export (an example of which is given later in the DPRK-Egyptian transaction) is the ability to design and construct a missile manufacturing facility, as well as the missiles themselves. Relatedly, the capacity to train a foreign entity how to organize and indoctrinate its military to use a missile in military operations is also of great importance.

North Korean (DPRK) Missile Capabilities

Despite its technological backwardness, the DPRK has managed to produce a variety of missiles. It is capable of supplying materials for missile bodies, warheads, and propellants. It can manufacture and assemble effective short and intermediate range missile systems. Known missile production entities include the Changgwang Credit Corporation, the Lyongaksan Machineries and Equipment Export Corporation, the No Dong 1, SCUD Development Project, and the Ordnance Factory in Chongin.[3]

The DPRK's electronics capabilities are still primitive, in spite of acquisition of a UN Development Program-supported integrated circuit factory known as the Pyongyang Semiconductor Manufacturing Factory. (The plant involved was an obsolete facility obtained from India, the only supplier willing to circumvent CoCom controls.[4] It has no ability to develop infrared seeker systems, although it must be producing an infrared system used on SA-7s made in the DPRK, whether by imitation or import-and-assembly. Its high precision technological capabilities remain elementary.[5]

The DPRK's missile program is also hampered by lack of funds and by its poorly skilled work force. That the DPRK continues to commit so many valuable and scarce resources to such a large scope and scale missile program—especially when considered in combination with its nuclear research and development program—indicates its high priority to the North Korean leadership. But neither Kim Il Sung's "on-the-spot" guidance nor his voluntarist ideology can overcome these absolute limitations. These constraints dictate that the DPRK can climb only to the obsolete rungs at the low end of the missile research and development ladder.

DPRK Surface-Surface Missiles

The DPRK missile program began with shorter range ballistic weapons such as artillery shells and multiple rocket launchers, progressing on to longer range and more potent SSMs and SAMs. The main precursor of the North Korean SCUD B program involved the first SSMs obtained after the 1967 DPRK-Soviet agreement to resume military aid.[6] The first FROG (free-rocket-over-ground) missiles were transferred about 1969-70 when the Soviets transferred FROG 3, FROG-5 and FROG-7A missiles.

In the mid-1970s, the DPRK initiated a program to indigenously produce a local version of the FROG-7A. It remains unknown publicly whether North Korea ever actually produced any FROG missiles. The Soviets had supplied only high explosive warheads with the original FROG missiles. One American source contends that the North produced a chemical warhead for the FROG systems.[7]

One military analyst suggests that the DPRK effort to reverse-engineer the FROG-5 was a direct response to US forces deploying *Lance* missiles in the South or (more likely) the US transfer of *Nike Hercules* SAMs and *Honest John* SSMs to the ROK after 1976.[8] However, the *Lance* was first deployed (for a short period during exercises) to the ROK in 1971, well before the DPRK initiated its FROG program. The *Lance* was not stationed in the ROK until February 1987 and was withdrawn in late 1991/early 1992. The United States transferred *Nike Hercules* after 1976, after the DPRK began to develop its own FROGs. The *Hawk* was not transferred until 1979.[9]

SCUD B. As of February 1991, the DPRK allegedly had produced about 50 SCUD B missiles per year since 1987.[10] A 1989 US study, however, estimated that the DPRK produces 88-110 SCUD B missiles per year.[11]

A South Korean source states that the DPRK imported Soviet-made SCUD missiles from Egypt in 1983.[12] A US source puts the transfer much earlier, in 1976, when the North ended its program to upgrade the FROG-7A.[13] Sales to Iran also played an important role in financing the DPRK program (see below).

In 1984–87, the DPRK test fired a variant of a North Korean produced SCUD B missile.[14] As of mid-1992, all tests were over the Sea of Japan.[15] Since 1987, a missile plant near Pyongyang has produced the operational version of the missile.[16] One report times the deployment of operational

SCUD B missiles in the DPRK military as late 1988.[17] North Korea likely deploys the missiles in brigade-sized units of 12-18 launchers.[18] It has been suggested that the DPRK used 156 heavy duty logging trucks imported from Nissan as transporters for mobile SCUDs.[19]

As the SCUD missile is not very accurate, the DPRK deployment has generated speculation as to its possible arming with nuclear or chemical warheads. American officials believe that it would take the DPRK many years to develop a miniaturized nuclear device that would fit on top of a SCUD rather than onto a truck, railroad boxcar, or military transport plane.[20] In July 1991, the ROK Ministry of Defense claimed that the North had already produced more than a 1,000 tons of chemical warheads for its SCUD brigades.[21] This estimate may be hyperbolic as the North is said to field only 54 surface-surface missile launchers[22] and at its estimated annual output of fifty SCUDs, has produced only about 250 SCUD Bs (including exports) since 1987.

In 1990, South Korean newspapers reported US media stories that two units of SCUD B missile launch pads were being built in the Demilitarized Zone itself. These sites were reportedly surrounded by SA-5 SAM launchers and radars. In February 1991, a South Korean government official stated that the DPRK had at least 12 launchers stationed 40–50 km north of the Demilitarized Zone.[23]

Modified SCUD. South Korean sources state that the DPRK began developing a modified version of the SCUD in 1988. (This missile is sometimes referred to as the SCUD-PIP or "product improved.") The major DPRK motivations for developing the extended range SCUD B included: (1) a drive to earn foreign exchange (or to barter missiles for oil or rescheduled debt to oil suppliers such as Iran); (2) the inability of the DPRK-produced SCUD B to hit rear areas of the ROK and US bases in Japan as well as Japan itself; (3) a wish to offset ROK ballistic missiles acquired from the United States; (4) a desire to compensate for its abandonment in the late eighties by its major security patron, the former Soviet Union; (5) the acquisition of political prestige among developing countries; and (6) a desire to achieve regional power status by virtue of its missile reach.

Although the DPRK military receives a notional budgetary allocation, it is largely self funding. To this end, it controls a major portion of the North Korean industrial base, including exports such as SCUD missiles. Thus, the missile export push from North Korea may relate as much to the DPRK military's desire to alleviate its own budgetary squeeze as to reducing the current account deficit of the whole DPRK.

Joseph Bermudez suggests that Egypt and the DPRK agreed in the mid-seventies to cooperate in upgrading the SCUD B after the Egyptian-Soviet security alliance ruptured in 1976. However, technological deficiencies forced the partners to rely on the PRC to supply the requisite design expertise and a better gyroscope for the improved guidance system.[24] The PRC connection was reportedly canceled in 1978.

In the early eighties, Egypt and the DPRK are said to have exchanged information and technicians to permit the missile to be reverse-engineered and upgraded, leading to the transfer of a small number of Egyptian SCUD Bs to the DPRK in about 1981.[25] An unconfirmed report in 1988 stated that the DPRK helped Egypt's defense industry to build its own SCUD B production plant and sent a number of technicians to Egypt to work on the project.[26] According to intelligence sources cited by Bermudez, the PRC also supplied rocket engine design, production, metallurgical, and airframe technology to the DPRK-Egyptian project.[27]

A 1989 Associated Press journalist suggested that the DPRK stepped into the breach after Egypt pulled out of a joint project with Argentina and Iraq to produce the *Condor II/Badr 2000* intermediate-range missile. The article cited an Israeli military analyst as saying that the DPRK might be renewing old Soviet SCUDs for Egypt, or upgrading them with improved components such as guidance systems.[28]

The North may also have attempted to obtain necessary technology for the program on the gray or black markets. In 1984, for example, two people were charged in New York with attempting to smuggle to the DPRK electronic components used in missile-guidance and night-vision systems.[29] A Japanese source claims that the DPRK also tried, in 1986–88, to acquire electronic equipment and information on cruise missile guidance systems from Japanese-Korean scientists, organizations, trading companies, and from Japanese researchers invited to visit the North. The report also cited an unconfirmed story attributed to a US official source that the DPRK had obtained the blueprint for part of the *Nike* SAM guidance system for ¥300 million.[30] Some analysts explain Japan's October 1988 expansion of its ban on missile system exports to cover missile-related components (including production machinery, rockets, guidance systems and propellants) as a response to these DPRK efforts.[31]

The modified missile was expected to be ready for manufacture and deployment sometime in 1992.[32] The new missile is reportedly 15.1 meters long and 1.3 meters wide with a range of greater than 600 km. Bermudez states that the SCUD-PIP entailed enlarging the fuel and oxidizer tanks, modifying the rocket motor, and adding a new guidance system.[33] [*Bermudez refers to this missile as the "SCUD Mod B" in his chapters on Egypt and Iran—ed.*]

The South Korean press reported in 1991 that US intelligence sources confirmed that the modified SCUDs were loaded at a military test site north of Pyongyang in May 1990 and that the DPRK was preparing a test firing from a coastal region of North Hamkyong Province.[34]

In November 1990, the US media reported US intelligence leaks that the North was preparing a second test from near No Dong of the modified SCUD after the first test ended in apparent failure in an explosion at a launch site near To Kol on the east coast. These articles also identified two radar sites about 30 km from the launch site for missile test tracking. The US sources estimated the range of the missile to be 520–780 km depending on the size of the warhead.[35] In October 1991, the DPRK finally successfully test-fired the missile into the Sea of Japan.[36]

DPRK Cruise Missiles

The DPRK probably also fields 12-15 SS-C-2b SAMLET anti-ship cruise missiles (that arrived from the Soviet Union some time after 1967) as well as Chinese HY-2 SILKWORM missile batteries.[37]

The US Defense Intelligence Agency states that the SAMLET coastal defense missile has been observed in North Korea since September 1965. The missile is 8.3 meters long and weighs 2.75 tons with a range of 90 km. It cruises at an altitude of 1 km at 0.8 mach. It is guided by autopilot with mid-course beam radar and radar terminal homing. The DPRK became capable of manufacturing the SAMLET sometime between 1975 and 1985.[38]

The DPRK Navy's missile attack boats were equipped by the Soviets with SS-N-2A/STYX anti ship missiles after 1967, even though there is no known local manufacture nor export of these missiles by the DPRK.[39] The STYX missile is 6.6 meters long and cruises at 90–300 meters at 0.9 mach. It has a maximum range of 45 km and carries radar or infrared homing seekers.[40] The missile has a 0.5 ton high-explosive warhead.[41]

There is no evidence that the DPRK has replicated the Chinese version of the STYX, the SILKWORM.[42] Two US analysts have suggested, however, that the DPRK initially produced SILKWORM components in the mid-seventies, and later produced entire systems including motors and guidance systems (incorporating Chinese supplied parts) in the early eighties. The DPRK has served as a conduit for Chinese arms shipments to Iran and possibly Iraq. In 1986, Iran obtained SILKWORMs which it fired at ships anchored in Kuwaiti waters the following year. Under intense international pressure, the PRC agreed to halt the supply, but the Iranians continued to field the weapon.

North Korea's willingness to supply Iran enabled China to deny in 1987–88 that it was exporting SILKWORMs, by claiming that third parties beyond its control were providing the missiles.[43] The SILKWORMs were shipped reportedly either by cargo vessel or via Iranian B-747 cargo planes flying from Pyongyang via the PRC directly to Iran, overflying Afghanistan or the former Soviet Union.[44] In December 1986, the Iranian Government obligingly rescheduled the entire DPRK debt for oil.

DPRK Surface-to-Air Missiles

The DPRK deploys a dense network of 54 surface-to-air missile sites. Excluding the SA-7, it has about 800 air-defense missiles, including the SA-2, SA-3, SA-5. There are also more than 5,000 hand-held SA-7 surface-to-air missiles.[45]

SA-2 GUIDELINE SAM. North Korea may have acquired the SA-2 because it was frustrated by the increasing numbers of US U-2 high altitude overflights of the North flown from Japan and Taiwan.[46] North Korea is believed to have two types of this missile, the SA-2b and SA-2f.[47] The SA-2/GUIDELINE missile provides medium range, medium altitude point defense for cities and airfields and a barrier defense along the Demilitarized Zone.[48] It has a maximum altitude of 27.4 km and a maximum range of 35–50 km.

One source states that the Soviet Union provided the SA-2 to the DPRK as early as 1960 and that the first operational KPA battalion entered service in 1962–63. Five battalions were operational by 1965, equipped with some 250 SA-2 missiles. The Soviet supply dried up during the early sixties due to the Sino-Soviet dispute, but resumed after 1967 and continued until the mid-seventies.[49] One US report states that the SA-2 system was upgraded by the Soviets in 1985.[50] It is also possible that the DPRK obtained the Chinese upgrade of the SA-2 in the mid-seventies. US analysts believe that such a missile was fired at a US SR-71 spy plane in August 1981.[51] In the mid-eighties, the DPRK reportedly transferred this technology to Egypt to facilitate Egypt's variant of the SA-2, the *Morning Bird* missile.[52]

Joseph Bermudez suggests that the DPRK obtained technology from the PRC that enabled it to indigenously maintain, modify and upgrade its SA-2s. After the Soviets refused to deliver upgrades of the system, the DPRK asked China to supply its own reversed-engineered version of the SA-2. The Soviet refusal may have been the pivotal event that motivated the DPRK to establish an indigenous missile capability.

SA-3 GOA SAM. In the mid-eighties, DPRK-Soviet security relations improved. In 1985, the Soviet Union supplied the DPRK with the SA-3 (and associated launchers) which provides short-range defense against low-flying aircraft or helicopters for major cities.[53] It has a maximum altitude of 12–18 km and a range of 18–22 km.

SA-5/GAMMON SAM. North Korea is said to have imported about thirty SA-5s and the related TIN SHIELD early warning/ground intercept radar from the former Soviet Union after 1987.[54] Fired from a launch pad, the SA-5 can intercept aircraft at altitudes of 0.3 to 30 km and has a horizontal range of 250–300 km.[55]

In 1987, the DPRK deployed the SA-5 missiles in the southern sector along with early warning radars.[56] A US account stated that a new batch of

SA-5s was installed in April-May 1988 at four sites about 60 km north of the Demilitarized Zone. An official noted that they could hit air traffic into Kimpo International Airport and were part of the war of nerves against the ROK during the Olympic Games.[57]

SA-7 GRAIL SAM. The shoulder-fired SA-7 is portable and is used to attack low-altitude, low-speed aircraft. A South Korean source states that the SA-7 was introduced from the Soviet Union in 1974.[58] It has a maximum altitude of 5.5 km, a maximum slant range of 6 km and a maximum speed of mach 1.5. It uses infrared guidance. South Korean authorities claim that the North has deployed 12 of these mobile units 40–50 km north of the Korean Demilitarized Zone while the Pentagon stated in 1990 that 54 SA-7 units exist. The SA-5 and SA-7 SAMs are deployed in 50 bases spread over North Korea and around key sites such as airports and military facilities. South Korean sources state that the DPRK has produced about 100 SA-7 SAMs per year since 1979 at an ordnance factory in Chongin.[59]

South Korean (ROK) Missile Capabilities

South Korea's capabilities to manufacture and export missiles derive primarily from its modification of missiles transferred by its security patron, the United States. Consequently, the ROK has not imported theater or intermediate range missiles to date nor developed self-reliant missile design and production capabilities (see Table 6.1).

Since the mid-seventies, however, the ROK has developed indigenous missile production capability to manufacture rockets and parts or systems for exports. In the longer run (after 2000), the ROK will likely become an active participant in the world aerospace and space industries. At that time, the ROK would be space booster rocket- and therefore ICBM-capable. To date, however, the ROK Government has not committed itself to that goal. Nor has the ROK exported any missiles. It has little to offer the international missile market in the short run.

ROK Acquisition and Modification of US Missiles

Since 1953, the United States has deployed a long list of ballistic and cruise missiles in the ROK. Until the mid-seventies, it retained sole control over weapons, crucial communications and intelligence assets, and major missile delivery systems. To compensate for his withdrawal of US troops, President Jimmy Carter authorized US *Nike Hercules* and *Hawk* missiles left by departing US forces to be transferred to ROK forces.

Nike Hercules *Missile.* The indigenous ROK missile research and development capability began with a US Military Aid and Advisory Group-supervised maintenance facility for US *Hawk* and *Nike Hercules* missiles which commenced in 1972.[60] The ROK Army's missile maintenance

TABLE 6.1 South Korean Firms with Missile-Relevant Capabilities

Name	*Activity*
Doo Won Heavy Industrial Co.	Missile Body
Sam Sun Industrial Co.	Kooryong Multiple Rocket Tube
Daewoo Heavy Industries	Aircraft Fuselage and Parts
Tong Myung Heavy Industries Co.	Hydraulic system for *Nike Hercules* missile and launcher; multiple rocket launcher
Chun Ji Industrial Co.	Missile Components
Hankuk Fiberglass Co.	Major Missile Products
Samsung Aerospace Industries	Rockets and Propulsion Systems

Source: Korean Defense Industry Association, *Korean Defense Business Directory*, Seoul, no date, circa 1991.

depot was known as PROJECT SILVER RIVER.[61] These efforts were organized as the ROK Army Nike-Hercules Cooperative Engineering Program and the ROK Army's Nike Hercules Improvement Program.

ROK personnel were trained in 1975 by the US military and Raytheon Corporation to operate and improve a ROK commercial missile maintenance operation established in late 1974. The techniques transferred to the South Koreans included electronics, conventional warheads, and conversion to surface-surface operation.[62] Training of ROK Army personnel in the *Nike* system began in January 1975. A core group of fifty-five ROK Army personnel was sent to Fort Bliss, Texas, and Redstone Arsenal, Alabama, where they learned the mechanics of the system. Another 106 South Korean maintenance personnel were trained at the *Nike Hercules* Training Center at Taegu in South Korea. South Korean troops augmenting US forces in Korea provided 703 less highly trained personnel who were infused into the six US firing batteries. In May 1977, US Forces Korea was transferring *Nike Hercules* battalions to the ROK[63].

On July 1, 1977, the 2nd Battalion of the US 44th Air Defense Artillery—then the largest *Nike Hercules* battalion in the world—was turned over to the ROK Army which redesignated it the 38th ADA (Air Defense Artillery) of the ROKAADCOM (Republic of Korea Army Air Defense Command). Even then, these weapons remained under US operational control due to the combined command arrangement implemented in 1978.[64]

In 1977, the ROKAADCOM had two air defense artillery brigades. The 1st Brigade was assigned two Basic *Hawk* battalions, a *Nike Hercules* battalion, and a weapons battery. The 2nd Brigade had a Basic *Hawk* battalion, a weapons battery, and a newly transferred *Nike Hercules* battalion.[65] In 1978, the ROK military procured from US forces in Korea two additional *Nike Hercules* batteries.[66]

Upon receipt of the *Nike Hercules*, the South Korean military promptly test fired it in its surface-surface mode on September 26, 1978 in South Chungchong Province. Many accounts of this event have incorrectly characterized this activity as modifying the US missile. However, the *Nike Hercules* had been assigned a ground-to-ground mission ever since 1960. All that was required of the ROK military was to reset the target range, azimuth, and elevation in the target tracking radar, and dial the correct settings on the computer. In ground-to-ground mode, the missile is fired, tracked by the missile tracking radar, and steered toward an aiming point above the target. At the right moment, the missile is commanded to dive so as to hit the target on a ballistic trajectory. The US Army claims "pin point" accuracy for this role.[67]

The whole operation was carried out by the ROK Agency for Defense Development.[68] The upgrade reportedly included solid state electronics for greater reliability, and improved conventional warhead munitions.[69] The range is said to have increased from the original 150-odd km to about 250 km.[70] One unconfirmed account mentions reports hinting of South Korean-Taiwanese collaboration on this project.[71] Gerald Steinberg notes that while it is technically difficult, the range of a modified *Nike Hercules* system could be extended significantly by vertically stacking three identical stages (and smaller stages can be clustered horizontally). Stacking limits the performance of individual stages; requires more non-burnable structure; may increase drag due to larger cross sections associated with clustering; and demands better attitude control, all of which make it unlikely that hybrid systems will appear early in a modification program.[72]

As *Ground Defence International* commented in 1979, "It may not be too difficult [for the ROK] to obtain a nuclear charge and thus produce a fine tactical nuclear weapon." As they noted laconically, doing so would also be "quite dangerous."[73] Certainly, the Korean *Nike Hercules* could deliver a 0.1–5 ton warhead a considerable distance.

In 1991, the ROK had 200 *Nike Hercules* missiles organized into two battalions at 10 sites.[74]

Kooryong *Multiple Rocket Launcher*. In the same year, the ROK Army advertised its development and successful testing of a domestically produced multiple rocket launcher, the 130 mm, 30-round *Kooryong* MRL manufactured by Daewoo Heavy Industries. The rocket propulsion system for the *Kooryong* MRL was developed by Samsung Aerospace Industries in December 1977 for the ROK Army.[75] This weapon can fire a high explosive, variable time warhead to a range of 32 km. The weapon was deployed in 1990 in 18-launcher MRL battalions at corps level.[76] As of mid-1992, Korean and American officials state that the ROK has not exported any *Kooryong* MRLs because its price is uncompetitive.

Hawk *Missile*. The US Army introduced the *Hawk* missile into South Korea in August 1960. The MIM-23B *Improved Hawk* has been deployed with the US Army since 1972. The *Hawk* is an all-weather low to medium altitude air defense SAM with a range of about 40 km. It uses a proximity-fuzed warhead with 73kg of high explosive.[77]

In 1977, 40 ROK Army officers already experienced in Basic *Hawk* operations were sent to Fort Bliss, Texas, where they were trained in Improved *Hawk* maintenance.[78] In May 1977, many of the *Hawk* battalions had already been turned over to the ROK as part of the force compensation package associated with Carter's withdrawal policy.[79]

By January 1978, the US cost-free transfer to the ROK of missiles had been limited to one battalion of *Improved Hawk* equipment.[80] The final congressional budgetary authorization for cost-free transfer of missiles and other equipment to the ROK did not pass until late 1978. In May 1978, the US Defense Secretary stated to the Senate Foreign Relations Committee that US personnel in Korea would be assigned to assist ROK personnel learn to operate the *Improved Hawk* system. Guidance was actually issued on October 27, 1978 that stated that technical and operation-type training would be conducted as on-the-job training. About 20 US Eighth Army personnel were assigned, in June and July 1978, to the ROK Air Defense Artillery School at Taegu to conduct *Hawk* training for ROK troops.[81]

On July 20, 1982, the 2nd Battalion of the US 71st Air Defense Artillery transferred its mission and *Hawk* missiles to Battalion 188 of the ROKAADCOM.[82] In February 1982, the Reagan Administration proposed the sale of 170 *I-Hawk* missiles and 723 rocket motors to the ROK for $68 million. In 1985, the U.S. offered to sell the ROK modification kits for 28 battery sets of the *Hawk* product-improved version plus spares and services for $61 million. In March of 1987, another offer was made for the same equipment for an estimated $84 million.[83]

In 1991, the ROK had 110 *Hawk* missiles organized into three battalions at 24 sites.[84]

Honest John *Missile*. When the *Honest Johns* were first transferred to the ROK military remains uncertain. In 1972, the ROK already had one *Honest John* missile battalion.[85] In 1976, the US Army had decided to deactivate its *Honest Johns* in the ROK, even before President Jimmy Carter's election.[86] Certainly, the *Honest Johns* had been transferred by the time the Pentagon audited the activity in September 1978.[87]

The transfer of the *Honest John* system to the ROK was conducted by a single US representative who documented that every article transferred was in exactly the same condition (used, usable without repairs, and good).

The audit report refers to the transfer of an *Honest John* battalion, *Honest John* rocket warheads, and *Honest John* rocket motors to the ROK.[88] One military journal states that the ROK Army has modernized the *Honest John* with a new guidance system and transformed it into a SSM.[89] It has also been reported that the modified *Honest John* was tested by the ROK military in 1978.[90]

In 1979, the last active US *Honest John* battalion retired from South Korea. Its equipment and missiles were turned over to ROK Army forces.[91] Given the alleged short warning times of North Korean attack, the *Honest John* missile is of dubious military utility because its propellant must be warmed with a special electric blanket for 24-48 hours prior to firing.

In 1991, the ROK had 12 *Honest John* missiles organized into two battalions.[92]

Lance. In 1973, shortly after the nuclear-capable *Lance* missile entered the US Army's arsenal, the missile was included in US Forces Korea's operational planning and was briefly deployed to Korea during annual exercises. The US Army stationed its first battery of *Lance* missiles in the ROK on February 9, 1987. The battery became operational in early March.[93] Although the ROK Army requested the *Lance* from the United States during the Carter withdrawal program, this request was refused.[94] The last US *Lance* unit withdrew from the ROK in early 1992, probably as part of the US withdrawal of tactical nuclear weapons from Korea at that time. As far as is known, ROK forces played no direct role in *Lance* deployments in Korea.

Harpoon *and* HARM *Missiles.* In 1978, the ROK purchased *Harpoon* anti-ship missiles and air-to-air missiles.[95] The ROK program to develop a locally made fighter-bomber aimed to obtain US *Harpoon* anti-ship missiles and the HARM (high-speed anti-radiation missiles).[96] The ROK Navy is now armed with *Harpoon, Standard,* and *Exocet* missiles imported from foreign suppliers.

Atlas Centaur *IRBM.* Although Carter reversed his withdrawal policy in 1978, the ROK military continued to seek additional ballistic missile capability. In 1979, for example, it tried to acquire the US *Atlas Centaur* IRBM. First deployed by the United States in 1959, the *Atlas Centaur* could lob a W-38 nuclear warhead over 7,000 km with one-mile accuracy.

It remains unclear whether the missile software, designs, and hardware that the ROK had bought were actually transferred or blocked by the State Department under pressure from the US Congress. The sale reportedly included nose cone materials, alloys, guidance systems, specifications, engineering drawings, instructions, and assembly equipment.[97]

Patriot *Missile.* After the 1991 Gulf War, the ROK expressed interest in acquiring the *Patriot* SAM, and the *Patriot* was deployed briefly to the South during US-ROK exercises in 1992.[98] However, the fact that the *Patriot* is a point-defense weapon of little use in defending large areas and has almost no time to react to a DPRK SCUD attack led the ROK government to not seek the *Patriot* after all.[99] Relatedly, the ROK government registered as an ally interested in participating in joint research with the US Strategic Defense Initiative Organization but no concrete capability is believed to have come of this connection.

Indigenous ROK Missile Research and Development Capabilities

Under President Park Chung Hee, the ROK began to gather the requisite resources to design and develop its own missiles. Indeed, a CINCPAC study team noted in May 1971 that the Research Agency for Defense Science (established in August 1970 to increase defense industrial self-sufficiency) was allocating scarce personnel and laboratory resources to "relatively sophisticated areas such as guided (missile) weapons and laser application"—even before basic production engineering functions had been addressed.[100] The Agency's staff included Ku Sang Hae, a doctoral graduate of the University of Saskatchewan and specialist in the field of rocket engineering.

In December 1975, the ROK Government purchased the Lockheed Aircraft Corporation's complete facilities for manufacturing solid-fueled rocket motors. Most of the production equipment of the now-defunct Lockheed Propulsion Company (then near Redlands, California) was shipped to South Korea in 1978. The ROK paid two million dollars for the equipment which produces motors for only two purposes; either for propelling military missiles and rockets; or for space launch rockets. Lockheed had tried unsuccessfully for more than a year and a half to obtain US Government approval for the sale and to set up a training program to teach ROK personnel how to manufacture solid rocket propellant, the same kind used in *Minuteman* and *Polaris* missiles. Lockheed later dropped the plan to provide training and technology transfer to the ROK and sold its plant to the Berkeley-based Pacific International Corporation which managed to obtain a US Commerce Department license to export the equipment.[101]

The ROK continued its own ballistic missile research and development program until about 1980 when it was discontinued for lack of finance and due to US pressure.[102] In the late eighties, influential South Korean defense intellectuals advocated that the ROK should develop military capabilities requisite to a strategy of offensive deterrence against the DPRK. Kim Cholhwan of the National Defense College, for example, argued in 1989 that the ROK should develop CSWS-class SSMs with multipurpose cluster warheads and a 200 km range, as well as intermediate range (400 km) anti-ship guided missiles. He also called on the ROK to acquire 2,000 km range SSMs with land, air and submarine launchers to counter what he called the ROK's secondary threat, Japan and China.[103]

ROK SAMs and SSMs. The ROK missile program revived in 1990 when the Agency for Defense Development initiated a program to indigenously manufacture a SAM to replace the existing *Nike Hercules* SAMs, and an SSM to replace the US-supplied *Honest John* and US-controlled *Lance* missiles in South Korea. The SAM project entails fabricating a version of the French defense firm Thomson-CSF's *Crotale* SAM. The *Crotale* is a SAM designed for anti-aircraft defense for armored formations and surface vessels. The South African government funded the development of the missile and—apart from the French military—is the major user of the terrestrial version (with other export sales up to 1989 to Abu Dhabi, Chile, China, Egypt, Greece, Kuwait, Libya, Pakistan and Saudi Arabia). The missile is 2.89 meters long, 0.15 meters wide, flies at mach 2.3, weighs 85 kg, and has a maximum range of 13 km. Thomson-CSF DSE was selected as prime contractor for the main weapon system.

The ROK version reportedly will use ducted motors to propel and maneuver the rocket. Goldstar Precision is developing a semi-active homing head and an infra-red proximity fuse. Live tests were planned for late 1991. Daewoo Heavy Industries Aerospace Product Division is also involved in developing the missile. Samsung Aerospace Industries signed a contract in November 1989 with Thomson-CSF to build the SAM system under license. Samsung has two facilities located at Changwon, and a third being built at Sachon.[104] Samsung was to deliver operational missiles in early 1992.[105]

The ROK is also developing a group of SSMs with ranges from 100-900 km. Samsung is heading a consortium of companies to produce the SSMs. The ROK may be developing penetration warheads for these missiles.[106]

Role of Agency for Defense Development. The ROK Agency for Defense Development is crucial to both these efforts, providing funds, managing research and development programs, and integrating systems developed under contract by different private firms (as with the *Kooryong* MRL mentioned earlier). This mix of public and private enterprise in the South contrasts with the North Korean model of military-owned and managed missile enterprises.

Aerospace Sector

In the eighties, the ROK military pushed for greater autonomy and self reliance from its US counterpart. Anticipating eventual US withdrawal, the ROK military is developing greater self reliance in command, control, communications, and intelligence systems; maritime patrol aircraft; airborne early warning aircraft; electronic warfare; ground-based air defense; and artillery target acquisition radars.[107]

The growth of its aerospace industry will endow the ROK with a variety of missile-relevant capabilities. South Korea aims to have a $10 billion annual aerospace industry by 2000. The program began in 1978 when then ROK President Park Chung Hee promulgated the Aerospace Industry Development Act.[108] It was followed in 1987 by the Aerospace Industry Development Acceleration Act. In December 1985, the Aerospace Industry Committee (later reformed into the Committee of Aerospace Industry Aid) was comprised of the Ministries of Defense, Trade and Industry, and Science and Technology.[109]

In 1989, the Ministry for International Trade and Industry published a sectoral development strategy that stated three goals. These were that the ROK would: (1) develop domestic capability through licensed production for domestic needs; (2) partake in international commercial aircraft co-development; and (3) become a world-favored maintenance depot and parts manufacturer.

In April 1990, President No Tae Woo created a new aerospace committee and drafted an Integrated Aerospace Industry Governing Law.[110] This law created new offset guidelines to increase the level of technology transfer and buy-back provisions under licensed production agreements. It also created a cooperative framework between government, private industry, universities, and research institutes backed by a special governmental committee.[111]

The aerospace program was part of a national effort to upgrade ROK high technology capabilities in new materials, microelectronics, bioengineering, chemicals, and optics as well as aircraft. In time, these dual-use technologies could enhance ROK military technology in missile-related guidance, communications, intelligence, and fire control systems.[112]

As of 1990, the ROK had 17 aerospace enterprises of which five have invested major resources in aircraft projects that include missile-relevant technologies. These firms are Samsung Aerospace Industries, Daewoo Heavy Industries Aerospace Production Division/Daewoo Sikorsky, Korean Air's Aerospace Division, Sammi Augusta, and Hyundai.[113] In addition, another eight firms, with ties to 100 odd lesser and local aerospace firms, are responsible for airframes, engines, avionics, airframe accessories, and parts production. In addition to these specific manufacturing capabilities, the aerospace sector has also established research and development capabilities that could be drawn on in a ROK missile/booster rocket program. These include: Daewoo's research and development center at Taejon (established in 1988); the government funded Korea Aerospace Institute (October 1989); and the Korea Aerospace Research Institute (1989).[114]

Although missiles are not part of this aerospace program, it endows the ROK with the technological basis to make its own booster rockets and ballistic missiles. The pace of this accretion, however, is greatly retarded by the 90 percent plus shortage of scientists and engineers needed to fulfil existing plans and priorities of the aerospace sector, let alone missile or booster rocket ventures.[115] Thus, the ROK's major capabilities to enter the missile market will likely emerge from dual-capable technologies acquired directly for its endeavors in space—the subject of the next section.

ROK Space Systems

In January 1985, the ROK Ministry of Science and Technology announced a draft decade-long space development plan comprised of three phases: planning, technology development, and industrialization of the technology. A MOST official stated that the draft plan recommended that the ROK shoot domestically-produced satellites via Korean-made rockets into outer space by the early nineties.[116]

In 1987, the director of the ROK Astronomy and Space Science Institute declared that the Institute would concentrate on developing rocket-launching technology to fire a rocket for observation purposes into space by 1991. He also stated that South Korea aimed to launch a research satellite into orbit in 1996 using a Korean booster rocket. He added that the ROK should have developed a sophisticated space launcher rocket and commercial communications satellite by 2001. He revealed that a key element of the strategy is the repatriation of some 200 Korean space scientists active in the US space industry to tackle technological development essential to a ROK space program.[117]

By 1989, space and aeronautics technologies were two of four core technologies in the ROK high-technology strategy. (The other two were transit and ocean technology.) The basic space concept was said to be to secure the skilled personnel and essential technology to produce domestic satellites and to complete 80 percent of the development of a ROK satellite launcher by 2001.

In 1989, the ROK government announced that it would fund scientific research into system and structural rocket design; solid and liquid propellants; and ignition, guidance, and control technologies. The first phase of the ROK program called for a small rocket to be developed for aerial observation purposes over Korea by 1995; and a rocket to launch a Korean-built satellite by 2000. The satellite program called for the development of a 50–100 kg satellite by 1995, and a 100–200 kg satellite for scientific exploration and communications experiments by 2000.[118] In December 1989, the Ministry of Science and Technology announced at a meeting with ROK President No Tae Woo that it would actively pursue joint research with France and West Germany in a variety of high technologies, including space sciences.[119]

On February 16, 1990, the ROK Minister of Science and Technology, Yi Sang-hui, announced that an earth observation satellite built with Korean technology will be launched in 1993. The US$116 million project includes joint development by 1996 of a rocket with foreign suppliers. It would be used to launch a 200–400 kg Korean satellite into 500 km orbital altitude by 1999. (The Koreans plan to use the US *Pegasus* launch system that fires the rocket from a plane flying at a 12 km altitude, thereby obviating the need for a launch site).[120]

The project is intended to enable South Korea to obtain observation equipment and computer technologies to analyze information gathered in space. The project is to be coordinated by the Korea Research Institute of Aerospace (KRIA, set up in October 1989) on behalf of the Korea Advanced Institute of Science and Technology, the Agency for Defense Development, universities, and industry. The KRIA declared that it intended to pursue joint research with agencies in the United States, Japan, and France to achieve its objectives.[121] The following November, the ROK military called for domestic development of its own military spy satellite to compile various data on North Korea.[122]

In spite of these developments, the ROK still lacks the basic technological infrastructure, legal framework, and commitment of governmental resources needed to enter space. A national space strategy has yet to emerge to overcome the various obstacles facing the ROK in this regard. One ROK official emphasized that the first generation of satellites will be an *ad hoc*, commercial endeavor, not a national space strategy.[123]

Korea Sat 1 *and* 2. South Korea's satellite plans crystallized in late 1991 when Korea Telecom called for bids to launch two identical domestic satellites in April and October 1995 into geosynchronous orbit. Both satellites will combine communications and direct broadcasting. The ROK wants its own satellite rather than leasing satellite services to obtain a high transmitting power so that the receiving antenna can be reduced to 30–40 cm in width at an affordable price. In comparison, a receiving dish for the *Asiasat* broadcasts is a meter in diameter.

Korea Telecom is taking the lead in funding and managing the satellite program, in large part because it is financially healthy and self-financing out of revenues. Korea Telecom already has a strong research and development capability to support the program. Nonetheless, as of late 1991, it had committed less than US$1 million—what one official termed a minuscule "piggyback" program on the basic space mission. Nonetheless, the ROK will launch its first scientific satellite, KITSAT-1, in July 1992; and plans a second in 1993.[124]

Korea Telecom, a public corporation, intends to maximize the transfer of satellite systems engineering and launch technology to Korean firms as part of the satellite supply contract.[125] It is therefore encouraging foreign bidders to team up with South Korean partners. The supplier will contract to transfer to south Korean firms systems engineering skills, including the associated capability to design, construct, maintain, and operate a satellite ground station that will be completed six to nine months before *Korea Sat 1* is launched. There were four bidders for the first two satellites: GE with Goldstar/KAL; Hughes with Samsung; Space Systems (formerly Ford Aerospace) with Hyundai; and British Aerospace with Daewoo. GE Astro was awarded the contract to build the first satellite.

Korea Telecom anticipates that the ROK will launch a second generation satellite in the late nineties, although no official commitments have been made to a follow-on program. A basic space law is being drafted, however, to establish a legal basis for a second phase in the space program.

Other ministries have expressed an interest in such space affairs as earth sensing and scientific satellites. The Ministry of Science and Technology has started to work on remote sensing, but the activity is more of a watching brief than an active program. As of early 1992, no funds were committed to the program.

Korea Sat *Launch*. In November 1991, Korea Telecom issued a request for proposals for the 1995 satellite launches. Korean officials state that the main criterion for awarding the contract will be cost. In the long run (post 2000), however, Korean officials believe that the ROK will build its own space booster rocket in spite of the expected tight controls on technology transfer in the immediate future. Thus, the launch contract will include technology transfer conditions, although ROK officials have a realistic appreciation of the likely constraints that suppliers of launch services will impose on this demand. "No-one is willing to share the technology," stated one official, "except the Russians who need cash and are a new factor, and perhaps China."

Constructing an indigenous satellite booster rocket would render the ROK an ICBM-capable state. To achieve this goal, the ROK would have to circumvent the missile technology control regime led by the United States.

It also would have to deal with the DPRK's reaction. Major General Kim Yong Chol, Director, General Staff Committee of the DPRK Ministry of Defense, stated in October 1991 that the DPRK is acutely aware of and monitors closely the South Korean space and booster rocket program. The DPRK's response, however, "is not to compete in technology. "So it's wrong," he added, "to think that when South Korea makes something, then we have to make it. We do things in our own way."

The general was equally clear that the DPRK perceives the ROK's program as a military threat: "We also think that if they have such a program, or want to have it, that this is preparation for war. It is not clear if it can be used against North Korea or not. Developing such a capability is already a threat. Especially during a confrontation, it logically means another threat to us. Even without forward deployment, they could easily target Pyongyang," he said.[126]

In sum, South Korea wants to obtain, import and manufacture missiles for at least five reasons: (1) to deter North Korean missile and conventional military attack on the ROK; (2) to attack North Korean cities and important military targets in wartime; (3) to flex its muscles at a regional level, especially toward Japan; (4) to counter putative political-diplomatic prestige accruing to the DPRK by virtue of its missile capabilities and trade; and (5) to advance its aerospace industry for long-run economic advantage. In the future, the private structure of the South Korean defense industry may also facilitate "marginal" missile exports in the gray market, in the search for private profit by spreading investment costs over larger production runs.

In early 1992, the ROK had not committed itself formally to observing the norms and practices established by the MTCR. It has not acted in ways contrary to the regime either. ROK and US officials are optimistic that the ROK will maintain its conservative stance in this regard.

Korean Missile Transactions

The rest of this essay focuses on missile exports. It is divided into two parts. The first describes the missile exports of the North and its motivations for becoming a major missile supplier. The second reviews the various sets of disincentives to missile exports that confront both the ROK and the DPRK, although with very different outcomes in each case. The greater attention given to the DPRK's missile trade is inevitable because the ROK has not exported missiles.

Unfortunately, information on the security perspectives and policy-making process of the DPRK security elite is less available and reliable than for the ROK. This section on the DPRK's motivations is therefore based on secondary and even tertiary accounts and sources sometimes marred by disinformation and partisan bias. The reader is cautioned that major portions of the following account of the DPRK's missile exports cannot be confirmed.

DPRK Missile Import Motivations

The DPRK imported missiles: (1) to obtain military deterrence; (2) to prepare for warfighting; (3) to realize regional great power aspirations; and (4) to obtain profits and prestige accrued by re-exporting missiles.

Military Deterrence. The DPRK ballistic missile program deters three kinds of military threats. First, the northern security elite wants to deter a US-ROK combined missile attack. Second, the DPRK leadership develops missiles to enable it to deter a US-ROK nuclear or chemical attack by threatening to fire a chemical or (in the future) nuclear warhead. Third, Pyongyang may seek to offset the deterioration of its conventional military power relative to that of the ROK and US-ROK combined forces on the peninsula by deploying weapons of mass destruction.

Warfighting. In wartime, the DPRK could use its missiles in a variety of missions. First, the DPRK could emulate the Iraqi strategy of firing missiles to wage psychological warfare against urban populations, thereby creating massive refugee flows and complicating US-ROK military movements and logistic support. Second, missiles are useful (if accurate enough) to attack high value, large, and vulnerable targets (such as cities, large military bases, airfields, troop concentrations, or industrial facilities including nuclear power plants). The poor accuracy of its theater missiles, however, means that the DPRK cannot credibly threaten most ROK and US military targets such as hardened artillery emplacements, command posts, ammunition or nuclear weapon storage sites, etc.

Regional Power Projection. Undoubtedly, an ability to fire missiles at US bases in Japan (and possibly Russia in the future) is an important goal of the North Korean leadership. The DPRK's extended-range SCUD-B missile reportedly can already reach western Japan. In November 1991, Japanese Vice Defense Minister Akira Hiyoshi described the DPRK missile (combined with the DPRK's potential nuclear capability) as Japan's top security threat—a statement that would confirm and enhance the importance of this capability in the minds of most North Koreans who harbor bitter memories of Japanese colonialism and active support for the UN Command during the Korean War.[127]

DPRK Missile Export Motivations

Like its imports, the DPRK's missile exports are also driven by multiple motivations. These include: (1) offsetting the cost of missile and other military imports; (2) earning scarce foreign exchange with which to import other items essential to regime survival (especially oil and food); (3) developing a network of political-military relationships with which to counteract ROK diplomatic and mercantile triumphs, especially in the Middle East; and (4) responding to internal political-bureaucratic factors, especially the need of the DPRK military to finance itself.

DPRK Missile Export Policy

North Korea rejects criticism of its missile exports as "preposterous fictions" fabricated by the United States, calling the latter the "caudillo of the merchants of weapons of mass destruction."[128] It even denies outright that it exports any missiles. "Essentially," an official statement asserts, "our country, proceeding from its peace-loving foreign policy, values friendship and unity with other countries and *has not sold any types of weapons.*"[129]

In reality, the DPRK has extensive capabilities to transfer missile production and organizational techniques as well as missile hardware (production technology or actual missile parts or systems). It has already engaged in both types of exports.

The organizations most likely to export missiles are the Weapons Bureau of the Korean People's Army which researches and develops weapons and administers weapons supply for each service; and the Military Munitions Production Bureau, which controls the production plans and production of munitions for each service.[130]

The rest of this section reviews the DPRK's export activities relating to China, Iraq, Syria, Iran and Libya. Most of this activity occurred during the eighties and represented a major national effort by the DPRK.

DPRK-China Connection. In March 1977, Secretary of the Korean Worker's Party Kang Song-san visited the PRC's Lop Nur nuclear test site and reportedly attended a reception hosted by the 7th Machine Industry Ministry, the agency that developed China's ballistic missiles (This ministry was renamed Ministry of Space Industry in 1982; and combined into the Ministry of Aerospace in 1988.). The substance of the DPRK-PRC missile technology connection remains wholly speculative, however.[131] As noted earlier, the DPRK has imported Chinese missiles to sustain its own missile deployments and development programs, and also acted as an intermediary for Chinese missile exports to the Middle East. Beyond that, little is known.

DPRK-Iraq Connection. In February 1991, the US State Department expressed concern at reports that the DPRK had sold more than 100 SCUD missiles to Iraq in 1988.[132] Pyongyang immediately denounced the US statement as a "cock and bull story" and claimed that the United States had fabricated "a fiction about 'supply of missiles'" to denigrate the DPRK's opposition to the Gulf War.[133]

A few months before the Gulf War, an Iraqi military delegation reportedly visited Pyongyang in quest of North Korean missiles and launchers. Nothing seems to have transpired from this unconfirmed event.[134]

As of late September 1992, almost none of the 60,000 pages of documents seized from Iraq by UN inspectors had been translated, although many of them reportedly describe the missile supplier network.[135] When this task is complete, more information may emerge as to the DPRK-Iraqi missile connection.

DPRK-Syria Connection. The Syrians reportedly sought SCUD missiles from the DPRK when the Soviet Union failed to provide long range missiles with which to strike Israel after the 1982 Lebanon war.[136] By about 1985, Syria is said to have developed chemical warheads for its stock of SCUDs. Joseph Bermudez has speculated that the DPRK was a direct or indirect supplier of this technology after the United States blocked Chinese supply to Syria and Libya (bankrolled by Libya's Qadafi) of 140 M-9 missiles. Syria may have negotiated also with the DPRK to purchase a variant of the SCUD B missile in late 1989 or early 1990. About 24 missiles and 20 launchers were reported to have been delivered to the Syrian port of

Latakia in early March 1991 after the North Korean vessel *al-Yarmouk* sailed around the Cape of Good Hope to avoid transiting the Gulf where it would have had to reveal its cargo.[137]

DPRK-Iran SCUD Transfer. During the Iran-Iraq war, the DPRK was a major arms supplier to Iran.[138] In June of 1987, Iran bought $0.5 billion of arms from the DPRK, including 90-100 DPRK-produced SCUD-B missiles. Iran used these missiles in the "war of the cities" in February-April 1988, firing approximately 77 SCUD-B missiles at Iraqi cities. The DPRK may have also assisted Iran to establish a SCUD-B manufacturing facility of its own.[139] It has been conjectured that the DPRK may have transferred chemical warheads or technology to Iran in 1988.[140]

In 1989, the DPRK and Iran issued a communiqué that referred to a joint commission for economic, scientific and technical cooperation, an indication of the warm relations between the two countries.[141] Bermudez and Carus suggest that Iran not only had an option to buy DPRK-produced SCUD-B missiles, but also agreed in 1985 to finance the North Korean program (see the chapter on Iran).

This latter arrangement illuminates two aspects of the DPRK-Iranian connection. First, it explains why the first combat-ready DPRK-produced missiles were apparently exported rather than deployed in the North itself.[142] Second, it accounts for the DPRK's willingness to absorb the high political costs of becoming Iran's major arms supplier. Iraq and other Arab states, where the North had nurtured a diplomatic advantage relative to the South, denounced the DPRK's opportunism. Chung-in Moon has argued that this episode marked the DPRK's metamorphosis from "a vanguard of radical ideology to a profit-seeking entrepreneur."[143]

In February 1992, US sources stated that a North Korean freighter was heading for Syria with an estimated US$100 million of missiles and other cargo in a second attempt to deliver the shipment. (An earlier shipment reportedly was abandoned in 1991 after it was identified publicly and Egypt barred the ship from entering the Suez Canal.) In the first week of March 1992, the Bush administration reportedly examined the military option of boarding two North Korean cargo ships heading for the Iranian Gulf port of Bandar Abbas, allegedly loaded with SCUD C missiles for Syria and Iran.[144]

In response, Iran warned the United States against interfering with ships destined for its ports. Israel threatened to prevent the shipment from arriving. An earlier threat led Pyongyang to recall a vessel in October 1990.[145] The *Dae Hung Ho* eluded US surveillance in the Gulf region by hugging the Iranian coast and docked in Iran in early March.[146] It remains unclear whether the United States lost track of the vessel, accepted that the ship was not carrying SCUD-B missiles, or concluded that it lacked authority to intercept the vessel.[147]

DPRK-Libyan Connection. In the first week of June, 1991, a ROK military source suggested that Libya had agreed to finance the development of a SCUD missile with a 1,000 km range. A few days later, however, the ROK Ministry of Defense denied that it ever suggested that Libya had such an arrangement with the DPRK and stated categorically that: "The South Korean Government has no knowledge of any military cooperation between Pyongyang and Tripoli."[148] In September 1991, an Egyptian paper reported again that the Libya had contracted with the DPRK to purchase missiles along with 300 SCUDs to be provided to Iran and 20 SCUDs to Syria.[149]

Disincentives to DPRK and ROK Missile Exports

The DPRK is an imprudent and reckless exporter of missile technology and weapons. It has not hesitated to supply missiles to states at war. Nor has it balked at selling missiles in conflict-ridden regions which were made more unstable by the diffusion of missiles. In contrast, the ROK has refrained from missile exports. It is useful to examine the factors which explain why the two Koreas have behaved so differently with respect to missile exports.

DPRK Disincentives

The DPRK has not halted marketing missiles in spite of at least seven disincentives that might be expected to persuade it to do so. These include:

Security Allies. The DPRK's allies have not constrained the DPRK. China used the DPRK for its own missile exports and refused to stop Pyongyang from exporting Chinese-supplied missiles. The former Soviet Union had little power (and sometimes little motivation due to its conflict with the United States) to stop the DPRK from exporting missiles during the Cold War.

Ideological Barriers. The DPRK has not allowed ideology to interfere with its missile exports. This is hardly surprising as the DPRK is the only state committed to Kim Il Sungism and his *chuche* philosophy.

Global Non-Proliferation Regimes. The DPRK is still not fully committed to the NPT nor to the supplier consensus represented by the participants in the MTCR.[150] The latter regime is led by its archenemy, the United States, a situation that does not encourage DPRK participation. In April 1992, however, while denying that the DPRK exports SSMs, Deputy Prime Minister and Foreign Minister Kim Yong Nam told a group of visiting Americans that the North is willing to observe the guidelines of the Missile Technology Control Regime. "Other countries have associated themselves with it," he stated, "Why not us?"[151]

External Sanctions. The DPRK is relatively invulnerable to the immediate effects of external political and economic sanctions. Being bankrupt, its economy exhibits low levels of external trade and financial flows. Being autarchic, it can continue to produce the minimal requirements for national survival and domestic political stability for years. Being repressive, it can ruthlessly and quickly dispose of emerging domestic unrest stimulated by economic shortages. Sanctions are not a credible threat to weaken the regime. Moreover, Pyongyang is acutely aware that Seoul does not want and cannot afford the DPRK to implode, imposing the costs of reunification on the South.

Domestic Public Opinion. Many political analysts deny that a domestic public opinion exists in the DPRK. They argue that the notion of a North Korean civil society that constrains the policies and actions of the leadership is a misnomer. Rather, the North Korean state pervades and dominates civil society to an extent unparalleled in the world.

Moreover, the North Korean elite—totaling perhaps 10,000 people of whom a couple of thousand are really important cogs in Kim Il Sung's machine—is divided and fragmented by a variety of control mechanisms. It is therefore incapable of stalling or even opposing the implementation of policies developed and dictated at the highest level of the extraordinarily centralized North Korean authority structure that culminates in the two Kims, father and son.

Regional Arms Control. In the absence of a regional security and arms control framework that includes the DPRK and its adversaries, the DPRK has few non-military means to reduce its perceived external security threats.

Rapprochement with the South. The DPRK has not shown itself to be enthusiastic about embracing the ROK in the short to medium term (before 2000). Indeed, the security elites of the two countries who fought during the civil war remain mortal enemies. The North let slip a series of opportunities in 1991–92 to accelerate the process of political-economic rapprochement with the South, including major trade and investment in the North led by the ROK and including Japan.

The crucial obstacle to north-south progress has been the alleged nuclear weapons program of the North at Yongbyon. It appears that the North has decided that major economic reforms needed to absorb external economic aid and investment would threaten the regime's survival.[152] Having elected to go slow on reunification, the North has little incentive to implement the nuclear safeguards accord and IAEA inspections. Seoul therefore has little marginal leverage over Pyongyang's activities, including its missile exports.

These seven possible disincentives, therefore, have failed to constrain the DPRK trade in missiles. What about the ROK?

ROK Disincentives

Three factors have dissuaded the ROK from entering the missile market to date. These are (1) the influence of the United States; (2) the ROK's desire to be perceived as a responsible member of the world community; and (3) the opportunity costs of a major missile program. The rest of this section analyses briefly each of these constraints.

Security Alliance. Until recently, the US-ROK security alliance has been the major disincentive to an active ROK missile program and exports. Whenever the ROK probed US resolve that it should not become missile-capable, the United States used its dominant status in the alliance to impose discipline on Seoul. The existence of a hegemonic ally to the ROK compares with the lack of one in the DPRK alliance relationships.

Global Regimes. The ROK leadership values greatly its reputation as a peaceful trading state committed to global and regional communities. Its membership and implementation of its NPT obligations have been exemplary since the mid-seventies, except for a few attempts to nibble at the margins by obtaining reprocessing technology.

The ROK will also observe the terms of the Missile Technology Control Regime when it comes to exporting any indigenously developed missiles or booster rockets. The major powers cannot expect the ROK to forego eventual development of its own missiles and booster rockets, however.

Opportunity Costs. Given the US military presence in the South, the ROK military has not had to offset DPRK missile capabilities with its own missiles. Rather, it has been able to rely on US-controlled missiles deployed in the ROK, or on US missiles transferred or sold to South Korea. The ROK military had—and still has—more important military priorities than investing scarce resources in major missile programs. This constraint will weaken as the ROK economy grows, and as civilian, dual-capable, aerospace capabilities are nurtured and as the US commitment seems to decline.

Conclusion

The North and South Korean states have very different policies about obtaining and exporting ballistic missiles. These diverging strategies could be described as vertical and horizontal, respectively. Isolated and largely left to its own devices, the North Korean state spent the last two decades producing and profiting from its own military missiles. It launched a frontal assault to surmount the lower rungs of the missile ladder.

In contrast, the South Koreans benefited from a security patron which deployed advanced missiles in and around Korea, relieving the ROK of any urgent military need to offset the DPRK's missile capabilities. Consequently, the ROK chose to position itself in crucial industrial and commercial segments of high technology sectors, including space and aerospace industries. In the next decade, this strategy will enable the ROK to step sideways onto the missile ladder at a much higher level of capability than the DPRK. The Missile Technology Control Regime imposed by the major suppliers of missiles and booster rockets will have to deal with an indigenous ROK or unified Korean capability within a decade or less.

The motivations driving the DPRK to produce and export missiles are persistent. The incentives for the ROK to manufacture dual capable rocket technology and its disincentives to export missiles are equally enduring. It follows that integrating both Koreas into a global missile arms control regime will entail reduction in the basic insecurities that afflict the ROK and the DPRK. It will also require introducing missile-related issues into North-South arms control negotiations in Korea; regional security fora that address missile technology diffusion; and adjustments to the global MTCR that link regional missile control measures with global controls on missile research, development, testing, deployment, and trade.

A major outstanding issue is reunification. This essay has assumed that reunification will occur slowly (over one or two generations). The likely sequence of reunification is political-symbolic links; cultural and social exchange; economic and environmental joint activities; political-institutional integration; and only lastly, military reunification.

If reunification should be rapid, non-violent (that is, without a north-south war whatever the mode of succession or transformation of the North), and soon, then a new missile power in Asia could emerge very quickly. This outcome would result from the fusion of the DPRK's capability to manufacture military missiles and its expertise, and marketing networks on the one hand with the ROK's military and industrial technology and investment resources on the other.

Whether separate or fused, Korean missile programs make it urgent to develop regional and global frameworks for missile non-proliferation which offer new incentives to forego missile development, deployment, and trade. A regional nuclear free zone and/or a global or regional ballistic missile test free zone are two such frameworks that bear investigation. Both, however, are beyond the scope of this essay.

Notes

1. Nautilus Pacific Research, 746 Ensenada Ave, Berkeley, CA 94707, USA. tel: 1 510 5269295; fax 1 510 5269297. Des Ball, Seth Carus, Andrew Mack, Janne Nolan, William Potter, and Sandy Spector generously shared information used in this study. Nautilus researchers Megan van Frank provided research assistance; Lyuba Zarsky and an anonymous reviewer critical comments; and Cassandra Morrow production support. Korean (North and South), American, and Australian officials graciously granted interviews that are drawn upon in this essay. Finally, the author acknowledges funding of Nautilus' on-going work on missile and nuclear

proliferation from the Alton Jones, Fund for Tomorrow, Merck, and Ploughshares foundations; and organizational support from the Nautilus Board of Directors.

2. For an overview of these issues, see J. Nolan, *The Trappings of Power, Ballistic Missiles and the Third World*, Brookings Institution, Washington DC, 1990; and O. Wilkes, M. van Frank, and P. Hayes, *Chasing Gravity's Rainbow, US Ballistic Missile Testing and Kwajalein Atoll*, Centre for Strategic and Defence Studies, Australian National University, Canberra, 1991.

3. US State Department, Bureau of Politico-Military Affairs, "Imposition of Missile Proliferation Sanctions Against North Korean and Syrian Entities," *Federal Register*, volume 57, no 130, July 7, 1992, p. 29924; US Department of Commerce, Bureau of Export Administration, "Expansion of Foreign Policy Controls; Missile Technology Destinations," *Federal Register*, volume 57, no 116, June 16, 1992, p. 26774.

4. Interview, UN Development Program official, Pyongyang, October 4, 1991.

5. *The Korea Herald*, January 29, 1991, p. 2; *JPRS-TND-91-002*, February 5, 1991, p. 8.

6. G. Jacobs, "North Korea's Arms Industry, Development and Progress," *Asian Defence Journal*, March 1989, p. 31.

7. J. Bermudez and S. Carus, "The North Korean 'Scud B' Programme," *Jane's Soviet Intelligence Review*, April 1989, p. 177.

8. G. Jacobs, "North Korea's Arms Industry: Development and Progress," *Asian Defence Journal*, no 3, 1989, p. 32.

9. See P. Hayes, *Pacific Powderkeg, American Nuclear Dilemmas in Korea*, Free Press, New York, 1990.

10. "DPRK's Advanced Weapons Analyzed," *Hanguk Ilbo (Korea Daily)* February 8, 1991, p. 8; *JPRS-TND-91-008*, May 31, 1991, p. 8.

11. J. Bermudez and W.S. Carus, *Missile Development in the DPRK*, (mimeo), Woodmere, New York/Washington DC, April 26, 1989, p. 17.

12. "DPRK's Advanced Weapons Analyzed," *Hanguk Ilbo*.

13. J. Bermudez and S. Carus, "The North Korean," p. 177.

14. "DPRK's Advanced Weapons Analyzed," *Hanguk Ilbo*.

15. J. Bermudez, "New Developments in North Korean Missile Programme," *Jane's Soviet Intelligence Review*, August 1990, p. 345.

16. "DPRK's Advanced Weapons Analyzed," *Hanguk Ilbo*,.

17. J. Bermudez and W.S. Carus, *Missile Development in the DPRK*, (mimeo), Woodmere, New York/Washington DC, April 26, 1989, p. 12.

18. US Defense Intelligence Agency, *North Korea, The Foundations for Military Power*, Washington DC, October 1991, p. 62.

19. D. Sneider, "Japanese investigate use of trucks sold to North Korea," *Defence News*, June 15, 1988, p. 14.

20. B. Gertz, "North Korea fortifies air defenses," *Washington Times*, November 28, 1991, p. 3.

21. *Yonhap Radio* (Seoul), "North Said to Possess 1,000 Tons of Warheads," July 15, 1991; *FBIS-EAS-91-135*, July 15, 1991, p. 23.

22. US Defense Intelligence Agency, *North Korea*, p. 42.

23. "DPRK's Advanced Weapons Analyzed," *Hanguk Ilbo*.

24. J. Bermudez, "New Developments in North Korean Missile Programme," *Jane's Soviet Intelligence Review*, August 1990, p. 343.

25. J. Bermudez and S. Carus, "The North Korean," p. 180.
26. "Korea helps Egypt build Scud-B," *Flight International*, July 16, 1988, p. 19.
27. J. Bermudez, "New Developments," p. 344.
28. N. Tatro, "North Korean Missile Help Sought By Syria, Egypt," *Associated Press*, December 29, 1989.
29. J. Bermudez and S. Carus, "The North Korean," p. 177.
30. Soichiro Aso, "Monthly Discusses DPRK Nuclear Technology," *Shokun* (Tokyo), May 1990, p. 78–91; in *FBIS-EAS-90-077*, April 20, 1990, pp. 50–55.
31. J. Bermudez and W.S. Carus, *Missile Development in the DPRK*, (mimeo), Woodmere, New York/Washington DC, April 26, 1989, p. 14.
32. J. Bermudez, "New Developments in North Korean Missile Programme," *Jane's Soviet Intelligence Review*, August 1990, p. 345.
33. *Ibid.*
34. "DPRK's Advanced Weapons Analyzed," *Hanguk Ilbo*.
35. B. Gertz, "North Korea set to test missiles," *Washington Times*, November 12, 1990, p. A3.
36. Associated Press (Seoul), "North Korea Successfully Test-Fires Mobile Scud Missile," October 4, 1991.
37. J. Bermudez and S. Carus, "The North Korean," p. 179.
38. US Defense Intelligence Agency, *North Korea, The Foundations for Military Strength*, Washington DC, October 1991, pp. 3-3 and 35.
39. G. Jacobs, "North Korea's Arms Industry, Development and Progress," *Asian Defence Journal*, March 1989, p. 31.
40. US Defense Intelligence Agency, *North Korea*, p. 44.
41. US Defense Intelligence Agency, *North Korean Armed Forces Handbook*, DDI-2680-37-77, Washington DC, July 1977, p. 3-3; released under a US Freedom of Information Act request.
42. J. Bermudez and W.S. Carus, *Missile Development in the DPRK*, (mimeo), Woodmere, New York/Washington DC, April 26, 1989, p. 7.
43. US Defense Intelligence Agency, *North Korea*, p. 24.
44. J. Bermudez and W.S. Carus, *Missile Development in the DPRK*, (mimeo), Woodmere, New York/Washington DC, April 26, 1989, p. 25.
45. US Defense Intelligence Agency, *North Korea*, p. 42.
46. J. Bermudez, *North Korean SAM Forces*, (mimeo), Merrick, New York, May 15, 1988, p. 1.
47. U.S. Defence Intelligence Agency, *North Korean Armed Forces Handbook*, p. 2-67.
48. US Defense Intelligence Agency, *North Korea*, p. 51.
49. G. Jacobs, "North Korea's Arms Industry, Development and Progress," *Asian Defence Journal*, March 1989, p. 31.
50. J. Bermudez and W.S. Carus, *Missile Development in the DPRK*, (mimeo), Woodmere, New York/Washington DC, April 26, 1989, p. 8.
51. B. Gwertzman, "U.S. Expresses 'Serious Concern' Over Firing of North Korea Missile," *New York Times*, August 27, 1981, p. 4.
52. J. Bermudez, *North Korean SAM Forces*, (mimeo), Merrick, New York, May 15, 1988, p. 3.
53. US Defense Intelligence Agency, *North Korea*, p. 51.

54. J. Bermudez, *North Korean SAM Forces,* (mimeo), Merrick, New York, May 15, 1988, p. 4.

55. "DPRK's Advanced Weapons Analyzed," *Hanguk Ilbo.*

56. US Defense Intelligence Agency, *North Korea,* p. 51.

57. P. Almond, "North Korea places missiles near DMZ," *Washington Times,* June 7, 1988, p. 1.

58. "North's Production, Export of Weapons Described," *Hanguk Ilbo,* February 26, 1991, p. 15; *FBIS-EAS-*91-041, March 1, 1991, p. 30.

59. "DPRK's Advanced Weapons Analyzed," *Hanguk Ilbo.*

60. US Senate, *U.S. Troop Withdrawal from the Republic of Korea, A Report to the Committee on Foreign Relations by Senators Hubert H. Humphrey and John Glenn,* US Government Printing Office, Washington, 1978, p. 53.

61. US Forces Korea/Eighth US Army, *1976 Annual Historical Report,* Seoul, 1977, p. vi; released under a US Freedom of Information Act request.

62. J. Nolan, *Trappings of Power, Ballistic Missiles in the Third World,* Brookings, Washington DC, 1991, p. 50.

63. US House of Representatives, Committee on Armed Services, *Review of the Policy Decision to Withdraw United States Ground Forces from Korea,* (Hearings), US Government Printing Office, Washington, 1978, p. 35.

64. P. Roming, "Partners in Defence, 38th Air Defence Artillery Brigade, Republic of Korea Army Air Defence Command," *Air Defence,* July–September, 1977, pp. 7–8.

65. *Ibid.* p. 7.

66. US Department of Defense, "Report on Korea 1978," mimeo report to US Congress, 1978, p. 4; released under a US Freedom of Information Act request.

67. US Army, "Improved Nike Hercules in Surface-to-Surface Role," *Field Manual 44-95,* Figure 2-12.

68. Kim Ki-sok, "The Development Process of National Defence Science and Technology and Directions of Future Development," January 1989, pp. 36–51; in *FBIS-EAS-*89-056, March 24, 1989, p. 25; Ha Young-sun, "South Korea," in J. Katz, ed, *Arms Production in Developing Countries,* Lexington Books, 1984, p. 228.

69. "Koreans seek military air challenges," *Aviation Week and Space Technology,* October 22, 1979, p. 63.

70. "Nuclear Bombs of Peace-Loving People," *Choson Ilbo* (Seoul), August 9, 1989, p. 2; *JPRS-TND-*89-017, August 29, 1989, p. 3.

71. "Aircraft Industry—Major Developments," *Armada International,* December 1985.

72. G. Steinberg, "Two missiles in every garage," *The Bulletin of the Atomic Scientists,* October, 1983, p. 48.

73. "South Korea," *Ground Defence International,* no. 58, November 1979, pp. 36–37.

74. International Institute for Strategic Studies, *The Military Balance, 1991–1992,* Brasseys, London, 1991, p. 169.

75. M. Banjamin, "South Korea's Aerospace Industry," *Asian Defence Journal,* December, 1990, p. 83.

76. J. Gordon, "ROK Artillery—Present and Future," *Field Artillery,* February 1990, p. 14.

77. General Dynamics, *The World's Missile Systems*, Pomona, California, 1982, p. 93.

78. P. Roming, "Partners in Defence, 38th Air Defence Artillery Brigade, Republic of Korea Army Air Defence Command," *Air Defence*, July–September, 1977, p. 8.

79. US House of Representatives, Committee on Armed Services, *Review of the Policy Decision to Withdraw United States Ground Forces from Korea*, (Hearings), US Government Printing Office, Washington, 1978, p. 35.

80. US Senate, *U.S. Troop Withdrawal from the Republic of Korea, A Report to the Committee on Foreign Relations by Senators Hubert H. Humphrey and John Glenn*, US Government Printing Office, Washington, 1978, p. 46.

81. Defense Audit Service, "Second Summary Report on the Interservice Review of U.S. Force Reductions in Korea," Report no 79-117, Arlington, Virginia, July 25, 1979, p. 13; partly declassified under a US Freedom of Information Act request.

82. F. Weichel, "The Last To Leave," *Air Defence*, July–September, 1982, p. 32.

83. Jane's, *Missiles*, DMS Market Intelligence Report, Alexandria, Virginia, 1989; United States international section, "Hawk Missile," pp. 3–4.

84. International Institute for Strategic Studies, *The Military Balance, 1991–1992*, Brasseys, London, 1991, p. 169.

85. W. Cunningham, *Arms Control in Northeast Asia*, Case Study, Senior Seminar in Foreign Policy, Foreign Service Institute, US State Department, May 1972, p. 4; declassified under a US Freedom of Information Act request.

86. US Senate, Subcommittee of the Committee on Appropriations, *Military Construction Appropriations for Fiscal Year 1980, Hearings*, US Government Printing Office, Washington DC, 1979, p. 181.

87. Defense Audit Service, "Summary Report on the Interservice Review of U.S. Force Reductions in Korea," Report no. 953, Arlington, Virginia, September 29, 1978, p. 1; partly declassified under a US Freedom of Information Act request.

88. Defense Audit Service, "Third Summary Report on the Interservice Review of U.S. Force Reductions in Korea," memorandum to Assistant Secretary of Defense (Comptroller), CINCPAC, and Defense Security Assistance Agency, Arlington, Virginia, October 12, 1979, p. 2; partly declassified under a US Freedom of Information Act request.

89. "South Korea," *Ground Defence International*, no. 58, November 1979, p. 36.

90. J. Nolan, *Military Industry in Taiwan and South Korea*, St. Martin's Press, New York, 1986, pp. 73–75.

91. T. Cochran et al, *Nuclear Weapons Databook, U.S. Nuclear Forces and Capabilities*, Ballinger, Cambridge, Massachusetts, 1984, p. 283.

92. International Institute for Strategic Studies, *The Military Balance, 1991–1992*, Brasseys, London, 1991, p. 169.

93. Commander, US Forces Korea, "Quarterly Report to SecDef," cable to CINCPAC 050310Z, March 1987; partly declassified under a US Freedom of Information Act request.

94. US Senate, *U.S. Troop Withdrawal from the Republic of Korea, A Report to the Committee on Foreign Relations by Senators Hubert H. Humphrey and John Glenn*, US Government Printing Office, Washington, 1978, p. 46.

95. US Department of Defense, "Report on Korea 1978," mimeo report to US Congress, 1978, p. 4; released under a US Freedom of Information Act request.

96 "FX Fighter Program to Set Stage for Air Force Modernization Plan," *Aviation Week and Space Technology*, June 12, 1989, p. 195.

97. See Rep A. Beilenson, letter to US Secretary of State, August 20, 1979; released under US Freedom of Information Act request to author.

98. S. Rosenfeld, "Korean Gamble," *Washington Post*, December 20, 1991.

99. D. Sanger, "Jittery Asia Has Visions of a Nuclear North Korea," *New York Times*, April 7, 1991, p. E-2.

100. CINCPAC Study Team, *An Evaluation of Possible U.S. Support to Republic of Korea Research, Development, Test and Evaluation Activities*, Honolulu, May 25, 1971, pp. 16; E-7.

101. "South Korea Summary," *DMS Market Intelligence Report*, Greenwich, Connecticut, 1978, p. 12.

102. Interview, former US ambassador to South Korea.

103. Kim Chol-hwan, "Trends in Weapons Systems' [sic] Development," *Kukpang Kwa Kisul*, January, 1989, pp. 52–65; *FBIS-EAS-89-055*, March 23, 1989, pp. 38–40.

104. M. Banjamin, "South Korea's Aerospace Industry," *Asian Defence Journal*," December, 1990, pp. 83–84.

105. E. Dantes, "Missile Threat," *Asian Defence Journal*, December, 1990, p. 50.

106. *Ibid.*

107. J. Morrocco, "South Korea Drives Toward Greater Military Autonomy," *Aviation Week and Space Technology*, June 12, 1989, p. 177.

108. M. Banjamin, "South Korea's," p. 82.

109. *Ibid.*

110. *Ibid.*

111. "Korean Aerospace Firms Seek Greater Role in World Market," *Aviation Week and Space Technology*, June 12, 1989, p. 203.

112. US Congress, Office of Technology Assessment, "The Defence Industry of South Korea," *Global Arms Trade, Commerce in Advanced Military Technology and Weapons*, OTA-ISC-460, US Government Printing Office, June 1991, p. 137.

113. M. Banjamin, "South Korea's Aerospace Industry," *Asian Defence Journal*, December, 1990, pp. 83–4; *Aviation Week and Space Technology*, "Daewoo Expands Machining Base To Increase Production Capacity," June 12, 1989, p. 219.

114 M. Banjamin, *ibid.*, pp. 80 & 82.

115. *Ibid.* p. 82.

116. "Space Development Committee to be Formed," *Yonhap Radio*, January 22, 1985; *JPRS-KAR*-85-009, January 31, 1985, p. 77.

117. "Korea to Launch Nation's 1st Research Satellite by 1996," *The Korea Times*, May 21, 1987, p. 1.

118. Yu Ul-sang, "A Challenge to High Technologies—a Report on the "Public Hearing to Determine National Policy-Level Research Priorities," *Tong-A Ilbo* (Seoul), September 7, 1989, p. 10; in *FBIS-EAS*-89-228, November 29, 1989, p. 44.

119. "Cabinet Ordered to Develop Science, Technology," *Yonhap Radio* (Seoul), December 12, 1989; *FBIS-EAS*-89-238, December 13, 1989, p. 34.

120. "Observation Satellite to Upgrade Technology," *Yonhap Radio* (Seoul), February 16, 1990; in *FBIS-EAS-90-034*, February 20, 1990, p. 44.

121. "Observation Satellite," *Yonhap Radio* (Seoul).

122. "Government Team Studies Unification in Germany," *Korea Times*, November 9, 1990, p. 1; in *FBIS-EAS-90-218*, November 9, 1990, p. 31.

123. Interview, Korea Telecom official, Seoul, October 14, 1992. This interview is the source for the information provided in the next two sections unless otherwise stated.

124. Australian Space Office, Department of Industry, Technology and Commerce, "Pacific Rim Developments Towards Business in Space," paper to Space Commerce 92, Montreux, Switzerland, March 1992, p. 6.

125. "Korea Sat Bidding Starts," *Asia Pacific Space Report* (Hong Kong), May, 1991, p. 3.

126. Briefing to author from Major General Kim Yong Chol, Director, General Staff Committee, DPRK Ministry of Defense, Pyongyang, October 4, 1991.

127. "N. Korea is Japan's Biggest Threat—Japan Official," *Reuters*, November 21, 1991.

128. "U.S. Reports of Missile, Technology Sales Denied," *Pyongyang Korean Central Broadcasting Network*, January 24, 1992; *FBIS-EAS-92-016*, January 24, 1992, p. 21.

129. *Ibid.*; Author's emphasis.

130. Kim Wom-pong, "North Korean Armed Forces, North Korean Military Officers and Organizations and Systems," *Gunji Kenkyu* (Tokyo), March 1986; *JPRS-KAR-86-018*, May 14, 1986, pp. 60, 64.

131. J. Bermudez, "North Korea's Nuclear Programme," *Jane's Intelligence Review*, September 1991, p. 408.

132. "Information Provided on DPRK Scud Missiles," *Yonhap Radio* (Seoul), February 2, 1991; *JPRS-TND-91-003*, February 25, 1991, p. 7.

133. "U.S. 'Disinformation' Over Scuds 'Intentional,'" *KCNA* (Pyongyang), February 2, 1991; *FBIS-EAS-91-023*, February 4, 1991, p. 10.

134. J. Bermudez, "Syria's Acquisition of North Korean 'Scuds,'" *Jane's Intelligence Review*, June 1991, p. 249.

135. G. Millhollin, "Hunting for Saddam's bomb," *The Age* (Melbourne), March 21, 1992, p. E4.

136. J. Bermudez, "Syria's Acquisition of North Korean 'Scuds,'" *Jane's Intelligence Review*, June 1991, p. 249.

137. *Ibid.*

138. "Asia: North Korean Arms Exports Rising," *Defence and Foreign Affairs Weekly*, April 2, 1984, p. 2.

139. J. Bermudez, "New Developments," and "North Korea's Nuclear Programme," *Jane's Intelligence Review*, September 1991, pp. 345 and 410; and G. Jacobs, "North Korea's Arms Industry, Development and Progress," *Asian Defence Journal*, March 1989, p. 35.

140. J. Bermudez and W.S. Carus, *Missile Development in the DPRK*, (mimeo), Woodmere, New York/Washington DC, April 26, 1989, p. 13.

141. "Joint Communiqué Published," *KCNA Radio* (Pyongyang), May 17, 1989; *FBIS-EAS-89-094*, May 17, 1989, p. 19.

142. J. Bermudez and S. Carus, "The North Korean," pp. 177–8.

143. Chung-in Moon, "Between Ideology and Interest," in Jae Kyu Park, Byung Chul Koh, Tae-Hwan Kwak, eds., *The Foreign Relations of North Korea: New Perspectives*, Westview Press, Colorado, 1987, pp. 383, 406–7.

144. "Scud Move," *The Age* (Melbourne), March 7, 1992, p. 6.

145. T. Walker, "Iran warns US to leave ships alone," *The Age*, March 19, 1992, p. 1.

146. T. Walker, "N Korea ship docks in Iran," *The Age*, March 12, 1992, p. 8.

147. "Why U.S. Failed to Intercept Ship," *The People's Korea* (Tokyo), March 28, 1992, p. 1.

148. "Ministry Denies DPRK-Libya Scud Contract," *Yonhap Radio*, June 7, 1991; *FBIS-EAS*-91-111, June 10, 1991, p. 17.

149. "North Allegedly Sold Scuds to Iran, Syria," *KBS 1 Radio Network* (Seoul), September 21, 1991; *JPRS-TND*-91-016, October 29, 1991, p. 19.

150. See my *Moving Target, Korea's Nuclear Potential*, Working Paper, Department of International Relations, Australian National University, Canberra, 1992; and my *The Republic of Korea and the Nuclear Issue*, paper to Conference on the Security of the Korean Peninsula in the 1990s, Australian National University, Canberra, February, 1992.

151. S. Harrison, et al., "Preliminary Report Carnegie Endowment Delegation Visit to Pyongyang, Democratic People's Republic of Korea," (mimeo), Washington DC, May 1992, p. 5.

152. Confirmed during the author's trip to Pyongyang in November 1992 and by A. Buzo, "The Pyongyang Myth," *Far Eastern Economic Review*, December 3, 1992, p. 21.

7

China's Case: Ballistic Missile Proliferation

Hua Di

Primitive ballistic missile (BM) technology was proliferated from the Soviet Union to China in the late 1950s. Three decades later, China began to proliferate advanced ballistic missiles and relevant technologies to certain Third World countries.[1]

Unlike widely spread and operationally fired Soviet SCUDs, Chinese-made BMs were never launched in any military conflict in the world.[2] China's BM proliferation, nevertheless, has become one of the hot topics of international security.

This paper traces the records of China's BM proliferation and tries to explain China's attitude toward this issue. The technical facts given in this paper are mainly based on my past professional experience. The policy arguments, although they may coincide with China's official stand, reflect solely my private points of view.

China's BM Exports

An Early Story

China encountered foreign demand for BMs 17 years ago. In April 1975, during Kim Il Sung's visit to Beijing, his Defense Minister, General Oh Jin U, inquired whether China could provide North Korea with tactical BMs. With the Soviet SCUD-A already in their arsenal, the North Koreans were seeking a longer-range BM to cover all of South Korea from the deep interior of the North.

China did not have any tactical BMs at that time, even though in December 1959 it received from the Soviet Union a prototype of the R-11FM missile which was a submarine-launched version of the SCUD-A. The R-11FM, capable of carrying a 950 kg payload over 162 km, was a prepackaged liquid propellant missile with a pressurized propellant-feeding propulsion system and fully inertial strap-down guidance system. The Chinese did not reproduce the R-11FM missile. Nor had they developed their own tactical BMs, because the military preferred to focus on long-range strategic weapon systems.

The North Korean request came after China had succeeded in developing its first generation long-range strategic missiles. It invoked the Chinese military's own interest in tactical BMs. They said a few tactical BM strikes could block remote mountainous passes along the Sino-Soviet border to prevent Soviet troops, which had air superiority, from breaking through there. In late 1976, a R&D program, code-named DF-61, was approved by General Chen Xilian, then in charge of the Central Military Commission's (CMC) day-to-day affairs after Deng Xiaoping was ousted in January 1976.

With six-ton launch weight, one meter in diameter and nine meters in length, the single-stage road-mobile DF-61 was designed to have 600 km range when equipped with a 1,000 kg conventional warhead. Conventional warheads with cluster bomblets and with fuel-air explosive were among considerations. A nuclear version, for Chinese use only, would carry a 500 kg payload over 1,000 km.

The DF-61 program, however, aborted in 1978, when Chen Xilian lost his power in the CMC because of his blind loyalty to Mao's failed Cultural Revolution. The intended BM proliferation to North Korea, which was purely a political deal—not for money but for distancing Pyongyang from Moscow—was put aside and never resumed.

Economic Incentives

In 1991, a western correspondent wrote from Beijing: "China may annoy the United States by selling weapons to volatile areas, but this is neither new nor rooted in ideology. The army sells weapons for reasons associated not with communism but with capitalism; its budget is falling as a share of the economy, and it wants to earn hard currency."[3] The observation is largely correct. It would be more precise to say that China's arms export is a national, not private, economic endeavor associated with socialist modernization, not international communist revolution. While the People's Liberation Army (PLA) sells its decommissioned weapons, or surplus stockpile due to drastic troops reduction, the nation's defense industries have also been enthusiastic in earning hard currency to finance their conversion and modernization.

In 1979, when economic reform started, the Chinese Communist Party's Central Committee issued a guideline stipulating that the defense industries be managed according to four principles of *junmin jiehe, pingzhan jiehe, junpin youxian, yimin yangjun* (combine military with civilian [products], combine peacetime with wartime [production], give priority to military products, use civilian [sales] to foster military [R&D]). However, practice soon after showed that the revenues from selling civilian products were far from enough to foster military R&D. The defense industry administrators had to extend the principle of *yimin yangjun* to *yijun yangjun* (utilizing military [sales] to foster the military [R&D]). Aside from converting part of production capability to civilian use, they began to tackle the international arms market.

To learn to become international arms suppliers for money, not for ideological reasons, the Chinese began with selling conventional weapons and munitions. In 1979, the Ministry of Ordnance established China's first arms trade organization named China North Industries Corporation (NORINCO). In 1980, the Central Military Commission and the State Council officially approved this approach to handling the arms export business.

The Ministry of Space Industry (MSI) followed the same path.[4] Among items for export were satellite-launching service from its First Academy, anti-aircraft missiles from its Second Academy, and anti-ship missiles from its Third Academy. It set up a foreign trade branch called China Great Wall Industry Corporation (CGWIC) to export space technologies and launching service. Another company called China Precision Machinery Import-Export Corporation (CPMIEC) was established for sales of all kinds of missiles manufactured under the MSI's jurisdiction. The First Academy, which is responsible for the development of BMs and satellite carriers was given the cover title of Beijing Wan Yuan Industry Corporation (BWYIC) to be a sub-contractor in any dealings relevant to the academy.[5]

By mid-1984, however, the First Academy had not received any foreign contracts for satellite launching, while feeling severe financial difficulties due to insufficient domestic military orders.[6] Facing a two-thirds cut in the R&D appropriation for 1985 and watching the Second and Third Academies' success in sales of anti-aircraft and anti-ship tactical missiles, the First Academy decided to develop tactical surface-to-surface BMs for export. The Soviet's long record of sales of primitive SCUDs to the Third World also contributed to this decision. Later, the "war of the cities" between Iran and Iraq gave another impetus to the Chinese ballistic missile export effort.

BMs Developed for Export

Engineers in the First Academy deemed that, based on technologies developed in R&D for strategic BMs, they could quickly and cost-effectively develop short-range BMs much better than the SCUDs. On April 28, 1984, the First Academy decided to start R&D on a tactical surface-to-surface BM, code-named M-9. The "M" stands for missile, an English word, which indicates that it is developed for export. On May 14, the MSI assigned the First Academy to be prime contractor for tactical BMs. On December 5, the Commission on Science, Technology and Industry for National Defense (COSTIND), which supervises the nation's defense ministries, approved the development of tactical BMs. On March 4, 1985, a feasibility study of the M-9 program was completed. In October, the Chinese began the M-9's general design. Ten months later, on August 15–17, 1986, they proceeded to hold a technical meeting to coordinate all the M-9's sub-systems.

The M-9 is a 600 km-range single-stage solid propellant road-mobile BM one meter in diameter, 9.1 m in length, weighing 6,200 kg at lift-off. The missile is vertically launched from a transporter-erector-launcher vehicle. It has an inertial strap-down guidance system with on-board computer to exercise fully digitized control. The control system allows easy re-targeting at the launching site and eliminates any need for weather correction. To enhance the weapon's accuracy and penetration capability, a miniature propulsion system is applied on the warhead to adjust its terminal velocity and reentry attitude and to change its flight trajectory and range.

The Chinese were so eager to export the M-9 to earn hard currency that they displayed it at the First Asian Defense Exhibition (ASIANDEX) in Beijing on November 4–11, 1986, two months before the M-9's entire design work was completed. Nominally, the M-9 was exhibited at the ASIANDEX by the ministry's CPMIEC, not the First Academy's BWYIC.

The engineers in the First Academy were delighted that the M-9 had attracted attention and admiration from international visitors at the ASIANDEX. At that time, no one informed the Chinese that seven major industrialized countries were holding secret talks to limit BM proliferation. Nor had the West voiced any official opposition to China's intention, expressed at the ASIANDEX, to sell the M-9. The Missile Technology Control Regime (MTCR), a result from the talks, was made public on April 16, 1987, three years after the Chinese had set off to develop the export-oriented M-9. The question is, however, would the Chinese have advertised the M-9 had they smelt the western MTCR talks in advance?

The international high appraisal of the M-9 had raised the Chinese military's interest in acquiring tactical BMs. On November 8, 1986, before the closing of the ASIANDEX and two years after the M-9 program had started, the MSI gave the M-9 a domestic code-name, DF-15, and thus included it in the DF-series of land-based BMs for the PLA's rocket forces—the Second Artillery.[7] For export, the MSI's document said, it would remain as M-9.

On March 2, 1987, the MSI decided to start producing M-9s for flight tests. The M-9 became one of three priorities in the MSI's 1987 R&D plan. The other two priorities were a second generation solid propellant mobile

IRBM, called DF-31, and a modified geostationary satellite launcher, code-named CZ-3A. To stress the importance of the M-9/DF-15 program in earning hard currency, the First Academy's director characterized the tasks to his subordinates by saying that, *"yao qian, gan dongfeng shiwu; yao ming, gan changzheng sanhao* (to earn money, work for the DF-15; to earn fame, work for the CZ-3)."

The Chinese, experienced in building with large strategic BMs, were so confident in their ability to deal with small tactical BMs that they signed a preliminary agreement with Syria on the sale of the M-9 even before the missile was flight-tested. Indeed, the M-9 has never failed in its flight tests since the first one in June 1988. The Syrians paid a deposit and the First Academy spent the money to build a library and guest houses.

At the 1986 ASIANDEX, it was disclosed that there existed a whole "M-family" of tactical ballistic missiles.[8] In fact, at about the same time as the M-9 was under development, two other units within the Ministry of Space Industry also began to develop export-oriented tactical BMs.

One unit was Base 066. Located in Dangyang County, Hubei Province, the base was affiliated with the Third Academy (Anti-Ship Missile Academy).[9] The base specialized in developing solid-propellant boosters for non-ballistic tactical missiles. Allured by the prospect of earning hard currency, it started in 1985 to design a tactical BM called M-11 for export. The missile was also code-named DF-11 for the Chinese army. Base 066 invited experienced engineers from the First Academy to help solve technical problems relevant to the missile's guidance and flight control systems. The M-11 program lagged some two years behind the M-9 and was not successfully flight-tested before mid-1990.

Jane's Strategic Weapons Systems reported that the M-11 was displayed in a photograph at an exhibition in 1988. The missile reportedly had two solid propellant stages, terminal guidance and a range of 300 km.[10] *Proliferation Watch*, issued by the US Senate Committee on Governmental Affairs, specified that the M-11 was exhibited at the 1988 Chilean FIDA 88 Arms Show.[11]

Another tactical BM designed for export was a variant of a surface-to-air missile (SAM). Its R&D program was initiated by the Second Academy, which has been responsible for building China's SAMs. It proved that, in addition to the sale of SAMs, its HQ-2 SAM could be converted into a short-range surface-to-surface BM at low cost.[12] A technical meeting, held on April 11–12, 1986, confirmed the feasibility of the conversion program. On April 17, MSI minister Li Xue ordered the Great Wall Corporation to provide a loan for the program, code-named 8610, and made the Second Academy the 8610's prime technical contractor.

The 8610 is a two-stage missile with a range below 200 km. It adopted the HQ-2's two-stage propulsion system. The first stage is a solid propellant booster, while the engine on the second stage uses storable liquid propellants. The control system, however, is completely different from the HQ-2's and needed to be developed from scratch. This added difficulties to the R&D and became the main bottleneck in the 8610 program.

It is not known whether the 8610 was given a designation in the DF family of BMs for the Chinese military. Although it was designed for export, it is also not known whether the 8610 has a code name in the M family. Four types of tactical BMs, M-7, M-9, M-11 and M-18 were reportedly developed by the Chinese and the M-18 version was also reportedly displayed.[13] The report described the M-18 as a two-stage missile larger than the M-11. [*A model of the M-18 was displayed at the 1988 ASIANDEX—*ed.] There is no information identifying the M-7, if such a missile really exists, with the 8610. A basic question, however, is how many types of tactical BMs have the Chinese developed: three or four?

What BMs Were Sold and to Whom?

The increasing western opposition to BM proliferation has made the Chinese try hard to conceal their commercial BM activities. On December 11, 1989, when asked about China's intention to sell M-9s to Syria, a spokesman from the Chinese Foreign Affairs Ministry answered: "China has always kept a serious attitude toward the problem of selling medium-range missiles. Except for the sale of a few [ballistic] missiles to Saudi Arabia, China did not intend to sell medium-range missiles to Mideast countries."[14] The evasiveness of the answer was evident. The spokesman did not specifically touch upon the M-9 which he was asked about. Instead, he was talking about medium-range missiles which, in China's official definition, mean missiles ranging between 1,000–3,000 kilometers.

During his official visit to Egypt, Chinese premier Li Peng announced at a press conference on July 6, 1991, that "I can definitely say that China had not sold any [ballistic] missiles to Syria."[15] Yet, a month later, it was reported that, "according to some western military intelligence reports, up to 24 M-9 missile launchers were recently sighted in Syria. The missiles... were built in China with research and development funds largely provided by Syria."[16] The Chinese did not confirm the report, nor did they deny either the delivery of M-9s to or the receipt of the M-9's R&D funds from Syria.

Although not completely confirmed, the sale of the designed-for-export M-9 at least to Syria seemed possible. For a breach of contract, China would have to return to Syria the down payment with a certain penalty. Not only would the loss of hard currency be enormous but the long-time friendship between Chinese and Syrian defense industries would be jeopardized. The Syrians, for example, had leaked Soviet technologies to China by secretly transferring to Beijing several SA-6 anti-aircraft missiles they received from

Moscow in the late 1970s. The SA-6's solid propellant rocket/ramjet propulsion system was unique in the world's missile technology. The Chinese did reverse engineering on the SA-6 missile.

Four months before the alleged M-9's appearance in Syria, it was reported in April 1991 that "U.S. intelligence agencies have recently spotted inside Pakistan what appeared to be a number of launch vehicles for Chinese-made M-11 ballistic missiles"[17] This has been the first and so far the only case regarding delivery of *short-range* BMs to a Third World country that Beijing has officially confirmed. The M-11 was way behind the Syrian-financed M-9 in R&D, and Pakistan probably did not fund the M-11 program.

Nevertheless, what was sold to Pakistan is still a puzzle. Responding to questions at the National Press Club in Washington, the Chinese Ambassador to the United States, Mr. Zhu Qizhen, gave a confusing reply. He said that "we have sold some conventional weapons to Pakistan, including a tiny amount of short-range tactical missiles. I think here you call it M-11. We don't call it M-11, but since you say M-11, let's say M-11."[18] "We don't use the name M-11. It is a United States code name, M-11," he added, "Let's say if it is M-11 this is within the range of the MTCR; that is, the range is only a little more than 200 kilometers."

In fact, the M-11 is the Chinese, not the American, code name. Mr. Zhu was obviously not familiar with China's weapons programs. Disconnection between Chinese foreign affairs officials and arms export managers was deeply rooted.[19] In fact, Beijing has recently tried, by establishing in November 1990 a supervising body called the Leading Group of Military Products Export, to put China's arms export under stricter central control and to make all concerned units better-informed.[20] This is probably why Mr. Zhu became knowledgeable about the sale to Pakistan and about the range of the sold missile.

However, the M-11 was designed to have a range of 300 kilometers. The Chinese had not developed a 200 km-ranged BM other than the 8610. The Chinese BM seen in Pakistan could not be the 8610 because it is still under development and its launcher is clearly different from that of the M-11. The Chinese may have reduced the range of the M-11s sold to Pakistan by fitting them with heavier warheads. If so, the M-11, specially retrofitted to reduce its range, may carry a payload weighing more than 500 kilograms. However, the current MTCR guideline restraining the transfer of rocket systems "capable of delivering at least a 500 kg payload to a range of at least 300 km" is ambiguous. It may be interpreted as not banning sales of missiles carrying a warhead, though heavier than 500 kg, to a range shorter than 300 km.

The key implication of Zhu's speech is that China did not ignore the MTCR even though it was not an MTCR party at the time of his statement.

It admits sales of BMs not violating the MTCR guidelines, but denies that China has exported BMs which simultaneously exceed both 300 km range and 500 kg throw-weight boundaries, except for the shipment of DF-3 intermediate-range BMs to Saudi Arabia in 1985-1988.

The DF-3's sale was handled by Polytechnologies Incorporated, a company under the jurisdiction of the Equipment and Technology Department of the PLA's General Staff. According to one source from Beijing, the amount of the revenue from the sale was kept in high secrecy. Even the heads of the COSTIND, the MSI and the Second Artillery, who helped the export by dispatching technicians and officers to train Saudi Arabian personnel, were not told how much had been earned by Polytechnologies.[21] The sale also brought to China a political side-product: the establishment of Sino-Saudi Arabian diplomatic relations in 1990.

The single-stage DF-3, capable of carrying a 2,150 kg nuclear warhead over 2,650 km, has been deployed in the PLA's Second Artillery since May 1971. The Chinese continued to improve the DF-3, and in 1986 they extended the missile's range to 2,800 km and code-named the modified version DF-3A.[22] The missiles, shipped to Saudi Arabia, were the outmoded DF-3s replaced by the DF-3As from the PLA's arsenal. The DF-3 was never equipped with a conventional warhead. Beijing, however, had never intended to sell the DF-3's nuclear warhead, either.[23] The questions are: How could the Chinese have so quickly developed a conventional warhead for the DF-3 to be exported, and had the effectiveness of the conventional warhead been sufficiently flight-tested? Moreover, the effectiveness of a conventional warhead, even if it weighs more than 2,000 kg and strikes upon a civilian soft target, would hardly justify the cost of the missile.

The DF-3 uses liquid propellant which is filled in the missile after it is erected on the launching pad. The propellant filling is time-consuming. The missile's pre-launch alignment, equipment test-check, and range-setting also take time.[24] The DF-3's total pre-launch exposure time is no less than two and a half hours, not including the time of transportation from storage to the launching site, which makes the missile vulnerable to an opponent's preemption.

According to a technical document issued in May 1983, the DF-3's life span is limited to 14 years after it rolls out from the factory, mainly due to aging problems of synthetic material and electronic units in the missile. The DF-3s sold to Saudi Arabia were produced before 1986. Therefore, they will have to retire by the end of the century. All in all, Saudi Arabia's deployment of dozens of conventional-tipped and vulnerable DF-3s does not have much strategic significance. Neither Israel nor Iran has expressed serious concerns about the DF-3s. The DF-3s also failed to deter Iraq from launching its SCUDs against Saudi Arabia during the recent Persian Gulf War.

Attempted Sales

There were several attempts to sell China's BMs or BM technologies which did not materialize for various reasons. In August 1984, a group of Chinese BM specialists from the MSI's First Academy visited Brazil and Argentina to lecture on BM technology. They were promoting sales of China's DF-5 ICBM for use in space programs. The Brazilians returned a visit to China in December to negotiate the procurement of the DF-5 technology. Actual cooperation intended to start in 1985.[25] The business, however, failed due to the buyer's shortage of hard currency.[26]

In early 1988, an arms broker from the Mideast signed a preliminary contract with the CGWIC to equip China's unguided sounding rockets with conventional warheads and to ship them to Iran, which was in desperate search of BMs to retaliate against Iraq's SCUD attacks. Though not accurate, the unguided BM was cheap and adequate for counter-city purposes. The deal would be paid by Iran in crude oil. However, while the sounding rocket was being re-equipped and the CGWIC was tackling how to resell the crude oil, the Iran-Iraq war ended and the contract was canceled.

Another contract was signed between China and Iraq on building a liquid propellant rocket engine test-firing facility. Engineers of the First Academy's engine test-firing station had completed the design. But, before the construction started, the latest Persian Gulf war doomed the project.

Potential BM Export Possibility

On October 12, 1982, China successfully flight-tested a submarine-launched BM (SLBM), the JL-1.[27] The JL-1 is a two-stage solid propellant missile capable of carrying a 600kg warhead over 1,700km. The technological breakthrough in solid fuel rocketry encouraged the Chinese to develop a new generation of mobile, thus more survivable, BMs to replace the old generation of fixed-based liquid propellant strategic weapons. From the JL-1 SLBM, the Chinese soon made a land-based version, code-named DF-21. The two-stage road-mobile DF-21 was first flight-tested on May 20, 1985, and became operational in the same year.

Among others in the new generation of road-mobile BMs still under development, there is a medium-range BM, called DF-25. The DF-25 would have 1,700 km range and carry a 2,000 kg conventional warhead. The DF-25 is expected to be deployed in the mid-1990s.

The maximum ranges of the DF-25 and the DF-21 are almost the same. However, the DF-21's 600 kg payload is too small for a conventional-tipped BM to be effective. This is why the Chinese started to develop the heavy-headed DF-25. The Chinese military, with insufficient long-range air strike force, would use the DF-25 to provide quick fire support over long distances.

The advanced DF-25 may become a best seller on the international BM market in the late 1990s, if an arms-sales control regime acceptable to China is not established sooner. Particularly, Saudi Arabia may choose the road-mobile DF-25 for its future generation of conventional rocket forces to replace the DF-3 at the end of the 1990s.

Another question posed to the Chinese was how to decommission the old generation of liquid propellant strategic BMs. A part of the answer was the sale of the DF-3s to Saudi Arabia. However, further export of these outmoded and soon-to-retire liquid propellant BMs seems unlikely. Fortunately, all Chinese satellite carriers, the CZ-1, CZ-2, CZ-3 and CZ-4, are based on their DF-4 and DF-5 BMs.[27] Instead of selling the BMs, the Chinese have been active in utilizing them to offer satellite launch services for hard currency.

The Marketing of Satellite Launch Service

On July 16, 1983, the MSI suggested in a report to the COSTIND to enter the international satellite launch service market. Many preliminary agreements and letters of intent were signed with foreign customers. However, no substantial economic benefit was achieved until recently.

The Chinese earned the first big amount of hard currency revenue on April 7, 1990, using the CZ-3 to launch a geosynchronous communication satellite, the *Asiasat-1*, made by Hughes Aircraft Company and owned by a Hong Kong-based consortium. The service brought in about $7.5 million net profit. The CGWIC usually offers the CZ-3 service at $30 million (about 70 percent of the West European and 60 percent of the American service charge) and still can retrieve 25 percent net profit.[29]

Four more foreign communication satellites are on the waiting list.[30] One is an Arabian communication satellite, the *Arabsat*. It was originally scheduled to be launched at the end of 1991 but has so far been delayed. An Indonesian communication satellite is scheduled for 1992. 75 percent of the launching fee will be paid by Indonesia in palm oil, chemical fertilizer and plywood.[31] Two Australian communication satellites, the *Aussat-Bs*, are to be carried by the four-booster-reinforced CZ-2E in 1992 and 1993 successively. All the four communication satellites are made by Hughes so that, to be eligible to handle the satellites, the Chinese need to apply for Washington's permission which is relevant to China's compliance with the MTCR guidelines.

China's aerospace industry's export has been increasing rapidly since 1985.[32] The industry's total export of civilian and military products in 1985 was US$20 million. It increased to $300 million in 1990. The Aerospace Ministry was expected to earn $400 million in 1991 and has set a target for its 800,000 staff to export $1.5–2 billion worth of products and services in the year 2000. The same people, same research institutions and factories, and same technologies are used in China's missile and space programs. Therefore, more capacity converted into civilian production and more hard currency earned from international space services would mean less sales of missiles.

China's Attitude Toward BM Proliferation[33]

Beginning on September 6, 1944, and continuing during the last few months of World War II in the European theater, thousands of V-2 missiles, each carrying a 1,000 kg conventional warhead, struck London. The British, though suffering physically and psychologically, did not kneel down. Nazi Germany could not reverse the trend of the war. In contrast, two atomic bombs, delivered by bombers to Hiroshima and Nagasaki on August 6 and 9, 1945, forced Japan to surrender in a week. Apparently, what is essential is not the delivery system but what is delivered.

There are many ways, ground, air and naval, to deliver destructive power, either conventional or non-conventional, upon a potential target. A human being with a suitcase, to give an extreme example, may constitute a system capable of delivering a miniature nuclear or non-nuclear explosive device. BMs are just one kind of delivery means. Why should they be singled out to be barred from the international market for delivery vehicles?

By itself, a ballistic missile (better to call it ballistic rocket) is not a weapon and cannot cause severe destruction, let alone mass destruction. A BM is only part of a weapon system, either conventional or non-convectional, depending upon what kind of warhead it carries. Why should we confuse delivery means with means of mass destruction by raising the BM proliferation issue to an equal footing with the issue of nuclear proliferation?

BMs, unless equipped with nuclear warheads, are less cost-effective than strike aircraft by many standards: accuracy, payload capability (thus destructive power), and ability to attack mobile targets.[34] To use chemical warheads, for example, the wind direction in the area of a potential target must be considered. BMs cannot adjust themselves to the wind direction, but aircraft pilots can while on site. When carrying nuclear warheads, BMs are merely as effective as strike aircraft. Why should strike aircraft, not BMs, be permitted to be marketed?

Whether a weapon system is defensive or offensive, and is a stabilizing or destabilizing factor, are also arguable. In 1980 when invading Iran, Saddam Husayn did not utilize his BM superiority. Years later, in 1988, when forced onto the defensive under Iranian counter-offensive, he launched SCUDs in a "war of the cities" to stop, not to win, the war he was going to lose. Had Iran won the war, as international opinion then expected, the balance in the Middle East would have been upset. Did the SCUDs play a stabilizing role in this case? In 1990, during its offensive against Kuwait, Iraq did not use SCUDs, either. However, Iraq launched SCUDs in 1991 when it was in a desperate defense. In both cases, were the SCUDs offensive or defensive? Were not Saddam Husayn's armored vehicles, artillery pieces, combat aircraft and helicopters (not his ballistic missiles) the factors that twice destabilized the situation in the Mid-East?

The main non-proliferation task should be to curb the spread of non-conventional, especially nuclear, warheads. BM proliferation, while undesirable, should not divert our attention from the nuclear proliferation issue, and must be considered along with curbing the spread of other advanced delivery systems.

Differences in social wealth and social value between developed and underdeveloped countries have probably contributed to the exaggeration and misperception by the West about BM's effectiveness, which resulted in overemphasizing the importance of BM non-proliferation. Striking New York, a conventionally tipped BM would destroy assets worth tens of millions of dollars. However, damage caused by the same missile to a developing nation's population center would hardly justify the missile's production and operation cost. A report that twenty or so American soldiers were killed by a SCUD in Saudi Arabia shocked public opinion in the United States. A third world nation would feel nothing extraordinary even if two hundred of its citizens fell victims of a missile attack. Actually, the thousands of Iranian people killed during the "war of the cities" have not made Tehran active in supporting the MTCR. Inaccurate, cheap and easy to acquire, BMs with any kind of warheads, as well as other weapons suitable for countervalue strategy, are indeed weapons of the poor against the rich.

The United States itself has engaged for decades in sales of, for example, submarine-launched BMs—the *Polaris* and the *Trident*—to the United Kingdom. Whatever the reasons for these transfers, they, too, constitute BM proliferations, though between developed countries. Isn't it discrimination that what the rich have done is not allowed to take place between the poor?

The U.S. Congress has passed a bill to impose economic sanctions on countries violating the MTCR. But, if developing countries, led by China, create a control regime banning sales of strike aircraft, would the United States abide by it? Of course, having no economic sticks, Beijing would not be capable to play power politics as the United States is unjustly doing.

One of the principles of the market economy recommended to China by the West suggests that everyone do business in areas of his comparative advantage. In the international weapons market, one of China's strong suits is its conventional tactical BMs. The Chinese would argue to let others deal with their strong suits, say, strike aircraft. But, so long as others are selling strike aircraft, China can legitimately sell BMs.

Evolution of China's Attitude

China's position against nuclear weapons proliferation has been firm and clear since the 1980s. Western accusations in this regard have been either groundless or out of misunderstanding. Meeting with Hans Blix, IAEA Director General, Chinese Premier Li Peng said: "China will not proliferate nuclear weapons. China will continue its cooperation with the IAEA on the peaceful use of nuclear energy." On the question of nuclear cooperation with other countries, Li replied: "China has always followed a prudent and responsible policy and stipulated certain regulations in this regard."[35] During Japanese premier Toshiki Kaifu's visit to Beijing in August 1991, Li Peng announced that China had decided in principle to sign the Nuclear Non-Proliferation Treaty (NPT).[36] Since early 1992, the PRC has become an official member of the NPT.

In contrast, Beijing did not clearly promise to stop its BM proliferation until recently. At a press conference in Beijing on March 27, 1991, Foreign Minister Qian Qichen said: "Now, nuclear weapons proliferation is prohibited in the world. There exists an international convention on the prohibition of biological weapons. An agreement banning chemical weapons is being negotiated. As to the export of conventional weapons, no regulations so far exist." "As to the issue of missile technology control regime," he added, "fifteen countries recently held a meeting in Tokyo, Japan, and China was not a participant. It cannot be required that agreement reached among a part of countries be obligatory to a non-participant country."[37] The statement implies that nuclear weapons technology should not be proliferated, but missiles can be sold so long as other conventional weapons are flooding the international market.

What Qian expressed was an annoyance at the attempt of imposing regulations stipulated by the world's big powers on China. With regard to nuclear and missile proliferations, two factors need to be remembered. First, China, the only developing country and the late-comer in the five-member nuclear-missile club, has felt discriminated against since the 1963 Limited Test Ban Treaty and the 1968 NPT. Its feeling of unequal treatment persists at the present. The practice that major powers negotiate a treaty behind China's back and then, after they sign it, "invite" China to join it must not be repeated. Second, China invested huge resources in its defense industries to the detriment of its economic development before the 1980s. As economic construction programs become the national priority, it was natural and imperative that revenues be retrieved from the heavily invested and not yet sufficiently converted defense sectors to help drive the entire national economy.

Beijing's statements on China's conventional arms sales were elusive. They usually stated that China's arms export policy is serious, prudent, and responsible, and that the arms sales are very small and limited to defensive weapons so as not to destabilize the situation. China has, in fact, been exercising certain prudence and responsibility expressed in, for example, declining Qadafi's request for nuclear weapons and in not selling BMs to him.[38]

While the United States is urging China to restrain arms sales, China reciprocally "calls on big arms export countries to take a restrained attitude toward arms export."[39] Moreover, the Chinese righteously point out that the United States—the world's biggest arms exporter since 1990—wants to "control others' but not its own" arms sales, and ask "who in the world should first control arms sales."[40] Yang Shangkun, the PRC's president, said, "American opinion censures us for selling weapons. Yet the United States also sells weapons. Why does it not censure itself?...So there is a question of fairness here. ...China has a saying, 'Only magistrates are allowed to set fires. Ordinary people are not allowed to light lamps.' You are strong, so you can sell without constraint. We are not so strong, and we sell very much less. Yet you denounce us every day. We feel uncomfortable."[41] The essential question is: Who authorized the United Stated to be an arbitrator in all these matters? Who gave the United States the right to stipulate what can or cannot be sold and to whom?

Moreover, unlike the disgusting 1989 bloody suppression of mass demonstrations, China's export of conventional weapons has enjoyed popular support in the country. People comment: "Others are selling weapons, why not we Chinese?" Particularly, those working in defense industries are delighted with every sale of their products abroad, seeing in it their contribution to the nation. They have long felt guilty in spending so much national wealth on weapons R&D over the past three decades. When talking about the sale of DF-3 IRBM to Saudi Arabia, they hailed: "*gande piaoliang* (beautifully done)."

Uncle Sam's "stick," like trade sanctions under the Missile Technology Control Act proposed by a congressional provision attached to the 1990 defense spending bill, seemed only capable of spoiling possible compromise. History proves that in adverse circumstances Chinese communists tend to be confrontational and the Chinese people unite around the government. They prefer to "die standing" rather than to "live kneeling." Worse still, the Chinese, angered at the U.S. imperialist behavior, might export more BMs, not for economic gains but just to display China's backbone to the world.

Nevertheless, this time the U.S. power politics succeeded. In June 1991, the United States imposed sanctions against the licensing of high-speed computers and sophisticated satellite parts to China. The U.S. Congress also threatened to suspend China's most-favored-nation status. Under the pressure, China was forced to pledge its compliance with the MTCR during

U.S. State Secretary James Baker's visit to Beijing in November 1991. A written guarantee was given to the U.S. government in early 1992.

Two factors contributed to China's policy change in regard to the MTCR. First, ignorant bureaucrats in Beijing's Foreign Ministry, who lack technical expertise, did not know how to argue against their arrogant counterparts in Washington. Second, the changing and booming Chinese economy has made the nation less reliant on arms sales, particularly BM exports. By 1991, China's foreign exchange reserve exceeded 40 billion dollars, and the aerospace industry had converted 65 percent of its production from military to civilian.[42]

Beijing has started to formulate its new policy position since 1991, under the changed situation in the Mideast after Operation Desert Storm and in the world after the disintegration of the Soviet Union. Chinese Deputy Foreign Minister Qi Huaiyuan told his Japanese counterpart Owada in Tokyo on March 13, 1991, that Beijing was ready to cooperate with tighter controls on conventional arms (not only ballistic missiles) trade within the framework of the United Nations (not the US-initiated MTCR).[43] Speaking to the World News Media Association in Washington on May 7, Chinese Ambassador Zhu Qichen announced that "China stands for a fair, reasonable and effective solution of the arms proliferation issue, including missile exports, through comprehensive and equal consultations among all countries, not through a decision made by a few countries."[44] Li Peng further explained that "comprehensive" means control over all countries and with regard to all kinds of weapons.[45] He added that it ought not control one kind of weapon while leaving another kind of weapon of equal lethality and the same nature uncontrolled.

Beijing's present official guideline can be concisely summarized in eight Chinese characters: *gongping, heli, quanmian, junheng* (fair [or equal], reasonable, balanced, overall [or comprehensive]).[46] This guideline was accepted by all five permanent members of the UN Security Council in a communiqué released after their two-day meeting in Paris in July 1991. The communiqué said the five "undertook to seek effective measures of non-proliferation and arms control in a fair, reasonable, comprehensive, and balanced manner on a global as well as on a regional basis."[47]

Conclusion

Tactical BMs do not play an essential role in China's national defense. China invested quite a bit in tactical BM programs mainly for export. The cost of this investment must be offset, even if the expected profit is to be abandoned. It was unfair that China was not notified when talks on the MTCR started in 1983 and when China started developing tactical BMs for export in 1984. It was unfair to impose the MTCR on China, although China has promised not to violate its current guidelines.

The current MTCR, stipulated by a few western countries, leaves much to be desired. BMs, if not nuclear-tipped, are not weapons of mass destruction. It is unfair that the sales of strike aircraft are unrestricted. Their export must be discussed within the framework of general restrictions of all arms sales by the United Nations. Any future regime negotiated otherwise would not be comprehensive and balanced. However, if all major suppliers of all kinds of weapons are willing to cut off arms sales and if other hard-currency earning channels are more open to Beijing, an international regime on arms-sales control, not only on missile technology control, can be successfully negotiated with China's active participation.

Notes

1. For details on China's ballistic missile programs, see John Lewis and Hua Di, "China's Ballistic Missile Programs: Technologies, Strategies, Goals," in *International Security*, Vol. 17, No. 2, Fall 1992, which I cite extensively in the first part of this paper.

2. The SCUDs were used at least in four wars: the 1973 Mideast war, the war in Afghanistan, the Iran-Iraq war, and the recent Persian Gulf war. Also, in April 1986, Libya launched two SCUDs against an American military base in Italy. (See Pan Jusheng, "Spread of Ballistic Missiles," *Conmilit*, No. 175, August 1991, p. 80.)

3. Nicholas D. Kristof, "China Takes on the Role of Enemy No. 1 to the West," *New York Times*, September 22, 1991.

4. The ministry was responsible for R&D of all but anti-tank and air-to-air missiles. It was called the Seventh Ministry of Machine Building before May 4, 1982, and became the Ministry of Aerospace Industry in April 1988 when it merged with the Ministry of Aeronautics.

5. Wan Yuan came from *wan yuan lu* (ten thousand sources road), the name of a street outside the First Academy's compound.

6. The Chinese decided to enter the international satellite launching service market on June 15, 1983.

7. The "DF" stands for *dong feng* (east wind), which is designated to all Chinese land-based BMs.

8. *Conmilit*, No. 123, 1987, p. 2.

9. In the latter half of the 1980s, Base 066 split off from the Third Academy as an independent missile research and industrial complex.

10. "M Family," *Jane's Strategic Weapons Systems*, ed. by Duncan Lennox, 1990, Jane's Information Group, *JSWS*-Issue 04, China: Offensive Weapons.

11. "China's Record of Proliferation: Missile," *Proliferation Watch*, Vol. 2, No. 2, March–April 1991, p. 3.

12. The "HQ" stands for *hong qi* (red flag) which is designated to all of China's surface-to-air missiles.

13. "M Family," *Jane's Strategic Weapons Systems*.

14. *Renmin Ribao* (*People's Daily*), overseas edition, December 12, 1989, p. 1.

15. *Shijie Ribao* (*World Journal Daily News*), July 7, 1991, p. 2.

16. "Road to Damascus," *Far Eastern Economic Review*, August 22, 1991, p. 6. See also, Nicholas D. Kristof, "Potent Office Weaves Web in China Arms," *New York Times*, August 21, 1991, p. A16.

17. R. Jeffrey Smith, "U.S. Reports Chinese Missile Launchers Sighted in Pakistan," *Washington Post*, April 6, 1991, P. A17.

18. See the Reuters Transcript Report (ao898 reutt.rw. BC-Text-China-3rdadd 06-27-0542), June 27, 1991.

19. For details, see John W. Lewis, Hua Di and Xue Litai, "Beijing's Defense Establishment: Solving the Arms-Export Enigma," *International Security*, Vol. 15, No. 4, Spring 1991, pp. 87–109.

20. Yan Kong and William C. Potter, "Comments on Beijing's Defense Establishment," *Eye on Supply*, No. 4, Spring 1991, p. 75. Also see "Saudi King Accepted Invitation to Visit Mainland," *Shijie Ribao*, July 13, 1991, p. 10

21. Another source from Beijing alleged that Saudi Arabia had paid US$3.1 billion for the whole deal of building up Saudi Arabian IRBM troops, including delivery of 31 DF-3 missiles (one for training), construction and installation of all necessary equipment and facilities for storage, maintenance, transportation and launch of the missiles, and training technical and operational personnel.

22. One source states that the DF-3A had a range of 3,000 km. See Li Ke and Hao Shengzhang, *"Wenhua Da Geming" zhong de Renmin Jiefangjun* [*The People's Liberation Army in the "Great Cultural Revolution"*], (Beijing: Zhongkong Danshi Ziliao Chubanshe, 1989), p. 310.

23. *Renmin Ribao*, Overseas edition, reported that Chinese Foreign Affairs spokesman refuted on January 14, 1990, a U.S. CIA report about China's shipment of 12 nuclear warheads to Saudi Arabia as "totally groundless."

24. Four soldiers, each sitting near one of the legs on the launching pad, make coordinated adjustment of the missile's position to get it strictly vertical and to have its "shooting plane" accurately oriented toward the potential target. They use hand cranks and are aided by a gravitational leveling instrument and a theodolite collimator.

25. *Dangdai Zhongguo de Hangtian Shiye* [*Contemporary China's Space Cause*], (Beijing: Guofang Gongye Chubanshe, 1986), p. 527.

26. Currently, China and Brazil are cooperating on an earth resources satellite and are ready to start working on the prototype design. (Li Hong, "Up, Up and Away for a Record Five Satellites in 1990," *China Daily*, March 2, 1990, p. 1.) See the Chapter on Brazil.

27. The "JL" stands for *ju lang* (giant wave).

28. The three-stage CZ-3 and CZ-4 use the DF-5 as their first two stages, while the two-stage CZ-2 is just a modification of the DF-5. The three-stage CZ-1 uses the two-stage DF-4 as its booster, while the DF-3 is used as the DF-4's first stage.

29. Ruan Cishan, "Struggle for Hegemony in Launching Satellites," *China Times Weekly*, No. 274, May 26–June 1, 1990, pp. 56–57.

30. Li Hong, "China Set to Launch 5th Satellite This Year," *China Daily*, September 26, 1990.

31. "Chinese Communists Will Launch US-made Satellite for Indonesia," *Shijie Ribao*, February 18, 1991.

32. "Mainland Aerospace Industry Expands Export," *Shijie Ribao*, December 5, 1990, p. 11. Also see "Civil Output at Missile Plants," *China Daily*, July 3, 1991, p. 2.

33. See Hua Di, "The Arms Trade and Proliferation of Ballistic Missiles in China," in *Arms Sales Versus Nonproliferation: Economic and Political Considerations of Supply, Demand, and Control*," PSIS Proceedings, the 1991 AAAS Science and Security Colloquium, pp. 3–6, which I cite in this part of the paper.

34. See, for example, John R. Harvey and Uzi Rubin, "Controlling Ballistic Missiles: How Important? How to Do it?" in *Arms Control Today*, March 1992, pp. 13–18.

35. *China Daily*, April 2, 1991, p. 1.

36. Sheryl WuDunn, "China backs Pact on Nuclear Spread," *New York Times*, August 11, 1991, p. 1.

37. *Renmin Ribao*, overseas edition, March 28, 1991, p. 1.

38. About the Libyan request for a nuclear weapon, see *New York Times*, April 16, 1991. The same Mideast broker who in 1988 negotiated the sale of unguided rockets to Iran asked the CGWIC whether the DF-3, shipped to Saudi Arabia, could be sold to Libya, too. The Chinese categorically refused on the grounds that Qadafi was a leader of questionable responsibility and that the DF-3 could threaten Europe if deployed in Libya.

39. "Call on Big Arms Export States to Curb Arms Export," *Renmin Ribao*, overseas edition, March 28, 1991, p. 1.

40. See *Renmin Ribao*, overseas edition: "Look at Yourself in a Mirror Before Accusing Others," July 17, 1991, p. 6; and "Strange Phenomenon on the World Arms Market," August 22, 1991, p. 6.

41. "The United States Also Sells Weapons," *U.S. News & World Report*, May 27, 1991, p. 43.

42. Li Hong, "Aerospace Trade Goes to Public Products," *China Daily*, February 1, 1992, p. 1.

43. *Japan Times*, March 18, 1991.

44. *Renmin Ribao*, Overseas edition, May 9, 1991.

45. "Li Peng Said at a Press Conference in Cairo," *Renmin Ribao*, overseas edition, July 8, 1991, p. 6.

46. From my interview with Colonel Pan Zhenqiang, Deputy Director of the Institute for Strategic Studies of the PLA's National Defense University, in October 1991 at Stanford University. Also see, "China Clarifies View on Arms Control," *China Daily*, July 10, 1991, p. 1.

47. "Security Council Concurs on Arms Cuts," *China Daily*, July 11, 1991, p. 1.

8

Iraq's Case: The International Missile Trade and Proliferation

Mark H. Kagan[1]

Introduction

In September 1981, Iraq invaded Iran and started what was to become the seven-year Iran-Iraq War. In August 1990, Iraq invaded Kuwait and started what was to become the seven-month war for Kuwait (although the armed hostilities of "Desert Storm" did not start until January 1991).

Iraqi President Saddam Husayn saw each invasion as a bold stroke which would solve major political and economic problems and solidify his claim to preeminent political leadership in the Arab world. Each "bold" stroke, however, turned out to be a disaster for Iraq, although the aftermaths of each war were strikingly different.

In 1981, the Iraqi armed forces were barely able to maintain and operate their mostly Soviet-made equipment. Soviet military personnel were essential for training, maintenance and even operations by the Iraqi military, although their numbers and activities were restricted by an intensely paranoid Iraqi regime. Moreover, the rudimentary Iraqi military-industrial infrastructure was only capable of producing some spare parts and ammunition.

Nine years later, when Iraq invaded Kuwait, it possessed a military-industrial infrastructure whose size and technical sophistication rivaled those in many Western countries. Furthermore, Iraq had gone from being barely able to operate its limited supply of Soviet FROG-7 and SCUD-B missiles, to having perhaps the largest and most ambitious ballistic missile program in the Third World outside of China. Iraq produced ballistic missiles which proved crucial, though not decisive, in ending the Iran-Iraq war on Iraqi terms. In the fall of 1989 it also launched the three-stage *Al-Tammuz* rocket, which was to be a prototype for a satellite launch vehicle. The missile program was part of an extraordinarily ambitious effort to create a comprehensive aerospace industry capable of producing military and commercial aircraft, satellites, and space launch vehicles.

The war for Kuwait, "Desert Storm," left that infrastructure largely in ruins. Furthermore, under the terms of United Nations Security Council (UNSC) Resolution 687, most of the surviving infrastructure—specifically, those elements that were involved in Iraq's ballistic missile, nuclear, biological, and chemical weapons programs—are supposed to be destroyed. Since the middle of 1991, the United Nations Special Commission on Iraq (UNSCOM) has been carrying out this search and destroy mission, in the face of persistent Iraqi non-cooperation and obstruction.

Under the terms of Resolution UNSC 687, Iraq is also forbidden from engaging in the future acquisition or production of ballistic missiles and all weapons of mass destruction. In addition, a long-term monitoring regime is to be established by UNSCOM to ensure that Iraq will abide by these restrictions.

Like Hitler in 1939 and the Argentine junta in 1982, Saddam jumped the gun when he invaded Kuwait in 1990, when waiting another year or two might have brought very different results. In another 12 to 18 months, his scientists and engineers would probably have completed assembly of at least one nuclear device. The Allied coalition which conducted "Desert Storm" would have been much harder to assemble another year into the post-Cold War era. Fortunately, Saddam followed the wrong precedents.

Background

Iraq initiated an indigenous missile program for all the usual reasons, plus a few peculiar to its own situation. In the early 1980s, Iraq was engaged with Iran in what was seen by both sides as a death-struggle. The Iraqi air force had proved to be remarkably ineffective in most of its bombing missions against Iranian targets, despite possessing a large and well-balanced arsenal of French and Soviet aircraft. In 1985, Iran began using Soviet-made SCUD missiles against Iraqi urban targets, principally Baghdad. Iraq also possessed Soviet-supplied SCUD missiles, but Tehran and other targets were beyond their range.

Iraq already began assembling the components of a missile program as early as 1982, but the 1985 Iranian attacks gave it special impetus. The Iraqi reasons for producing missiles included the following:[2]

- Long-range missiles could reach Iranian urban targets, especially Tehran, and thus avenge Iranian missile attacks on Baghdad.

- Planes could be shot down. At that time, missiles could not, and Iran certainly did not have the capability.
- The speed and lack of warning of missile attacks made them psychologically more devastating then the actual damage they caused merited.
- Iraqi pilots generally flew too high to make effective bombing attacks in order to avoid anti-aircraft defenses, whereas missiles "ignored" air defense systems. Missiles could also miss their targets, and often did, but missile accuracy was a technical problem that could be solved with time, money, and technology.
- The infrastructure for operating a modern air force was much more complex and expensive than that required for a missile force. Missiles also did not require expensively-trained pilots and they might bring quicker results.
- Building missiles was within the reach of Iraqi industry, although much needed to be acquired. Building bombers was not within reach and would not be for years, if ever. While Iraq could buy the planes from foreign suppliers, its long-term aim was military self-sufficiency.
- An air force is a potential coup weapon, while missiles are not. While Saddam was not about to get rid of his air force, creating a missile force did not add to his concerns about being overthrown by a military coup.
- Finally, becoming a missile power enhanced Iraq's claims to leadership in the Arab and Third Worlds. Not coincidentally, it also enhanced Saddam Husayn's prestige and legitimacy.

Transactions

Iraq was never a participant in the international missile or missile technology marketplace as a supplier, only as a consumer. There is no information in open literature to indicate that Iraq served as a transshipper of missile technology, even in the *Condor II/Badr 2000* project with Argentina and Egypt. The *Condor II* program was an indigenous Argentine program to develop ballistic missiles and satellite launch vehicles (see Scott Tollefson's chapter). Iraq secretly joined it as a means of shortcutting its own missile development program, but its contribution was primarily financial, in return for the technological fruits of Argentine efforts. Iraq secretly joined the Egyptian *Badr 2000* missile program for the same reasons. All three countries shared in their research and development results, but Iraq was primarily a consumer in the exchanges.

It is possible that those in charge of the Iraqi missile program looked forward to trading missile technology to other countries for additional high technology infusions, mainly through joint ventures. A factor that was almost as important, in the Iraqi context, was that the possible sale of ballistic missiles to other Third World countries would have contributed to Iraq's self-image as a leading Arab, regional, and Third World power. It would also have given Saddam the chance to stick his thumb in the eyes of the "imperialist Western powers" who were behind the Missile Technology Control Regime (MTCR), and thus, by definition, were viewed as hostile to Iraq.

At the First Baghdad International Fair for Military Industrialization in April-May 1989, Iraq publicly exhibited for the first time models of the *Al-Husayn* and *Al-'Abbas* missiles. These were probably Iraqi modifications of the SCUD-B. However, according to Simon Henderson, photo analyses by foreign intelligence agencies of the missiles exhibited at the fair indicated that one missile was actually an unmodified SCUD-B, while the other was an *Al-Husayn*.[3] The Iraqi Minister of Industry and Military Industrialization, Husayn Kamil Hasan (al-Majid), stated at a press conference held during the fair that Iraq was

> ...studying requests from a number of states to purchase Iraqi weapons. ...Weapons will be given to Arab states or to friendly states that support the Arabs....Iraq is working for the benefit of the Arab nation and will not turn down any Arab state wishing to purchase weapons....Iraq has informed its brothers that it can supply their needs at low prices....Iraq is doing this to make things easier for the Arab states, to help them overcome their problems, and to contribute to real stability in the Arab region.[4]

In retrospect, it would seem that Husayn Kamil was referring to the other Iraqi-produced weapons that were shown at the exhibition, not to ballistic missiles. Exhibiting the missiles seemed to be part of the exhibition's public relations effort to demonstrate Iraq's technological capabilities. This would encourage technically advanced countries to take Iraq seriously in the arms technology market, and foster agreements for joint or co-production and technology transfers. It is not known if Iraq was ever approached by another country for the sale of missiles or missile-related items and services. A plausible possibility might have been Libya, but this would only be speculation.

During the 1980s, Iraq set up an enormous world-wide procurement network to obtain weapons, spare parts and ammunition. This network also was created to obtain the technology to produce these items; as well as nuclear, biological, and chemical (NBC) weapons; and missiles. While Iraq was prepared to go through normal legal channels to get what it wanted, it had absolutely no compunctions about engaging in illegal and covert activities to obtain what it needed. It is most disturbing that much of what Iraq obtained for its missile and NBC weapons programs was obtained overtly and legally.

There was probably no "master plan" in the technology acquisition process. It began in an *ad hoc* fashion in the first years of the Iran-Iraq war, and quickly expanded under the direction of a number of government departments. The one common element that characterized this process, and the acquisition strategies that Iraq followed, was the availability of cash. There were apparently no limits on what Iraq was willing to pay to suppliers. This free-spending philosophy only began to change in the two years prior to the invasion of Kuwait, when Iraq began to experience serious cash-flow problems due to its accumulated war debts.

The availability of almost unlimited financing was crucial to the success of the Iraqi technology acquisition program. Multiple and complex agencies and departments required money. Covert operations, which were liberally used to obtain more problematic items, are—almost by definition—expensive. The Iraqis frequently paid two, three, or four times the value of the equipment or technology acquired; either to ensure quick responses or because of the sensitivity of the items.

Iraqi efforts to acquire equipment and technology would still not have been so successful in such a short time span if there had not been such enthusiastic willingness on the part of governments and companies to supply Iraq's needs. During the early to mid-1980s, this was justified, mainly in the West, on the grounds of keeping Iraq from being defeated by the radical Islamic Republic of Iran. It did not hurt that at the same time, Iraq became a good market for hundreds of companies. The U.S., British, French, West German, Italian, and Brazilian governments (among others) saw to it that financing for contracts was facilitated. In the late 1980s, however, particularly after the end of the Iran-Iraq war, this economic justification became a vicious circle. By then Iraq had fallen billions of dollars behind in payments for previous contracts. However, companies continued to seek new contracts with Iraq, and governments continued to provide easy financing arrangements, hoping to be paid eventually for older contracts, and to avoid Iraqi threats of default if new contracts were not forthcoming.

The Iraqis also spent lavishly on consulting fees, salaries and benefits for the thousands—perhaps tens of thousands—of foreign engineers, scientists, technicians, and workers whom they recruited for their military-industrial complex.

There were seven basic strategies of equipment and technology acquisition, which will be described below. They could all be summarized as one strategy of "beg, buy, borrow, or steal." The most important consideration was "doing whatever worked." The second most important consideration was not allowing anything to stand in the way of success. Whatever it cost, the Iraqis paid, whether it was cash or in kind. They did not hesitate to resort to subterfuge, espionage, or possibly even murder.

Usually it was not necessary to go to such extremes to get the technology, equipment, or skilled manpower that Iraq sought. During the 1980s, Western governments, especially those of the United States, Great Britain, France, and West Germany, made it easy for Iraq to acquire technology and equipment that was undeniably destined or suitable for military and aerospace uses. This often was done despite self-imposed embargoes on the sale of military equipment and technology to Iraq. It was also frequently carried out with the cooperation of high-ranking officials who were more concerned about "free-trade" and trade balances than they were about weapons' proliferation.

Western companies, without whom the Iraqis could not have established—let alone built up—their enormous military-industrial infrastructure in less than nine years, stepped all over each other in their eagerness to "exploit" the Iraqi market. Just as the Iraqis often went to great and illegal lengths to acquire what they needed, so, too, did many of these companies engage in shady, fraudulent, or illegal practices to supply their valued customer.

Iraq had an unprecedented programmatic philosophy of redundancy to ensure success and security. Just as Iraq used multiple methods to obtain enriched uranium for its nuclear program (a total of four methods have so far been discovered by UN inspection teams), and built multiple military R&D and production installations; so too it used multiple and simultaneous missile acquisition strategies. Sometimes this was done intentionally so as to maximize the chances for success. Sometimes it was done unintentionally by competing or multiple agencies, in situations that could be described as "the left hand not knowing what the right hand was doing."

The seven acquisition strategies follow.

Government to Government

At the overt level, this involved formal government-to-government arrangements between Iraq and other countries for technology transfers, equipment sales, training and education of personnel and students, joint R&D programs, and joint or licensed production. The most important countries involved in such relationships with Iraq were Brazil, China, Egypt, France, and the Soviet Union.

At the covert level, this strategy involved secret agreements between the Iraqi and other governments when public disclosure would have proved embarrassing to one or both governments. It may have been carried out to evade international control efforts on the transfer of sensitive technology (e.g., the MTCR) and the threat of possible sanctions. Here, the most important countries were Argentina, Brazil, East Germany, Egypt, Libya and South Africa. Argentina and Egypt were particularly notable for their involvement in the *Condor II/Badr 2000* missile program.

Government to Private Company

At the overt level, this involved direct agreements or contracts between the Iraqi government and foreign private or government-owned companies. Both parties may have felt the need to be discrete at times, but did not feel compelled to conceal or disguise the existence or nature of these arrangements. Contracts covered almost every area in the Iraqi acquisition drive: technology transfers, construction of facilities, equipment sales, training and education of personnel and students, and joint production and licensing arrangements.

Some of the more prominent examples of such arrangements, though not necessarily always in the missile field, involved Industrias Cardoen (Argentina); Consultco Ltd. (Austria); HOP (Brazil); Dassault and Thomson-CSF (France); BAS Tools and Deltacam Systems (Great Britain); SNIA-BpD (Italy); Conchem and the CONSEN Group (Switzerland); Electronics Associates and Hewlett Packard (United States); and Gildemeister Projecta and MBB (West Germany).

The Zug-based CONSEN Group played a major role in Iraq's European activities. Both by itself, and through its association with the Zug-based firms of Desintec, Condor Projekt and the IFAT Corporation, the CONSEN Group spread a world-wide network for the procurement of technology and equipment for the Iraqi missile program.[5] Its most notable achievement on behalf of the Iraqis was the role it played as manager of the *Condor II* missile project. Through its involvement in this project, the CONSEN Group was able to funnel equipment, technology, and skilled personnel from a variety of sources to Iraq's Sa'ad 16 missile complex.

The Austrian engineering company Consultco designed the enormous R&D and production facility known as Sa'ad 16, just outside the northern Iraqi city of Mosul. Sa'ad 16, which covered 40,000 square meters, was involved not only in the design, modification and production of missiles, but also in the production of chemical and conventional weapons. Elements of Iraq's nuclear program were also located there. The West German company Gildemeister Projecta was project manager and general contractor for equipping the complex.[6] MBB, also of West Germany, was the main contractor for the acquisition of equipment.

Literally hundreds of companies in dozens of countries were involved in these types of arrangements. Most of the contracts concluded with these companies were legal, according to the laws and regulations of their respective countries, and conducted in the full light of day. In the case of Gildemeister, this was not always the case. For example, according to *Der Spiegel*, the company was unable to get an export permit for shipping a wind tunnel to Sa'ad 16 in 1985. In order to get around West German regulations preventing issuance of the license, the company simply changed the export documents to conceal the military end-uses of the wind tunnel and informed the Iraqis by letter that: "The equipment that will be supplied will conform to the original contract."[7]

These arrangements and transactions usually involved the cooperation and encouragement of the companies' governments. For example, the U.S. Department of Commerce and the British Department of Trade and Industry issued hundreds of export licenses between 1985 and 1990 to American and British companies, respectively, for sales to Iraq. These sales often involved technology and equipment whose military or dual-use applications were easily identifiable. These licenses were often issued over the vociferous opposition of the U.S. Department of Defense or the British Ministry of Defence, and sometimes without their knowledge.

At the covert level, the Iraqi government often entered into agreements with foreign private or government-owned companies in which it concealed the actual end-use of the technology or equipment it purchased. Quite often, the deception was not very subtle or sophisticated, but it usually did not have to be. The foreign company either was deceived or it "looked the other way." Iraq usually found it most congenial and/or necessary to carry out such an acquisition strategy in France, Italy, the United States, and West Germany.

Where it was necessary, and the foreign company was willing, the Iraqi government might also make arrangements in which both sides concealed their connections, activities and/or the technology or equipment involved. This was done in order to evade foreign laws against the transfer of sensitive, dual-use, or military technology or equipment. It was not unusual for companies that were involved with Iraq in overt arrangements to also participate in covert arrangements of this type, either simultaneously or at different times. Examples of companies that were involved in such arrangements included the Swiss CONSEN Group and IFAT Corporation,[8] and the West German H&H Metalform and Karl Kolb GmbH.

Iraqi State Agency to Private Company

A number of Iraqi government agencies, which were actually part of the Ministry of Industry and Military Industrialization (MIMI), concluded deals with foreign companies. Among these agencies were the Nasr State Establishment for Mechanical Industries, the Technical Corps for Special Projects (Teco), and the State Organization for Technical Industries (SOTI).

These organizations were set up for legitimate bureaucratic and organizational requirements of the Iraqi military-industrial complex. However, their existence as separate agencies often helped to mask their connections with MIMI or the Ministry of Defense and their purchasing activities on behalf of those ministries. This was particularly useful in providing cover for the purchase of problematic equipment or concluding possibly controversial contracts. The Technical Corps for Special Projects, for example, was actually responsible for running Sa'ad 16; Project 124, (which was the plant responsible for the modification of SCUD missiles to enhance their range—what were later dubbed the *Al-Husayn*); and Project 395 (or DOT) which was the name given to the overall *Condor II* project in Iraq.[9]

If necessary, these state agencies deliberately concealed their connections to MIMI or the Defense Ministry. Nor were they reticent about concealing or lying about the ultimate end-use of items or technology which they purchased from a foreign company.[10]

On the other hand, they often did not have to resort to such methods. For example, between 1985 and 1988 the U.S. Department of Commerce Bureau for Export Administration approved hundreds of export licenses for shipments of dual-use and military equipment to Iraq, with a significant percentage going to Sa'ad 16. This came *after* the Commerce Department received a letter from the Director of the Sa'ad General Establishment, dated 27 February 1985, which accompanied the first license requests. The letter described the complex, which contained 76 labs and workshops, most of which dealt with such fields as fuel production, vibration and friction effects, stability of mixtures, aerodynamics, turbo machines, microwaves, etc. During 1985–88, the U.S. Commerce Department granted export licenses to the following companies for the following items, all of which went to Sa'ad 16.[11] This is only a fraction of the total items for which export licenses were granted:

- May 1985: An American firm sought to export electronic equipment, including 18 GHz electronic counters, and six 275 MHz oscilloscopes. (Approved without condition.)
- December 1985: The Wilton Co. sought to export a 10 MHz–40GHz scalar network analyzer system. (Approved without condition.)
- June 1987: A U.S. company sought to export a 19.9 Mbit computer system "for process control and data evaluation." (Approved without condition.)

Electronic Associates Inc. shipped parallel analog processors, televideo graphics displays, and a hybrid analog-digital computer. Upon U.S. Congressional inquiry, however, the Commerce Department was unable to find the supporting documentation for the sale in its files or computer.

Hewlett Packard made multiple deliveries of electronic voltage regulators, sophisticated computers, and programmable equipment designed for signal analysis, measuring, test, and calibration.

In addition to the scalar network analyzer system, Wilton sold electronic test and measuring equipment to the flight-test laboratory at Sa'ad 16.

Iraqi Government Purchase of Foreign Companies

The Iraqi government purchased a number of companies in Western countries, primarily in Great Britain and West Germany, in order to openly acquire certain useful technologies directly. These companies could also provide equipment, project management and/or training for Iraqi personnel. One of the most important companies acquired under this strategy was the British machine tool company, Matrix Churchill.

The Iraqi government also purchased a number of companies in the West to use as second and third party companies. This was done in order to evade foreign laws forbidding the transfer of technology or equipment to Iraq. Some of these were holding companies. Others were used to place orders with third companies to conceal the ultimate destination or end-use of the purchased items or technologies. Sometimes the companies were aware of what was going on; sometimes not; and sometimes they suspected but looked the other way.

Another variation of this strategy was the establishment of front companies. Iraqi agents (actually government or intelligence officials) set up front companies in Western countries, which then carried out the same activities described above. The European center for such covert and semi-covert activities was Great Britain. The two most important front companies were the Technology and Development Group (TDG) and Meed International.[12] TDG was set up by Dr. Safa al-Habubi, an Iraqi engineer and former head of the Nasr State Establishment for Mechanical Industries. Meed International was set up by an Iraqi national, Anis Mansur, and a British national, Roy Ricks. TDG's most important action was the purchase of the British machine tool company, Matrix Churchill Ltd.

In fact, the British government was aware of the role of Matrix Churchill in the Iraqi procurement network. This came out in the November 1992 trial of three former Matrix Churchill officials, who were charged with violating export guidelines. The prosecution's case collapsed, however, when it was revealed that the British government had secretly decided to allow the company to continue its activities for two reasons: (1) the Trade Department argued that exports of machine tools by Matrix Churchill should continue lest other countries, such as West Germany, France, Italy, and Switzerland would supplant Great Britain's role in the Iraqi market; and (2) MI5, the British counter-intelligence agency, was using Matrix Churchill as a means of acquiring intelligence information on Iraq's military procurement network and its weapons programs.[13]

Company to Company Agreements

A number of Iraqi state-owned companies negotiated directly with foreign companies for equipment or technology transfers. These companies were either a part of the Iraqi military-industrial infrastructure, or they were front companies set up by the Military Industries Commission (which became, in 1986, part of MIMI). These companies were used to provide cover or false *bona fides* for ultimate end-uses in the military industries.

The Industrial Projects Company and the Technical Consulting Company were two such companies which furthered this strategy. The Industrial Projects Co. was actually set up by MIMI Minister Husayn Kamil Hasan, at the direction of President Saddam Husayn, as a procurement organization.[14] Also included in this category is the University of Mosul, which acted as a conduit for material and technology transfers for the Sa'ad 16 missile complex. Mosul University was probably one the best covers for Iraqi technology acquisitions, since it would take a very suspicious company official, intelligence analyst, or customs agent to suspect a major academic center of being engaged in questionable activities.

Espionage

Iraqi intelligence agents covertly and overtly tried to buy restricted technology in foreign countries, either directly or by paying commissions to foreign nationals. Agents also stole the technology; sometimes they did both.

The Iraqi government also used second-party espionage to acquire technology. The most notable example was the Egyptian operation initiated by Egyptian Defense Minister Abu Ghazala, which involved an Egyptian-American rocket scientist, 'Abd al-Qadi Hilmi, who was employed by the American Aerojet Company.[15] Hilmi smuggled missile blueprints and restricted materials from the U.S. to Egypt for the joint Egyptian/Argentine/Iraqi *Condor II/Badr 2000* missile program. Hilmi was ultimately arrested in June 1988 and convicted of trying to illegally export carbon-carbon, a restricted material used to make rocket nose cones, to Egypt. Abu Ghazala was later "retired" by the Egyptian government. However, it can be assumed that Egypt shared the fruits of its operation with Iraq, either by direct transfer or by virtue of its cooperation in the *Badr 2000* program.

Recruitment

The seventh acquisition strategy, which involved Iraqi recruitment of thousands of foreign scientists, engineers, and technicians, is not usually considered to be within the realm of technology. This would be a grievous oversight, for personnel of this type are "technology" at its most basic and its most esoteric.

The Iraqi military-industrial infrastructure was based on a large, well-educated and talented cadre of *Iraqi* scientists and engineers. Many, if not most of them, had studied and trained in top universities in Western and Eastern Europe, the United States and the former Soviet Union. In an interview broadcast on American television on *CBS 60 Minutes* in November

1991, David Kay, of the International Atomic Energy Agency (IAEA), said some "world class physics" had been carried out by Iraqi scientists in their nuclear program.

Among these Iraqis are such outstanding people as Lt. Gen. 'Amer Rashid al-'Ubaydi and Lt. Gen. Dr. 'Amer Hamudi Hasan al-Sa'di (sometimes referred to by foreign companies that dealt with them as "the two Amers"). Al-'Ubaydi was Deputy Minister of Industry and Military Industrialization, and headed the Iraqi aerospace and electronics projects. Al-Sa'di was the First Deputy Minister for Industry and Military Production, responsible for the day-to-day management of the Military Production Authority. Given a degree of autonomy that was unprecedented and unimaginable anywhere else in Iraq by MIMI Minister Husayn Kamil Hasan (who was also a son-in-law of President Husayn), they were responsible for creating an amazingly sophisticated industry in an amazingly short time.

Nevertheless, it would still have been impossible to achieve a fraction of their accomplishments without the services of thousands of foreign expatriates. In what was still a Third World country of only 18 million people, Iraq simply did not have the educated and trained people to fulfill Saddam's vast ambitions in the missile, nuclear, biological, and chemical weapons fields.

The foundation for Iraq's recruitment program was laid in 1974 with the formation of a three-man committee headed by then Vice President Saddam Husayn, Vice Premier 'Adnan Hamdani, and Chief of Staff General 'Adnan Khayrullah. Their aim was to establish an Iraqi program to produce weapons of mass destruction, starting with chemical weapons. This was later expanded to include nuclear and biological weapons, as well as an indigenous armaments industry. The committee contracted with a Palestinian non-profit organization based in Beirut, Lebanon, called Arab Projects and Developments (APD). APD's task was to recruit thousands of Arab scientists, engineers, and technicians around the world for the Iraqi program.[16]

In 1979, APD folded when Beirut succumbed even further to the Lebanese civil war. Moreover, by 1989, only Saddam Husayn remained alive from the original three-man committee. He had executed Hamdani in July 1979 and Khayrullah, who was also his cousin and had become his son-in-law, died in "an unfortunate helicopter accident" in April 1989. But the pattern and scope of recruitment initiated by APD continued, although it was now expanded to recruit anyone who was interested in and needed by Iraq's military-industrial infrastructure. The personnel came from everywhere, not just from the Arab world. Iraq was willing to pay three, four, or five times the going salary to get what it wanted—just as it did when it came to equipment or technology.

Iraqi Missiles and Weapons of Mass Destruction

With the exception of China, Iraq had the most ambitious program for the development of nuclear, biological, and chemical weapons in the Third World during the 1980s. Marrying such weapons to its ballistic missiles would have made eminent sense, given the missiles' inaccuracy (see below concerning chemical weapons) and Saddam's ambitions to make Iraq at least a regional power. In fact, Saddam's scientists and engineers were engaged in such a program when the Kuwait war broke out.

The inspection teams of the IAEA and have generally concluded that Iraq was only 12–18 months from constructing at least one nuclear device when hostilities started. Since most estimates before the war said that it would take Iraq at least another five to ten years to build an atomic bomb, the revelations of actual Iraqi progress in the nuclear field were astonishing and dismaying. It was an appalling failure of intelligence and applied non-proliferation.

It would not have required much more time to sufficiently downsize the bomb's components to mount it on one of the larger Iraqi missiles, such as the *Al-'Abid* or *Al-Tammuz,* or to harden it to stand the stresses of ballistic flight. The IAEA and UNSCOM inspection teams have discovered Iraqi records indicating that most of the theoretical work had already been done, and only awaited development and testing.

Iraq seems to have been well along in its development of chemical warheads for its missiles. Again, however, Saddam jumped the gun in his invasion of Kuwait, for advancement in development did not mean workable weapons. One of the most prominent unanswered questions of the Kuwait war was, why didn't Iraq use chemical warheads on the missiles that it fired at Israel and Saudi Arabia? The simple answer seems to be that Iraq had not yet developed the technology for doing so.

Producing a workable chemical warhead for a ballistic missile is a delicate and complex engineering task.[17] Chemical agents in either liquid or slurry form contained in a warhead will cause significant deviations in the flight path of a missile. Given the inherent inaccuracy of the SCUD-B, and the Iraqi-produced *Al-Husayn* and *Al-'Abbas* missiles, this was not a small problem. Another problem that must be solved is the design and production of fuzes that will detonate the warhead at altitudes which will vary, depending on the agent. Different agents require different concentrations and spreads to maximize their effectiveness. The warhead must detonate at the proper altitude, or the agent dispersal will be ineffective.

An Iraqi engineer who claimed to have formerly worked in the *Al-Husayn* and *Al-'Abbas* missile programs, and who claimed that he was still briefed irregularly on the Iraqi missile program by military officials, said in a February 1991 interview that Iraq had still not succeeded in manufacturing chemical warheads for its ballistic missiles.[18] The engineer said that

Saddam Husayn had called for an "immediate" solution to the existing difficulties with fitting the missiles with poison gas. He described Saddam's threat to launch SCUD missiles filled with poison gas against Israel as "a mere poker game at this point."

The engineer stressed that the technical difficulties involved the "relative inaccuracy of the SCUD missiles." The SCUD attacks on Israel had shown that there was a "large deviation" between the target and the object that was hit. However, this must not happen in the event of a poison gas attack, "because such an attack must not hit Jordan." He added that it was difficult to attach a heavy gas container to a warhead without causing a ballistic deviation. He also noted that there were problems in the area of electronics, which may have been a reference to the safing and fuzing problem.

The interview, which was published in the West German newspaper, *Frankfurter Allgemeine,* was apparently either overlooked or ignored at the time. We have not been able to find a credible source, official or unofficial, who could or would give an adequate explanation for this oversight.

UN inspection teams did discover 30 missile warheads that were either filled with chemical agents or were to be used as chemical warheads.[19] They were never tested and it is not known if they would have worked. Fourteen of the warheads were filled with a mixture of isopropanol and cyclohexanol. The organophosphorus component (DF) required to produce the nerve agent would be added only just prior to use. The resulting agent would have resulted in an "Iraqi cocktail" of the nerve agents GB and GF. This was the famous "binary" weapon that Saddam referred to in his flamboyant and inflammatory speech of 2 April 1990, when he threatened that he would "burn half of Israel with his binary weapons." The other sixteen warheads were filled with a mixture of nerve agents GB and GF.

The question does arise as to why these warheads were not fitted on some of the missiles that were actually fired at Israel and Saudi Arabia during the Gulf war. There would have been no better time to flight test them, and Saddam's general recklessness does not indicate that he had any compunctions against using them, at least against Israel. The Iraqi missile attacks against Israel were primarily a political tactic aimed at breaking off the Arab partners from the Allied coalition. The missile attacks were not successful in goading Israel into attacking Iraq, but a chemical attack, even if unsuccessful, might have been a sufficient provocation.

There are three possible answers to this question. First, that the order actually did go out, but because of the almost total collapse of the Iraqi communications network, it did not reach operational units. Second, the order might have gotten through but, as was possibly the case in Kuwait, the officers on the ground pretended that they had not received the orders. Finally, it has been suggested that the Israeli nuclear deterrent might have succeeded in staying Saddam's hand in this case.[20]

Even if Iraq had fired some of its missiles with the above-mentioned warheads at Israel or Saudi Arabia during the war, and even if they had worked, their *military* effectiveness would have been minimal. For many reasons that are beyond the scope of this chapter, it is really misleading to include chemical weapons in the category of "weapons of mass destruction." Furthermore, ballistic missiles are a very cost-*ineffective* means of delivering chemical weapons, given their inaccuracy and relatively small payloads.[21] Nevertheless, they would make splendid terror weapons against civilian populations, which may, after all, be all that Saddam requires.

Structure

There is little to say in the Iraqi context with regard to export licensing regulations and procedures and relevant governmental actors in the export licensing process. They simply did not exist, because Iraq was not an exporter of missiles or missile technology. The same largely applies to the role of the private sector, major firms, quasi-governmental actors, and multinationals regarding missile exports. However, even if Iraq had been an exporter of missiles or missile technology, the question would not have applied. In the highly centralized Iraqi economy, the only actors involved would have been government or government-controlled agencies. Even the Technical Consulting Company and the Industrial Projects Company, which were ostensibly private companies, were actually mere fronts for the Ministry of Industry and Military Industrialization in its military procurement program.

Norms

Iraq had no declared policies regarding missile exports except for a general hostility to restrictions on trade which hindered its drive to establish and expand its missile production program. Undoubtedly the same attitude would have applied in the future had Iraq reached the point where it was willing to sell missiles or missile technology to other countries.

From the Iraqi viewpoint, such restrictions, and specifically the MTCR, were part of an international "Zionist, imperialist conspiracy" to infringe on its sovereignty, maintain Israeli domination in the Middle East, and prevent Iraq from achieving its rightful place as leader of the Arab world. It was probably not a coincidence that Iraq launched its three-stage *Al-'Abid* rocket in September 1989 at the same time that the signatories of the MTCR were meeting in London.

This viewpoint was simply part of the Iraqi *Ba'th* political ideology, which viewed the world in paranoid and Manichean terms. The regime is obsessed with conspiracies, both internal and external, directed against Iraq, the *Ba'th* regime, and Saddam Husayn. The boundaries between reality and imagination in this area have long since ceased to exist in a deliberately fostered atmosphere of suspicion, paranoia, distrust and terror.[22]

As we noted in the "Transactions" section, Iraq set up an enormous world-wide weapons and technology procurement network during the 1980s. In the course of their operations, Iraqi agents and operatives had no compunctions about engaging in illegal and covert activities if necessary. Everything could be justified in an operation that sought to "beg, buy, borrow, or steal" what was sought for its military-industrial infrastructure. As we noted earlier, the Iraqis did not allow anything to stand in the way of success. Whatever it cost, the Iraqis paid, and they did not hesitate to resort to subterfuge, espionage or even murder.

Conclusion

Numerous investigative reports on the Iraqi missile and NBC programs have been published in Western Europe and the United States since 1988. UNSCOM and IAEA inspection teams have discovered and confiscated thousands of Iraqi documents which have revealed much about the activities and cooperation of governments and companies in the build-up of the Iraqi military-industrial complex. Although Iraqi officials have never ceased to hamper and harass the activities of the inspection teams, and much documentation still remains hidden or has been destroyed, the records discovered so far indicate that hundreds of companies around the world overtly and covertly participated in Iraq's military-industrial programs. Dozens of investigations into these activities by various ministries of interior or justice and by public prosecutors or police departments have been taking place in the United States, Great Britain and Germany. Investigations are being carried out by congressional and parliamentary committees and commissions in the United States, Germany and Great Britain. These have raised serious questions of governmental incompetence and cover-ups concerning past dealings with Iraq. Perhaps the most serious of these investigations has concerned the activities of the Atlanta branch of the Italian bank Banca Nazionale del Lavoro, which illegally provided over $2 billion in loans to Iraq to finance purchases of dual-use equipment.

Many company and government officials have expressed shock and surprise concerning these revelations during the past several years. Their reactions have frequently recalled the scene in the movie *Casablanca* in which the French police captain, Louis Renault, exclaimed that he was "shocked, absolutely shocked, to find out that there was gambling going on in this establishment." Seconds later, much to his discomfort, one of the waiters brought the captain his not inconsiderable night's gambling winnings.

Iraq constructed a sophisticated missile program in less than eight years from what might be described as a standing start. It is true that the missiles were based on foreign technology and that the program relied heavily on expatriate workers. However, unlike several other countries that have or had ballistic missile programs, such as Argentina and Egypt, Iraq's missiles had flown, and they were getting better and more sophisticated by 1991.

Perhaps ironically, the development of Iraq's program had much in common with the U.S. and Soviet missile programs during the 1940s and 1950s, in that all had the "Made in Germany" label on them. They all relied heavily on outside materials—for the Americans and Soviets, it was captured German V-2 rockets; for the Iraqis it was SCUD missiles obtained from the Soviet Union, China, and North Korea. The SCUD itself was a direct descendant of the V-2. They also all relied heavily on German scientists and engineers, though from different generations.

Iraq's recruitment of unemployed German and Brazilian aerospace and nuclear engineers and technicians for its missile and nuclear programs during the 1980s does not bode well for the control of proliferation in these fields in the future. The end of the Cold War and collapsing economies in the former Warsaw Pact countries have made available thousands of Soviet and East European aerospace and nuclear engineers and scientists. A lesser number from the West will also be looking for employment as defense budgets decline.

Meanwhile, the destruction of Iraq's military-industrial infrastructure has also made thousands of well-educated and well-trained Iraqi scientists, engineers and technicians available to this international market. If they want to continue working in their chosen fields, they presumably will have to leave Iraq and go to countries that are running their own missile and NBC weapons programs. This is a problem that is not covered under the long-term UN monitoring regime, and it also does not bode well for the future of controlling missile and NBC weapons proliferation.

Iraq's belligerence and minimal cooperation with UNSCOM and the IAEA since the end of Desert Storm also indicate that Saddam Husayn still contemplates rebuilding Iraq's capabilities to produce ballistic missiles and weapons of mass destruction. Iraqi actions point to a policy of wearing down the resolve of the international community so that the long-term monitoring regime envisioned under UNSC 687 will either be withdrawn or so emasculated that Iraq will be able to resume its prewar activities with minimal interference.

Saddam Husayn might also take a page out of his German mentors' manual and use a strategy that was carried out by the German Ministry of War following World War I.[23] Under the terms of the Treaty of Versailles, Germany was forbidden from possessing or constructing U-boats, tanks, chemical weapons, and military aircraft, such as fighters and bombers. However, during the 1920s, the German Ministry of War, without the knowledge of the rest of the government, engaged in research, development and production in these fields in a number of foreign countries, including the Soviet Union and the Netherlands. In the 1920s, German naval engineers in Holland designed and built submarines for the navies of Argentina, Brazil, Finland, Spain, and Turkey.[24] German engineers and scientists went to the Soviet Union where they helped design tanks, military aircraft and chemical weapons. German advisers to Chinese warlords also made sure that orders by their employers for commercial aircraft went to German firms. When Germany rearmed in the 1930s, the German scientists and engineers who had worked on these secret foreign projects returned to Germany, and quickly re-established R&D and production facilities in formerly forbidden areas.

In fact, these secret German activities were not so secret after all; reports on these activities were duly filed during the 1920s and early 1930s by attachés to their respective ministries in Great Britain, France and the United States. However, the governments which should have been concerned chose to look the other way, whether they could have done anything or not. The rest is history. The precedent is particularly disturbing because of the way Western governments chose to look the other way concerning Iraq's activities during the 1980s. Furthermore, despite the supposed lessons of the Iraqi case, Western countries seem to be following almost identical policies concerning *Iran's* missile and NBC weapons programs in the 1990s, in their rush to sell high-tech and dual-use technology to Iran.[25]

Iraq's defeat in the war for Kuwait does not seem to have chastened Saddam Husayn at all. In fact, his continued survival, as well as that of his regime, has apparently allowed Saddam to believe that he actually won the war. His continued belligerence toward the international community, his lack of cooperation with the UN and IAEA, and the public revival of Iraqi claims to Kuwait in the fall of 1992 all support such a conclusion. Despite his "victory," he is obsessed with taking revenge on his enemies, while his megalomaniacal ambitions for leadership of the Arab world are apparently undiminished.

When the first draft of this chapter was written in the fall of 1991, we predicted that Saddam might try to follow a strategy similar to the German example between the world wars on the basis of two assumptions: that Saddam would remain in power, and that he would try to do everything he could to get around the restrictions imposed by UNSC Resolution 687. Nearly a year and a half later, Saddam is still very much in power and Iraq has done and continues to do everything it can to get around UN restrictions and demands. Moreover, there have been unconfirmed reports that Iraq has been secretly setting up operations in Algeria, Jordan, Morocco, and Tunisia to purchase arms and equipment and continue its forbidden weapons programs.[26]

It would seem that Prince Metternich's remark about the restored Bourbon monarchy in France could be applied both to Iraq *and* to the countries that so willingly supplied its needs before the Kuwait war: "They have learned nothing and they have forgotten nothing." Therefore, Iraq (and Iran) should not be discounted when the problem of missile proliferation is raised in the future.

Notes

1. I would like to thank Christopher Scheithauer, for his assistance in the research for this paper, and Seth Carus, Bill Elliott, Charles Flowerree, Ben Garrett, Leo Laughlin, and James Leonard for their helpful comments.

2. See W. Seth Carus, *Ballistic Missiles in the Third World: Threat and Response* (Washington, DC: Center for Strategic and International Studies; and New York: Praeger, 1990); Janne E. Nolan, *Trappings of Power: Ballistic Missiles in the Third World* (Washington, DC: The Brookings Institution, 1991), pp. 52-8 and 81-6; and Uzi Rubin, "Iraq and the Ballistic Missile Scare," *Bulletin of the Atomic Scientists*, October 1990.

3. Simon Henderson, *Instant Empire: Saddam Hussein's Ambition for Iraq* (San Francisco: Mercury House, Inc., 1991), p. 126.

4. Iraqi News Agency, Baghdad, in Arabic, 1 May 1989, as translated in *FBIS-NES*-89-083, 2 May 1989.

5. Alan George, "Flight of the Condor," *The Middle East*, April 1989.

6. "My Cousin in Baghdad," *Der Spiegel*, 28 January 1991, as translated in *FBIS-WEU*-91, 30 January 1991.

7. *Ibid.*

8. See transcript of *Condor-II*: Windrem television show, 28 April 1989.

9. See "Sa`ad 16: Iraq's Military `Business Park'," *MidEast Markets*, 1 May 1989, and "Iraq Goes It Alone on Condor II," *MidEast Markets*, 15 May 1989.

10. For example, see "With God's Help," *Der Spiegel*, 15 October 1990, as translated in *FBIS-WEU*-90-200, 16 October 1990.

11. *Middle East Defense News*, Vol. 4, No. 5/6, 17 December 1990.

12. See "Iraqi Arms Purchasing: A Network in Europe Revealed," *MidEast Markets*, 18 September 1989; Alan George, "Iraq's London Procurement Fronts," *Defence*, December 1989; Tim Kelsey, "Crisis in the Gulf: The Men Who Made Saddam Dangerous: The Procurement Network Was Rarely Intercepted; Risks and Rewards Were High," *The Independent*, 26 August 1990; and Frederick Kempe, "Germans Had Big Role in Helping Iraq Arm, Internal Report Shows: Minister Cites Sales of Gear That Let Hussein Create Chemical, Other Weapons; Firms Knowledge is at Issue," *The Wall Street Journal*, 2 October 1990.

13. Eugene Robinson, "Spy Says British Knew of Iraqi Arms Plans: MI5 Man Testifies in Rare Breach of Secrecy," *Washington Post*, 31 October 1992; John Steele and Philip Johnston, "Inquiry Urged After Collapse of Arms Trial," *The Daily Telegraph*, 10 November 1992; and Eugene Robinson and R. Jeffrey Smith, "Profits Lured Britain to Accept Iraqi Deals: Papers Note U.S. Role in Arms-Related Sales," *Washington Post*, 24 November 1992.

14. Insight Team, "The Trail of Secrets: Revealed: How a Scientist Unwittingly Helped Iraqis Perfect Their Atom Bomb," *London Sunday Times*, 16 December 1990.

15. "US Scientist Receives Four-Year Sentence," *Jane's Defence Weekly*, 16 December 1989.

16. Adel Darwish and Gregory Alexander, *Unholy Babylon: The Secret History of Saddam's War*, (New York: St. Martin's Press, 1991), pp. 102-5.

17. Steven J. Zaloga, "No Chemical Scuds?" *Armed Forces Journal International*, March 1991.

18. "Use of Scud With Poison Gas Still Impossible," *Frankfurter Allgemeine*, 4 February 1991, as translated in *FBIS-NES*-91-024, 5 February 1991.

19. Rolf Ekeus, "Report by the Executive Chairman of the Special Commission Established by the Secretary-General Pursuant to Paragraph 9(b)(i) of Security Council Resolution 687 (1991)": S/23165, 25 October 1991, p. 28.

20. Johan Molander, Special Adviser to the Chairman, UN Special Commission on Iraq, in talk before the Committee for National Security, Washington, DC, 13 November 1991.

21. Julian Perry Robinson, "Chemical Proliferation in Perspective," in Trevor Findlay, ed., *Chemical Weapons & Missile Proliferation: With Implications for the Asia/Pacific Region* (Boulder & London: Lynne Rienner Publishers, 1991), pp. 27-32.

22. For an excellent description of this atmosphere, see Samir al-Khalil, *Republic of Fear: The Politics of Modern Iraq* (Berkeley: University of California Press, 1989), Chapter 2: "A World of Fear."

23. Barton Whaley, *Covert German Rearmament, 1919-1939: Deception and Misperception* (Columbia, MD: 1981).

24. David Miller, *Submarines of the World* (New York: Salamander Books, 1991), p. 69.

25. Steve Coll, "Technology From West Floods Iran: Equipment Intended for Civilian Projects Has Military Uses," *Washington Post*, 10 November 1992; Steve Coll, "German Exports Helping Iran Rebuild, Rearm: Bonn Approves 80% of Requests to Sell Tehran High-Tech Goods," *Washington Post*, 6 December 1992.

26. For example, see "He's Up to His Old Tricks Again," *Time*, 30 December 1991, which reported on an article published in the London-based newsletter, *Africa Confidential*. According to the newsletter, Iraq had set up an arms-manufacturing and arms-acquisition operation in Tunisia. Furthermore, State Department officials said that "Iraq was using Tunisia as a clearinghouse for black-market weapons purchases to confound the United Nations team monitoring Iraq's chemical and nuclear arms program."

9

India: Emerging Missile Power

Timothy V. McCarthy[1]

After devoting large sums of scarce financial resources to build its rocket expertise, India is now poised to enter the select club of states having both a robust civilian space industry and viable "missile-based" defenses. With its increasing capabilities to design, build and test missiles and nuclear weapons, India emerges as a possible 21st century world power, whose strategic policies must be taken into account by other, more mature, nuclear and missile states. India also emerges as a potential supplier of sophisticated missile technologies whose export behavior could affect the maintenance and viability of existing nonproliferation regimes. How and why India has become a missile power are the central questions this study seeks to examine.

This chapter consists of three sections. The first examines the history of the Indian missile program and assesses its current status and capabilities. The second section analyses New Delhi's motivations for missile development. The final section looks at the capacity and likelihood for India to emerge as a supplier of missile and space technologies. Included in this discussion is a review of economic and other incentives for India to enter the world's missile market, India's perceptions of the Missile Technology Control Regime (MTCR) and India's export control policies and structures.

History and Current Status of the Missile Program

From initial studies and research to the wide variety of missile systems currently in development, Indian efforts to design and build surface-to-surface missiles (SSMs) span nearly three decades. Lacking resources (and in many cases an established military requirement from the armed forces), India's military R&D establishment first sought basic knowledge in rocketry and to increase awareness among service personnel of missilery and its military applications. With these very basic first steps, each successive phase of New Delhi's missile development effort has involved greater resources, more specific system development goals and closer cooperation with service end-users. Today, India is ready to deploy its first short-range ballistic missile (SRBM), is capable of fielding a 2500km-range medium-range ballistic missile (MRBM), and has the technological infrastructure to undertake development of intercontinental ballistic missiles (ICBMs) and cruise missiles.

Indian SSM research began in the early 1960s under the direction of the Defence Research and Development Organization (DRDO), which was established on January 1, 1958.[2] A department of the Ministry of Defence, DRDO is the primary source for all Indian military R&D, with a mandate to "enable the nation [to] become self-reliant in weapons, weapon systems and equipment through research in wide-ranging areas of modern technology."[3] Maj. Gen. B.D. Kapur, DRDO's first Chief Controller, played an integral role in India's initial missile efforts. Kapur helped establish both a foreign training program for Indian scientists (which included the study of space and rockets) and a curriculum of basic rocketry science for service personnel at the Institute of Armament Studies.

Following an "information-gathering" trip to the United States in early 1962, where he toured R&D centers, SAC bases, missile training sites, and NASA facilities, Kapur stopped in Switzerland to meet with representatives from the Zurich-based firm Contraves. The meeting produced an Indo-Swiss agreement to design and manufacture an intermediate range surface-to-air missile (SAM) known as "Project Indigo."[4] However, at the same time Kapur was meeting with the Swiss, New Delhi was also negotiating with the Soviet Union for purchase of SA-2 SAMs. The Indians opted for the Soviet system and "Project Indigo," which would have been a first attempt to actually build a missile system, was canceled.[5]

Although it never came to fruition, "Project Indigo" did provide impetus for a more broad-based Indian missile research program.[6] That effort was institutionalized in a Kapur-drafted plan, approved by the Defence Committee of the Cabinet sometime in mid-1962, to create a "missile establishment" in India. Located at the "Special Weapons Establishment" in Hyderabad, the plan called for a group of scientists "to study missilery so that they could advise the services at the appropriate time."[7] There is no evidence that developing a deployable SSM was one of the goals of the project. Initially directed by Air Commodore V. Ganeshan, the project began by launching experimental rockets to study their ballistic behavior. In 1963, "a number of two-stage rockets" were fired from Hyderabad and "work on the development of rocket propellant was carried out at the [DRDO] explosives laboratory."[8]

In 1965, the ad-hoc Electronics Committee provided the impetus for sustaining these early developments. Headed by Dr. Vikram Sarabhai, then Chairman of the Atomic Energy Commission and later the first head of the Indian Space Research Organization (ISRO), the Committee concluded that India should move forward with a missile production program. The Committee noted that since a base for rocket manufacture had already been established with licensed production of the French *Centaure* Sounding Rocket[9], work should proceed in developing propellants and guidance systems.[10]

The Devil Program

Because it involved a greater concentration of manpower and financial resources than previous research efforts and was the first attempt to develop an operational SSM, the "Devil Program" can be considered the next significant milestone in New Delhi's missile program.[11] The project began in the early 1970s and involved Indian attempts to convert SA-2s into SSMs. Reportedly involving over 880 experts, the project developed two liquid propulsion rocket motors by 1974. However, following the failure of several prototype systems,[12] the project was canceled in 1978. The liquid-fuel motors developed under the "Devil Program" later became the basis for the propulsion systems on India's first operational SSM, the *Prithvi*.

Failure of the "Devil Program" was based on several factors.[13] The project was "ill-conceived" according to one Indian official, as it was headed by an Air Force officer with "good political connections" but who did not have the support of the military bureaucracy. No General Staff Qualitative Requirements, or GSQRs, were issued for the project, meaning that the armed services did not envision a specific need for the system and therefore did not advocate its development. Moreover, the Rs 2-3 crore (US $700,000–1,000,000)[14] per year devoted to the project (though greater in relative terms than earlier projects) was not enough to create the critical mass of a technical and manufacturing infrastructure to develop a deployable missile.

The Integrated Guided Missile Development Program (IGMDP)

In July 1983, New Delhi authorized a Rs 380 crore ($133 million) Integrated Guided Missile Development Program (IGMDP) to make India independent in missile design and production. The plan, which has now received a total of over Rs 788 crore ($275 million), involves the development of four missile systems: *Trishul*, a short-range SAM; *Akash*, a medium-range SAM, *Nag*, a "fire-and-forget" anti-tank guided missile; and *Prithvi*, a battlefield support SSM. Development of *Agni*, an IRBM, is being undertaken "concurrently" with the other IGMDP systems.[15]

Although the IGMDP draws upon the knowledge gained and technologies developed under India's earlier missile efforts, it represents a clear departure from those undertakings in several respects. The project signals a dramatic change in the way missile research is done in India for it is a well-funded, broad-based effort, involving not only the defense laboratories but also technical institutions, universities, Defence Ministry ordnance factories, and public and private sector firms. The IGMDP also represents the first Indian attempt to develop several missile systems simultaneously. Moreover, the closer cooperation between the services (especially the Army) and the R&D institutions created specific system development goals at the onset of the project. Therefore, apart from the missiles that are developed within the program, the IGMDP's enduring legacy may well be its creation of a vast missile design and production establishment within India that is more integrated with and responsive to the needs of the armed forces.

Like previous Indian programs, the IGMDP is a DRDO effort, with substantive research and design work being carried out by the Defense Research and Development Laboratory (DRDL). Dr. A.P.J. Kalam, DRDO's director, heads the missile development program, having recently replaced Dr. V.S. Arunachalam, who held the DRDO directorship for over a decade. A Rs 100 crore ($35 million) Research Centre, Immarat (RCI) was built 6km from DRDL for developing advanced missile technologies in cooperation with university scientists. Reportedly, RCI will also incorporate missile production facilities.[16] There are now over a thousand scientists and engineers working on missile-related projects at the two facilities.[17]

Missile flight testing takes place at several sites: six of the first eight *Prithvi* tests took place at the Shriharikota (SHAR) test range, which is under the control of ISRO's Vikram Sarabhai Space Center (VSSC). The first two *Agni* tests were conducted at the Interim Test Range (ITR) facility located at Baliapal in eastern Orissa state. Several of the facilities which form the ISRO Telemetry, Tracking and Command Network (ISTRAC), such as those at SHAR and Car Nicobar island, were used to monitor *Agni*'s maiden launch. U.S.-built INSAT communications satellites, which fall under ISRO's control, were used to transmit *Agni* launch data.[18]

ISRO and DRDO. The use of ISRO's test and tracking facilities reflects the close, though not integral, relationship between the missile program, its related defense production agencies, and the civilian space program. There appears to be significant cooperation in the manufacture of certain key rocket components. In the early 1980s, ISRO signed a memorandum of understanding with the Public Sector Undertaking (PSU, a government-owned firm) Bharat Electronics, Ltd. (BEL), for "technical cooperation in the field of development and production of electronic equipment and components for space applications."[19] BEL is run by the Defense Ministry. Apparently, the agreement established a separate and dedicated production division within BEL.[20] Another PSU, Mishra Dhatu Nigam Ltd. (Midhani), produces maraging steel (M-250) for the Polar Satellite Launch Vehicle's (PSLV) lower stages.[21] Perhaps the most important cooperative relationship ISRO has with any Defense Ministry PSU is with Hindustan Aeronautics, Ltd. (HAL). ISRO funded a dedicated Rs 32 crore ($11 million) facility at HAL's Aerospace Division in Bangalore to manufacture alloy structures and tankages for the PSLV.[22] HAL also "designed and supplied systems" for the Satellite Launch Vehicle (SLV) project[23] while the engine division supplied titanium alloy bottles for the PSLV.[24]

The missile and civilian space program, however, are not sister organizations. U.S. government analyst indicated, "There is unlikely a very close relationship between ISRO and DRDO; they are separate empires although their technological base overlaps."[25] Indeed, they compete for resources. The IGMDP is clearly taking money that otherwise would be used in the civilian program. Meanwhile, it appears that defense has taken precedence over the civilian use of rocket technology. DRDO is recruiting young talent and "visionary scientists" such as Dr. Kalam, formerly head of ISRO's SLV-3 program, away from the ISRO. According to one VSSC employee, ISRO is left with scientists and engineers that are "burnt-out and aging."[26] According to a 1988 U.S. Embassy assessment,

> We believe that most ISRO scientists agree with the official [government of India] policy of keeping separate India's military and civilian rocket programs. They argue that ISRO is not developing military missile technologies in its civilian space program even though certain technologies can be shared by both....They are supported by defense scientists who maintain that using the ISRO rockets would involve major modifications, [and] that they would rather design and are designing military missiles from scratch.[27]

The cable also states that some ISRO scientists believe that "without explicit military backing, ISRO's rocket program will not gain sufficient momentum to achieve its aims." In this view, India's relative weakness in rocket technology is due to its civilian rather than military focus. The U.S. assessment concludes that development of military missiles is not "antagonistic" to a peaceful space program and that it is "natural for scientists and engineers, working on similar problems....to discuss problems and successes [and to share] information about their projects."[28]

The characteristics and implications of the most important delivery systems under development in India are discussed below.

Prithvi. In *Prithvi*, DRDO is upgrading and integrating many previously-developed technologies into a system that compares favorably to other missiles of the SCUD class. At the same time, *Prithvi* development expands India's knowledge base to include, for the first time, series manufacture of a missile whose range exceeds that of standard field artillery.

The *Prithvi* is a single-stage, short-range battlefield support missile that is 10 meters long with a body diameter of 1.1 meters. According to Dr. Kalam, Thirty-four R&D organizations designed and developed the missile and 22 PSUs, ten ordnance factories, and nine private-sector industries are involved in system or subsystem production.[29] Described by Indian scientists as having the "best warhead-to-weight ratio of any missile in its class," *Prithvi* comes in two versions: the 150 km range SS-150 which can carry a 1,000 kg warhead, and the 250 km range SS-250 which can carry a 500 kg warhead.[30] A possible third version, which some analysts speculate is a surface-to-air variant of the same system, is the *Prithvi*-3.[31] The missile's minimum range is reportedly 40 km.[32]

New Delhi authorized *Prithvi* development in July 1983, but actual work began in October 1984 under the direction of Major General V. J. Sundaram, who previously worked on solid fuel propulsion technologies.[33] The system's first flight test was from SHAR on February 25, 1988; at this writing, eight tests have been conducted, the last three from the ITR in Baliapal.[34] According to Kalam, *Prithvi* must undergo at least ten full-range test launches before deployment can begin.[35]

The missile's frame is a locally developed light-weight aluminum alloy, manufactured by Bharat Aluminum Company (BALCO), and the aerodynamic wings are a magnesium-based material. The oxidizer and fuel tanks are also made of aluminum alloy.[36] The propulsion system, an upgraded version of that developed under the earlier SA-2 conversion "Devil Program," consists of two gimbaled and regeneratively cooled engines with programmable total impulse. The system affords flexibility in payload weight and range.[37] *Prithvi* uses a hypergolic liquid fuel combination of red fuming nitric acid oxidant and xylidiene G-fuel—the Solid State Physics Laboratory (SPL) developed India's indigenous G-fuel manufacturing process, and both propellants are now produced at the Explosives Research and Development Laboratory, Pune.[38] The services approved the liquid propellant handling and fueling system for *Prithvi* in 1984–85.[39]

At the heart of *Prithvi*'s guidance and control system is an on-board computer "based on" an Intel 8086 microprocessor.[40] According to Dr. Kalam, *Prithvi*'s strap-down inertial navigation system is also used in the *Agni* IRBM.[41] Per a 1987 agreement, Hindustan Aeronautics Ltd. (HAL) manufactures the DRDL-designed gyroscopes for *Prithvi*. HAL also produces accelerometers for the various IGMDP missile systems.[42] *Prithvi* uses two radars: one modified surveillance radar for targeting and a modified FLY-CATCHER radar for guidance.[43]

During the boost phase, *Prithvi* maneuvers by thrust vector control using the two gimbaled engines, which presumably allows for full attitude control of pitch, yaw and roll movements.[44] Four cruciform delta wings and four stabilizing fins provide control during the free ballistic phase; HAL's Lucknow division produces the actuators used in both phases.[45] DRDL is known to be working on terminal guidance for both *Prithvi* and *Agni*, although development of such a system involves formidable technical, financial, and even testing obstacles.[46] *Prithvi* accuracy approaches a circular error probable (CEP) of 0.1% of range, or 250m at its maximum range of 250 km.[47]

Prithvi can carry several types of warheads, including unitary high explosive, prefragmented, minelets, and cluster munitions. The first static warhead test, probably of the unitary HE type, was conducted at Pokharan, Rajasthan in March 1990.[48] Reportedly, DRDL is studying fuel-air explosive (FAE) warhead feasibility for both *Prithvi* and *Agni*, and it is therefore possible that *Prithvi* will deploy with FAEs.[49] Given the missile's throw-weight, particularly at shorter-ranges, *Prithvi* may also be nuclear-capable.

In a "concurrent production program", facilities for series manufacture were established during *Prithvi*'s developmental flight-test program. Bharat Dynamics Ltd. (BDL)—a Defense Ministry-owned firm located near DRDL in Hyderabad—will build the system, reportedly at a rate of 40–50 missiles per year.[50] Following the failure of the "Devil Program", many of the scientists and engineers working on the project moved to BDL, providing the firm with ample in-house production expertise.[51] BDL began tooling up for system production as early as May 1989 and, according to V.S. Arunachalam, the Army placed orders for *Prithvi* around the time of the missile's second test flight in September 1989.[52] *Prithvi* production costs will be Rs 1.6 crore ($563,000) per missile.[53]

Approximately five to ten percent of *Prithvi*'s components are imported; DRDO currently has enough of these goods in stock to complete "initial" production runs.[54] These imports, according to one analyst, consist primarily of precision sensors, a few special alloys and materials, and microprocessors.[55] Given the history of progress in the Indian missile program, it is safe to assume that many of these components will eventually be produced within the country. Indigenous production of these goods would, at least initially, increase the costs of *Prithvi* and the other IGMDP systems.

DRDO officials say *Prithvi* will deploy with the Army in 1993.[56] Mounted on a 8 x 8 *Kolos Tatra* Transporter Erector Launcher (TEL) produced by Bharat Earth Movers, Ltd., *Prithvi* missiles will be organized in "Heavy Rocket Regiments" consisting of 12–18 TELs, and associated fueling, reload (with perhaps 1 reload missile per TEL), and command equipment.[57] If production targets are met, India could deploy three to five such regiments by 1995.[58]

Prithvi could be employed against static targets such as the large maintenance areas required by Pakistani Army Reserves, command centers,

Pakistani airfields and fixed air defense sites.[59] Such targets would include Pakistan's Kamra and Chalala air bases, the Lahore airfield and the command headquarters at Bahawalpur.[60] Close collaboration between Army and Air Force strike units—which to date is lacking in the Indian armed services—would be required for such missions, *Prithvi* also might be used as a "close support" weapon against reserve formations moving up after armored penetrations.[61] Even in this mode, the effective use of *Prithvi* would prove difficult unless India strengthened its reconnaissance capabilities. Nonetheless, given a nominal 60-minute reaction time[62] and a 60-minute reload time, a *Prithvi* regiment would theoretically be able to deliver 12–18 tons of HE to targets at 150 km range within two hours upon arrival at a pre-surveyed launch site. *Prithvi* will therefore provide the Indian Army with a needed boost in operational firepower, particularly when operating without strike aircraft.

Agni. Like the *Prithvi*, the *Agni* relies on propulsion and motor case technologies developed under previous missile and space programs. However, some new technologies developed for *Agni* (such as an indigenously designed heat shield), as well as the system's intermediate-range capability, are indicative of India's success in its drive toward an increasingly sophisticated missile design infrastructure. *Agni*'s development may also be indicative of a change in what New Delhi views as the appropriate military response to its nuclear- and missile-armed neighbor, the People's Republic of China (PRC).

Agni is a two-stage IRBM with a length of 18.4 meters and a body diameter of 1.3 meters at its widest point. According to Dr. Kalam, *Agni*'s maximum range is 2,500 km with a 1,000 kg warhead, but the missile can carry heavier payloads to 1,500km.[63] The *Agni* project is directed by R. N. Agarwal, and developers had reportedly spent a total of Rs 38 crore ($13 million) on the system by mid-1990.[64]

Following a series of technical delays, *Agni*'s maiden launch was from the ITR in Orissa on May 22, 1989. The missile traveled 1,000 km during its first flight, which was designed to test heat shield, inertial guidance and stage separation technologies.[65] Following two flight postponements in 1990, the missile was tested for the second time on May 29, 1992. Although Indian officials first claimed the test was a success and that the missile followed its projected course exactly, DRDO later acknowledged that the "mission objective of the final maneuvering could not be fulfilled due to the premature ignition and separation of the second stage."[66]

Agni's first stage motor is an exact copy of the proven first stage on ISRO's SLV-3 which, in turn, is based on the design of the U.S. *Scout* rocket.[67] *Agni*'s second stage is a shortened *Prithvi* stage, modified for high-altitude operations.[68] Small thrust control motors are used as an auxiliary propulsion system for keeping the missile stable during its terminal phase.

DRDL designed *Agni*'s control and guidance system in collaboration with the India Institute of Science (Bangalore) under the Joint Advanced Technology Program.[69] The complete guidance package is carried in the missile's re-entry vehicle,[70] and is essentially an upgraded version of that used on the *Prithvi* SSM. The *Agni* proved "embarrassingly accurate" during its first test, landing just one meter from its target point according to one report.[71] If the report is true, the test was very likely a statistical fluke. While Dr. Kalam credits *Agni* with a 60 m CEP,[72] one would expect that the upgraded *Prithvi* guidance package reportedly carried on *Agni* would provide accuracies of roughly 1.5 km at a 1,500 km range or 2.5 km at a 2,500 km range.

Agni's auxiliary propulsion systems could increase these notional accuracies, but the missile would need to be equipped with mid-range course correction and terminal guidance packages to obtain the accuracies claimed by Dr. Kalam and other Indian officials. Some reports do suggest that DRDO is examining satellite navigation (such as GPS) and stellar inertial guidance for mid-course updating.[73] In addition, the Indian Defense Ministry's announcement that *Agni*'s second launch tested "the technology of advanced maneuvers during the re-entry phase to achieve high accuracy"[74] may be a reference to a terminal guidance system. The Indians, however, have not yet given any firm indication of the specific type of terminal guidance they are developing.

Unlike *Prithvi*, *Agni* has no declared user service nor has there been any public announcement regarding production funding.[75] Estimated production cost of a single *Agni* missile is Rs 3 crore ($1 million).[76] A total of three *Agni* development flights were planned at the onset of the project, and it is possible that final production and deployment decisions will be revealed following this initial series of tests. In 1989, Kalam stated that *Agni* could enter series production within five years.[77] According to testimony given by Rear Admiral Edward Sheafer, Director of U.S. Naval Intelligence, India could deploy "some" *Agni* IRBMs by the turn of the century.[78]

Indian officials, however, continue to say *Agni* is a "technology demonstrator" which has not yet been converted into a missile project.[79] According to former Defense Minister K.C. Pant, *Agni* is a means to "test some of the advanced missile technologies developed indigenously....Being an experimental R and D vehicle, the goals of *Agni* are technological."[80] This could be, as some Indian analysts have speculated, a reference to the *Agni* project as an interim step towards developing technologies relevant to a future ICBM.[81] This public ambiguity also serves a political purpose since it imputes a latent Indian IRBM capability—which must be taken into account by any aggressor nation—without actually having to fund full production.[82] In any event, there is little evidence that the foreign powers concerned with New Delhi's growing missile capabilities actually believe such statements. As one respected team of Indian analysts put it, "No sect, clan, tribe or nation which falls under its shadow" will believe *Agni* is a "technology demonstrator."[83]

Perhaps the most controversial element of the *Agni* program is its apparent design purpose: to afford India the capability to deliver nuclear weapons against several important Chinese targets. The 1974 Pokharan test demonstrated India's ability to design nuclear explosives, but New Delhi has since maintained an ambiguous policy regarding weaponization. Nuclear-equipped *Agnis* could provide a deterrent, counter-value capability *vis a vis* China by their ability to credibly threaten the industrial centers of Chengdu, Lanzhou and Xi'an or the space launch facilities at Xichang in Siquan province. Indian aircraft do not have the necessary ranges to reach such targets nor do they offer the assured penetrability of missiles. There are of course a whole range of political and policy issues surrounding an overt Indian nuclear deployment which go beyond the decision to develop the missile itself. What *Agni* does offer is a viable delivery option if and when India decides to move from a fully conventional defense posture with respect to China, to one that incorporates a nuclear deterrent capability.

Indian officials have not publicly made a positive, direct link between *Agni* and nuclear weapons. For instance, following the May 1989 test, Prime Minister Rajiv Gandhi denied that *Agni* was a nuclear delivery system, saying instead that the missile could afford India "the option of developing the ability to deliver non-nuclear weapons with high precision at long ranges."[84] Equipped with mid-course or terminal guidance systems and armed with cluster or large FAE warheads, a missile of this class could provide a deep strike weapon against targets beyond the range of aircraft or where the use of manned bombers would be imprudent.[85] Clearly, China (or Pakistan) would have to take into account New Delhi's conventional retaliatory capability in any plans to attack or threaten to attack the country. It remains in doubt however, whether such conventionally armed *Agnis* could inflict the level of punishment necessary to provide an "assured deterrence" against either power.

Indian ICBM. There is very little public or official information available regarding a potential Indian ICBM. On the same day as *Agni*'s first launch, press reports did claim that Indian defense scientists "would begin work on an ICBM with a range exceeding 5,000 km."[86] While there is no clear evidence that this is the case, Dr. Kalam has said that, "if given the resources and the okay, it is possible for India to build an ICBM" and that India would develop the missile "when required."[87] According to R.N. Agarwal, *Agni*'s guidance system and vehicle structure would be roughly the same for an ICBM although the "stage structure and configuration would have to be changed."[88] Missile analyst Seth Carus suggests that the powerful solid fuel motors developed by ISRO for the PSLV's first stage may be used in an Indian ICBM design.[89]

The strategic and political implications of an Indian ICBM capability outstrip those related to the *Prithvi* SRBM or *Agni* IRBM. First, it is nearly unthinkable that the resource and manpower investment required to develop an ICBM would be dedicated to a long-range *conventional* weapons carrier; no missile of this class has ever been fielded without nuclear warheads. ICBM deployment would therefore be a strong signal of New Delhi's intention to move to an overt or declaratory nuclear weapon posture and hence, provoke an overt nuclear arms race in South Asia. Second, a 5000 km range, nuclear-armed missile—clearly able to target Beijing—would clearly evoke a condition of mutual deterrence between India and the PRC. The strategic relationship between the two powers would be altered irrevocably. Third, an ICBM would extend New Delhi's missile reach throughout southeast and northeast Asia and the Middle East. Although there may be no intention to target these areas, a long-range Indian missile capability would be a cause of concern to regional actors and elicit, at the very least, a negative political backlash against New Delhi.

Short-Range Rockets. Along with its longer-range SSMs, India is developing artillery rockets and multiple-launch rocket systems (MLRS). Work on an indigenous version of the Soviet BM-21 122 mm MLRS began in 1977, and the Defense Ministry chose BDL to produce the new system in 1983–84.[90] DRDL developed the rocket's propellant charge, while the Armament Research and Development Laboratory (ARDE) designed its high-explosive fragmentation warhead.[91] The rocket may also carry an FAE warhead, possibly for use in mine-clearing operations.[92]

The *Pinaca*, a longer-range MLRS, is also in the development stages. According to Dr. Arunachalam, *Pinaca* has had several successful test flights, but more tests are needed before user evaluation trials proceed.[93] Work on the system, which has a 45 km range and a warhead "several times" that of the BM-21, is being undertaken at ARDE.[94]

Indian Cruise Missile. Although India does not currently produce cruise missiles, the Indian navy does deploy Soviet STYX anti-ship cruise missiles on several classes of ships, including its *Kashin* destroyers and *Osa*-class missile boats. During the 1971 war, these missiles proved very effective in attacks on Pakistani ships in Karachi harbor. In a bid to upgrade their anti-ship capabilities, the Indians sought more modern U.S.-made *Harpoon* missiles in the mid-1980s, but the Americans turned down the request.[95]

No cruise-type system is being developed under the IGMDP, although India has considerable experience in developing Remotely Piloted Vehicles (RPV) and Pilotless Target Aircraft (PTA). In the 1970s, India acquired expendable target drones from the United States and 300 man-months of technical consultation on such systems from a German company.[96] Work on a PTA, the *Lakshya*, began in the early 1980s, with launch trials beginning in 1983–84. Initial prototypes were powered by a license-produced Microturbo TRI 60-2 turbojet engine used in the French C-22 PTA, with a BDL RGB-25 JATO rocket booster providing launch assistance.[97] More recent models are powered by HAL's PTAE-7 turbojet engine; these later models apparently use the same JATO booster.[98] The PTA is six meters long with a Mach 0.75–0.85 speed, and can carry a 150 kg payload for one hour. India also produces the *Kapothaka*, a mini-RPV, and a Low-Level Missile Target Drone (LLMT).

DRDO studies of cruise missile technologies are currently underway, but a decision to actually develop such a system has not reached the cabinet level. The problem of lack of available funding must first be overcome before more detailed development begins.[99] The DRDO concept study reportedly envisions a vehicle with GPS-type update and terminal guidance, capable of carrying a 450 kg warhead.[100] This type of system would provide more effective fixed-point targeting than *Prithvi*, but would be vulnerable to air defenses. The Indians could more easily build a rudimentary land-attack missile—for attacks against large area targets—based on the *Lakshya* air frame and a simple inertial guidance system.[101] In the absence of nuclear warheads, however, neither of these first generation Indian cruise missiles would be strategically significant, though they could obviously provide the Army or Air Force with greater targeting and delivery flexibility. Clearly, the proven combat effectiveness of its Soviet STYX missiles provides an incentive for India to develop its own anti-ship missile. When deployed, such systems could have an impact on the naval balance in the Indian Ocean.

Motivations

Indian motivations for initiating and maintaining its missile program may be grouped into two general categories. The first category involves national security and military-strategic considerations, i.e., the relatively straightforward notion that SSM capabilities enhance Indian military power which, in turn, serves either to deter aggression or allow for the more successful prosecution of war should deterrence fail. The second category views the missile program in terms of New Delhi's push for economic, scientific, and technical "self-reliance," a broad-based national strategy that seeks to prevent excessive foreign influence over its political, economic and social well-being. Though separated for analytical purposes, these categories should not be thought of in mutually exclusive terms. India's ability to indigenously design and develop sophisticated weapons systems (such as missiles and combat aircraft) is the product of its long-term strategy to build technical knowledge and scientific manpower. Ultimately, the nation's ability to ensure its own security and to conduct an independent foreign policy is dependent on the degree to which it is self-reliant in defense.[102]

Security Motives

Although its external strategic environment has undergone several changes since independence, India's "traditional defense posture" has consistently centered around the perceived threat emanating from the subcontinent's other regional powers, Pakistan and China.[103] India has fought three major wars with Pakistan; religious, ethnic and territorial disputes continue to be a source of conflict between the two states. India has also fought a war with China. Unresolved border questions involving territory in north and northeastern India contribute to tension between New Delhi and Beijing. Both qualitative and quantitative increases in defense capabilities inject an additional element of friction into South Asia's most important triangular relationship.

Of course, changes in the global political environment have had an impact on India's security posture and defense policies. Sino-American rapprochement (along with the Bangladesh crisis) brought closer relations between the Soviet Union and India, as exemplified by their 1971 Friendship Treaty. More recently, the Soviet invasion of Afghanistan emphasized strategic commonalties between Washington, Islamabad and Beijing on the one hand and Moscow and New Delhi on the other. Moreover, arms races and tension in the Middle East, Vietnam's military campaigns in Southeast Asia, Chinese involvement in that region, and the threat of nuclear proliferation on the subcontinent contribute to New Delhi's perception of an "extended strategic environment" and serve to complicate and broaden more traditional security concerns.[104]

To what extent is India's missile program driven by its perception of threat from the external strategic environment? With respect to Pakistan, two connections may be made. First, it is reasonable to assume that Pakistan's purchase of F-16s and other sophisticated weaponry—as part of two June 1981 arms agreements with Washington—did not escape the eyes of IGMDP planners. Given the fact that reactive acquisitions tend to characterize the Indian-Pakistani security nexus,[105] this significant increase in Islamabad's military capabilities must have provided a stimulus for India's missile, as well as other defense programs.[106] In the same vein, Pakistan's nascent missile capability may also add to India's own perceived missile requirements.[107] Second, although Indian officials assert (probably correctly), that the country has the capability to defeat Pakistan at every level of conventional military confrontation,[108] the addition of battlefield missiles such as the *Prithvi* further diversifies Indian strike force capabilities.

Simply put, *Prithvi* and other SSMs under development strengthen India's ability to fight and win a war with Pakistan.

India's threat perception from China is two-fold: a direct military threat (which includes nuclear-armed missiles), and perhaps a more likely scenario, the potential for Chinese political, logistical or even military intervention on Islamabad's behalf in the event of another Indo-Pakistani war. Indian concern over Chinese nuclear and missile capabilities is nothing new. Shortly after assuming office in 1966, Chief of the Army Staff Gen. P. P. Kumaramangalan stated that given the military threat from China and its growing nuclear capability, "We should go in for missiles; there is no question about that."[109] Public statements by at least some retired and active duty Indian officers during the 1970s echoed Kumaramangalan's thinking about missile development.[110]

China continued to upgrade its missile capabilities throughout the 1980s, including the deployment of the JL-1 SLBM. Many Indian military officials and analysts say their own missile program is largely a response to the PRC's growing capability, as well as Chinese missile deployments in Tibet.[111] The potential for nuclear-armed *Agnis* or ICBMs to provide a credible counter-strike in the face of nuclear threats—a capability India has sought since the mid-1960s—may be the ultimate motivation for the missile program. Conventionally armed IRBMs may also be a means to convince the Chinese that assistance to Pakistan during a conflict with India would not be without costs.

More generally, Indian military planners are well-aware of the technological revolution in modern warfare and the integral role missiles play on the modern battlefield. This recognition provides its own compulsion for indigenous development of anti-tank, air defense and surface-to-surface missiles. The IGMDP, in the words of K.C. Pant, aims at "building up our missile-based defenses."[112] Though not fully articulated, at least in the public literature, the concept of "missile-based defenses" clearly ties India's overall military capabilities to its progress in developing and integrating missile systems into the services. The considerable resources devoted to the IGMDP indicate that New Delhi intends to keep pace with the technological revolution in warfare.

The Gulf War and the defeat of Iraq adds an immediacy to the missile program on at least two fronts. The war, according to Dr. Kalam, proved the cost-effectiveness of missile systems by demonstrating their ability to cause considerable damage to strategic installations.[113] Moreover, according to one Indian analyst, the war emphasized India's and the Third World's strategic vulnerability *vis a vis* the United States and other militarily advanced nations. This perception reinforces the need to acquire even more advanced technologies and provides an incentive to increase military R&D, especially in the area of ballistic missiles.[114]

Self-Reliance

The objective of self-reliance appeals to a nation that detests being in a position of dependence as a result of its colonial history. "Self-reliance" does have a distinctive ideological connotation in the Indian context, but it may also be seen as one means to achieve the substantive objectives of economic and technological development, and the insulation of Indian foreign policy from external pressures. The Indian missile programs both reflect and are inspired by the push for industrial and economic self-reliance.

Soon after the independence of India, the nationalist leadership decided to license-produce or indigenously develop defense and other equipment to the greatest extent possible.[115] Reliance on high-technology and defense imports, they reasoned, could only lead to their country's continued economic inequality relative to the developed nations. India has therefore focused on high-tech sectors such as atomic science, space applications—and in defense—aircraft and missiles once thought the preserve of only the most advanced countries. DRDO's 1962 plan calling for the study of missilery is indicative of this tendency. There was no perceived threat from China nor was there an immediate threat from Pakistan; strictly military-strategic factors did not provide the plan's motivating force.[116]

The IGMDP does not have an overt economic development motive analogous to the space or nuclear programs. But success in high-technology defense industries does have a positive impact on other productive activities in the economy. This spillover effect provides the country with skilled scientific manpower,[117] a "technology culture," and direct technology transfer from one sector to the next. Maintaining Indian abilities in specific fields, (i.e., space or missilery) generates confidence and technological acumen which contributes to other, less-advanced, sectors of the economy.[118] For instance, in 1991 Defense Minister Pawar decided to open defense laboratories to Indian industry "as a way to develop new technologies and to increase the quality of their products." [119] Pawar intends for the culture of high quality and reliability found in these labs to be passed on to the private sector. As discussed below, ISRO has a similar policy of directing advanced technologies to the private sector.

Defense and industrial self-reliance has obvious implications for India's conduct of foreign policy. Former Prime Minster Indira Gandhi once described Indian non-alignment as "a policy not an objective. The objective is freedom of judgment and of action to safeguard the nation's basic interest."[120] One operational goal of non-alignment is to inhibit the ability of developed states to derive political benefit from technology transfer.[121] India thus views indigenous weapons production as a means to insulate itself from political pressures which foreign suppliers could exert.[122]

India's reliance on external sources of high-technologies, including those related to missile and space development, has in many cases reinforced this view. In the late 1980s, stringent restrictions were attached to Indian use of a U.S.-built Cray XMP-14 super computer, and in July 1990 the export license for another Cray was denied.[123] More recently, Washington applied sanctions on India after ISRO purchased cryogenic engine technology from Russia, and then announced that it would deny export applications for goods going to Indian space or missile-related entities.[124] As long as the missile and space programs rely on certain high-technology imports, they will remain vulnerable to an exporter's ability to attach conditions to their supply. New Delhi views such sanctions as a clear attempt to modify their own internal and external behavior, and that vulnerability compels greater self-reliance in programs integral to the defense and development of the country. The IGMDP is an attempt to protect India from dependence on outside, unreliable suppliers.[125]

One final aspect of self-reliance expressed in some Indian circles is that an indigenous missile program—and the high-technology goods it develops and incorporates—increases Indian foreign policy flexibility and impact. DRDO's Dr. Kalam reasons that the advanced industrial countries are only willing to supply "second-hand" technology, and with such technology "...you can never hope to catch-up or have access to state of the art equipment; you will always be behind."[126] He believes that in world affairs "technology respects technology and strength respects strength."[127] Indian power is dependent on its *own* ability to make progress in high-tech sectors such as missiles and space. One practical effect of the missile program, notes one Indian analyst, is that *Agni*'s development will lead to greater democratization of the international decision-making process since there now can be no future arms control negotiations without New Delhi's participation.[128]

Exports and Export Controls

India does not yet export missiles, nor has it ever been a major exporter of defense equipment. India's well-developed missile and space infrastructure now provides an opportunity to enter this potentially lucrative international market. The Indian government could sell complete systems (e.g., *Prithvi* SSMs or launchers), DRDO technologies and expertise, or technologies now license-produced by Indian private industry. Unintended "leakage" of privately-produced dual-use and missile technologies through the Indian export control system is a further concern. Potential Indian missile sales will be affected by financial incentives, market conditions, Indian proliferation attitudes, and the structure and viability of the Indian export control system.

The primary incentive for India to export missiles is financial gain. Lack of foreign exchange poses severe problems for the Indian economy as a whole; in the fall of 1991 for instance, foreign exchange reserves were barely enough to cover two weeks worth of imports.[129] Missile profits could pump badly needed hard currency into the economy to pay for critical technology imports or to underwrite various defense programs. Financial repercussions of the Gulf war, including loss of remittances from Indian workers in the region, loss of Indian exports to the Gulf states, and higher prices for oil imports accentuated the hard-currency crisis.[130]

New Delhi is seeking to rapidly expand defense sector exports as one among several policies to alleviate the country's foreign exchange problems; missile-related sales may become part of this policy. Following two to three years of abysmal defense export performance,[131] a decision was made in the late 1980s to re-ignite defense sales.[132] Defense Minister Pawar said in 1991 that India expected to emerge as "an important exporter of defense equipment within the next two years" with targets of $160–190 million worth of sales "in the near future."[133] A committee under the chairmanship of the Assistant Secretary of Defense for Production and Supplies has been established to increase exports.[134]

Indian analysts have cited ideological and political implications of nonalignment and "Nehruvian morality," for the low level of defense exports.[135] Perhaps more important is India's inability to deliver a significant volume of high quality goods that meet a demand in the international marketplace. India has, however, sold patrol boats and helicopter trainers to Nepal and Bangladesh and reportedly supplied small arms and ammunition to Malaysia, Nigeria, Jordan, Lebanon and Oman.[136] The Indians are also offering low-end of the market defense items such as uniforms and stores.[137]

If export targets are to be met, India must look to sell high value-added items. The Main Battle Tank, Advanced Light Helicopter, and Light Combat Aircraft all fall into this category but are still under development. Unlike these projects, the missile and space programs can immediately offer quality goods at competitive prices. Both programs have benefited from significant capital investment but have yet to recover any appreciable external returns.[138] Both programs provide export options that India is likely to explore.

No senior Indian official has made an unambiguous policy statement dealing strictly with sales of ballistic missiles. Former Defense Minister Pant said publicly that one aim of the IGMDP is to "sell equipment and systems in the international market competitively, and to conduct joint production of missiles with other countries."[139] Pant did not, however, mention a specific class of missile. One Indian official interviewed for this study said that while the *Prithvi* SSM was not developed specifically for export, sales of this missile would be reviewed on a "case-by-case basis."[140] The director of U.S. Naval intelligence has stated that "*Prithvi* might attract buyers,"[141] and one U.S. intelligence officer believes that, "In all likelihood,

India's missile systems will be available for export to selected countries by the year 2000."[142]

The market for Indian missiles or missile technology might include any one of the 17 countries, named in an Office of Naval Intelligence estimate, that have or will have ballistic missiles by the year 2000. These countries include Egypt, Libya, Saudi Arabia, Syria and Yemen.[143] Developing countries seeking to advance their space launch capabilities, such as Brazil, may also be potential markets. Of course, New Delhi would have to seriously weigh the profound international repercussions attendant to ballistic missile sales in any decision to export systems or technologies.

Export of non-ballistic systems or technologies is also an option. A $210 million SA-6 *Kvardat* overhaul facility is being established by the Army Corps of Electrical and Mechanical Engineers, Meerut.[144] India can earn foreign exchange by extending the 10-year lifespan of the SA-6 for other users. India may be able to export the *Trishul* and *Akash* SAMs being developed under the IGMDP. The *Lakshya* PTA, priced at $290,000, will also reportedly be available for export.[145]

Reflecting a more general trend in Indian defense exports, the Director of U.S. Naval Intelligence has stated that the country is "beginning to export special weapons-related technology as a means of obtaining desperately needed hard currency."[146] DRDO has the expertise and technical resources to produce and integrate sophisticated missile systems which can be exported. The RCI recently joined with the Technical Information Forecasting and Assessment Council of the Department of Science and Technology to market advanced composites, such as carbon-carbon fiber. Composites will be produced at the Composite Production Centre (COMPROC) at RCI, which will be operated jointly with Indian industry.[147] Finally, many private industries supplying materials and technologies to the IGMDP could export their products.

Space Exports

A diffusion of advanced production and process technologies to the Indian industrial sector—technologies conceivably available for export—can clearly be seen in the Indian space program. Technologies used in launch vehicle production are part of the legitimate civilian infrastructure, yet they have "dual-use" applicability for military purposes. While the present study has not emphasized the Indian space program, it could become a proliferation problem.

As a matter of ISRO policy, hardware fabrication for all Indian space programs is carried out, to the greatest extent possible, through subcontracting to Indian industry.[148] Through technical consultancy, technology transfer, and long-term buy-back programs, ISRO has introduced hundreds of launch vehicle and process technologies to public and private firms. A major objective of this ISRO-industry partnership is to "promote and tap export markets for space goods and services."[149]

A few examples illustrate the lengthy list of technologies.[150] More than 400 industries of varying size have participated in the Augmented Satellite Launch Vehicle (ASLV) and PSLV projects. For example, the Midhani PSU is the prime contractor to supply maraging steel cases for the PSLV, but the firm uses subcontractors such as Rourkela Steel Plant for plate rolling and Leos Mercantile Corporation for finishing and polishing. Walchandnagar Industries Ltd. also contributes to motor case hardware fabrication. Bharat Forge Ltd., Poona, developed 600mm diameter titanium alloy hemispherical forgings. Echjay Industries, Rajkot, successfully produced and qualified titanium alloy rings of similar size through an ISRO-developed ring rolling process. Other industries are involved in special processes for spherical dome manufacturing, roll welding and maraging steel heat treatment. Industry is also providing tools and techniques for large scale propellant processing. A 100-ton-capacity plant for UDMH and MMH propellants was established by Andhra Sugars Limited, Tanuku, and an HTPB plant was built by National Organic Chemical Industries Limited (NOCIL). Other propellants used by ISRO, such as ammonium perchlorate and nitrogen tetroxide are provided by industry through a long-term buyback program. Industry is also providing "crucial support" for production of inertial guidance systems and liquid propulsion engines. Aerospace Materials, Tamil Nadu, is now working to commercialize production of long lengths of carbon phenolic cloth;[151] production of ablative silica cloth for rocket nozzles and silica phenolic inserts for the *Vikas* engine is already underway. In addition, many SHAR launch pad facilities, such as the towers, flame deflectors, auxiliary power supply and materials handling equipment were all subcontracted to civilian industry.

The most direct push for exports of space equipment has come directly from ISRO. Antrix Corp., a new space company acting under ISRO auspices and using HAL as a major subcontractor, is being formed to market goods such as remote-sensing data, ground equipment, and propellants. According to the general manager of HAL's aerospace division, the company will receive no subsidies from the Indian government and will have "a free hand to take any work."[152]

To date, India has achieved some success in space technology exports. As part of the collaborative agreement with France on the *Viking* engine development, India provided 500 accuracy pressure transducers to Arianespace.[153] Brazil, Indonesia, and China are reportedly interested in purchasing Indian remote sensing data and launcher propellant while South Korea has reportedly expressed interest in ground equipment.[154] Given relatively low production costs in India, the country is likely to find a niche in the international space market.

Proliferation Attitudes

The extent of Indian space or missile technology sales to countries of proliferation concern will be determined, in part, by perceptions of international control regimes, India's export control system and, more generally, Indian views of the proliferation problem. For the purposes of this study, it is especially important to note Indian attitudes toward the MTCR.

India is not a member of the MTCR nor has it given any specific, public indication that it would readily identify with the regime's guidelines and parameters. India's objections to the MTCR closely parallel its oft-repeated objections to the NPT and other international "supplier cartels." Opposition to what one analyst has termed a "global hegemonistic institution"[155] centers around several inter-related issues.

First, Indians see the MTCR as a "discriminatory" regime in that it implicitly (and in the case of the NPT, explicitly) allows some nations to have a certain class of weapon system that others are forbidden to have. The MTCR ignores regional factors and legitimate security interests of non-member states. New Delhi does support "non-discriminatory" regimes, i.e., those that involve weapon system prohibition for all states. India is a party to the biological weapons convention and has expressed support for a similar ban on chemical weapon stockpiling and technology transfer precisely because the regulations in such regimes prohibit all states from possessing such weapons.[156]

Second, India believes the MTCR takes too narrow an approach to control the global arms race and is thus an ineffective means of conflict management. In this view the MTCR, or any other regime which seeks merely to control the *flow* of weapons-related technology, does not consider the more general political factors which are the basis of conflict; nor does it address the conceptual basis of the legitimacy of war and arms transfers as instruments of national policy.[157]

The Indians seek a global disarmament approach as a broader and thus more effective solution to the arms control problem. In his 1988 address to the Third Special Session on disarmament of the UN General Assembly, Prime Minister Rajiv Gandhi proposed a comprehensive plan to totally eliminate nuclear weapons by the year 2010, a ban on space weapons, and a global and significant reduction in conventional weapons. He emphasized however, that "There are no technological solutions to the problems of world security."[158] Because the MTCR does not take a comprehensive approach, it has proven ineffective, as evidenced by the ability of states such as Pakistan, Saudi Arabia, Syria and others to obtain ballistic missiles after the accord was signed.

Third, because the MTCR seeks to control the transfer of certain dual-use technologies, it impedes the ability of Third World countries to access such technologies for non-military programs and hinders their economic progress. According to Air Commodore Jasjit Singh, "Every control that is exercised...on technology transfer or its dispersion by definition effects and/or retards the development process."[159] In the face of pressing developmental needs in such states, the inability to access technologies for economic growth could prove politically destabilizing and thus could offset any potentially positive effects on an international or systemic level.

Finally, India objects to the "self-righteous" attitudes of developed countries. These attitudes are characterized by the attempt to apply arbitrary norms embodied in the MTCR on states who were not privy to the establishment of those norms at the onset of the accord. Indians are quick to note that it was not they but the Western countries who transferred dangerous technologies to Iraq. MTCR members, in other words, cannot expect India to adhere to a regime which the creators themselves violate.

Objections to the MTCR notwithstanding, Indian decision-makers are not oblivious to proliferation problems or the dangers inherent in the transfer of military technologies to certain states. V. S. Arunachalam said that the "vulnerability of technology in the wrong hands and the need to protect technology so that it doesn't lead to further escalation of the arms buildup are vital concerns to our political leaders."[160] Despite the IGMDP's inherent export capabilities, an External Affairs spokesman recently said that India "had not transferred or sold any of the technologies involved [in the IGMDP] in spite of many requests to do so."[161] In 1989, Iraq reportedly attempted to study the Indian missile program and offered to host Indian experts in order to acquire missile technology.[162] More recently, the Iraqis made a "lucrative offer" for Indian missile technology during the Gulf crisis.[163] In both cases, the Indians rejected these offers. By refusing to transfer missiles or missile technologies New Delhi is, in effect, informally observing the MTCR even though it does not subscribe to the regime.[164] The character of India's approach toward controlling exports of weapons technology can best be seen in the Indian export control system.

Export Control System[165]

The Indian export control system consists of both formal and informal structures. The formal system consists of a regularized export control bureaucracy centered on a published list of items and technologies, the export of which is either banned or controlled. At this level, the export licensing process is relatively transparent if not particularly efficient; anyone who accesses the published list of controlled items can be apprised of allowable exports. At the informal (and perhaps more important) level is a political process which considers the export of certain technologies in a case-by-case fashion. Here, the export licensing process is not subject to public scrutiny nor are the criteria for export decision-making published. The institutional basis at this level consists of the various agencies which have either direct or indirect control over certain technologies—such as the Department of Space, Defense Ministry, or Ministry of External Affairs—and reaches to the highest levels of the Indian political decision making structure.

India's Ministry of Commerce is the nodal agency for formal Indian export control. Actual implementation of export policy is carried out by the Office of the Chief Controller of Exports and Imports. A list of controlled commodities is published periodically that contains two schedules of items: those that are banned totally, and those that are regulated to varying degrees by the Commerce Ministry. All other exports are permitted, provided they do not violate any other Indian laws or are not subject to control by agencies outside of the Commerce Ministry, such as defense exports.

The export control schedule states that the objective of the government in detailing items and procedures is "to promote exports to the maximum extent, *but in such a manner that the economy of the country is not affected by unregulated exports of items essentially needed within the country*."[166] In other words, the list has a specific internal focus. The schedule also states that export can be made to any destination in the world and that "no discrimination is made between one country and another" in the issuance of licenses.[167] No missile-related technologies, propellants, or materials, as enumerated in the MTCR appendices, appear in either the banned or controlled list. Moreover, none of the so-called "precursor chemicals" enumerated by the Australian group are found on the list. Indian companies therefore are free to export these items. This is particularly impressive, because many nuclear-relevant metals, ores and compounds are on the export ban list.

It is therefore clear that agencies other than the Commerce Ministry make key decisions concerning missile and space-related exports. Here, the informal level of export controls takes precedence. In the absence of a clearly articulated national security policy and export guidelines, the Ministry of Defense and Department of Space have the initial responsibility for regulating technologies they have developed or control.[168] Sales of such items are not however, an internal ISRO or DRDO matter; export approval for missile technologies would have to follow a "standard procedure of departmental review."[169] An export request would be raised to the Cabinet Secretariat or a sub-committee of Secretaries for a recommendation. Depending on the specific case, the ministries of External Affairs, Defense, and Commerce, as well as the Department of Space would be involved in the decision-making process. Depending on the sensitivity or size of the sale, the decision would ultimately have to be ratified by the Defense Minister, Prime Minister, or the Cabinet.[170]

This procedure is rather cumbersome and quite lengthy. Indian industry is itself angry with the current licensing process since "they don't know what they can or can't export." Moreover, the relevant ministries are reluctant to open the process in order to effect greater transparency in the export control system.[171] These many layers of bureaucratic red tape do, however, provide a mechanism for control of sensitive exports, particularly since currently there are few requests for such export licenses.[172]

Although India is unlikely to publicly identify with the MTCR (at least in the near future), it must act with its guidelines and parameters in mind. New Delhi is unlikely to export ballistic missile systems that exceed MTCR range and payload specifications due to its own sensitivity to the proliferation problem and to the international political costs that such transactions would involve. As noted above, India may consider *Prithvi* exports on a "case-by-case basis" and may be expected to export the *Lakshya* PTA and *Pinaca* MLRS, since their specifications fall below MTCR Category I guidelines.

The potential for Defense Ministry sales of sub-systems and technology cannot be discounted. Shrinking military budgets, the desperate need for hard currency, and the need to recoup some of the sunk capital costs of the IGMDP provide powerful incentives for the Ministry to seek customers for their technologies. The ambiguous *government-wide* position regarding missile technology sales increases the possibility for such exports since it may allow the Defense Ministry more latitude in dealing with foreign buyers.

ISRO is moving forcefully into the space applications and launch vehicle technology market. One can expect such ventures to be moderately successful, given ISRO's relatively inexpensive and technically sophisticated products.

Perhaps the greatest potential for Indian proliferation exists in the area of privately-produced goods, i.e. those manufactured items supplied by contractors to both DRDO and the Department of Space. As space-related manufacturing, materials, and testing technologies are diffused throughout Indian industry, it will be increasingly difficult for the cumbersome export control process to maintain control over sales. With increased private production of sensitive items, "informal" controls may be overwhelmed—it will be nearly impossible for each sensitive item to be a approved or disapproved by the Cabinet. Export controls will then be left to "formal" export control authorities, primarily the Ministry of Commerce,[173] but the current export list and control procedures are clearly lacking in terms of proliferation controls. Non-discriminatory licensing procedures, lack of a detailed export control list, and the many categories of technologies left off the list, may provide room for private sales to states of proliferation concern.

Conclusion

The foregoing analysis leads to several general conclusions and policy recommendations.

First, India now has a robust capability to design and develop a variety of missile systems, and will continue its efforts to indigenously produce those missile components it currently imports. In all probability, the import content of its missiles will (gradually) be reduced to the point where it will achieve relative independence in missile design and manufacture.

Second, India's 10-year missile program, the IGMDP, is entering its final phases. Therefore, decisions regarding future missile developments—such as series manufacture of the *Agni,* development of a solid-fuel *Prithvi,* or ICBM development—will be made (or revealed) within the next year or two. It is likely that development of land-attack or anti-ship cruise missiles will be a high priority. Of course, any decisions will be influenced to a significant degree by the availability of funds to continue the program.

Third, India has a good proliferation record and it should not automatically be assumed that it will enter the world's missile market. However, economic pressures provide a powerful incentive for missile exports, and an export control system that is currently inadequate to regulate sales of privately-produced, missile-related items may allow for unintended leakage of sensitive technologies.

Fourth, technology embargoes and sanctions may have some near-term effect in slowing New Delhi's missile program, but its missile-related infrastructure has been developed to the point that it is no longer feasible for outside interests to bring the program to a halt. The motives that have driven missile development for three decades remain, and Indian decision-makers will continue to view the program as a vital element in national security and foreign policy strategies. MTCR members and other concerned states should therefore focus their energies on seeking some ground for nonproliferation accommodation with India while recognizing that it is indeed a missile power. Nonproliferation policies might include the offer of assistance in establishing export control structures, legal or technical advice on the make-up of the MTCR annexes, and perhaps more importantly, seeking Indian input into global nonproliferation strategies. The Indians should be made fully and forcefully aware, however, that ICBM development/deployment will have a severe impact on their external relations; an ICBM capability could threaten a whole host of states that are not central to the Indian security sphere and would thus be regarded as highly destabilizing.

Fifth, as a quid pro quo for either formally or informally adopting MTCR guidelines and prohibiting missile-related exports, the United States might provide Indian access or subcontracting work to SDI or theater missile defense programs.[174] India's focus on defensive systems might help to slow the missile proliferation momentum on the subcontinent. The central question facing the international community is not whether India will have significant missile capabilities, but rather how best to deal politically with India as a missile power and how to ensure that India does not become a missile exporter.

Notes

1. The author would like to thank current and former U.S., Indian and other officials and analysts interviewed for this study. I would also like to thank Glynn Wood, Peter Lavoy and Joe Bermudez for their helpful comments and Neal Carter, Greg Gerardi and Chris Fitz for their editing suggestions.

2. Substantive work is actually carried out by the Defence Research and Development Laboratory (DRDL).

3. Indian Ministry of Defence, *Annual Report, 1987–88* [hereafter, *Annual Report*], p. 61.

4. B.D. Kapur, *Building a Defence Technology Base* (New Delhi: Lancer International, 1990), pp. 79–81, 115–119.

5. India ordered its first SA-2 battalions in 1962, with deliveries beginning in 1965–66. See Steven J. Zaloga, *Soviet Air Defence Missiles* (Alexandria, VA: Jane's Information Group, 1989), p. 55.

6. Buoyed by his U.S. trip and subsequent negotiations with Contraves, Kapur writes that he was *"seized with the intention to build up Missile R&D facilities in India."* The Indo-Swiss SAM was to have served as the basis of the development effort. Kapur, p. 122 (emphasis in original).

7. Kapur, pp. 98–99.

8. *Annual Report, 1963–64*, p. 75. These tests appear to be separate from those being conducted for civilian space research at the Thumba Equatorial Rocket Launch Station, or TERLS.

9 India began the *Centaure* program under a 1964 agreement with France's Sub-Aviation. U.S. Congress, House, Committee on Science and Technology, Subcommittee on Space Science and Applications, *World Wide Space Activities* (Congressional Research Service Report), 95th Congress, September 1977, p. 120. By 1969, the Chemical Engineering Division of the Bhaba Atomic Research Center was producing the composite type solid propellant for the *Centaure*, with the know-how provided by the French government. U.S. Department of State Airgram, American Embassy New Delhi to Department of State, *Rocket Propellant Production in India*, A-716, 16 October 1969.

10. Raju G.C. Thomas, *The Defence of India: A Budgetary Perspective of Strategy and Politics* (Delhi: The Macmillan Co. of India, Ltd., 1978), pp. 165–166.

11. Information on the Devil Program may be found in *The Hindu* (Madras), July 14, 1988, p. 7; Hong Kong *AFP*, May 26, 1989, reported in Foreign Broadcast Information Service, *Daily Report: Near East and South Asia* [hereafter *FBIS-NESA*], May 30, 1989, p. 61; and Manoj Joshi, "Agni: Importance and Implications," *Frontline*, June 10–23, 1989, p. 5.

12. *Hindustan Times* (Delhi), February 27, 1988, pp. 1, 5; reported in *FBIS-NESA*, March 7, 1988, pp. 55–6.

13. The following is based on author interviews with Indian officials.

14. A crore equals 10 million. Approximate U.S. dollar figures are shown at the July 31, 1992 official rate of 1 rupee = 0.0352 dollars. These dollar figures do not account for exchange rate fluctuations over the past 20 years and therefore are provided for comparative purposes only.

15. Indranil Banerjie, "The Integrated Guided Missile Development Program," *Indian Defence Review*, July 1990, p. 99. Many analysts include *Agni* as one of the systems being developed under the IGMDP. However, one official Indian source does not include *Agni* in its report that "Under the [IGMDP] development of four types of missile systems has been undertaken...", *Annual Report 1987–88*, p. 63.

16. *The Hindustan Times*, February 27, 1988, pp. 1, 5; reported in *FBIS-NESA*, March 7, 1988, pp. 55–56.

17. Banerjie, p. 100.

18. Seth Carus, *India's Ballistic Missile Program* (unpublished paper), Naval War College Foundation, January 10, 1990, p. 12.

19. *Annual Report, 1982–83*, pp. 60–61. This report also notes that "similar cooperation exists between the defence labs and BEL."

20. P. Sundarsan, "ISRO and Indian Industry—A Growing Partnership," in R.K. Mishra, ed., *Indian Industries: Problems and Prospects*, 1986–87, (New Delhi: United India Periodicals Ltd, Patriot Publications, 1987), p. 247.

21. *Ibid.*, p. 245.

22. C.V. Gopalakrishnan, "HAL Gears for Dynamic Phase," *The Hindu Survey of Indian Industry*, March 1990, p. 35. The division will produce 13 structures, including the core-based shroud, an iso-grid panel and the center portion of the heat shield.

23. *Annual Report, 1981–82*, p. 49.

24. *Annual Report, 1987–88*, p. 42.

25. Author interview.

26. Author interviews and Amarnath K. Menon, "In a Tailspin," *India Today*, May 31, 1992, p.77.

27. U.S. Embassy, New Delhi, Political Section, *Indian Space Program*, Cable to U.S. Department of Defense #30510, January 6, 1988, para. 62. What appears to be a very similar message was routed to the State Department on December 31, 1987 [hereafter, State Cable]. The author thanks Dr. Peter Lavoy for providing these documents which he obtained from the National Security Archives Nonproliferation Project.

28. State Cable, December 31, 1987, para. 96.

29. *Patriot* (Delhi), August 10, 1991, p. 1; reported in *FBIS-NESA*, August 19, 1991, pp. 58–9.

30. *The Hindustan Times*, February 27, 1988, pp. 1, 5; reported in *FBIS-NESA*, March 7, 1988, pp. 55–6; and *Milavnews*, April 1991, pp. 15–16.

31. In his announcement of the fifth *Prithvi* test launch in August 1991, Defence Minister Pawar described the system as a "surface-to-air" missile. *Times of India* (Bombay), 8/8/91, pp. 1, 11 and *Milavnews*, September 1991, p. 11.

32. Banerjie, p. 103.

33. *Times of India* (Bombay), April 10, 1989, p. 12; reported in *Joint Publications Research Service-Nuclear Developments* (hereafter *JPRS-TND*), June 14, 1989, pp. 19–20 and Banerjie, p. 104.

34. *Prithvi* tests were conducted on 2/25/88, 9/27/89, 2/11/91, 7/3/91, 8/7/91, 5/5/92, 8/18/92 and 8/29/92. The last two tests were from the *Prithvi*'s mobile transporter-erector-launcher (TEL).

35. *Milavnews*, September 1991, p. 15.

36. Mohammad Iqbal, "Missile Proliferation in South Asia," *Regional Studies*, Spring 1990, p. 15 and Hormuz P. Mama, "Progress on India's Tactical Missiles," *International Defense Review*, July 1989, p. 963.

37. Pushpinder Singh, "India's Agni Success Poses New Problems," *Jane's Defence Weekly*, June 3, 1989, p. 1052; and Mama, p. 963.

38. "Agni IRBM Details Revealed," *International Defense Review*, March 1989, p. 247. Hypergolic propellants are spontaneously ignitable and therefore do not require a separate ignition system. India was importing G-fuel through at least 1981. See *Annual Report 1980–81*, p. 37. Fuel production information from P. Sharma, "Towards Self-Reliance in Defence," *The Defence Review*, 1984, p. 261; and Singh, p. 1052.

39. *Annual Report, 1984–85*, p. 76.

40. Banerjie, p. 104.

41. *Patriot*, August 10, 1991, p. 1; reported in *JPRS-TND*, August 19, 1991, pp. 58–9.

42. *Times of India* (Bombay), September 28, 1989, p. 1; reported in *JPRS-NESA*, November 13, 1989, p. 59.

43. *Asian Recorder*, September 1, 1991, p. 21881, from a report carried in *Hindu* (Madras).

44. It is possible to control pitch and yaw with the use of one gimbaled engine, since the thrust vector of the rocket nozzle runs through the vehicle's axis. However, roll control usually requires two or more engines or rotary vanes. See George P. Sutton, *Rocket Propulsion Elements*, Fifth Ed. (New York: John Wiley & Sons, 1986), pp. 161–162.

45. *Jane's Defence Weekly*, July 15, 1989, pp. 88–89.

46. For reports on Indian terminal guidance developments, see *The Economist*, March 26, 1988, pp. 31–2; Edmond Dantes, "Missiles in Gulf Buoy India's Defense Drive," *Defense News*, February 2, 1991, p. 3; and Singh, p. 1052. For terminal guidance technical and testing difficulties, see Donald Mackenzie, *Inventing Accuracy: A Historical Sociology of Nuclear Missile Guidance* (Cambridge, Mass: The MIT Press, 1990), pp. 236–237, 420–421.

47. *All India Radio General Overseas Service* (Delhi), July 20, 1991, as reported in *JPRS-TND*, August 8, 1991, pp. 18–19.

48. Banerjie, p. 104.

49. Manoj Joshi," The Indigenous Effort," *Frontline*, April 13–26, 1992, p. 51 and Joshi, June 10–23, 1989, p. 8. DRDO work on a FAE mine clearing rocket began in 1980–81. *Annual Report, 1980–81*, p. 64. In 1988, a DRDO spokesman claimed that scientists had "already developed and proved" a "high-explosive incendiary weapon." *Hong Kong AFP*, March 3, 1988; reported in *FBIS-NESA*, March 4, 1988, pp. 54–5.

50. Banerjie, p. 104.

51. Author interview.

52. *Delhi Doordarshan Television Network*, September 27, 1989; reported in *FBIS-NESA*, September 28, 1989, p. 45.

53. *Delhi All India Radio General Overseas Service*, July 20, 1991; reported in *FBIS-NESA*, August 8, 1991, pp. 18–19. This figure does not include production costs for fuel and oxidizer trucks, mobile launchers or command and control vehicles.

54. Author interview with Indian official,

55. Banerjie, 101.

56. *Hindu* (International Edition), August 29, 1992, p. 13.

57. IDR Research Team, "Weapons and Equipment State: Are We Getting Our Money's Worth?" *Indian Defence Review*, July 1988, p. 145. This is a familiar pattern the world over. For instance, Iraqi SCUD brigades consisted of 18 TELs organized into 3 battalions, with three batteries in each battalion and two TELs in each battery. *The Iraqi Army: Organization and Tactics*, National Training Center, Handbook 100-91, prepared by the S-2, 177th Armored Brigade and the Operations group of the NTC, January 3, 1991, p. 9.

58. Indian officials foresee no *technical* production problems, but are concerned over availability of moneys for a full production run. Author interviews.

59. IDR Research Team, p. 145.

60. W.P.S. Sidhu, "Tactical Gap," *India Today*, September 15, 1992, p. 84.

61. IDR Research Team, "Weapons and Equipment: An Overview," *Indian Defence Review*, July 1989, p.209.

62. This is the reaction time of the Soviet SS-1c/SCUD-B, a system the *Prithvi* closely resembles. Headquarters, Department of the Army, *The Soviet Army: Troops, Organization and Equipment*, FM100-2-3, July 1984, pp. 65–67.

63. Amarnath K. Menon, "We Can Design Any Missile," *India Today*, June 15, 1989, p. 12.

64. Banerjie,. p. 106.

65. Data from the test revealed that the 3 meter carbon-carbon heat shield performed well. *Delhi Domestic Service*, May 26, 1989; reported in *FBIS-NES*, May 30, 1989, pp. 60–61; and *Patriot* (Delhi), August 10, 1991, p. 1; reported in *FBIS-NESA*, August 19, 1991, pp. 58–9.

66. Michael Battye, "Indian Missile Test Imperfect," *Reuters*-0110, May 30, 1992. For original claims of success, see Nageshwar Patnaik, "India Test-Fires Medium-Range Missile," *Reuters*-0135, May 29, 1992.

67. Defense Intelligence Agency, *Background Paper on Indian Missile Capabilities for Mr. R.L. Armitage, Office of the Assistant Secretary of Defense*, DIA/DT-20, 23 February 1988, p. 1.

68. "Emphasis was on Re-entry Technology—R.N. Agarwal," *Frontline*, June 10–23, 1989, p. 14.

69. *International Defense Review*, March 1989, p. 247. Proliferation analyst Gary Milhollin claims that India received critical assistance in guidance and other technologies such as composite production from the (former) West German aerospace agency DLR. Reportedly intended for India's space launch vehicle program, the assistance was instead used in the *Agni* project. Gary Milhollin, "India's Missiles—With a Little Help From Our Friends," *Bulletin of the Atomic Scientists*, November 1989, pp. 31–35. Defense Minister K.C. Pant denied these assertions. See report of Pant's statement before the Lok Sobha in *Delhi Domestic Service*, July 24, 1989; reported in *JPRS-TND*, August 14, 1989, p. 23.

70. *Delhi General Overseas Service,* May 23, 1989; reported in *FBIS-NES,* May 24, 1989, p. 53.

71. Banerjie, p. 106.

72. *Milavnews,* March 1991, p. 11.

73. See "An Embargo Cannot Throttle Us—Dr. Abdul Kalam," *Frontline,* June 10–23, 1989, p. 11; and Joshi, June 10–23, 1989, p. 9.

74. *Delhi All India Radio Network,* May 30, 1992; reported in *FBIS-NESA,* June 1, 1992, p. 48.

75. In an interview with the author, an Indian official close to the missile program stated that "no decision has been made to produce or deploy" the missile. See also Dantes, p. 3.

76. Amarnath K. Menon, "We Can Design Any Missile," Interview with Dr. Kalam in *India Today,* June 15, 1989, p. 12.

77. *Ibid.,* p. 12.

78. Statement of Rear Admiral Edward D. Sheafer before the Seapower, Strategic and Critical Materials Subcommittee of the House Armed Services Committee, February 5, 1992, p. 76.

79. See for instance Dr. Kalam's statement in *Asia-Pacific Defence Reporter,* March 1991, p. 26.

80. *Times of India* (Bombay), July 18, 1989, p. 8; reported in *JPRS-NESA,* September 6, 1989, p. 62.

81. See, for instance, Banerjie, p. 106.

82. Author interview with Indian official.

83. IDR Research Team, July 1989, p. 211.

84. *Delhi Domestic Service,* May 22, 1989; reported in *FBIS-NESA,* May 22, 1989, p. 54.

85. For instance, use against very heavily defended airfields or command centers.

86. *Asian Defence Journal,* July 1989, p. 99, quoting a Press Trust of India report. For a similar report see also *Hong Kong AFP,* May 28, 1989; reported in *FBIS-NESA,* May 30, 1989, pp. 60–61.

87. *Patriot* (Delhi), January 12, 1990, p. 4; reported in *JPRS-TND,* February 16, 1990, p. 22 and *Asia-Pacific Defence Reporter,* March 1991, p. 26. See also Sadananda Mukherjee, "India Has ICBM Ability," *Jane's Defence Weekly,* February 3, 1990, p. 191.

88. *Frontline,* June 10–23, 1989, p. 15.

89. Carus, pp. 27–28.

90. *Annual Report, 1983–84,* p. 73 and IDR Research Team, January 1989, p. 166. This second source notes significant troubles in developing and producing the system whose costs are now 2.1 times the import price.

91. IDR Research Team, January 1989, p. 166.

92. Joshi, April 13–26, 1992, p.51.

93. Interview with Arunachalam in *Defense News,* February 24, 1992, p. 86.

94. Joshi, April 13–26, 1992, p. 53.

95. Author interviews with American and Indian officials.

96. *Ibid.,* p. 52.

97. Kenneth Munson, *World Unmanned Aircraft* (London: Jane's Publishing Co., Ltd., 1988), pp. 38, 54.

98. *Ibid.*, p. 54. PTAE-7 tests began in 1987–88. *Annual Report, 1987–88*, p. 62.

99. Author interview with Indian official.

100. Joshi, April 13–26, 1992, pp. 52–53.

101. For a discussion of cruise missile technologies available to developing countries see Eric H. Arnett, "Cruise Missiles in the Developing World," in Eric H. Arnett and W. Thomas Wander, eds., *The Proliferation of Advanced Weaponry: Technology, Motivations and Responses*, American Association for the Advancement of Science, 1992, pp. 105–119.

102. Raju G.C. Thomas, *Indian Security Policy* (Princeton, NJ: Princeton University Press, 1986), p. 6.

103. The following is based largely on Thomas, pp. 1–50; see also Akhtar Majeed, "Indian Security Perspectives in the 1990s," *Asian Survey*, November 1990, pp. 1084–1098.

104. Thomas, 1986, pp. 30–31.

105. *Ibid.*, pp. 21–22.

106. India did buy French *Mirage-2000s* as a direct response to Pakistani acquisition of F-16s.

107. In 1991, Defense Minister Pawar stated that Pakistan's acquisition of Chinese M-11 missiles posed "a serious threat to India." Pawar's statement before Lok Sobha in *Times of India* (Bombay), July 20, 1991, p. 7; reported in *JPRS-TND*, September 21, 1991, pp. 11–12.

108. Author interviews.

109. *Indian Express*, June 13, 1966. The U.S. government apparently agreed. In a Congressional testimony, Secretary of State Dean Rusk declared that "they (Chinese) are now developing nuclear weapons and missile delivery systems...These weapons can ultimately be deployed to attack Peiping's Asian neighbors." See *U.S. Policy Toward China*, Statement before the Far East and the Pacific Subcommittee of the House Foreign Affairs Committee, March 16, 1966. A week earlier, Defense Secretary McNamara told the Joint Committee on Atomic Energy that within two years China would have a nuclear "warhead delivery capability" within a 700-mile radius. Quoted in Congressional Quarterly, *China: U.S. Policy Since 1945* (Washington, D.C.: Congressional Quarterly, Inc., 1980), p. 161.

110. See, for instance, Brig. A.C. Cariappa (Retd.), "Missiles In Conventional Warfare," *Hindu*, November 25, 1973, p. 6 and Group Captain A.L. Bary, "National Approach to Missiles," *Tribune*, November 22, 1978.

111. See, for instance, R.R. Subramanian, *India, Pakistan, China: Defence and Nuclear Tangle in South Asia* (New Delhi: ABC Publishing House, 1989), p. 60 and Dantes, p. 3.

112. *Delhi Domestic Service*, May 26, 1989; reported in *JPRS-TND*, June 14, 1989, p. 20.

113. Dantes, p. 3.

114. J. Mohan Malik, "India's Response to the Gulf War Crisis: Implications for Indian Foreign Policy," *Asian Survey*, September 1991, pp. 847–861.

115. Amit Gupta, "The Indian Arms Industry," *Asian Survey*, September 1990, pp. 846–861.

116. The project was initiated several months before the disastrous October 1962 war with the PRC [*and two years before China's first successful nuclear test*—ed.].

117. Gen. Kapur, for instance, writes that the "deep, intricate implications [of self-reliance] involve a phase wise development concerned with training a body of manpower within the country...such innovators are the...wealth producers of the country." Kapur, p. 69.

118. Vikram Sarabhai, *Management for Development: A Collection of Papers*, Kamla Chowdhry ed., (Delhi: Vikas Publishing House, 1974), p. 7.

119. *Hindu* (International Edition), November 1991, p. 3.

120. Quoted in *Delhi Domestic Service*, October 30, 1981; reported in *FBIS, Daily Report-South Asia*, November 2, 1981.

121. H.C. Sarin, *Defence and Development* (New Delhi: USI National Security Lectures, 1979), p. 16.

122. P. Khokhar, "Arms Proliferation in the Third World: The Rationale for Defence Exports From India," *Journal of the United Service Institution of India*, January–March 1990, p. 82.

123. For a discussion of the super computer deal from the Indian perspective, see Ashok Raj, "U.S. High-Tech Diplomacy and the Indian Supercomputer Deal," *Strategic Analysis*, September 1987, pp. 735–757. The License denial date is from *Defense & Foreign Affairs Weekly*, August 13–19, 1990, p. 1.

124. See *Statement of the U.S. Department of State/Office of Assistant Secretary*, May 11, 1992; *Federal Register*, (Vol. 57, No. 116) June 16, 1992, pp. 26773–26774; and *Export Control News*, June 30, 1992, pp. 15–18.

125. Author interview with Indian official.

126. Quoted in Banerjie, p. 100.

127. Quoted in Cecil Victor, *India: The Security Dilemma* (New Delhi: Patriot Publishers, 1990), p. 62.

128. K. Subrahmanyam, *Hindu* (Madras), May 22, 1989. For another expression of this view, see R.R. Subramanian, p. 101.

129. From budget speech given by Manmohan Singh before Lok Sobha, reported in *Indian Express*, March 1, 1992, pp. 13–14.

130. See "Gulf War—How it Will Hit Us," *Business India*, January 21–February 3, 1991, pp. 62–72 and "The Foreign Exchange Squeeze," *Business India*, April 1–14, 1991, pp. 46–52.

131. Following 1986, when defense exports totaled $44 million, value of defense exports dropped to $5 million in 1987. There were no recorded export earnings in 1988 and 1989. U.S. Arms Control and Disarmament Agency, *World Military Expenditures and Arms Transfers*, 1990, Released November 1991, p. 108.

132. See former Defense Minister Pant's announcement that India plans to increase defense exports in *Hong Kong AFP*, January 30, 1989 as reported in *FBIS-NES*, January 31, 1989, p. 45.

133. "India Boosts Electronics Capability; Hopes for Export Hike," *International Defense Review*, October 1991, p. 1135. This target figure would represent roughly a 600% increase in sales based upon 1990 reported figures of $28 million.

134. *Asia-Pacific Defence Reporter*, April 1991, pp. 22–23.

135. See for instance Gupta, p. 858.

136. Maj. Brian S. Tolle, "The Rise in Indian Defense Exports," *How They Fight: Armies of the World*, United States Army Intelligence Command, ATC-RD-2600-105-91, July–November 1991, p. 23.

137. Author interview with official of U.S. embassy, New Delhi.

138. One team of analysts concluded that the IGMDP costs have been so high that the ability to continue the program is in question. The solution is to "export or perish." IDR Research Team, July 1988, p. 146.

139. *Delhi Domestic Service*, May 26, 1989; reported in *JPRS-TND*, June 14, 1989, p. 20.

140. Author interview.

141. Sheafer statement, p. 75.

142. Tolle, p. 24.

143. *Jane's Defence Weekly*, March 16, 1991, p. 366.

144. "India Faces Critical Spares Shortage of Soviet Arms," *International Defense Review*, December 1991, p. 1308. The Soviets apparently provided complete drawings and other documents to the Indians for indigenous fabrication of SA-6 spares.

145. *World Weapons Review*, June 27, 1990, p. 2.

146. Sheafer statement, p. 74.

147. Hormuz Mama, "India Offers Plastics," *International Defense Review*, March 1992, p. 44.

148. Government of India, *National Paper of India for the Second U.N. Conference on Exploration and Peaceful Uses of Outerspace* (UNISPACE 82) (Bangalore: Government of India, Publications and Public Relations Unit, ISRO, 1981), [hereafter, UNISPACE] p. 36.

149. Sudarsen, p. 245.

150. The following is largely drawn from Michael X., "Industry's Crucial Role in Space Programme," in R.K. Mishra ed., *Indian Industries: Problems and Prospects, 1986–87* (New Delhi: United India Periodicals, Ltd., 1987), pp. 269–274; Sundarsan, passim.; and UNISPACE, passim.

151. *Hindu* (International Edition), July 4, 1992, p. 16.

152. Andrew Lawler, "India to Begin Commercial Sales of Space Goods," *Space News*, May 4, 1992, pp. 1, 21.

153. UNISPACE, p. 45.

154. Lawler, op. cit, p. 21.

155. See Ravi Shastri, "The Spread of Ballistic Missiles and Its Implications," *Strategic Analysis*, May 1988, pp. 157–168.

156. See, for instance, Indian reaction to President Bush's Middle East arms control initiative in *Hindu* (Madras), June 13, 1991, p. 8 as reported in *JPRS-TND*, August 8, 1991, pp. 16–18.

157. See, for instance, the comments of Air Commodore Jasjit Singh in *The Global Diffusion of Military Technology*, Workshop Proceedings sponsored by the Center for International Cooperation and Security Studies, University of Wisconsin-Madison, December 6–8, 1991, pp. 28–32.

158. India earlier advocated similar proposals. In a May 1984 declaration Argentina, Mexico, India, Thailand, Greece and Sweden called for cessation of the development, production and deployment of nuclear weapons as well as the means to deliver them. *Izvestiya*, August 10, 1985, p. 5; as reported in *Worldwide Report*, February 4, 1986, pp. 49–53.

159. Singh, p. 30.

160. Arunachalam's *Defense News* interview, p. 86.

161. *Patriot* (Delhi), January 29, 1992, p. 1, as reported in *JPRS-TND*, March 26, 1992, p. 31.

162. *Defense & Foreign Affairs Weekly*, June 25–July 1, 1990, p. 4.

163. Author interview with Indian official.

164. Author correspondence with S. Chandrashekar, August 3, 1992.

165. The following is based largely on author interviews and S. Chandrashekar, "Export Controls and Proliferation: An Indian Perspective," in Gary K. Bertsch, Richard T. Cupitt and Steven J. Elliot-Gower, eds., *International Cooperation on Nonproliferation Controls: Prospects for the 1990s and Beyond* (forthcoming), Center for East-West Trade Policy and Department of Political Science, University of Georgia, March 1992.

166. The list is published in Government of India, Ministry of Commerce *Import & Export Policy*, V. 2, Export Control and Procedures, April 1990–March 1993; p. 1 [emphasis added].

167. Exceptions to this rule are exports to South Africa and Fiji due to a complete Indian ban on trade with these countries.

168. Chandrashekar, p. 20.

169. *Ibid.*, pp. 22, 27.

170. Correspondence with Chandrashekar.

171. Author interview.

172. Correspondence with Chandrashekar.

173. Author interview.

174. This was suggested to the author by an Indian official interviewed for this study.

10

Israel: Case Study for International Missile Trade and Nonproliferation

Gerald M. Steinberg

Capabilities

Israel has been active in research and development of ballistic missile technology, as well as production, testing, and deployment of such systems for many years. The Israeli government created a Science Corps in the military in 1948, and this group was active in developing the technological base for the components necessary for missile production. The Science Corps evolved into the National Weapons Development Authority (Rafael), which developed and launched sounding rockets. More advanced experimental systems, incorporating solid state electronics and telemetry, were tested in the late 1950s and early 1960s.

The indigenous scientific and technological base for the development of missile technology grew throughout this period. The Technion (Israeli Institute of Technology) in Haifa specialized in aeronautical and missile engineering, and the activity at the Weizmann Institute and other Israeli universities and research institutions added to this foundation. Research and applications for military requirements took place in the laboratories of Rafael, the Israeli Aircraft Industry (IAI), Israel Military Industries (known in Hebrew as *Ta'as*) and many other smaller firms.

Between 1955 and 1967, cooperation with France, and particularly with the firm Marcel Dassault, led to development of technology to manufacture solid rocket motors, and these became the foundation of the Israel tactical and strategic missile programs. Later, Israel developed the technology for the inertial guidance systems which are necessary for navigating the warhead to its target. The various tests and engineering models of air-to-ground, air-to-air, and surface-to-surface missiles were known under the generic name of *Luz*.[1] The MD660 surface to surface missile was produced under a co-production agreement with Dassault.[2]

In 1967, the first Israeli-made tactical missile (the *Shafrir* air-to-air system) were tested in combat. Other tactical missiles, such as the *Gabriel* ship-to-ship missile (with radar homing) were also developed. These systems were used by Israeli forces in the wars against the Arab states during this period, and in the mid-1970s became a major source of export income. Based on the lessons learned from the use of these weapons in combat, other highly advanced tactical systems, including the *Shafrir* 2 and *Python* 3 AAMs, the *Popeye* air-to-ground missile, and *Barak* naval missile defense system were developed in the 1980s.[3] According to a report in *Jane's Weapons Systems*, in the 1970s Israel produced a short-range rocket known as the *Ze'ev* (Wolf) with a range of less than five kilometers and a warhead of 70 kilograms.[4]

The technology base which led to the production of a wide range of tactical missiles also served as a foundation for strategic intermediate-range ballistic missiles (IRBMs). No official Israeli source has acknowledged the existence of these weapons, but they are widely referred to in the press as the "*Jericho*." The *Jericho 1* is believed to have been deployed in the early 1970s, when Syria, Egypt, and other Arab states began to receive Soviet SCUD missiles. After the 1973 war, in which Syrian and Egyptian forces made substantial progress, Israel sought to reinforce deterrence and reestablish escalation dominance. In 1975, the US refused to sell Israel the *Pershing-1A*, and while Washington agreed to provide *Lance* battlefield missiles, these did not solve the strategic problems. In response, Israel proceeded in the development of an indigenous IRBM capability. The *Jericho 1* reportedly has a payload of 1,000 kilograms and a 500 kilometer range.[5]

According to published reports, the more advanced and longer-range *Jericho* 2 was tested and deployed beginning in 1987. The *Jericho* 2 is credited with a range of 2,000 to 2,800 kilometers, and, according to Fetter, the *Jericho* 2 "can probably deliver at least 2 tonnes on any Arab country."[6]

Israel is also developing a ballistic missile defense system known as the *Arrow*. Although most of the funding is being provided by the United States, research and development are taking place in Israel, with the Israeli Aircraft Industry as the prime contractor. The *Arrow* is designed to destroy incoming warheads at an altitude of 20 to 40 kilometers, and is expected to cost $2 to $5 billion.[7] On September 24, 1992, after three tests that were at least partial failures, a fully successful test of the *Arrow* was conducted. The sophistication of the *Arrow* program and technology provide additional evidence of the overall Israeli capability to develop and produce ballistic missiles.

Israeli firms have also developed and produced the *Barak* ship-defense missile system.

The Israeli Space Program

In September 1988, Israel launched its first satellite into orbit. The *Ofek* (*Horizon*) 1 satellite, which weighed 156 kilograms, was launched by the three-stage solid fueled *Shavit* (*Comet*). Although few details regarding the launch vehicle were released, it is likely that the *Shavit* is based on or identical to the *Jericho* 2 missile.[8] (The United States, Soviet Union, and China also used modified ICBMs for space launchers.) *Ofek* 2, with similar characteristics, was launched in April 1990, and a third satellite was expected to be launched in the Spring of 1992.

The Israeli space program is likely to grow in the near term, with an increasing emphasis on military applications. In a Knesset discussion following the intelligence failures preceding and during the Iraqi war (and the failure of the United States to locate the Iraqi nuclear facilities and missile launchers), Israeli Defense Minister Moshe Arens announced plans to develop reconnaissance satellites.[9]

Israel has also expressed interest in commercial space activities, including the provision of launch services for small payloads in low-earth orbit. IAI has advertised the capabilities of the *Shavit* (apparently despite the misgivings of the Defense Ministry and the military, who opposed the publicity and feared that public discussion would compromise national security). An Israeli communications satellite is scheduled for launch aboard a European Space Agency *Ariane* launcher in 1994.

A civilian organization, the Israeli Space Agency (ISA), was created in 1983, to support scientific and engineering activity. The ISA has developed working relationships and agreements with NASA, the European Space Agency, and other countries. In 1989, a cooperation agreement was reached with the Soviet Union, and joint projects have continued with the Commonwealth of Independent States. Israel, Denmark, and the CIS signed an agreement to launch a scientific research satellite from Baykanur in 1995. The Israeli team is developing an ultra-violet telescope for the system.[10] In the longer term, the Israeli space program can be expected to expand to include larger launchers capable of placing larger payloads into low-earth orbit and, ultimately, into synchronous orbits.

Transactions

Motivations

In general, Israeli exports of military technology and weapons are driven by a combination of security and economic requirements. Israel is an extremely small country, with very limited resources, and threats to security and national survival are primary considerations. Economically,

Israel cannot compete with the weapons purchased by the Arab oil exporters, and the United States is the only major source of weapons or military technology. To provide an assured and independent source of weapons, Israel has developed a highly sophisticated and technologically intensive arms industry.[11] Like other states which produce major weapons systems, Israel seeks to reduce the costs of this development by exporting, licensing and co-producing indigenously developed weapons and technology.[12] According to an Israeli government source, more than 20 percent of total industrial exports come from weapons and military technology, and Israeli Aircraft Industry, which is the country's largest industrial firm, is reported to be dependent on exports for up to 80 percent of its revenues.[13]

The development and production of ballistic missile technology is closely linked to Israeli military doctrine and policy. The Israel Defense Forces (IDF) have always sought to offset the overwhelming quantitative advantage of the Arab states by emphasizing advanced weapons. This technology was also an important element in the development of the Israeli deterrent capability. In the 1950s, Prime Minister David Ben-Gurion was concerned that the Arab nations would eventually be able to develop a conventional force sufficient to overrun the Jewish state. In response, he embarked on the development of a deterrent capable of inflicting "massive retaliation" on any Arab state or coalition which threatened Israeli survival.[14] The development of missile technology, in general, and strategic ballistic missiles in particular, were essential elements in this deterrence strategy.

The events of 1967 accelerated the development of the Israeli deterrent, including ballistic missiles. In May 1967, massive tank and infantry forces were mobilized along Israel's borders with Egypt, Syria, and Jordan, and Egypt's President Nasser threatened "a war of annihilation." Although an Israeli pre-emptive attack removed this threat, at least for the short term, the fear of a multi-front Arab attack has remained. This fear was reinforced in the 1973 Yom Kippur War, when Egyptian and Syrian forces penetrated Israeli defenses in the Sinai and Golan Heights.

The effort of the Arab states to develop ballistic missiles provided a second motivating factor for the Israeli program. In the late 1950s and early 1960s, Egypt obtained the assistance of German scientists in developing liquid fueled missiles[15] [*see Joseph Bermudez chapter on Egypt*—ed.]. Outside pressure forced an end to this effort, but in 1970, Egypt received a shipment of SCUD missiles from the USSR. In the mid-1980s, the Egyptian effort to manufacture missiles, code-named *Badr 2000*, was resumed with participation in the *Condor* missile project, along with Iraq and Argentina[16] [*see Scott Tollefson's chapter on Argentina*—ed.]. An Egyptian official was arrested in the US for attempting to smuggle carbon-carbon materials used for warheads. There are also reports that North Korea has provided help in indigenous production.[17] (Links between these states go back to the 1970s, when Egypt supplied some SCUDs to North Korea, which "reverse-engineered" a local production plant, and then exported the missiles and technology to Iran and Syria.)[18]

In the 1970s and 1980s, many other Arab and Islamic states sought, and many obtained, ballistic missiles. Libya financed the West German OTRAG group's testing efforts in Zaire,[19] and purchased SCUDs from the USSR; while Iran obtained SCUDs from Libya, Syria, and North Korea. In 1985 Saudi Arabia bought 30 to 50 CSS-2 IRBMs from China.

Following the signing of the Camp David accords in 1978, Syria became the primary threat to Israel, and Damascus obtained ballistic missiles during this period. In the 1973 war, Syrian forces fired some short-range FROG-7 missiles at air bases, but missed their targets. The first SCUDs arrived in 1974 from the USSR, and following the 1982 war, the Soviets supplied SS-21 missiles to Syria.

Iraq began to purchase SCUD missiles from the Soviet Union in 1976.[20] Saddam Husayn also sought longer range SS-12 missiles from the USSR and was an active partner in the *Condor* project. With significant foreign assistance, the Iraqis were also able to extend the range of the SCUD-B, which they called the *al-Husayn* missile. During the 1991 Gulf war, Iraq launched 39 such missiles at Israeli cities. A larger missile, the *Tammuz*, was tested in December 1989.

Thus, the major Arab states surrounding Israel all obtained ballistic missiles during the 1970s and 1980s. Many also developed chemical arsenals for these weapons. These threats increased the motivation for Israeli deployment of ballistic missiles for deterrence purposes. The Israeli ballistic missile arsenal was not designed for the purposes of war-fighting, nor for prestige. For war fighting, the Israelis continue to rely on their air force, which is more cost effective. The absence of any public discussion about ballistic missile capability eliminates the potential role of prestige as a motivating factor.

Major Purchasers

For Israel, as for most other arms producers, exports are of major economic and political importance. Lacking assured suppliers, Israel was forced to invest scarce resources in indigenous production of weapons. Some 20 to 25 percent of the Israeli industrial work force is employed in this sector and IAI is the largest firm in the country, with over 15,000 employees. Economically, exports of weapons and technology provide a vital means to offset these costs.[21]

However, most of the most lucrative markets for arms exports are closed to Israel. With the exception of Iran under the Shah, the Arab and Islamic states in the Middle East, which are the major importers of weapons from the United States and Western Europe, do not purchase any Israeli products, including weapons.[22] (As long as these states maintain a state of war, there is also no Israeli interest in arming them further.) While billions of dollars of oil revenues go to pay for arms purchases from the rest of the world's weapons makers, Israeli industry must find other purchasers and partners for joint production. Arms sales and military links were also seen as a means for developing political ties to countries with which Israel did not have diplomatic relations, such as Iran, China, and Ethiopia.

Arms sales are also very important for the Israeli economy. By volume, the bulk of Israeli arms sales involve small arms and ammunition, but the most profitable exports are those systems which have the highest value added. Advanced technology in general, and missiles in particular (for which there are few alternative suppliers), can be a major source of revenue. Thus, there are many reports of Israeli exports of technology and joint research programs applicable to missile development. However, a Congressional Research Service report of February 1989 notes, "there are no indications to date of any exports of either Jericho or Jericho II" missiles.[23]

Iran. In the 1970s, Iran was a major market for Israeli arms and technology. During this period, when the *Jericho* was under development, the Shah of Iran was seen as a potential partner for this very costly project. Iran was a source of petroleum (the Arab oil exporters refused to sell to Israel, and Jerusalem has always sought to develop a long-term relationship with a major producer in the region). Iran is a non-Arab state, a would-be regional power, and seen as a counter to Iraq, which has always been a leader of the radical Arab anti-Israel coalition. Under the Shah, Iran became a tacit ally and part of the peripheral strategy pursued by the Israeli leadership. According to documents taken from the Israeli and American embassies in Teheran after the revolution, Iranian military officials were briefed on the *Jericho* and viewed test launches.[24] According to some reports, Project Flower, as the joint venture was named, was designed to produce a short-range tactical missile (150–200 kilometers), but the evidence is unclear.[25] With the fall of the Shah in 1979, the project ended. Although some arms sales took place to Iran after the revolution, these consisted of spare parts and no missile technology was involved.

South Africa. The collapse of the Shah's government forced Israel to expand the search for alternative partners to offset the high costs of military research, development, and production. Israeli links with South Africa apparently began after the 1973 Yom Kippur war. African states with which Israel had trade and military relationships were pressured by the Arabs to break all contact with Israel. Here, as in the case of Iran, energy imports also played a role, and Israel purchased coal and other goods from South Africa. Israeli exports reportedly included military technology and arms, including small arms, licensing agreements to produce the *Reshef* missile gunboats, and perhaps ship-to-ship missiles. Most of these long-term agreements were concluded in the mid-1970s, prior to the 1977 United Nations embargo on weapons (but not technology or components), but continued for many years thereafter.

The details of the Israeli-South African military relationship, including reports regarding missile technology, are largely speculative and often inaccurate. For example, numerous reports claiming that Israel had sold *Kfir* combat aircraft to South Africa have proven to be false. (The South African *Cheetah* is similar to the *Kfir,* since both are based on the French *Mirage.* Since French arms sales to South Africa are far greater than from Israel, there is no conclusive link between the two aircraft.) In April 1987, the US government estimated that Israel delivered $400–800 million worth of military technology to South Africa, indicating the size of the market, but these reports are also highly uncertain.[26] A report published by the Stockholm International Peace Research Institute concluded, "Contrary to what is often claimed, the Israeli government formally adhered to the mandatory embargo of 1977 [on arms sales to South Africa...]."[27] However, since the embargo covered weapons but not technology, Israel, like many other suppliers, could have transferred technology without actually violating the embargo.

In recent years, many of the reports of Israel-South Africa links focused on missile technology. South Africa has conducted a surface-to-surface ballistic missile research and development program, acquiring components and know-how from many sources. (According to the *Financial Times,* South Africa may also have sold missile technology to Iraq.[28]) Israel is reported to be a supplier, although, as Landgren notes, "The foreign technology needed for the missile industry was acquired from FR Germany, France, Israel, and possibly the United States, in that order."[29]

The links with Israel in this area apparently date to the 1970s, when the South African *Skerpioen* (*Scorpion*) ship-to-ship missile first appeared. Analysts note that "The actual identity of this missile is not quite clear—*Jane's Fighting Ships* says it is 'believed to be' the South Africa name for *Gabriel* 2. *Skerpioen* has also been described as a joint venture by Israel and South Africa, presumably based on *Gabriel* 2."[30]

More recently, there have been increasing reports of joint Israeli-South African development and testing of ballistic missiles. A missile test was reportedly conducted in July 1989, off the coast of South Africa. The *Washington Post* cited reports (apparently leaked by US intelligence officials) that the plume "bore a striking resemblance to that of an Israeli Jericho missile, and testing equipment at the site also resembled that known to be used by Israel."[31] A study published by a group from Stanford University claims that the test was conducted from Overberg, a test range on the southern Indian Ocean, and suggests that this was a test of a South African version of the *Jericho.*

In October 1989, NBC News ran a story which purported to show links between Israel and South Africa in missile development and testing. This report provided no "hard" evidence, showing pictures of South African launch sites, but no indication of Israeli involvement. This story was also based entirely on a combination of speculation and leaks from US government officials, whose access to information was limited and whose assessments have not always been accurate. (In March 1992, the same reporter, Fred Francis, was a channel for other claims regarding Israeli arms transfers. These assertions were later acknowledged by the State Department to be entirely false.) In 1989, a United Nations investigation, which could have been expected to be the most critical of Israeli policy and to provide detailed evidence of Israeli sales to South Africa, found no direct evidence of an Israeli link with South African missile development. Its authors could only note that, like many other countries, "Israel has the know-how to have helped." Other reports allege that in November 1988, US Customs inspectors conducted a "sting" operation in which a South African arms merchant with ties to Israel tried to illegally export gyroscopes from the US, using a fictitious Israeli firm as a conduit. Although there was no claim of Israeli government involvement, the United States reportedly placed the export of gyroscopes to Israel under careful scrutiny.[32]

Jerusalem either denies the allegations regarding cooperation with South Africa, asserting that they are part of the Arab political campaign to delegitimize Israel, or refuses comment (this is the Israeli policy regarding all arms sales). In March 1987, following numerous published reports on military ties, the Israeli cabinet publicly reiterated its adherence to the UN embargo, and extended export limits to include new contracts involving military technology and components. On September 16, 1987, the embargo was extended to include civilian contracts and goods. However, government officials and defense-industry personnel pointed out that the costs of these policies for the Israeli economy would be very great. The daily newspaper *Ha'aretz* warned that the economic impact could potentially result in the loss of hundreds or even thousands of jobs and even in the closure of major firms.[33]

In July 1991, after another round of leaks from the US, senior Israeli defense ministry officials declared that Israel was following American policy with respect to South Africa, and would not "implement an independent policy in this subject." They indicated that even if economic sanctions and social contacts were relaxed, the restrictions on military links would remain in effect.[34]

On October 27 1991, the *Washington Post* reported that "U.S. Intelligence agencies recently determined that Israel exported key ballistic missile components to South Africa..."[35] Another American publication reported that Israel and South Africa had conducted joint tests of the *Barak* naval anti-missile system off the Natal coast in August 1991.[36] This test may be evidence of broader Israeli-South African military links, or may indicate that intelligence analysts are confusing tactical ship protection missiles with tests of ballistic missiles. In any case, as Aaron Karp notes, "South Africa does not have a mature long-range rocket programme, nor is it investing in one."[37]

China. In the 1980s, the sale of Israeli arms and military technology to the People's Republic of China also grew. Like Iran and South Africa, China was a source of energy (oil and coal). China was also an emerging world power, and military links were seen as a means of developing political ties, and of diminishing the extent of Chinese support for the PLO and the radical Arab states.

The Chinese were impressed by the high level of Israeli military technology, and their ability to upgrade and extend the useful lifetimes of outdated Soviet-designed weapons. A series of high-level visits and exchanges followed, and this apparently led to contracts for the sale of Israeli weapons and technology. In 1983, the Israeli daily *Davar* published a story on an Egyptian military delegation which was in China to purchase upgraded Soviet tanks, and found out they had been upgraded with Israeli technology, and killed the deal. By the mid-1980s, published reports claimed that in this period, Israel had sold $3 billion in weapons and military technology to the PRC.[38] Like Iran under the Shah, and South Africa, the PRC had limited access to other sources of weapons, and could provide the Israeli arms industry with the export contracts necessary for survival.

In 1988, reports surfaced alleging that Israel had sold missile-related technology to China. The London *Sunday Times* reported that Israel had signed a contract worth "a few hundred million dollars" to provide China with sophisticated warheads for missiles.[39] During this period, China began to develop a new generation of more accurate solid-fueled ballistic missiles and IRBMs, such as the M-11 and M-9. Hua Di, reported to be a Chinese missile engineer, claimed that Israel had provided guidance technology to China,[40] and a report published in the *Economist* on March 23 1991, claimed that Israel also helped China improve the accuracy of the CSS-22 [sic] IRBM.[41] In November 1991, Defense Minister Moshe Arens went to Beijing, and analysts speculated that he sought to persuade the Chinese to halt the sales of missiles and nuclear technology to hostile Arab and Islamic states.[42] Since the Chinese are dealing with both sides, it is possible that they provided technical specifications of the missiles sold to the Arab states, which would help Israel in developing counter systems and ballistic missile defense.

In March 1992, the Auditor General of the US State Department issued a report asserting that a "major recipient of American military aid" had illegally transferred weapons with American components, or based on technology developed in the US, to third parties, including China.[43] The unnamed state was clearly Israel. At the same time, the US press published a series of reports based on leaks from "senior intelligence sources" claiming that Israel had also transferred components from the *Patriot* BMD system (or even a *Patriot* missile) to the PRC. The US government teams dispatched to check the *Patriot* batteries in Israel determined that the reports were false. Israel disputed the claims, based on the State Department Auditor's report, that weapons developed and produced in Israel, such as the *Python 3* and *Popeye* tactical missiles, were based on "American" weapons, such as the *Sidewinder* and the *Maverick*. Although the overall approach is similar in many cases, as could be expected from operational requirements, Israel claims that, as noted above, the first air-to-air missiles, on which the *Python* is based, were developed and tested before the *Sidewinder*. Similarly, although one version of the *Maverick* and the *Popeye* are both television-guided air-to-ground missiles, the *Maverick* has a much shorter range, smaller warhead, and entirely different mission (which explains the American decision to purchase the *Popeye*.) Assistant Secretary of State Richard Clark noted "there is a history that goes back at least ten years of reports of such violations....Many of them were specious on their face. Many others were investigated by intelligence agencies for many years, without any smoking guns ever being shown to us."[44] Although personal conflicts between State Department officials seem to have been involved, some Israeli analysts also saw these reports as politically motivated and designed to weaken support in the US for military aid. This case provides a clear illustration of the caution which must be exercised in attempting to evaluate such reports.

Evaluation and Assessment

As long as Israel is forced to maintain a strategic deterrent to insure national survival, development and production of advanced weapons, including missiles and technology will continue. In a broad sense, exports of these products are necessary to offset the high cost of this activity, and the overall cost of maintaining Israel's technology-intensive weapons industry. This income is necessary to maintain the Israeli military industry, and without it, firms such as IAI, *Ta'as* and Rafael might not survive.

Although sales of small arms and ammunition to a number of states in Asia and Western Europe provide some income, they are not nearly as profitable as advanced weapons and technology. (Iran reportedly provided Israel with $280 million in oil as a first payment for the short-lived joint venture known as Project Flower in the late 1970s.[45]) The market for these systems, however, is limited. With the exception of the Arab and Islamic states, the number of countries which have a need for advanced weapons and related technology as well as the resources to pay for them is minimal.

As seen in this study, advanced Israeli systems such as missiles and related technology, are primarily of interest to "pariah" states such as South Africa and China.[46] These customers, however, are inherently risky, and carry high political costs. These markets are also unstable, and, as in the case of Iran under the Shah, the current regimes in Pretoria and Beijing may not survive in the long term. Furthermore, their successors (particularly in the case of South Africa) are likely to be hostile to countries that supplied arms and technology, such as Israel.

Reports of sales to China and South Africa have indeed been politically costly to Israel. Such reports were leaked, apparently deliberately, by the US government in order to increase pressure on Israel. This activity was reported to be an obstacle to the agreement on American participation in the *Arrow* project.[47] Following the publication of a series of intelligence leaks, President Bush was asked about these reports in a press conference held on October 28, 1989. In his reply, he stated his opposition to the "transfer of any military technology that should not be transferred. And if that's taken place, it would not enhance relations between us, or any country that does that."[48]

In 1990, the US Congress enacted the Missile Technology Control Act, creating penalties for foreign firms that violate the MTCR guidelines. This provided the Administration with additional leverage to use against Israel. In October 1991, the *Washington Post* reported that "A U.S. official confirmed in Washington that State and Defense Department officials have cited the risk of Israeli missile technology transfers in seeking to bar Israeli Aircraft Industries and other firms from competition for U.S. defense contracts or approval of import licenses for military technology."[49] The penalties were waived by the Bush Administration (as provided for under the legislation) when Israel signed a bilateral agreement with the US that included the MTCR guidelines (see discussion below). In addition, as noted, the transfer or sale of Israeli technology also carries the risk that it will be retransferred to the Arab states, as reported in the case of the Chinese missiles sold to Saudi Arabia.

Economically, civilian space exports and continued American funding for the development and production of ballistic missile defense systems such as the *Arrow* provide potential alternatives. Both programs could provide employment and growth in the Israeli aerospace industry, and allow for the maintenance of the infrastructure for the development and production of ballistic missiles. However, either alternative requires a long-term contract to insure continuation of the program for many years. If the United States commits itself to funding for the *Arrow* over a period of seven to ten years, including production, maintenance, and upgrading, this could provide a substantial alternative to the sale of missile technology. Similarly, if the Israelis were able to obtain a major contract for commercial launch services, this would also allow for an end to the sale of missile-related technologies to other countries.

Export Structure

Historically, the framework for Israeli arms exports has been relatively loose. As is the case with other arms producers and exporters around the world, the emphasis is on sales over regulation. Most of the major exporting firms and producers are government owned and are closely linked to and funded by the Ministry of Defense. The MOD operates SIBAT, the agency responsible for exporting arms and technology. In addition, each major firm, such as IAI, IMI, and Rafael has its own marketing unit, which often operates independently of SIBAT. Hundreds of retired generals are also involved in military exports, either as licensed agents or as representatives of Israeli and foreign firms. This multi-tiered structure was developed to encourage exports, and has been generally successful.

Formally, there have been a variety of mechanisms designed to regulate the sale of military technology and weapons, but in practice these frameworks have had a limited impact on policy. Since a leak could easily lead a potential customer to withdraw, secrecy is very important, so the number of people involved in decision making is very limited. In theory, all applications for exports require a MOD license, but these are often granted routinely after the negotiations have been completed (except were a sale might compromise military secrets).

In 1983, a joint committee including representatives from the MOD, Foreign Ministry, and Ministry of Industry and Commerce was created. This committee, however, was dominated by the MOD, and there is little evidence that the Foreign Ministry played a significant role. In most cases, agreements were presented for formal approval once negotiations were completed and contracts had been initialed.[50] (Ben-Gurion declared that arms sales would be approved "in all cases where the Ministry of Foreign Affairs has no objection," placing the burden of proof on this ministry.)[51]

In 1986, following revelations about the role of private Israeli arms merchants in the Caribbean and Israeli connections to the Iran-Contra affair, the regulations were tightened. A permit from the Ministry of Defense is now required before negotiations can begin or exports can take place.[52] As noted above, in March 1987, the Israeli government announced that no new contracts involving military sales and technology would be signed with South Africa. A subcommittee of the Knesset Committee on Defense and Foreign Affairs was created to exercise legislative oversight, but this subcommittee has only three members, and appears to have played a very limited role, if any.[53]

The sale and transfer of sensitive technologies involving the major firms is generally handled at a very high level, with the direct involvement of the Minister of Defense and even the Prime Minister. The negotiations with Iran and South Africa in the 1970s, and with China in the 1980s, were all under the direct control of the Minister of Defense. In 1991, Defense Minister Arens went to China, even before the establishment of diplomatic relations between the two states.

The MTCR

Israeli research, development, and testing of ballistic missiles, as well as the transfer of technology, have been a source of conflict with the United States for many years. Much of this conflict has been centered on the MTCR. Since this regime was created in 1987, the US government has pressured Israel to join, and to accept the limits on transfer of ballistic missile technology as called for by this agreement. Israel, however, has resisted on the grounds that acceptance of the limitations of the MTCR was not in its national interest. The economic cost would be substantial, and, proportionately, far greater than for any other country that has accepted the MTCR. In addition, there was no evidence that the MTCR was effective in stopping the flow of missiles to Israel's enemies in the region. Indeed, the technology and assistance provided by MTCR signatories such as Germany, Britain, and the US was instrumental in the development of the Iraqi missile program[54] which produced the extended-range Scud-B missiles that were fired at Israeli cities in 1991. Other major suppliers were not members of the MTCR, including the Soviet Union, China, and North Korea.

Nevertheless, American pressure continued, and, in October 1991, after the US government threatened to ban Israeli firms such as IAI from conducting operations in the United States, the Israeli government agreed to accept the terms of the MTCR and signed a bilateral agreement with the U.S. to this effect. According to reports published in Israel, the government initially agreed to implement the terms of the agreement by the end of 1992, but the Bush Administration demanded implementation beginning at the end of 1991. Here again, the US position prevailed. In December 1991, the arms exporting agency of the Ministry of Defense (SIBAT) published regulations which required special Ministry of Defense approval for all missile technology, and a license from the Ministry of Commerce and Trade for potential dual-use technology.[55]

Acceptance of the terms of the MTCR, regulations which were issued, and the accompanying regulation and licensing mechanisms, created Israel's most extensive control system for exports of arms and military technology. The regulations are very specific and wide-ranging, and include limitations on Israeli nationals with experience in military technology from accepting employment in foreign-owned firms (such as National Semiconductor and Motorola) which operate in Israel. SIBAT sent copies of the regulations to exporting firms, along with forms for the managers of these firms to sign and return. These forms include an acknowledgment of the receipt of the regulations, and a pledge to inform the Ministry of Defense of intentions to produce or export MTCR-related technologies.[56]

There has been criticism of the impact of the MTCR limitations on Israeli industry and science. One critic wrote that "Israel has an interest in exporting know-how. It would therefore have been expected that the authors of the regulations would have phrased them in a way which would have minimized the coverage [of the limitations]. But this is not the case. ... According to the regulations, an Israeli scientist working in the area of solid fuel for rockets would be prohibited from lecturing abroad about his research, even if this research had been published."[57] In the *Jerusalem Post,* another author wrote that as a result of the bilateral agreement, "The bureaucratic procedures are tremendous. ... In a country where defense exports comprise a major segment of the national economy, the need for responsible export controls must be carefully weighed against the importance of preventing bureaucratic barriers from becoming too stringent."[58]

At the same time, the acceptance of the terms of the MTCR and their enforcement created expectations in Israel regarding the behavior or other supplier states, particularly the US. Washington was expected to take more active military and diplomatic measures to stop proliferation of missiles to Arab states and to Iran. This proliferation became a major issue in Israel after the Gulf war, because of the terror which remained after six weeks of Iraqi missile attacks on Israeli cities and the constant threat of chemical weapons.

However, in the months which followed the Israeli agreement regarding the MTCR, the actions of the US and the other suppliers have not met Israeli expectations. In March 1992, North Korean ships carrying SCUD-C missiles, launchers, and equipment to manufacture these missiles, reached Iran and the missiles and launchers were transshipped to Syria. (The Syrian government received $2 billion from Saudi Arabia for joining the anti-Iraqi coalition, and used this money to purchase weapons. While the US was actively pressuring Israel to accede to the MTCR, the Syrian activity was not forcefully criticized in public by the Bush Administration. Economic sanctions on Syria were meaningless as the economic links with the US are minimal.) In August 1992, Israeli Prime Minister Rabin revealed that the missiles had already been deployed and tested.

The failure to prevent the delivery of these missiles or to respond to the tests was followed closely in Israel. The threat posed by the proliferation of missiles in the Middle East continues, and the failure to slow this process could have an important impact on the future of the MTCR in the region. Another point of contention involves Israel's status in the MTCR structure. Some Israeli officials apparently expected the bilateral agreement to lead to formal membership in the regime.[59] Israel applied for membership in 1992, but the US government did not provide the expected support. Thus, some Israelis noted that they were forced to pay the costs of the limitations, without gaining the political and other benefits.

Israel has also followed the "cat and mouse" game between Saddam Husayn and the UN inspectors which has taken place since the end of the Gulf War. Prior to and during the war, the US asked for Israeli "restraint" in response to the SCUD missile attacks. The Bush administration pledged to destroy Iraqi missiles and chemical weapons. The cease-fire agreement of April 1991 specified a period of 120 days in which all of Iraq's non-conventional weapons, related materials, and production facilities would be destroyed under the verification of the United Nations. However, the speed with which the American troops withdrew from the area removed the incentives for Saddam Husayn to comply. Over a year passed, and the Iraqi capability, including hundreds of SCUD missiles, an unknown number of launchers, and large-scale production facilities continue to exist. Although the UN inspectors made some apparent progress in March 1992, following the renewed threat of bombing, the Israeli concern will continue as long as the verified destruction of these weapons is incomplete.

The major achievement of American efforts with regard to missile proliferation in the Middle East appeared to be with respect to China, which had agreed to sell advanced solid-fueled M-9 missiles to Syria. The cost of the transaction is reported to be $285 million.[60] The mobile launchers for these missiles were reported to have been delivered to Syria in 1991 or 1992, but the missiles did not appear.[61] Repeated American pressure and threats of sanctions seemed to have persuaded Beijing to refrain from providing these missiles. The Chinese were also participating, albeit with apparent reluctance, in the Arms Control in the Middle East (ACME) talks of the five permanent members of the UN Security Council (the "P-5").

In September 1992, however, George Bush suddenly announced the sale of 150 combat aircraft to Taiwan, in order to seek support in his reelection campaign. The Chinese responded angrily, and the Chinese Foreign Minister declared that his country was withdrawing from the P-5 talks. There were also reports that China would suspend limitations accepted under the MTCR guidelines, and might reinstate the sale of M-9 missiles to Syria. A few days later, Bush announced the sale of F-15s to Saudi Arabia, further undermining Middle East arms control efforts and the prospects for Chinese restraint.

Conclusions

The morality of arms sales to countries such as Iran under the Shah, South Africa, and China has been criticized, both within Israel and outside. Israeli government officials have rejected these moral accusations as hypocritical, charging that the billions of dollars worth of arms, including fighter aircraft, ballistic missile technology, and even materials for chemical and nuclear weapons which are sold by the US and Western European states to the Arab countries at war with Israel are morally unjustifiable. Indeed, Israelis note that their economic and military requirements provide a far stronger rationale for arms exports than can be found for American, German, or French sales. Israel would not need to develop ballistic missiles if other states did not continue to arm the Arabs with massive quantities of both conventional and unconventional weapons. Without the need for the *Jericho*, there would also be no exports.

Israel continues to be faced with clear threats to national survival, and these threats are expanding to include countries such as Iran, Libya, and Algeria. As long as the Arab and Islamic world denies the legitimacy of the Jewish state, and is able to acquire advanced weapons, including massive quantities of conventional arms and non-conventional weapons and technology, the threat to Israel will continue. Israel will therefore rely on deterrence and the threat of massive retaliation to offset this threat of annihilation.

Ballistic missiles are an important aspect of this strategy, and the expense of these weapons will also force Israel to seek a means to recover some of the cost. Alternatives could be found, such as long-term joint development of the *Arrow* ATBM, or the availability of civil space contracts, but at present neither can be considered likely.

Similarly, Israel continues to view regimes such as the MTCR with skepticism. The MTCR provides a global framework, designed to slow or stop the proliferation of missile technology over a period of years and even decades. In contrast, Israel's perspective is short-term and focused specifically on the Middle East. National security concerns are based on immediate threats to survival resulting from the proliferation of long-range ballistic missiles and weapons of mass destruction in the region.

To date, global regimes, such as the NPT, the London Supplier's group, and the MTCR have not succeeded in preventing proliferation in the Middle East. Iraq acquired a significant nuclear threat while under IAEA inspections. Since the MTCR was created in 1987, the signatories, led by the United States, have failed to prevent Iraq, Syria, Saudi Arabia, or Iran from acquiring long-range ballistic missiles.

The Israeli ballistic missile capability, and thus, the need to export this technology, is the result of the threat to national survival posed by the Arab and Islamic states. Ultimately, the reduction or even end to the military threat is the best and only sure means of preventing Israeli missile development and exports.

Notes

1. Munya Mardor, *Rafael* (Hebrew), Ministry of Defense Publishers, Tel Aviv, 1981, p.225–294; see also Stewart Reiser, *The Israeli Arms Industry*, New York: Holmes and Meier, 1989, pp. 60–63.

2. "Missile Proliferation: Survey of Emerging Missile Forces," Congressional Research Service, Washington D.C., February 9, 1989, p.56.

3. See Gerald Steinberg, "Israel: high technology roulette" in *Arms Production in the Third World*, edited by Michael Brzoska and Thomas Ohlson, Stockholm, Sweden, Stockholm International Peace Research Institute (SIPRI), Taylor and Francis, 1986, pp. 163–193; also Reiser, *The Israeli Arms Industry*.

4. *Jane's Weapons Systems*, 1981–2, p. 373, cited by Reiser, fn. p. 224.

5. Steve Fetter, "Ballistic Missiles and Weapons of Mass Destruction," *International Security*, Vol. 16, No. 1 (Summer 1991).

6. Fetter; see also "Missile Proliferation: Survey of Emerging Missile Forces," CRS, Washington D.C., February 9, 1989.

7. Marvin Feuerwerger, *The Arrow Next Time? Israel's Missile Defense Program for the 1990s*, Washington DC: The Washington Institute for Near East Policy, 1991.

8. Steve Fetter, "Ballistic Missiles and Weapons of Mass Destruction." Fetter assumes that the *Jericho* 2 constitutes the first two stages of the *Shavit*.

9. *Jane's Defence Weekly*, March 16, 1991, p.379.

10. *Ha'aretz*, March 27, 1992.

11. For a history of the Israeli defense industry, see Shimon Peres, *David's Sling*, New York: Random House, 1970; Yigal Allon, *Shield of David: The Story of Israel's Armed Forces*, London: Widenfield and Nicolson, 1970; also Stewart Reiser, *The Israeli Arms Industry*, and Gerald Steinberg "Israel: High-Technology Roulette."

12. See Aharon Klieman, *Israel's Global Reach: Arms Sales as Diplomacy*, New York, Brassey's, 1985.

13. Aharon Klieman, *Israel's Global Reach: Arms Sales as Diplomacy*, p.97; and Ian Anthony, editor. *Arms Export Regulations*, SIPRI, Oxford University Press, 1991.

14. For an analysis of Israeli deterrence policy, see Avner Yaniv, *Deterrence Without the Bomb*, Lexington, Mass.: Lexington Books, 1987; and Shai Feldman, *Israeli Nuclear Deterrence*, New York, Columbia University Press, 1982.

15. *Assessing Ballistic Missile Proliferation and Its Control*, Center for International Security and Arms Control, Stanford University, November 1991, p.68. See also Aaron Karp, "Ballistic Missile Proliferation," *1990 SIPRI Yearbook*, Oxford University Press, 1990, pp. 376–7.

16. Martin Navias, Ballistic Missile Proliferation in the Third World, Adelphi Paper 252, London: IISS, Summer 1990.

17. *Assessing Ballistic Missile Proliferation and Its Control*, Center for International Security and Arms Control, Stanford University, November 1991, pp. 68–69. See also Navias, p.30, and the chapters on Egypt and Korea in this volume.

18. Aaron Karp, "Ballistic Missile Proliferation," *SIPRI Yearbook*, 1991, World Armaments and Disarmament, Oxford University Press, 1992.

19. Gerald Steinberg, "Two Missiles in Every Garage: The Proliferation of Ballistic Missile Technology," *Bulletin of Atomic Scientists*, Vol. 29, No. 8, October 1983, pp. 43-48.

20. *Ibid*. See also the chapter on Iraq in this volume.

21. For a detailed analysis of Israeli arms exports, see Klieman, *Israel's Global Reach*.

22. After the Iranian Revolution and the overthrow of the Shah, there were a few small Israeli arms shipments, largely in the context of the "Iran-Contra" affair. The objective of these transactions was not commercial, but rather was essentially political. The Israeli government sought to reestablish links with Iran, despite the Islamic fundamentalist government, and to provide military support for Iran to prevent an Iraqi victory in the Gulf War.

23. CRS, February 1989.

24. Text of the minutes of a meeting between Israeli Minister of Defense Ezer Weizmann and Iranian Minister of War Toufanian on 18 July 1977, reproduced by the Iranian government in *Den of Spies* from documents found at the U.S. Embassy and the Israeli Interests Office, Teheran. The Hebrew translation was published in *Ma'ariv* on April 18, 1986.

25. See Joseph Bermudez's Chapter on Iran in this volume.

26. Report of Secretary of State George Schultz to the US Congress, cited by Landgren; see also R. Pedhazur, *Ha'aretz*, Nov. 10, 1991, p.3 .

27. S. Landgren, *Embargo Disimplemented: South Africa's Military Industry*, SIPRI, Oxford University Press, 1989, p.103 .

28. *Financial Times*, May 24 1991, p.1,6 .

29. Landgren, *Embargo Disimplemented*, p.103.

30. Landgren, p.109.

31. *Washington Post*, October 27 1991, p.1.

32. *Ha'aretz*, March 20, 1992, p.1.

33. *Ha'aretz*, October 26, 1987, p.9.

34. *Ha'aretz*, July 15, 1991, p. 3B.

35. *Washington Post*, October 27 1991, p.1.

36. See *NAVINT*, Vol. 3, No. 22, Nov. 8, 1991, p.1.

37. Aaron Karp, "Ballistic missile proliferation," *SIPRI Yearbook: World Armaments and Disarmament*, Oxford University Press, 1981.

38. *Davar*, October 24, 1986 pp. 5–7, citing *Jane's Defence Weekly*, December 1984.

39. Cited by *Al-Hamishmar* (Hebrew), April 3 1988.

40. *Ha'aretz* December 19 1991. See Hua Di's Chapter on China.

41. *Economist*, March 23 1991, p.50.

42. Jackson Diehl, *Washington Post*, November 20, 1991.

43. United States Department of State Office of Inspector General, *Report of Audit: Department of State Defense Trade Controls*, Washington DC, March 1992.

44. *Report of Audit*, p.36.

45. See the Chapter on Iran in this volume.

46. While there are some Israeli sales to Taiwan, Singapore and Sri Lanka, these are limited to small arms and do not include major systems or ballistic missile technology. Similarly, Israeli firms have sold ammunition and spare parts to Western Europe, but again, these sales are limited in scope.

47. Reuven Pedhazur, *Ha'aretz,* July 15, 1991, p.3.

48. Transcript, NBC Nightly News, *Defense-Dialog,* US Department of Defense, Washington DC, October 30, 1989.

49. *Washington Post* October 4 1991.

50. Klieman, pp. 92–122.

51. *New York Times,* Dec. 7, 1986, cited by Anthony.

52. Kleiman, pp. 94–96; see also Ian Anthony, SIPRI.

53. See *Ha'aretz,* 17 March, 1992, p. 5a.

54. Mike Eisenstadt, *The Sword of the Arabs: Iraq's Strategic Weapons.* Washington Institute for Near East Policy, Washington DC 1990; and Gary Milholin, "Building Saddam Hussein's Bomb," *New York Times Magazine,* March 8, 1992. See Mark Kagan's Chapter on Iraq.

55. *Ha'aretz,* April 12, 1992.

56. *Ha'aretz,* April 12, 1992.

57. Arye Niger, "Not Every Detail Requires a Permit," *Ha'aretz,* March 19, 1992.

58. Brent C. Mitchell, "Giving arms exporters a helping hand," *Jerusalem Post,* April 23, 1992.

59. There is a great deal of confusion regarding the MTCR and Israeli expectations. Apparently accepting the American position, Defense Minister Arens said that "We are not talking exactly about joining it, but about declaring that we adopt its principles." (*JPRS-TND*-91-016, 29 October 1991, p.40) However, a few months later, Israel did apply for membership, and Israeli officials expected American support.

60. *Milavnews,* March 1991, p. 23.

61. *Ha'aretz,* July 7, 1992.

11

El Condor Pasa: The Demise of Argentina's Ballistic Missile Program

Scott D. Tollefson[1]

Introduction

This chapter will examine Argentina's meteoric rise and fall as a producer and supplier of missile technology. That rise can be traced to 1979, when Argentina's military government began to develop the *Condor I*, a "meteorological research" rocket.[2] Buoyed by the success of the *Condor I*, in 1982 Argentina embarked on one of the most ambitious missile programs in the developing world—the *Condor II*, a ballistic missile designed to carry a 500 kilogram warhead to a range of over 1,000 kilometers. The *Condor II* program collapsed in 1989, when it was virtually frozen for lack of funds, and it was completely deactivated in 1991 by the Argentine government.

The case study of Argentina is significant for at least three reasons. First, by the mid-1980s Argentina had become the most successful developer of ballistic missiles in Latin America. Although Brazil had a more advanced space program and a broader industrial base, its ballistic missile capabilities lagged those of Argentina. Second, Argentina's *Condor II* program was sustained by an unusual international partnership. Iraq funded most of the program, with Egypt acting as a middleman. Over 20 companies were involved in supplying technology to the *Condor* project, from West Germany, Italy, France, Spain, Switzerland, and Austria.[3] This chapter argues that the fragility of that partnership in the face of a changing international system helps explain the eventual failure of Argentina's ballistic missile program.

Third, Argentina is often regarded as the country in which the Missile Technology Control Regime (MTCR) has had the greatest impact in stifling an incipient missile capability.[4] The MTCR was instrumental in inhibiting the *Condor II* program, but the influence was more indirect than has been posited. This chapter focuses on the relationship between the MTCR and the shifting political (and especially civil-military) dynamics within Argentina to explain the breakdown of the *Condor II* program.

Motives and Disincentives

Various factors motivated Argentina's space and missile programs, and those factors changed over time. Under the military regime (1976 to 1983), the *Condor I* and the *Condor II* programs were driven primarily by security interests. The Argentine military government was concerned with the security threats posed by Chile and Great Britain. In 1978, Argentina nearly went to war with Chile over their competing claims to the Beagle Channel islands. In 1982, the Argentine military fought a war to wrest control of the Malvinas/Falkland Islands from the British, but was humiliated. Given such a perception of threat, the military viewed a ballistic missile as necessary for Argentina's security.

In developing the *Condor*, Argentina's military was also driven by political motives such as prestige. Argentina sought to "keep up" with Brazil, its traditional rival for supremacy in South America. Although tensions with Brazil never approached the level of those with Chile and Great Britain, there was concern within the Argentine military that Brazil's rapidly-expanding space program could pave the way for a ballistic missile capability. At the time, Brazil was also under military rule, which seemed to heighten Argentina's perception of threat.

With the inauguration of civilian President Raúl Alfonsín in December 1983 (Alfonsín was president until 1989), there was a reduction of the security threats used to justify the *Condor* program. In one of his greatest accomplishments as president, Alfonsín set out to defuse tensions with Chile and Great Britain—tensions that the military had exploited to gain political legitimacy. In 1984 Alfonsín settled the Beagle Channel islands issue with Chile through papal mediation. Although Alfonsín continued to press Argentina's claims for the Malvinas/Falklands, he did so through diplomatic channels. In relation to Brazil, Alfonsín and his counterpart, José Sarney, signed a series of agreements that reduced tensions in their nuclear programs, and opened the way for economic integration between the two countries.

During Alfonsín's term, economic factors became dominant in driving the *Condor II* program. The Argentine Air Force, which was primarily responsible for the *Condor* program, began to justify the program on the grounds that it brought hard currency and advanced technology to

Argentina. Their argument was compelling, given that the *Condor II* program cost Argentina virtually nothing, financially. Iraq provided most of the funding, while firms from Germany and other European countries supplied the lion's share of the technology.

Political motives also sustained the *Condor II* program under President Alfonsín.[5] From a bureaucratic politics perspective, Alfonsín supported the *Condor II* program in order to appease the Air Force at a time when he was overseeing the trials of senior military officers charged with human rights abuses in the "dirty war" of the late 1970s. Furthermore, the *Condor* program gave the Air Force a role that was perceived as apolitical and benign. This perception changed with time, and will be discussed later.

The political motives for supporting the *Condor* program were mainly domestic. Argentina's foreign policy-makers were uninformed about most aspects of the project. It cannot be argued, therefore, that the Argentine government utilized the rocket and missile programs as instruments of external political influence.

Eventually, both external and internal disincentives led Argentina to dismantle its ballistic missile program. Externally, the major disincentives facing Argentina as a missile producer and supplier were economic and technological. Iraq stopped funding the missile in 1989. The U.S. threat of economic sanctions increased the potential costs of maintaining the *Condor II* program. The eventual restrictions of technology transfers by the U.S. and other MTCR signatories hindered Argentina's economic development.

Changes in the international system and Argentina's response to those changes also affected the *Condor* program. The collapse of the Soviet Union, historically one of Argentina's major trading partners, reduced the appeal of Argentina's nonaligned foreign policy. Under President Saúl Menem (1989-present), Argentina opted for a "First World" foreign policy and withdrew from the Non-Aligned Movement. In order to establish close ties with the First World, Argentina had virtually no choice but to disband the *Condor* program. Access to investment, technology, and credit in the United States and Western Europe would have been jeopardized by the continuation of the program.

Argentina's decision to deactivate the *Condor* program was consistent with President Menem's foreign and economic policies and his attempt to reinsert Argentina into the West. Under Menem, Argentina sent four ships to the Persian Gulf in support of the United Nations blockade against Iraq. Menem has sought closer ties with the United States, renewed relations with Great Britain,[6] has made Argentina's nuclear program more transparent, and cooperated in a regional integration agreement with Brazil, Paraguay, and Uruguay.[7] Iraq's pariah status after its invasion of Kuwait in August 1990 was the final blow to the *Condor* program. The invasion not only removed virtually any possibility of renewing Argentine cooperation with Iraq but it also increased the international scrutiny of Argentina's past cooperative efforts with Iraq.

Domestic economic factors also affected the *Condor* program. Under Alfonsín, a weak economy made it virtually impossible to fund the program once Iraq withdrew its financial support. The Argentine Air Force was not able to underwrite the program, which needed an infusion of at least $100 million in cash.[8] Those economic constraints continued under President Menem.

Perhaps the most overlooked disincentives to Argentina's *Condor* program have been in the domestic political realm. Both Alfonsín and Menem took dramatic strides to reduce the political influence of the military. Under Alfonsín, the military's share of the budget was purposefully reduced, from 6.5 percent of Gross National Product in 1982, to 3.4 percent in 1989.[9] Menem continued that trend, and went a step further by privatizing many of the military's assets, including numerous defense enterprises.[10] Although Menem issued a blanket pardon for all military officers who had been convicted or were facing charges of human rights abuses, he took strong action against mutineers in the coup attempt of December 1990.

By deactivating the *Condor* program, therefore, Menem has reduced Air Force prerogatives and influence in a sensitive area. The *Condor* program had become an Air Force fief, in which virtually no information was shared with civilians, including the president, foreign minister, and economy minister. Now, Menem has established civilian control over Argentina's space program, and resisted repeated attempts by the air force to regain control. Furthermore, Menem has placed the Foreign Ministry firmly in charge of any international developments relating to the space program.

In sum, changes in both the international missile transfer regime, as evidenced by the growing clout of the Missile Technology Control Regime, and Argentina's political regime, have led to the demise of the *Condor* program. It is the relationship between external and domestic (Argentine) factors that best explains the motives and disincentives for that program. Ultimately, however, domestic political disincentives were the most important.

Chronology of the *Condor II* Program[11]

In 1979, the Argentine government contracted Germany's Messerschmidt-Bloekow-Blohm (MBB) to assist in developing the *Condor I*, under the guise of a weather rocket. The *Condor I* was designed to deliver a 400 kilogram warhead a distance of over 150 kilometers.[12] MBB recruited engineers from CONSEN, a Swiss-based company, who arrived in Argentina in

1981 to work on the *Condor I*.[13] In that same year, Italy's SNIA-BpD shipped solid rocket fuel to the project.[14]

The *Condor II*, a two-stage intermediate-range ballistic missile propelled by solid fuel, grew out of the *Condor I* rocket program, but was much more sophisticated. The Argentine Air Force was in charge of both *Condor* projects, through its Institute of Aeronautic and Space Research (IIAE—Instituto de Investigaciónes Aeronáuticas y Espaciales). Argentina signed preliminary contracts with European firms as early as 1982, and by 1984 the program was established. The Air Force and its firm, Technologia Aerospacial SA, completed contracts with Germany's MBB, under which MBB continued to be the major supplier of technology, providing the missile design and simulation laboratories, in addition to special computers for missile guidance systems. Italy's Fiat transferred solid rocket motors and sensors.[15] In 1984 Argentina's government contracted CONSEN as a technical advisor in the *Condor II* project. MBB's subsidiary, Transtechnica, also assisted.[16] France's SAGEM provided inertial guidance systems.[17]

The *Condor II* program was sanctioned by Argentina's national executive branch through secret decree 604/85 on 9 April 1985.[18] According to U.S. intelligence sources, the initial purpose of the *Condor II* project was to provide Iraq and Egypt with indigenous production facilities for intermediate-range ballistic missiles that would be comparable to the *Pershing 2*,[19] a far more advanced missile than Iraq's SCUD.[20] Iraq and Egypt were to acquire 200 missiles each.

Argentina's role in the *Condor* project was to develop solid fuel technology and test the prototype. Argentina was chosen in part because it received less scrutiny than Iraq or Egypt by the United States and other Western countries.[21] Argentina was to receive some *Condor* missiles and hundreds of millions of dollars for the sale of solid-fuel engines to Egypt and Iraq.[22]

In 1984 Egypt reportedly signed an agreement with Argentina to begin development of the *Condor II*.[23] Egypt secretly represented Iraq, which financed the project. The Egyptians called their version of the project the *Badr 2000*.[24] MBB was the primary contractor for the project and provided assistance in design and planning, as well as "simulation laboratories and mission-control units based on advanced American computers." CONSEN was also involved in the Egyptian venture. The Egyptian program acted as a front for Iraq's DOT, its solid-fuel missile program. Egypt served as a conduit for machinery deliveries to DOT by MBB and SNIA-BpD.[25] North Korea and various Soviet-bloc countries may have provided additional assistance to Iraq.[26]

In a parallel development, Iraq's Sa'ad General Establishment signed a contract in early 1984 with West Germany's Gildemeister Projecta for the design and construction of a missile research, development, and testing center, near Mosul, a city in northern Iraq. The project was named "Sa'ad 16."[27] Eventually, dozens of companies from Western Europe (especially Germany) became involved in delivering equipment and technological know-how to Iraq for Sa'ad 16.[28] (See Kagan's chapter on Iraq.)

Sa'ad 16 was Iraq's version of the *Condor* projects in Argentina and Egypt.[29] The Egyptian and Iraqi building plans were identical.[30] In the mid-1980s, many of the European firms and engineers that were active in the Argentine *Condor* program also were involved in the Iraqi and Egyptian versions of the program. A number of former MBB engineers actively sought technology for both the Sa'ad 16 and *Condor II* projects.[31] Vienna-based Consultco Ltd. and the German firm Gildemeister Projects Ltd. shared an office in Mosul, Iraq.

MBB was Gildemeister Projecta's main supplier of technology, and may have provided technology for fuel-air explosives, utilizing Egypt as an intermediary.[32] MBB's involvement in the Sa'ad 16 project is now a matter of public record, but under the ambiguous German laws at the time, it was unclear whether MBB and other German firms were acting illegally. MBB's subsidiary Transtechnica was the main equipment supplier, making three deliveries of lab equipment, the last in December 1988. According to various reports, the Iraqi "*Condor II*" manufacturing sites were completed between December 1988 and March 1989.[33]

The linkages between the Argentine, Iraqi, and Egyptian programs were evident on a managerial level. For example, the chairman of CONSEN's board of directors, Helmut Raiser, was a Zug explosives expert who previously managed Salzburg Bowas Induplan Chemie (a West German Bohlen-Halbach group subsidiary specializing in chemical plants). Raiser was also on the boards of directors of many of the companies later involved with IFAT and DOT.[34] IFAT, based in Zug, Switzerland, was a CONSEN affiliate.

In March 1984, the first of many U.S. firms was drawn into the broad *Condor* scheme.[35] IFAT sought to convince Honeywell (United States) to undertake a fuel-air explosive (FAE) study.[36] In September of the same year, Honeywell and IFAT signed a contract for two studies relating to payloads. IFAT specified a 360 kilogram net warhead weight. Honeywell was later questioned regarding allegations that one of its executives sold plans for a ring laser gyroscope to IFAT.[37] A 4 November 1984 memorandum from J.D. Beckman of Honeywell revealed that the Egyptians were developing a ballistic missile. IFAT received a deposit of $1 billion in a Swiss account.[38]

In further Egyptian-U.S. developments, samples of ceramic-ceramic and carbon-carbon composites were smuggled out of the United States to Egypt in late 1987 by the head of the Egyptian *Condor II* procurement team, Colonel Fuad al-Gamal. Such samples could be used to determine which of the materials worked best for nose cones and rocket nozzles.[39] Abdelkadr Helmy, a native of Egypt with U.S. citizenship, was found guilty in Sacramento, California of attempting to buy secret technology for the nose cones.[40]

In the mid-1980s, the United States vigorously protested the involvement of German firms in the *Condor* program. In 1985 the German government began to pressure MBB to withdraw from the *Condor II* program. In response, MBB left the Egyptian program but continued to participate in DOT.[41] MBB's subsidiary, Transtechnica, proceeded to make deliveries to CONSEN and CONSEN's Argentine clients. MBB denied any knowledge of those deliveries. Finally, in mid-1986, Transtechnica halted shipments to the *Condor II* project.[42]

According to U.S. intelligence sources, Argentina shipped between 12 and 30 *Condor* missile air frames to Egypt, from September 1988 to March 1989.[43] Other reports confirm such shipments.[44] In April 1990 it was reported that Argentina had produced five prototypes of the *Condor II* in the Falda del Carmen plant. The Argentine government itself admitted, in March 1991, to delivering eight *Condor* missiles to Egypt.[45] The U.S. government was most concerned with the solid fuel motor and guidance technology Argentina had sent to Iraq.[46]

The French magazine *L'Express* reported that Argentina's Intesa firm exported guidance components to Iraq that had been built by France's SAGEM. French President Mitterrand denied this report, however.[47] Other reports suggest that German cooperation with Argentina may have led to the use of German technology by the Iraqis in increasing the range of their SCUD missiles.[48]

Falda del Carmen, a $200 million plant, was built in the mid-1980s with Iraqi and Egyptian financial support, and is 700 kilometers northwest of Buenos Aires.[49] According to various reports, the *Condor II* missile was tested there some time between early 1988,[50] late 1988,[51] or April 1989.[52] However, U.S. officials who visited the site claimed that the test facilities look unused.[53]

The U.S. government assigned a high priority to slowing or halting the *Condor II* program. That pressure preceded the MTCR by at least two years.[54] The United States stepped up its opposition in October 1988, when U.S. Secretary of Defense Frank Carlucci warned Argentina's Defense Minister Horacio Jaunarena regarding the *Condor* project.[55] Israel, Great Britain, and Iran also pressured Argentina to curb the program.[56] That pressure eventually led to the liquidation of CONSEN and IFAT.[57]

In 1989, the *Condor* program began to collapse. Egyptian Defense Minister Abu Ghazalah was forced out of office when he was implicated in a conspiracy to smuggle missile technology out of the United States, in blatant violation of export control laws.[58] In June 1989 Egyptian President Hosni Mubarak announced to Britain's Prime Minister Margaret Thatcher that his country had severed all ties with the *Condor* project.[59]

On 19 September 1989, U.S. Assistant Secretary of State John H. Kelly confirmed that Egypt had terminated its cooperation with Iraq and Argentina on the *Condor II*.[60]

In the aftermath of the Iran-Iraq war (1980 to 1988), and in the face of falling petroleum revenues due to the low world price of oil, Iraq was forced to reduce its imports of arms and missile technology. In all likelihood, Iraq stopped funding the Argentine *Condor II* program in 1988. In May 1989 Iraq denied that it was still funding Argentine missiles,[61] which was probably true. Iraq seems to have decided in 1988 that it either no longer needed or could no longer afford the support of Argentina and Egypt in its quest for an intermediate-range ballistic missile.

On 5 December 1989, Iraq successfully launched a "satellite-carrier rocket system" from the space research center at al-Anbar. That system was composed of three stages, as opposed to the *Condor II*, which was a two-stage rocket. Iraq received assistance from Egyptian and Argentine scientists and engineers in the rocket's development.[62]

On 30 June 1989, the Italian government brought charges against nine former employees of SNIA-BpD, for selling medium-range missile technology to Argentina, Egypt, and Iraq. Documents disclosed that the Special Aircraft Research Company of Cordoba, Argentina, had signed a contract with SNIA-BpD in 1981. The Italian military searched the warehouses of SNIA-BpD and Rata (also in Italy) and discovered parts of the missile and components of the mobile nozzle with which the *Condor* missile was equipped.[63]

In September 1989, U.S. President George Bush and Secretary of State James Baker informally pressured recently-elected Argentine President Carlos Menem and his Foreign Minister Domingo Cavallo to suspend the *Condor* project.[64] According to one account, U.S. Ambassador to Argentina Terence Todman sent a letter to Defense Minister Antonio Erman Gonzalez that listed all of the failed promises that had been made to him by the Argentine government concerning the dismantling of the *Condor* program.[65]

In April 1990, Argentina announced that the *Condor II* program was being "paralizado" (halted). Foreign Minister Domingo Cavallo said the reason for this decision was to prevent the technology from falling into Iraq's hands.[66] On 20 July 1990, the Menem administration issued a secret decree that suspended contracts for selling missile parts to Egyptian and German firms.[67]

The Menem administration went a step further, and began to reveal past missile activities. In January 1991 Cavallo disclosed that as president, Alfonsín secretly authorized two executive branch decrees (Decree No. 604, of 9 April 1985; and Decree No. 1315, of 13 August 1987, also signed by then-Defense Minister Jaunarena), in which *Condor II* missile technology was transferred to Iraq in exchange for money. Decree No. 604 approved, "without reservations, several contracts and the formation of firms..."[68] Menem annulled the project shortly after coming to office.

By the end of 1990, therefore, Argentina was virtually out of the *Condor* program. Iraq continued to apply its *Condor* technology to build a prototype of the *Condor* missile, but was unable to adequately solve the technical problems relating to the guidance system.[69] By the time the Gulf War (Desert Shield) broke out in 1991, the Iraqis were in the process of extending the two-stage *Condor II* by another stage.[70] Argentine Vice President Eduardo Duhalde stated that his government "suspects" that Argentine-made *Condor II* missiles were used in the Persian Gulf war.[71]

The key date in the demise of the *Condor II* program was 28 May 1991, when Defense Minister Gonzalez announced the cancellation (as opposed to the halting) of the project. In a monumental shift in Argentine foreign policy, Gonzalez stated that Argentina would adhere to MTCR guidelines. He also announced the creation of a space commission that would be placed under the direct control of President Menem. Gonzalez noted, however, that all "non-bellicose" technology would be retained.[72]

The cancellation of the *Condor II* was supported by Minister of Economy Cavallo and Minister of Foreign Relations Guido di Tella.[73] On 3 June 1991, President Menem endorsed Gonzalez' statements and stated that "all parts of the *Condor* missile, in all of its versions and stages of development, will be deactivated, dismantled, reconverted, or unutilized, according to their use in peaceful applications."[74] On 10 February 1992, Argentine officials dismantled components of the *Condor II* missile under the direct supervision of U.S. inspectors.[75] Argentina was rewarded almost immediately, as U.S. Secretary of Defense Richard Cheney traveled to Buenos Aires and promised on 20 February that the United States would provide two ships, two Hercules C-130 planes, and would refit six other C-130s.[76]

In sum, the collapse of the *Condor* program was a gradual, yet sporadic process. Today the *Condor is* dead. In order for Argentina to resurrect the *Condor*, it would take a political decision at the presidential level, major funding, significant technology transfers, and considerable time—a combination of factors that grows increasingly remote. No factor is pushing Argentina in this direction. Furthermore, the costs of reactivating the *Condor* project only escalate with time.

Transactions

Argentina as a Transshipper

Argentina was an eager participant in the *Condor* program, at least until 1989. Argentina served as a transshipper of numerous missile-related goods and of technology to Egypt and Iraq. Argentina specialized in the second stage of the *Condor* rocket and solid fuel technology, and was also tapped to conduct the tests of the *Condor.* There are no instances recorded in which Argentina was approached for the sale of missiles or missile-related items and services, but declined.

All of Argentina's important trade agreements were carried out on a strict cash basis, in which Argentina performed a service for Iraqi money. There were no offsets or counter-trade involved in the transactions. Argentina and Egypt did discuss co-production possibilities, but little if any such activity actually transpired. Although Argentine officials had hopes of selling a missile in the world market, they never had a marketable product.[77]

Estimates vary, but Argentina may have received as much as US $1.5 billion to US $2.2 billion for its efforts in developing the *Condor II* missile,[78] although most sources place the figure at a more modest US $200 million to US $400 million.[79] The total cost of the *Condor* project between 1984 and 1991 is calculated to have been between US $3.2 billion[80] and US $5 billion, with Iraq providing most of the funding.[81] In 1991, the Atlanta branch of Banca Nazionale del Lavoro of Italy was under U.S. Congressional investigation for US $3 billion of Iraqi loan commitments. The funds were apparently diverted to the *Condor II* project.[82]

Argentina has not received any major funding for its missile or space programs since 1988. With the dismantling of the *Condor II* program, no revenues are expected from future missile exports. There is the potential for Argentina to sell some of its space technology, but any such revenues would be modest, and would be superseded by the costs of dismantling the *Condor II* program.

The Government's Role

Although the Argentine government was aware of the general nature of Argentina's missile trade, it was uninformed about many of the details. Economy Minister Domingo Cavallo stated that under Alfonsín and the retired Air Force chief of staff, Brigadier General Ernesto Crespo, there was "an illegal situation, a commitment to export technology without the participation of the Argentine Foreign Ministry and the Economy Ministry, as is established by law."[83] The Argentine Air Force worked in an institutional vacuum, and was accountable to no one — not even the Defense Minister or the President, who often had only limited knowledge of many aspects of the program. Much of the funding for the *Condor* missile program went directly to the Air Force, which operated in secrecy.[84] Consequently, any restrictions and guarantees that the state may have placed on missile-related transfers were virtually meaningless.

In 1992 it was reported that Argentina's original plans for the *Condor II* had disappeared from Air Force archives over an 18-month period. The Air

Force probably disposed of the documents to protect itself. As a result, the civilian government has virtually no records of the project.[85] Today, Argentina is not involved in any missile trade, so the question of state support for joint venture activities in missile production and transfers is less relevant.

In a sense, the entire *Condor II* missile project was an example of illegal and black market activity. For example, end use certificates for Egypt were purposefully ignored, as Argentine *Condor* technology was transferred to Iraq, often through Jordan. In Argentina, there was no effective civilian oversight of the Air Force and its companies, which operated with impunity. European firms took advantage of weak government supervision, and broke various laws. There is no evidence, however, that technology or goods from the *Condor* program were diverted to countries other than Iraq, Egypt, and Argentina.

In short, Argentina's missile export behavior has changed dramatically. The recklessness of the mid-1980s has given way to prudence and adherence to international standards. The Menem administration recognized that a continuation of rash behavior in the missile realm negatively affected Argentina's broader goals of approximation with the First World.

Capabilities

Missiles

Perhaps the most insightful point made by Cavallo in revealing the secret deals with Iraq is that "the technological development was not autonomous, but a compensation mechanism that allowed Argentina to obtain technology for its foreign partners under the condition that the technology transfer be made from Argentine territory."[86] This suggests that the *Condor* program was virtually an enclave—politically, economically, and technologically. Politically, as seen above, the civilian government had virtually no control over the program. In terms of economic benefits, the *Condor* program produced few linkages to the rest of the Argentine economy. In addition, there were no major technological spin-offs from the project.

At present, there are virtually no transactions taking place involving Argentine missile technology, equipment, components, and services. Argentina will probably continue to develop sounding rockets, as well as the *Alacran*, a multiple launch rocket system (MLRS). The *Alacran* would be capable of delivering a 100-kilogram payload to a distance of 200 kilometers—far under the MTCR threshold (500 kilograms; 300 kilometers). Although it is called a missile by the Argentines, U.S. government officials refer to it as a rocket, because it is unguided. U.S. government officials exhibit little concern over the *Alacran*.[87]

Space Program

Argentina has been involved in space activities since 1951, when a group of scientists created the Argentine Interplanetary Association.[88] Four decades later, however, Argentina does not have significant space launch capabilities. In early 1991, Argentine government officials declared that some of the *Condor* technology would be transferred to the space program. Felix Menicocci, the Third Secretary in Argentina's Foreign Ministry, Directorate of International Security, Nuclear and Space Affairs, argues that such an approach was taken in order to placate the opposition. Today, the funding for Argentina's space and *Alacran* programs is so limited that there is virtually no activity taking place in either.[89]

In May 1991, the Argentine government wrested control of the National Commission for Space Research (CNIE) from the Air Force, and placed it in civilian hands.[90] That decision led to Decree 995/91, which created the National Commission for Space Activities (CNAE—*Comision Nacional de Actividades Espaciales*). The CNAE eventually replaced the Space Investigations Commission. Defense Minister Erman Gonzalez announced that "all the installations and equipment" used for the *Condor II* project would be placed under CNAE, and would be used to produce a rocket capable of placing satellites in orbit.[91]

On 10 February 1992 the Argentine Air Force formally transferred the remnants of the *Condor II* project to the CNAE. CNAE is under presidential and Congressional control, and is responsible for all space-related activities. The chief of CNAE is Jorge Sa'ade, who hopes to make his organization the Argentine "NASA" (U.S. National Aeronautics and Space Administration).[92] Sa'ade announced in August 1991 that Argentina, Brazil, and Mexico would begin feasibility studies for the joint production of a satellite-launch vehicle.[93]

In other space-related developments, in August 1991 CNAE signed a framework agreement with NASA.[94] In the following month, the Applied Research Institute (INVAP) in Rio Negro province announced that it would join NASA in constructing a satellite, the SAC-B (Satellite Argentino Cientifico—the Argentine Scientific Satellite), which is scheduled to be launched from a U.S. space shuttle in 1994. INVAP will produce the guidance package of the new satellite, including precision instruments. The purpose of the satellite is to study solar rays and measure gamma rays.[95]

Argentina has sought to increase space cooperation with partners beyond the United States. Russian Vice President Aleksandr Rutskoy stated that his country will transfer space technology to Argentina.[96] The Spanish Defense Ministry's Aerospace Technical Institute may co-produce a satellite with Argentina at Falda del Carmen, where the *Condor II* was developed.[97] In addition, there are plans to have a joint *Mercosur* satellite for communications purposes. The satellite will be produced by Brazil, however. Such partnerships and arrangements are a far cry from the extensive *Condor* network that Argentina built up in the mid-1980s.

Bottlenecks

Argentina's major technological bottleneck in developing the *Condor II* was the system for guidance and control. At the time of the cancellation of the *Condor II* program, it was estimated that Argentina had at least five, and up to 30 *Condor II* missiles assembled or nearly assembled. Those missile lacked only a reliable guidance system.[98] Argentina began work on a guidance mechanism in 1988 after having developed a propulsion system, but by then Iraq had withheld its funding of the Argentine program.[99] Argentina faced other technical problems, but they were of far lesser concern.

Structures

Export Licensing

On 9 April 1992, the Argentine government adopted a new system for controlling the technology and materials used for missiles; and for nuclear, chemical and bacteriological weapons. That system was formalized in a ceremony on 27 April, attended by President Menem and U.S. Ambassador Todman. According to Menicocci, the new policy is based on MTCR guidelines, imposes strict controls and penalties, and will be updated in accordance with changes in the MTCR. End user certification will be required and monitored.[100]

Argentina's export licensing process for sensitive technology is being redefined. An initial draft of the bill stipulated that a single commission, headed by the Foreign Ministry, will approve the transfer of conventional arms, missiles, and space technology. The defense minister and CNAE will also be a part of the process. Of the seven representatives on CNAE's board of directors, only two are from the armed forces—one from the Air Force, and one from the Navy. In effect, the Argentine president and vice president head the commission. The Foreign Ministry's proposals have not been formally presented to the national legislature and the president, who must approve them.[101]

Role of Various Actors

In the mid-1980s, the Air Force was the most important actor in determining the export of Argentine missile products and technology. Today, the prerogatives of the Air Force have been reduced in this area, and although some retired military officers have made comments concerning the process, they are outside the formal decision-making structures.

Clearly, civilian elements within the government have the upper hand in formulating and implementing Argentina's space and space-related programs. The Foreign, Defense, and Economy Ministries are the most important actors in this process.

Private sector actors, quasi-governmental actors, and multinationals continue to exercise very little influence regarding missile exports or the space program. The major Argentine companies that were involved in the *Condor* missile program were linked to the Air Force, and with the demise of the program are no longer relevant actors. Those companies included the following:

1. Aerotech. As part of the CONSEN group, it sent "missile technology" to Iraq.
2. Conseltech. Also a part of the CONSEN group, it helped to import high-technology items into Argentina by organizing end-user certificates for the Argentine government which were then reportedly sent to Egypt and Iraq.
3. Intesa S.A. This company was bought out by CONSEN and restructured as a joint venture with IIAE, a technical agency of the Argentine Air Force. It may have passed missile guidance equipment from the French firm SAGEM to Iraq.
4. Technologia Aerospacial S.A. The Argentine Air Force used this firm to contract for the *Condor* project.[102]

Norms

Declaratory Policies

The Argentine government has stated emphatically that it will not produce or export ballistic missiles or missile-related services. At the MTCR meeting in November 1991, Argentina formalized its adherence to the MTCR and asked to be invited to the next meeting. Argentina has sought regulatory advice as it develops a new set of guidelines for technology transfers.[103] The Argentine government has expressed an interest in becoming a full-fledged member of the MTCR.

Prevailing Views

The decision to cancel the *Condor II* program elicited substantial opposition in Argentina, especially from the Air Force and the Radical party (UCR—*Union Cívica Radical*). In February 1991, retired Brigadier General Ernesto Crespo criticized the cancellation,[104] and stated that "Argentina will become a banana republic if it allows another nation to decide the future of the Condor II."[105] On 17 May 1991, the Argentine government punished Crespo with 30 days of house arrest for his unauthorized public statement. In a highly unusual move, Crespo requested his discharge from the armed forces. Later, Crespo debated Economy Minister Domingo Cavallo on the radio.[106]

In April 1991 Cavallo accused Air Force Chief of Staff General Jose Antonio Julia of being unwilling to fully cancel the *Condor* missile project, and urged that Julia be replaced. Julia was retained, but only after Defense Minister Antonio Gonzalez "reaffirmed his confidence" in Julia.[107] In a separate incident, Colonel Louis Guerrero, head of the *Condor II* project, said that there was an international campaign against Argentine production of the *Condor II* "because the United States never forgave us for transferring technology to Iraq that permitted that country to build its own missiles in a much shorter time."[108]

The Radical party protested the cancellation of the *Condor*. Leading the charge were two of the most important civilians in the development of the *Condor* missile: Alfonsín, former president and head of the Radical party; and Jaunarena, former minister of defense. Alfonsín "categorically rejected" the cancellation of the *Condor II* program, and argued that the government should continue the project "in defense of our sovereignty."[109] Jaunarena argued that "it makes no sense to renounce the *Condor II* if Chile, Brazil and other countries continue to strengthen their efforts in this kind of project."[110] Within the Congress, a bloc of Radical nationalist deputies were joined by other opposition legislators in asking the government to continue developing the *Condor II*, and to "reject foreign pressures to dismantle it."[111] Radical Senator Ricardo Lafferriere (of Entre Rios province) proposed that the *Condor II* project be declared "in the national interest" and that development be continued under "strategic congressional control."[112]

Despite such vitriolic statements in opposition to the government's decision to deactivate the *Condor* program, the decision is supported by the Peronist (*Justicialista*) party, which has a majority in both houses of Congress. In addition, the Navy, and more significantly the Army, have failed to openly support the Air Force position. It would seem that the Radicals would only be able to alter the current policy if they were able to gain control of the presidency and the national legislature. Such a prospect seems unlikely, but even if it did occur, it is doubtful that the Radicals would reverse the decision to cancel the *Condor*, given the changing cost-benefit calculation.

Links Between Nuclear and Missile Programs

Despite some argument to the contrary,[113] there appears to have been very little linkage between Argentina's nuclear and ballistic missile programs. One unidentified company involved in the nuclear program worked on some aspects of the missile program, but its involvement was not significant. Some minor *Condor* activity took place at Argentina's uranium enrichment plant in Pilcaniyeu. At no time did Argentina seek to produce a warhead, nuclear or otherwise.[114]

Conclusion

The dramatic changes that President Menem brought to Argentina's ballistic missile program should not overshadow a more gradual and enduring phenomenon—that of "social learning" on the part of the Argentines.[115] Regime change had a major impact on Argentine security, foreign, and economic policies. But regime change and democratic consolidation are gradual and uneven processes. Changes that began under Alfonsín, such as the reduction of military prerogatives, were accelerated under Menem.

Likewise, it took time for the efforts of the MTCR to influence the *Condor II* program. It is this relationship, between political regime change in Argentina and a strengthened missile proliferation regime (the MTCR) that best explains the eventual cancellation of the *Condor II* missile program, despite some opposition within Argentina. The "social learning" process suggests that the success in halting the proliferation of ballistic missile technology in Argentina can be reinforced by further consolidation of democracy, and by appropriate incentives from the international community.

Notes

1. The views expressed in this chapter are entirely those of the author, and should not be interpreted as representing the official views of the U.S. Department of Defense, the U.S. Navy, the Naval Postgraduate School, or any other government agency.

2. Alan George writes that "there was widespread suspicion from the beginning that the military applications were of far greater interest to Argentina." See "Flight of the Condor," *The Middle East*, April 1989, p. 20.

3. *Nuclear Developments*, 14 August 1989, p. 31, citing Alberto Cipriani, *L'Unita* (Milan), 30 June 1989, p. 6 ; *Nuclear Developments*, 14 August, 1989, p. 42, citing *Ansa* (Rome), 31 July 1989.

4. Henry D. Sokolski, "Export Control Policies and Processes," Statement Before the Joint Economics Committee, Subcommittee on Technology and National Security, U.S. Senate, 23 April 1991, p. 9. Sokolski is the Deputy for Non-Proliferation, Office of the Assistant Secretary of Defense, International Security Affairs, U.S. Department of Defense.

5. In an interview with the author, Rosendo Fraga (president of the Union for the New Majority Studies Center, Buenos Aires) claimed that President Alfonsín tried to gain political control of the Air Force and *Condor*, but failed. President Carlos Menem, in contrast, succeeded in subordinating the military. Fraga stressed

the (1) incapacity of civilians to oversee the missile and space programs; and (2) the incapacity of the military to restructure itself. Buenos Aires, 18 November 1991.

6. According to one account, one of the preconditions stipulated by Great Britain for resuming diplomatic relations with Argentina was the dismantling of the *Condor II* program. See "Book Details Background of Condor-2 Missile," (in Spanish), *Clarin* (Buenos Aires), 1 March 1992, p. 10, in *Foreign Broadcast Information Service, Latin America* (hereafter refered to as *FBIS LAT)* 92-044, 5 March 1992, p. 16. The article makes reference to a book by journalist Daniel Santoro.

7. Rosendo Fraga, "La Argentina en el Golfo Persico" [Argentina in the Persian Gulf], *Nacion*, 25 September 1990, p. 16.

8. Political counselor, U.S. embassy in Buenos Aires, interview with author, 19 November 1991.

9. U.S. Arms Control and Disarmament Agency, *World Military Expenditures and Arms Transfers, 1990*, released November 1991, p. 53.

10. See "Privatization of Military Enterprises Viewed," (in Spanish), *Clarin* (Buenos Aires), 17 February 1992, p. 14, in *FBIS LAT*-92-033, 19 February 1992, p. 27; "Military Industries Register $700 Million Loss," (in Spanish), *Clarin* (Buenos Aires), 22 January 1992, p. 18, in *FBIS LAT*-92-017, 27 January 1992, p. 26; and "Privatization Planned for Pampa Airplanes Maker," (in Spanish), *Clarin* (Buenos Aires), 14 May 1992, p. 32, in *FBIS LAT*-92-097, 19 May 1992, p. 22.

11. This chronology is a synthesis of relevant data in the International Missile Proliferation Project database at the Monterey Institute of International Studies.

12. *Nuclear Developments* 5 May 1989, pp. 34-36, citing Herbert Langsner and Alan George, *Profil* (Vienna), 24 April 1989, pp. 38-42.

13. Timmerman writes that "As time went on, Consen became little more than a stand-in for MBB, which was providing the bulk of the Condor technology. By channeling its sales and cooperation through Consen, MBB could claim ignorance of the real nature of the project, which it would later describe as a 'meteorological rocket.' It could also claim, as a review of MBB promotional literature shows, that its principal export markets were in the industrialized West (Consen companies were registered in Switzerland, Austria, and Monaco), when in fact MBB was fueling an indigenous Third World armament program." Timmerman, *The Death Lobby* (Boston: Houghton Mifflin Co., 1991): p. 152.

14. Snia-BpD, the National Industrial Applications Company, was formerly a subsidiary of Fiat; BpD is the Defense Division). BpD later claimed that the fuel was originally purchased from Baker-Perkins of Saginaw, Michigan. Timmerman, *The Death Lobby*, pp. 53-4, 152.

15. Nathaniel C. Nash, "Argentina's President Battles His Own Air Force on Missile," *New York Times*, 13 May 1991, pp. A1, A5; Nuclear Developments, 10 April 1989, pp. 33-34, citing *Der Spiegel* (Hamburg), 27 March 1989, pp. 170–173; *Nuclear Developments*, 14 July 1989, pp. 30-36, citing *Der Spiegel* (Hamburg), 12 June 1989, pp. 70-86.

16. *Nuclear Developments*, May 5, 1989, pp. 34-36, citing Langsner and George, *Profil* (Vienna), 24 April 1989, pp. 38-42.

17. Timmerman, *The Death Lobby*, p. 154.

18. *Nuclear Developments*, 25 February 1991, p. 13, citing *Somos* (Buenos Aires), 28 January 1991, pp. 1-4.

19. See Mel Elfin, "Behind the Condor Carbon-Carbon Smuggling Scam," *U.S. News & World Report*, 25 July 1988, p. 38.

20. Henry D. Sokolski, "Export Control Policies and Processes," Statement Before the Joint Economic Committee, Subcommittee on Technology and National Security, U.S. Senate, 23 April 1991, p. 9.

21. Jimmy Burns and Alan Friedman, *Financial Times*, 9 March 1992, p. 3.

22. Janne E. Nolan and Albert D. Wheelon, "Third World Ballistic Missiles," *Scientific American*, vol. 263, no. 2 (August 1990), p. 39; *U.S. News & World Report*, 25 July 1988, p. 38; *Nuclear Developments*, 25 February 1991, p. 13, citing *Somos* (Buenos Aires), 28 January 1991, pp. 1-4.

23. This information is according to company documents, and is cited in Timmerman, *The Death Lobby*, p. 155.

24. Timmerman writes that in naming their project the *Badr 2000*, Egypt suggested that "the new missile's range was 2,000 kilometers (in fact, Condor II is believed to have been designed to fly 1,000 kilometers, or around 600 miles)." Timmerman, *The Death Lobby*, p. 156.

25. *Nuclear Developments*, 5 May 1989, pp. 34-36, citing Langsner and George, *Profil* (Vienna), 24 April 1989, pp. 38-42.

26. *U.S. News & World Report*, 25 July 1988, p. 38; *Nuclear Developments*, 5 May 1989, pp. 34-36, citing Langsner and George, *Profil* (Vienna), 24 April 1989, pp. 38-42.

27. Timmerman, *The Death Lobby*, p. 156.

28. See *Nuclear Developments*, 23 August 1990, pp. 12-13, citing *Der Spiegel*, 14 August 1990, pp. 98-99.

29. Through telex, Gildemeister arranged for Bowas Induplan Chemie of Austria to hold a course on explosives to further the Sa'ad 16 project. Helmut Raiser, managing director and co-owner of Bowas, was involved with many firms which had openly contributed to the *Condor* program. The telex confirming these training courses by Bowas was the first concrete link between Sa'ad 16 and the *Condor* project. See *Nuclear Developments*, 5 May 1989, pp. 31-34, citing *Profil* (Vienna), 20 March 1989, pp. 36-38.

30. *Nuclear Developments*, 10 April 1989, pp. 33-34, citing *Der Spiegel* (Hamburg), 27 March 1989, pp. 170-173; *Nuclear Developments*, 14 July 1989, pp. 30-36, citing *Der Spiegel* (Hamburg), 12 June 1989, pp. 70-86; *Nuclear Developments*, 5 June 1989, pp. 34-36, citing *Profil* (Vienna): 24 May 1989, pp. 38-42; and *Nuclear Developments*, 5 May 1989, pp. 34-36, citing Langsner and George, *Profil* (Vienna), 24 April 1989, pp. 38-42.

31. *Nuclear Developments*, 5 May 1989, pp. 34-36, citing Langsner and George, *Profil* (Vienna), 24 April 1989, pp. 38-42; and Alan George, *Middle East*, June 1989, 21.

32. Barbara Starr and Heinz Schulte, *Jane's Defence Weekly*, 20 October 1990, p. 739; Sally Apgar, *Minneapolis Star-Tribune*, 16 December 1990; and *Nuclear Developments*, 25 November 1990, p. 25, citing *Der Spiegel* (Hamburg), 22 October 1990, p. 15.

33. Timmerman, *The Death Lobby*, p. 128. See also *Nuclear Developments*, 5 May 1989, pp. 34-36, citing Langsner and George, *Profil* (Vienna), 24 April 1989, pp. 38-42; and Alan George, *Middle East*, June 1989, 21.

34. *Nuclear Developments*, May 5, 1989, pp. 34-36, citing Langsner and George, *Profil* (Vienna), 24 April 1989, pp. 38-42.

35. See Elaine Sciolino with Dean Baquet, "An American Front Company Was Cog in Baghdad's Buildup," *New York Times*, 26 July 1992, pp. A1, A4; Lionel Barber and Alan Friedman, "A Fatal Attraction," *The Financial Times*, 3 May 1991, p. 2; and Jack Anderson, "U.S. Did Little as Iraq Acquired Missile Data," *The Herald* (of Monterey), 2 October 1991, p. 12A.

36. Timmerman, *The Death Lobby*, p. 164.

37. Sally Apgar, *Minneapolis Star-Tribune*, 16 December 1990, p. 19.

38. Alan George, *Middle East*, January 1991, pp. 15-16; and *Nuclear Developments*, 14 August 1989, p. 42, citing *Ansa* (Rome), 31 July 1989.

39. Mel Elfin, "Behind the Condor Carbon-Carbon Smuggling Scam," *U.S. News & World Report*, 25 July 1988, p. 38; and Timmerman, *The Death Lobby*, p. 290.

40. See Eric Ehrmann, "Guided Missile From Argentina," *Journal of Commerce*, 16 January 1990.

41. *Nuclear Developments*, 5 May 1989, pp. 34-36, cited in Langsner and George, *Profil* (Vienna), 24 April 1989, pp. 38-42; and *Nuclear Developments*, 5 May 1989, pp. 31-34, cited in *Profil* (Vienna): 20 March 1989, pp. 36-38.

42. *Nuclear Developments*, 5 May 1989, pp. 34-36, citing Langsner and George, *Profil* (Vienna), 24 April 1989, pp. 38-42.

43. *Nuclear Developments*, 25 February 25 1991, p. 13, citing *Somos* (Buenos Aires), 28 January 1991, pp. 1-4.

44. Adel Darwish and Gregory Alexander (pseudonym), *Unholy Babylon* (New York: St. Martin's Press, 1991), pp. 87-89.

45. *Milavnews*, March 1991, p. 1.

46. A U.S. investigator revealed on 8 March 1992 that the United States had received good information on the Argentine-Iraqi *Condor* connection from an agent working in a European-based firm, which Iraq used as a front company. Jimmy Burns and Alan Friedman, *Financial Times*, 9 March 1992, p. 3.

47. *Nuclear Developments*, 5 February 1991, p. 33, citing *Paris Domestic Service*, 20 January 1991; *Nuclear Developments*, 23 February 1991, p. 17, citing *Folha de São Paulo*, 6 February 1991, p. A12; and William Safire, "Beware the Condor and Iraq," *Minneapolis Star-Tribune*, 3 July 1990, p. A12.

48. *Milavnews*, June 1991, p. 2; *Arms Control Reporter*, March 1991; Eric Ehrmann and Christopher Barton, *The Christian Science Monitor*, 29 January 1991, p. 18; Nathaniel C. Nash, "Argentina's President Battles His Own Air Force on Missile," *New York Times*, 13 May 1991, pp. A1, A5; *Nuclear Developments*, 28 March 1991, citing Wolfgang Hoffman, *Die Zeit* (Hamburg), 25 January 1991, p. 31.

49. Daniel Santoro, "Como matar al Condor II" [How to Kill Condor II], *Clarin* (Buenos Aires), 22 April 1991, p. 12.

50. *Defense Electronics*, April 1988, pp. 19-20.

51. These were forecasts, and not reports of actual testing. See *U.S. News & World Report*, 25 July 1988, p. 38. See also *Nuclear Developments*, 25 February 1991, p. 13, citing *Somos* (Buenos Aires), 28 January 1991, pp. 1-4.

52. *Nuclear Developments*, 28 March 1991, p. 11, citing *O Estado de São Paulo*, 7 March 1991, p. 11.

53. See "Book Details Background of Condor-2 Missile," (in Spanish), *Clarin* (Buenos Aires), 1 March 1992, p. 10, *FBIS* 92-044, 5 March 1992, p. 16.

54. Henry D. Sokolski, "Export Control Policies and Processes," Statement Before the Joint Economic Committee, Subcommittee on Technology and National Security, U.S. Senate, 23 April 1991, p. 10.

55. *Nuclear Developments*, 25 February 25 1991, p. 13, citing *Somos* (Buenos Aires), 28 January 1991, pp. 1-4.

56. *Nuclear Developments*, 25 April 1989, p. 11, citing *Noticias Argentinas* (Buenos Aires), 5 April 1989; and *Nuclear Developments*, 25 February 1991, p. 13, citing *Somos* (Buenos Aires), 28 January 1991, pp. 1-4.

57. Adel Darwish and Gregory Alexander (pseudonym), *Unholy Babylon* (New York: St. Martin's Press, 1991): p. 98.

58. *Nuclear Developments* 23 May 1989, p. 2, citing *Davar* (Tel Aviv), 28 April 1989, p. 1.

59. Darwish and Alexander, *Unholy Babylon*, p. 90.

60. David B. Ottaway, *Washington Post*, 20 September 1989, p. A-32.

61. Timmerman, *The Death Lobby*, p. 257.

62. *Los Angeles Times*, 9 December 1989.

63. Microtechnica in Turin and IFAT Corp. in Zurich were also searched. See *Nuclear Developments*, 14 August 1989, p. 31, citing Alberto Cipriani, *L'Unita* (Milan), *30 June 1989, p. 6* ; and *Nuclear Developments*, 14 August, 1989, p. 42, citing *Ansa* (Rome), 31 July 1989.

64. *Nuclear Developments*, 25 February 1991, p. 13, citing *Somos* (Buenos Aires), 28 January 1991, pp. 1-4.

65. "Book Details Background of Condor-2 Missile," (in Spanish), *Clarin* (Buenos Aires), 1 March 1992, p. 10, in *FBIS* 92-044, 5 March 1992, p. 16.

66. *Newswatch*, November 1990, original source, *Reuters*.

67. *Nuclear Developments*, 25 February 1991, p. 13, citing *Somos* (Buenos Aires), 28 January 1991, pp. 1-4.

68. "Cavallo Gives Details of 'Secret' Deal With Iraq," (in Spanish), TELAM (Buenos Aires), 26 January 1991, 1003 GMT, in *FBIS LAT*-91-018, 28 January 1991, p. 26.

69. *Middle East*, January 1991, p. 12.

70. *Nuclear Developments*, 25 February 1991, pp. 48-51, citing *Der Spiegel*, 28 January 1991, pp. 3-4.

71. Statement made on 18 April 1991. See *Nuclear Developments*, 20 May 1991, p. 17, citing *EFE* (Madrid), 19 April 1991.

72. John Barham, *Financial Times*, 30 May 1991, p. 8; *Arms Control Reporter*, June 1991; *Milavnews*, June 1991, p. 2; *New York Times*, 8 June 1991, p. 14; and Holly Porteous, *Jane's Defense Weekly*, 8 June 1991, p. 948.

73. "Di Tella Justifies Cancellation of Condor 2," (in Spanish), *La Nacion* (Buenos Aires), 1 June 1991, p. 6, in *FBIS LAT*-91-112-A, 11 June 1991, p. 1; Daniel Santoro, "Como matar al Condor II" [How to Kill Condor II], *Clarin* (Buenos Aires), 22 April 1991, p. 12.

74. "No Mass Destruction Weapons," *Latin American Regional Reports: Southern Cone Report* (RS-91-06), 8 August 1991, p. 8.

75. "Minister Denies Reports on Dismantling Condor-2," (in Spanish), *TELAM* (Buenos Aires), 7 February 1992, 1130 GMT, in *FBIS LAT*-92-027, 10 February 1992,

p. 37. The title of the article refers to the Defense Minister's statement that the *Condor II* was undergoing a "review of the inventory" before being transferred to the civilian space agency.

76. "Cheney's Remarks on Military Cooperation Reported," (in Spanish), *Noticias* (Buenos Aires), 20 February 1992, 2230 GMT, in *FBIS LAT*-92-036, 24 February 1992, p. 22.

77. Official in U.S. Defense Attaché Office, Buenos Aires, interview with author, 18 November 1991.

78. *Nuclear Developments*, 28 March 1991, p. 11, citing Flavio Tavares, *O Estado de São Paulo*, 7 March 1991, p. 11.

79. See Nathaniel C. Nash, "Argentina's President Battles His Own Air Force on Missile," *New York Times*, 13 May 1991, pp. A1, A5; "Argentina," *Milavnews*, June 1991, p. 2; and John Barham, "Argentina to Scrap Condor Missile Project," *Financial Times*, 30 May 1991, p. 8.

80. U.S. intelligence estimate. See Janne E. Nolan and Albert D. Wheelon, "Third World Ballistic Missiles," *Scientific American* vol. 263, no. 2 (August 1990), p. 39; *U.S. News & World Report*, 25 July 1988, p. 38; and *Nuclear Developments*, 25 February 1991, p. 13, citing *Somos* (Buenos Aires), 28 January 1991, pp. 1-4.

81. Jimmy Burns and Alan Friedman, *Financial Times*, 9 March 1992, p. 3.

82. Lionel Barber and Alan Friedman, *Financial Times*, 3 May 1991, p. 2.

83. "Missile Project Viewed," (in Spanish), TELAM (Buenos Aires), 17 May 1991, 2134 GMT, in *FBIS LAT*-91-097, 20 May 1991, p. 29.

84. Nathaniel C. Nash, "Argentina's President Battles His Own Air Force on Missile," *New York Times*, 13 May 1991, pp. A1, A5.

85. Jimmy Burns and Alan Friedman, *Financial Times*, 9 March 1992, p. 3.

86. "Cavallo Gives Details of 'Secret' Deal With Iraq," (in Spanish), TELAM (Buenos Aires), 26 January 1991, 1003 GMT, in *FBIS LAT*-91-018, 28 January 1991, p. 26.

87. Official in U.S. Defense Attaché. Office, Buenos Aires, interview with author, 18 November 1991.

88. "Menem on Space Activities for Peaceful Purposes," (in Spanish), TELAM (Buenos Aires), 24 October 1991, 0114 GMT, in *FBIS LAT*-91-208, 28 October 1991, p. 24.

89. Interview with author, 30 January 1992, Monterey, CA.

90. "Ministers Decide to Deactivate Missile Program," (in English), *Buenos Aires Herald*, 5 May 1991, p. 1, in *FBIS LAT*-91-087, 6 May 1991, p. 34.

91. "Peaceful Uses of Condor-2 To Continue," (in Spanish), *Noticias* (Buenos Aires) 13 May 1991, 1334 GMT, in *FBIS LAT*-91-093, 14 May 1991, p. 32.

92. See *Proliferation Issues*, 9 December 1991, p. 3, citing *Noticias Argentinas* (Buenos Aires), 23 August 1991.

93. *Proliferation Issues*, 12 September 1991, p. 3, citing *Noticias Argentinas* (Buenos Aires), 23 August 1991.

94. "Government Appoints Members to Space Commission," (in Spanish), *Clarin* (Buenos Aires), 6 August 1991, p. 13, in *FBIS LAT*-91-156, 13 August 1991, p. 22.

95. "Research Institute To Build Satellite With NASA," (in Spanish), TELAM (Buenos Aires), 22 September 1991, 0016 GMT, in *FBIS LAT*-91-186, 25 September 1991, p. 29.

96. "Russian Military Know-How for `Peaceful Purposes'," (in Spanish), *EFE* (Madrid), 10 June 1992, 1346 GMT, in *FBIS LAT*-92-113, 11 June 1992, 21.

97. "Minister on Condor-2, Domestic Satellite Project," (in Spanish), Buenos Aires Radio Nacional Network, 11 June 1992, 1500 GMT, in *FBIS LAT*-92-114, 12 June 1992, p. 11.

98. Nathaniel C. Nash, "Argentina's President Battles His Own Air Force on Missile," *New York Times*, 13 May 1991, pp. A1, A5; and *Milavnews*, June 1991, p. 2.

99. *Financial Times*, 22 February 1992, p. 4.

100. Interview with author, 30 January 1992, Monterey, CA.

101. Menicocci, ibid.

102. Compiled by the International Missile Proliferation Project, Monterey Institute of International Studies, Monterey, California, "Draft List of Associated Firms," p. 1.

103. "Argentina's Perspective on Missile Proliferation: An Interview with Felix Menicocci," *Missile Monitor*, Number 2 (Spring 1992): pp. 10-11.

104. During his tenure as Air Force chief of staff, Crespo strongly supported the development of the *Condor*. *Arms Control Reporter*, March 1991; *Defense and Foreign Affairs Weekly*, 25 February-3 March 1991, p. 3; *Nuclear Developments*, 25 February 1991, p. 13, citing Mario Baizan, *Somos* (Buenos Aires), 28 January 1991, pp. 1-4; *Nuclear Developments*, 25 February 1991, p. 16, citing *Noticias* (Buenos Aires), 8 February 1991.

105. "Argentine Condor Missile," *Latin American Regional Reports: Southern Cone Report* (RS-91-05), 7 July 1991, p. 2.

106. "Aplicaron al brigadier Crespo 30 dias de arresto domiciliario [Brigadier Crespo Received 30 Days of House Arrest]," *Clarin*, 18 May 1991, pp. 2, 3; "Requests Discharge," (in Spanish), *Noticias Argentinas* (Buenos Aires), 17 May 1991, 1322 GMT, in *FBIS LAT*-91-097, 20 May 1991, p. 29; "Un Exocet de Cavallo" [An Exocet from Cavallo], *Clarin* (Buenos Aires), 18 May 1991, p. 2.

107. Luis Garasino, "Cortocircuito con Cavallo por el Condor II?: Aeronautica—Gonzalez ratificó a Julia" [Short circuit with Cavallo Because of Condor II?: Air Force—Gonzalez Confirmed Julia], *Clarin*, 18 April 1991, p. 13.

108. *Nuclear Developments*, 15 May 1990, pp. 9-10, citing *EFE* (Madrid), 28 April 1990.

109. "Alfonsín on Condor-2, Alignment With U.S. Policy," (in Spanish), *Noticias Argentinas* (Buenos Aires), 25 April 1991, 1710 GMT, in *FBIS LAT*-91-081, 26 April 1991, p. 20.

110. "Argentine Condor Missile," *Latin American Regional Reports: Southern Cone Report* (RS-91-05), 7 July 1991, p. 2.

111. "Government Asked to Continue Condor Project," (in Spanish), *Noticias Argentinas* (Buenos Aires), 24 April 1991, 2210 GMT, in *FBIS LAT*-91-080, 25 April 1991, p. 10.

112. "Condor in `National Interest'," (in Spanish), *Noticias Argentinas* (Buenos Aires), 24 April 1991, 2235 GMT, in *FBIS LAT*-91-080, 25 April 1991, p. 10.

113. Timmerman writes that "Argentina's military dictatorship launched the Condor program in the late 1970s at the same time it intensified research into nuclear weapons. The intent was to build a missile capable of carrying a nuclear warhead." Timmerman, *The Death Lobby*, pp. 150-151.

114. Views expressed by various officials in the U.S. Embassy and U.S. Defense Attaché Office, Buenos Aires, 18-19 November 1991.

115. The idea of "social learning" was stressed by Roberto Russell, director of the international relations program at the Facultad Latinoamericana de Ciencias Sociales (FLACSO), in an interview with the author in Buenos Aires, 16 November 1991. It refers to the capacity of a society to change its attitudes over time, based on perceived lessons from the past.

12

Alternative Approaches to Managing Missile Proliferation

Janne E. Nolan

Efforts to control the international diffusion of missiles and other advanced military technologies traditionally have focused on protectionist and punitive measures against countries pursuing military programs which the United States does not sanction. For example, the Missile Technology Control Regime (MTCR), an industrial country supplier cartel to restrict missile technology exports to the Third World, is the centerpiece of the current US efforts to stop the spread of ballistic and cruise missiles.[1] The main premise underlying this approach is that industrial nations can still exert decisive influence over developing countries by exercising technological coercion.

Whether or not this premise will prove an effective basis for American policy in the face of the progressive global diffusion of weapon production capabilities, it is likely to remain the focus of decision-making for the foreseeable future. The following analyzes how supplier instruments like the MTCR are currently designed, and alternative ways in which they could be improved.[2]

Export Controls: Background

Especially since World War II, the United States and its allies have used a variety of formal and tacit arrangements to restrict the diffusion of advanced technologies to regions or countries perceived as inimical. The United States typically has been the most aggressive supporter of such efforts, beginning with a unilateral policy of security export controls against Soviet bloc nations imposed in 1948.

A substantial network of multilateral institutions aimed at restricting technology dissemination to the Warsaw Pact evolved as part of the Cold War, including one of the most enduring mechanisms, the Coordinating Committee for Multilateral Export Controls (CoCom) which was established in 1949. Subsequent US legislation, such as the Export Control Act of 1949 and the Mutual Defense Assistance Control Act of 1951, reinforced the concept of international controls to protect against the dissemination of technologies deemed essential to the defense of the free world.

These efforts have been accompanied by more recent legislation and international agreements to control other aspects of military trade. These measures include prohibitions on exports of nuclear materials and technology under the 1970 Non-Proliferation Treaty (NPT), efforts to ban the production and use of chemical weapons, the 1976 Arms Export Control Act guiding world-wide military exports, and periodic efforts to organize embargoes against countries subject to international opprobrium, such as the United Nations prohibition on arms exports to South Africa.

The industrial countries have struggled with tensions in their policies guiding military exports for decades, seeking ways to manage the challenges posed by the military ambitions of hostile or unstable countries while continuing to seek political and commercial advantages from technology and arms sales. Even in the early days of the Cold War, the effort by the United States to restrict exports to the Soviet Union often were opposed by the European countries and Japan, whose commercial interests were cosmetically disguised as principled opposition to a policy of economic warfare against the East. Despite the appearance of a durable consensus among Western countries about the need to restrict East-West military trade, in fact, the practical implementation of this policy has been plagued by chronic domestic and inter-allied controversies.

However contentious in practice, East-West strategic trade controls at least have had the benefit of a coherent geographic and political framework, as well as relatively straightforward objectives. In the North-South context, efforts to manage military trade are impeded by the geopolitical complexity of the Third World, and by the absence of any common agreement about the objectives sought from export controls.

This is particularly the case with respect to conventional arms. The only instance in which an international embargo on conventional weapon sales can be said to have succeeded was the Tripartite Declaration of 1950, an agreement among the US, Britain, and France which imposed limits on arms exports to the Middle East. Vitiated five years later by the Soviet sale of arms to Egypt and the withdrawal of British troops from Suez, the Tripartite Agreement nevertheless was one of the few examples of the effective use of a supplier cartel on behalf of great power military objectives in the Third World. The conditions which made such a regime possible in

1950, including the limited ability of recipient countries to purchase or utilize advanced armaments, the small number of arms suppliers, and the clarity of purpose among the Western industrial states bent on containing conflict in a vital region, have long since been outstripped by regional and international realities.

The Control of Missiles

Ballistic missiles traditionally have been singled out for more stringent export control than is applied to other technologies, including high performance aircraft and naval platforms, in part because of the linkage between nuclear proliferation and advanced missile delivery capabilities. Surface-to-surface missiles were discussed as possible candidate systems for bilateral export restraint in the US-Soviet Conventional Arms Transfer negotiations during the Carter Administration, for example, and both the United States and the Soviet Union observed tacit restraint in transferring long-range missiles to allies in Korea and the Middle East throughout the 1960s and 1970s.

US policy has been particularly stringent with regard to sales of potentially nuclear capable surface-to-surface missiles or related technology to any countries outside of NATO and Japan. Although Israel received the *Lance* missile, for instance, its request to purchase the *Pershing Ia* intermediate-range missile in the early 1970s was denied. The US also discouraged Indian efforts to acquire the US *Scout* space launch vehicle for its civilian space program in 1965, recognizing that it could have military applications. The US did permit the sale of the *Nike-Hercules* surface-to-air missile to Taiwan and South Korea, which led to South Korea's successful conversion of this system to a surface-to-surface configuration despite strict end-use assurances from the Korean government.

The Soviet Union, for its part, transferred hundreds of SCUD-B ballistic missiles to its clients in the Third World beginning in the 1970s, and provided Syria with the more advanced SS-21 ballistic missile. Western European suppliers also have proven quite permissive about missile-related exports, including missile systems, space launch vehicles (SLV), and associated manufacturing technologies. French assistance helped Israel to build the *Jericho I* in the 1960s, and there have been numerous European programs to assist states with the development and production of SLVs, such as the provision of the French *Mammoth* propulsion system for production by Pakistan and India. European commercial ventures have been vital to missile programs in India, Brazil, Israel, Argentina, Iraq, and even Libya.

In furtherance of traditional US policy, President Reagan signed - National Security Decision Directive (NSDD)-70 in November 1982, calling for the investigation of ways to control missile proliferation. This led to agreement among seven industrial countries to establish consensual restraint guidelines for missile-related exports, formalized as the Missile Technology Control Regime in April 1987. Over time and particularly after Operation Desert Storm, the restraint of missiles became a far more central element of the Western diplomatic agenda, on a par with the international nuclear non-proliferation regime, efforts to control chemical weapons, and discussions with key states about ways to contain regional military tensions. The MTCR now has over twenty members. there are additional non-signatory states which have publicly pledged to observe MTCR guidelines and parameters [*see Appendix A*—ed.].

Prior to the initiation of the MTCR in 1987, there was no formal international apparatus to guide transfers of conventional technologies to developing countries. There is still very little interest in a regime which would curtail exports of weapons or dual-use non-missile technologies by international agreement. Despite their pertinence for the delivery of nuclear weapons, and, potentially, to ballistic missile development, controls on transfers of advanced aircraft and other types of missiles have been actively resisted by governments, including those which are adherents to the MTCR and the NPT.

Given the history of failed efforts to craft even modest agreements to control conventional technology transfers, the MTCR is a significant achievement. Judging from the experience of developing "trigger lists" for restricted equipment in nuclear non-proliferation efforts, which has always proven highly contentious domestically and internationally, the MTCR also should be seen as a triumph of unusual technical consensus. Those who crafted the regime have gone a long way in identifying the inputs which can contribute to missile development, and in securing agreement from eighteen countries about guidelines to control their dissemination. The MTCR also has helped to pinpoint the most difficult aspects of missile design and target these for special scrutiny. Guidance technology is generally agreed to be the most important "enabling" technology for countries aspiring to develop missiles.

The MTCR led to the development of a new bureaucratic infrastructure for monitoring one aspect of North-South missile technology flows, and to try to understand the synergism among particular dual-use technologies which, added together, could augment missile production capabilities.[3] The MTCR already has had some success in impeding missile programs. It is credited with helping to stop the Argentinean-Egyptian-Iraqi *Condor II* program, discouraging Chinese sales of the M-series of missiles, and forcing the West German government to crack down on private firms engaged in missile development efforts in Libya and Iraq. Partly as a result of congressional pressure and the threat of legislated sanctions, countries began to pay more attention to export violations beginning in the late 1980s, and some, such as the German government, emplaced entirely new procedures to ensure closer government scrutiny of technology exports.

Meetings between US officials and the newly formed governments in the former Soviet Union in 1991 also are reported to have included discussions of ways to establish controls on missiles, associated technologies, and other dual-use exports. Now that industrial production in the former Soviet bloc is no longer dominated by state-run enterprises, governments are facing the difficult task of developing domestic guidelines and enforcement mechanisms to monitor their newly commercial activities. Absent cooperation, liberalized trade between East and West could have serious implications for developing countries' access to technology. Given the high level of export dependency among most industrial countries, the easing of trade barriers among developed nations could significantly raise the level and volume of missile technology available for purchase globally.

Constraints on the Effectiveness of the MTCR

Unlike agreements in the nuclear area, such as the London Suppliers' Group, the MTCR has no international agency to monitor compliance, no enforcement mechanism, and no institutionalized arrangements for regular meetings among participants. Only five formal meetings of MTCR members have occurred since 1988, the most recent in November 1991, although bilateral meetings have taken place since that time on an *ad hoc* basis [*see Appendix B*—ed.].

Despite the much greater policy profile accorded this issue in the recent past, moreover, the relatively small number and low rank of officials who deal with this issue on a routine basis suggest that governments do not perceive missile non-proliferation to be among their highest foreign policy priorities. In the U.S., the inter-agency apparatus which has responsibility for the MTCR has suffered from a relative lack of bureaucratic clout. It has generally been left to mid-level bureaucrats to adjudicate disputes about adherence to guidelines.

Despite its modest scope, the MTCR nevertheless was enmired in some serious international controversies over its implementation in late 1989. Over strenuous US objections, the French insisted on their right to proceed with a sale to Brazil of liquid-fuel motor technology which could be useful for ballistic missile production, in return for a $60 million contract for the launch of two Brazilian communications satellites.[4] The contract was finally suspended after two years of dispute. West German involvement in developing guidance technology for the Indian *Agni* intermediate-range missile, however, continued, while a former Soviet space enterprise proceeded with a sale of cryogenic and rocket technologies to India in 1992, prompting the US to invoke mandatory trade sanctions against both entities.

Aside from difference among countries about their interpretations of their international obligations, there are four major areas where ambiguities in the text of the MTCR have helped fuel controversy, and which could be clarified in the interest of strengthening the regime.

First is whether the MTCR is solely an adjunct of the nuclear non-proliferation treaty, meaning that its restrictions apply only to exports to states with nuclear programs who are not NPT signatories. Some put forward this argument in trying to justify the Chinese sale of the CSS-2 intermediate-range missile to Saudi Arabia, for example. The United States and British governments have since reaffirmed that they do not believe that sales of missile technology are permissible even to states which are NPT members, but this is still a source of potential controversy which could complicate efforts to elicit additional support for the regime.

Second is the question of space cooperation, and what is and is not considered permissible under MTCR guidelines. Although the text of the MTCR states specifically that it is not designed to interfere with "legitimate" space programs, it also states that such efforts cannot be associated with the development of nuclear weapon delivery capabilities. Since the technologies for space launch vehicles and ballistic missiles are virtually indistinguishable, this would seem to preclude any activities in this area. France has obviously taken a different view; in the future, other countries may as well. The United States was trying to forge a common position on this issue in late 1989. Some agencies, including the U.S. Arms Control and Disarmament Agency, have argued that a blanket prohibition on exports of SLVs is not realistic, and that devising safeguards on the uses of space technology is preferable. Officials with responsibility for the MTCR in the Department of Defense, however, actively oppose any loosening of the interpretation that the MTCR prohibits SLV exports. This dispute continues, and is confusing to those who may be subject to competing views of US policy.

Third is the priority governments plan to give to national and international regulatory mechanisms for stemming missile proliferation as compared to counter military responses, such as promoting anti-tactical ballistic missile programs for key allies or even deploying strategic defenses nationally. Although these instruments are not necessarily mutually exclusive, they represent wholly different approaches to the problem which may not be politically or bureaucratically compatible in the long term.

Fourth is the question of national obligations imposed as a result of signing the MTCR. From its inception, the regime was designed to be consensual, with participating governments interpreting and adapting guidelines in national export codes. The MTCR is not intended to override national policy, and individual states are supposed to be responsible for end-use assurances. France's claim that it had the sovereign right to sell engine technology to various states because it could prevent diversion to military uses by imposing its own safeguards, nevertheless caused international friction.

Given the political sensitivity of a supplier cartel among developing countries, some ambiguity may be a virtue. No supplying government wants to state outright that Third World space ventures are inherently illegitimate, and some flexibility in the application of guidelines is needed to accommodate differences among sovereign countries.

The issue of enforcement, however, is very contentious politically, and publicized disputes over apparent violations of the letter or spirit of the MTCR will damage the credibility of the regime. The lack of binding enforcement authority prompted several pieces of legislation in the US Congress over the last few years which would impose punitive measures on countries and companies engaged in MTCR-restricted trade. Although different in the scope and nature of sanctions that could be invoked, these initiatives shared the common view that penalties on MTCR violators must be stiffened. For example, an amendment was attached to the 1991 mandatory sanctions on countries or companies that violated the MTCR; suspending their rights to trade with the US for specified periods.

Despite fairly broad bipartisan support in the Congress, some of the provisions prompted criticism from foreign governments and from the Bush administration. Imposing trade sanctions on foreign nationals, for example, including denying access to US government contracts and licenses to violators, is seen as excessive intrusion on Executive Branch authority, circumscribing the ability of the US to use non-coercive means to persuade states to comply with the MTCR, and, it is argued, to elicit the support of additional countries. Supporters of sanctions counter that trade restrictions are meaningless if they can be readily circumvented by renegade companies or countries, and that the US has the leverage to enforce compliance by threatening penalties which exceed the perceived benefits of violations.[5]

Regardless of one's view about the legitimacy or desirability of sanctions, to the extent that MTCR states are seen to be circumventing guidelines for unilateral advantage, it will impede the prospects for widening membership in the regime. Strengthening enforcement thus is an urgent priority if the missile regime is to survive, and its membership expanded. As the European countries move to integrate their economies into a single market, the idea of a selective cartel which does not even include all the countries of the region makes little sense. The general consensus would suggest that Eastern European countries and newly independent Soviet republics looking to the West for much-needed aid and technological assistance also might be induced to join.

Eliciting enduring support for the MTCR, however, is hindered by the absence of a common perception of the risks posed by missile proliferation.

Leaving aside opposition from states which perceive it as discriminatory, the MTCR lacks a publicly compelling rationale. As Joseph Nye has argued, the regime has inherently limited legitimacy because ballistic missiles, unlike nuclear or chemical weapons, are not widely perceived to carry "a moral stigma."[6]

Improving the Regime

Gaining wider support for the MTCR might be helped by a clearer articulation of its costs and benefits, the pragmatic calculus which makes the restraint of trade in missile and space technology a prudent course of action for the industrial nations. Aside from disparate perceptions of the military importance of ballistic missiles, some governments seem to have exaggerated expectations of the potential value of export contracts that would be lost as a result of adherence to MTCR guidelines. Although one cannot assign costs to the political antagonisms that sometimes result from denials of technology, the relatively modest impact on supplier revenues and profits from ceding missile sales could be demonstrated with reasonable precision. Emerging missile producers like Brazil may once have had ambitious plans to capture export revenues through missile sales, but recent assessments of the potential value of ballistic missile exports prompted Brazil to drastically scale back its missile investment efforts.

Similarly, consideration should be given to developing a mechanism by which allied defense planners could estimate the effects of missile proliferation on their own force requirements. If it is correct, as one analyst has argued, that "the costs of failing to control exports (to the Third World) are likely to be higher than the costs of the additional military capabilities required to make up for a free market in weapons-related technology," the case for a supplier cartel could be made more persuasively on national security and budgetary grounds.[7] Now that the diffusion of missiles is taken seriously as a military risk, it should inform requirements for such activities as overseas basing, interventionary capabilities, and ways to help clients counter military instabilities in regions of high tension.

The risks associated with the diffusion of space technology also could be articulated more clearly. Commercial satellite reconnaissance images available today can assist nations to plan attacks against adversaries, and contribute to the accuracy of their missile forces. US LANDSAT and French SPOT images are believed to have been used by military planners in the Iran-Iraq war, for example. Over time, accurate satellite images available from a wider number of commercial sources may play a more significant role in helping states to prepare and execute military operations. Space technologies also may help states conduct military operations more effectively, by improving command and control and communications capabilities. Although some would argue that greater openness among countries is a welcome, or at least inevitable, international trend, there is not much evidence that US policy has kept pace with the military challenges that also may be posed.

The diffusion of satellite and missile capabilities suggests at least the potential for more nations to acquire the means to conduct offensive operations in space. Some analysts in the Arab world have accused Israel of introducing a "space race" into the region through its participation in SDI-related collaborative ventures, such as laser and high particle energy research and the US-funded *Arrow* anti-tactical ballistic missile program. Although Israel denies it, there is a growing Arab perception of Israel's plans to use its satellite programs for offensive military space operations.

In the future, states which have missile programs might begin to look at their potential as anti-satellite systems. Following the Israeli test of the *Ofek* satellite, Iraqi president Saddam Husayn announced that Iraq had developed an anti-satellite system, and had tested a space launch vehicle. Although these claims were obviously fatuous, it suggests that efforts to acquire such capabilities, however quixotic, may be on the rise in developing countries.[8]

The acquisition of even rudimentary anti-satellite capabilities among a wider number of countries could certainly complicate, if not vitiate, any agreement among the great powers to develop a space operations regime or to limit space weapons. Even if the possibility of offensive space activities is still remote, the possession of such systems in additional countries may impose new complications in trying to develop international norms for the management of military space operations. Given its disproportionate reliance on space-based assets for a variety of security objectives, the US has every reason to pay close attention to the global diffusion of space technology.

One other trend in military technology is worthy of attention. As the industrial countries progress towards significant reductions in nuclear arsenals, accurate non-nuclear weapons with strategic range may begin to replace nuclear forces. The implications of non-nuclear counterforce capability accorded by precision-guided specialized warheads has been a subject of discussion in US strategy for several years. Unencumbered by the taboos associated with nuclear or chemical weapons, the proliferation of such systems may be difficult to prevent. As one analyst argued, "...while such technologies will not come to possess the psychological or status value of nuclear arms, the lower stigma attached to their acquisition is likely to lead to their widespread proliferation."[9] The acquisition of such systems could be destabilizing in regional contexts if they accord states with the ability to launch pre-emptive strikes and encourage aggressive military operations which would otherwise be seen as too risky with nuclear or chemical warheads.

The states which retain a margin of control over sensitive technologies can influence demand by raising the financial and political costs of their acquisition. There is little question that technology eventually will proliferate to countries which are determined to achieve certain military capabilities. The capability to produce and launch advanced missiles is still centered in a handful of nations, even if additional states, including Brazil, China, India, and Israel are beginning to produce such goods and may in time be able to undercut the current market hierarchy.

Trade restrictions, however, can delay this process and buy time to devise ways to contain the instabilities posed by global militarization, and to address the root causes of international conflicts. The added time also could be used to help states to develop force postures and doctrines oriented toward deterrence and stability, and to devise international norms for managing the potential risks posed by the diffusion of advanced weapon technologies.

In principle, the lists of controlled items compiled for the MTCR could be the basis for a more comprehensive approach to North-South technology diffusion, were there political support for such an objective. There is sufficient flexibility in the existing guidelines to accommodate new kinds of high risk technologies which may become more widely available in coming years, including equipment pertinent to warhead design, improvements in missile accuracy and range, targeting capabilities, and anti-satellite operations.

With the exception of a relatively few categories of items which could be restricted *a priori*, such as biological and chemical agents, decisions about what constitutes sensitive technologies will increasingly have to take into account the specific conditions in recipient states, including relative industrial capabilities, local or regional enmities, other military forces, and overall foreign policy objectives.

The US developed considerable operational experience in identifying and tracking technologies in the East-West context, and, though this is its weakest link, in enforcement of restraints. To be more effective, enforcement will have to be beefed up, from monitoring technology flows with shared intelligence, to imposing strict penalties for non-compliance, to joint efforts to pressure non-adherents to abide by the organization's guidelines. Although there may never be full agreement about the scope and desirability of technology safeguards, the existence of even general norms provides a foundation for adjudicating disagreements.

Although export controls may not be the optimum basis for policy in the long term, they can serve as a first step toward identifying other instruments for international cooperation. Consideration should be given to elevating a missile and other proscribed military trade regime to the status of an international agency, even if membership remains strictly consensual. Such an apparatus could serve as the source of expertise to anticipate the kinds of futuristic technology transfers which could have adverse consequences for global stability, such as precision-strike systems, biotechnologies, or anti-satellite systems, and to try to manage their dissemination in a more structured way.

It is not realistic to expect that a single agency can accommodate the diverse interests of dozens of states and remain effective. Like the nuclear non-proliferation regime, however, building an international regime for dual-use conventional technology could complement national policies and bilateral or regional diplomacy. The establishment of such a mechanism will have to be an evolutionary process, based on the development of flexible institutions which can adapt to rapid changes in the international system.

The sheer complexity of the international technology market, with its vast networks of legal and illegal suppliers, already is overwhelming the modest resources available in government to track technological developments and to develop effective policy instruments. With the growing international commercialization of inputs needed for modern weapon production, far greater cooperation between industry and government may be necessary simply to identify technologies deemed vital to security. As the European countries move to rationalize their high technology industries by melding commercial and defense activities, for instance, industry will have to play a larger role to ensure the security of defense-related innovations.

This kind of cooperation may be especially important in the case of Japan. As the world's leading source of advanced information technology, Japanese industry dominates an area which has become a central factor in a wide range of advanced military functions, including command and control, intelligence, targeting, and guidance. Absent Japanese industry and government support, any technology regime could be readily subverted by Japanese exploitation of market opportunities if undertaken without adequate consideration of the collective security interests of other industrialized states.

As the industrial countries move to greater integration of their defense industrial sectors, they will have to forge common agreements about the disposition and security of their shared technologies. Defense companies will have a direct interest in these agreements. Industry participation and support for such arrangements may be necessary both to help compile information about sources of technology and to help design and implement workable security safeguards which do not interfere unduly with desirable private enterprise.

A practical model for government-industry cooperation might be found in the area of chemical weapons. The Chemical Manufacturers Association, whose member account for almost ninety percent of all chemical production in the US, has been an active participant in devising the terms and mechanisms of a treaty to ban chemical weapons. Without the assistance of industry, it is safe to say that there would not have been the requisite resources and expertise to identify the thousands of items relevant to chemical weapons production and where they are produced, nor to evaluate the risks and benefits of alternative approaches to treaty limitations and their verification.

The chemical producers model may be particularly apt for the space industry. Commercial interests involved in promoting peaceful space cooperation have the most to lose from international opprobrium about the diversion of space technology for ballistic missiles or other offensive military uses. It may be in the immediate self-interest of such companies to assist governments to restrain missile programs in problematic states, by helping to identify relevant technological inputs needed for missile development and in devising safeguards which can discourage the adaptation of civilian equipment for military programs. Although some might see this as undue encroachment on sovereignty, this is one area in which a few suppliers still do have the leverage to influence the pace and content of space-related production programs.

Domestically, US policy initiatives for missile nonproliferation require more clearly stated objectives which can be supported by sustained bureaucratic attention. At a minimum, there must be sufficient consensus at the highest levels of government that the security threats posed by the diffusion of missile technology are worth the political costs which may be incurred in encouraging restraint. Leadership is vital to the conduct of multilateral diplomacy, to ensure that such efforts are consonant with overall foreign policy goals, and to resolve the bureaucratic disputes which inevitably arise as restraint policies impinge on traditional international relationships.

Enforcing the MTCR may require greater intelligence resources than are currently dedicated to this objective. Improved intelligence capabilities could help enforcement by shifting the emphasis of restraint policies toward prevention of proliferation, rather than the more demanding process of inflicting punishment after the fact. This is an important issue which should be raised with allies, in order to establish procedures for pooling intelligence assets. The economic and defense integration of Europe, along with the declining demands of East-West defense, may make this kind of collaboration easier in the future.

Another unresolved question is whether the United States is prepared to offer client states incentives for their forbearance in missile acquisition, and, if so, what kind. As of now, the absence of effective coordination among agencies which have jurisdiction over trade policy, security assistance, economic assistance, sensitive technology transfers, space policy, and arms control, among others, makes it difficult to examine mechanisms from which the US could derive leverage.

Agencies with responsibilities for international debt management and other concessionary transactions also need to be brought into the policy process to see if there may be ways to link financial incentives to desirable military restraints. At a minimum, the policies of the international lending agencies, such as the World Bank and the International Development Agency, should be reviewed to ensure that their assessments of countries' eligibility for credits and loans take into account the influence of the military sector, including the nature and relative burden of weapons development and production programs.

In the current international political environment, an effort to broaden the MTCR into an international treaty seems quixotic, at best. It would founder on objections by developing countries about its discriminatory nature, and on the difficulties of making the case that ballistic missiles are worthy of universal controls even though other delivery vehicles, including non-ballistic missiles and aircraft, are not. To the degree that the MTCR has been successful, in fact, its success has derived from the regime's modest and consensual nature, and from the fact that it was negotiated out of the glare of the international spotlight.

There are, however, similarities between a space cooperation treaty aimed at stemming missile diffusion and the nuclear non-proliferation regime, making the possibility of such an agreement, however remote, worth further examination. In both cases, there is general consensus in the respective areas that militarily-related technologies should be controlled, but that peaceful uses should be encouraged. If countries could be persuaded that involvement in an international space regime brings with it guarantees of needed technology and the potential for greater security, it might be possible to persuade some states to join in. This has led some to advocate the establishment of an international space organization to provide launcher services to countries which do not have their own space programs, or to those willing to abjure diversion of their space investment to military uses.

The difficulties of distinguishing between military and non-military space technologies may seem overwhelming, but similar challenges have plagued the NPT for years. Nuclear reactors and related processes, including enrichment technology and chemical separation facilities, have both civilian and military applications. In the case of the NPT, it has been possible to institutionalize safeguards against targeted technologies, and try to protect against diversion from civilian to military purposes through the monitoring activities of the IAEA. Following Desert Storm, however, the discovery that Iraq, an NPT-signatory, had pursued an elaborate, clandestine program for nuclear weapons development despite IAEA inspection demonstrated the need to strengthen the inspection regime. Proposals to give the IAEA the authority and resources to conduct "Strategic" inspection of suspect installations were under active consideration in 1992.

It is conceivable that a system of international safeguards could be developed as part of a space cooperation regime, with states permitting on-site inspections of space facilities in return for satellite data and launch services. An agency comprised of multinational inspectors, like the IAEA, could serve as the umbrella organization to conduct international inspections and verify compliance with the agreement.

There would be several, potentially intractable, problems. The degree to which countries would be willing to forgo efforts to acquire independent space launch capabilities would depend in part on the degree of concessionary assistance given to them by advanced countries. Given the problems faced by space industries in the developed nations, such subsidies are difficult to envision. More importantly, every developing country which currently has a space program also has a missile program, and they may not want to abandon their ambitions to be freed of great power control. An agreement on space activities, moreover, would not address other, equally vital channels of missile-related technology diffusion.

The one area in which the prospects for international agreement might be more promising is the regulation of anti-satellite capabilities. Acquiring operational anti-satellite capabilities is a distant prospect even for advanced countries, and certainly for any developing state. As Donald Hafner has argued, "By continuing to offer open and generous access to their own space services, the superpowers can reduce the incentives of third states to go off on their own and acquire independent capabilities that could be turned to ASAT purposes."[10] The price, however, may be for the United States and other industrial countries to impose ASAT restraints on themselves, an option which might be accepted if the threat of international ASAT proliferation were taken seriously.

Conclusion

As important a challenge as controlling missiles is finding the means to anticipate future technological change which could have even more pronounced effects on global security, including the diffusion of new generations of weapons such as precision strike systems. A more focussed strategy for managing the missile trade could help begin to address several such security challenges, identifying futuristic technologies whose significance to national security warrant efforts to protect them from market forces and encouraging accommodations among adversarial states to contain the demand for advanced weapons.

The MTCR has been plagued by its image as an idealistic arms control initiative designed to save the Third World from itself, rather than a prudent gesture to stem the deterioration of military environments in which the West may have to protects its own interests. Although it should be obvious, it perhaps needs to be reiterated that countries have abided by export restraints in the past because of an interest in containing military developments in areas in which their own forces might be placed at risk. This may not be an argument which wins supporters in developing countries, but it does have the virtue of reflecting the pragmatic self-interests embodied in the MTCR for industrial states.

In the future, alternative policy options to address the problems posed by missile proliferation will have to recognize the extent to which missile proliferation is already deeply rooted in international politics, and, as such, may not be seriously attenuated by selective supplier controls. The very limited number of examples of conscious military restraint among developing countries, including regional agreements such as the Treaty for the Prohibition of Nuclear Weapons in Latin America, does not inspire great optimism for restraint regimes which elicit the support of recipients, however. No such system of international controls has ever been fully articulated, or been deemed a sufficient international priority to warrant concerted negotiations among governments.

For now, the most significant impediment to missile proliferation stems from constraints within the developing countries themselves. The prohibitive expense of missile programs, exacerbated by suppliers' restraints, have stymied progress in several cases. As Jeffrey Richelson has argued with regard to satellite launch capabilities, "An investment of several billion dollars is required to establish a launch site, build the launch vehicles, develop the satellite, construct a ground control station or network, purchase the necessary computers and imagery enhancement software, and maintain a staff of photo interpreters."[11] Exceeding the resources of all but a handful of nations, such ambitious undertakings are likely to be structurally constrained for the foreseeable future.

As such, reducing global demand for missile technology by raising the economic and political costs of its acquisition is still a viable instrument of supplier policy, if there is agreement that the political frictions which may result are worth it. In the future, the MTCR could be strengthened by seeking agreement for more formal guidelines, along the lines of the London Suppliers' Group controlling nuclear exports, establishing routine procedures for consultation among participants, sharing intelligence, and developing durable international norms for broader areas of technology diffusion. To be credible, however, such a regime must be adhered to by a larger group of nations, and needs to elicit the support of developing, as well as developed states.

The majority of existing proposals for international agreements to control weapon technologies tend to reflect a great power bias, often with little sensitivity for the ambitions of developing states to become more equal partners in the international system. Too little is known about the nature of incentives which might draw states like India and Pakistan into a system of international cooperation. Although the great powers still have some capacity for exerting some leverage over smaller states, the perception of discrimination may become the greatest impediment to achieving more far-reaching cooperative efforts in the coming years. Building common norms which can elicit genuine international support will require taking the objectives of developing countries seriously, and recognizing that those interests are as enduring as they are diverse.

In the longer term, an export cartel like the MTCR is only one of several instruments which will have to be brought to bear on the broader problem of technological and weapon diffusion. In addition to efforts to encourage accommodations among combatant states and to contain the incidence and scope of regional conflicts, managing the transition to a more complex international system will require more coherent articulation of industrial countries' policies towards new power blocs in the Third World.

Notes

1. Signed in 1987, the MTCR had seven original members, including the United States, Japan, Canada, France, Germany, Italy and the United Kingdom. By consent, the states agree to abide by prohibitions on the sale of ballistic and cruise missile systems capable of carrying 500 kilograms of payload to a range of 300 kilometers or more. Eleven additional countries, including Austria, Australia, Belgium, Denmark, Finland, Luxembourg, the Netherlands, New Zealand, Norway, Spain and Sweden have joined as formal adherents since 1987. The Soviet Union, Israel and China are not members but have agreed to comply with MTCR strictures. With the breakup of the Soviet Union in late 1991, international efforts were underway to try to induce newly independent republics such as Ukraine and Kazakhstan also to acceded to these norms.

2. The following is adapted from the author's study *Trappings of Power: Ballistic Missiles in the Third World* (Washington, D.C.: Brookings Institution, 1991).

3. The list of restricted technologies was modestly updated and revised in November 1991. See "Missile Technology Control Regime (MTCR) Equipment and Technology Annex," November 4, 1991.

4. See, for instance, Ian Anthony, "Missile Technology Control Regime," in *Arms Export Regulations*, (Oxford: Oxford University Press, 1991), p. 226. In 1992, the French government suspended the sale, in part due to economic constraints in Brazil.

5. Senator Jeff Bingaman (D-NM), the principal sponsor of a bill in 1989 to impose sanctions on violators of the MTCR, argued that legislation to stem missile proliferation is no different than legislation on behalf of nuclear nonproliferation,

including the 1978 Nuclear Non-Proliferation Act. See Statement of Senator Jeff Bingaman, *National Security Implications of Missile Proliferation,* Hearings before the Senate Committee on Foreign Relations, 101 Congress, 1 sess, (Washington, D.C.: U.S. Government Printing Office, 1989, pp. 34–35.

6. Joseph S. Nye, Jr., "Arms Control After the Cold War," *Foreign Affairs,* vol. 68, Winter 1989–90, p. 60.

7. Benjamin N. Schiff, "Conventional Lessons from the Nuclear Export Policy Experience," paper prepared for the 1984 annual meeting of the International Studies Association, p. 2.

8. As Paul Stares has argued, "Any ballistic missile capable of delivering a nuclear warhead within range of a space object to inflict damage or otherwise interfere with its normal functioning is technically an anti-satellite weapon. This would include...any nuclear armed system with the requisite reach." Although it would be far more challenging technically, conventionally armed space launch vehicles could in principle be adapted to an ASAT role. As Stares argues, "States in possession of long range ballistic missiles and sufficiently powerful radio transmitters will always have the inherent capacity to destroy and interfere with the functioning of objects in space." See Paul B. Stares, "The Problem of Non-Dedicated Space Weapons Systems," paper prepared for the UNIDIR Expert Group on Problems of Definitions and Demarcations in the Prevention of an Arms Race in Outer Space, November 1989, p. 3.

9. Carl H. Bilder, "The Prospects and Implications of Non-Nuclear Means for Strategic Conflict," *Adelphi Papers 200* (London: International Institute for Strategic Studies), Summer 1985, p. 30.

10. Donald Hafner, "For the Benefit and in the Interest of All: Superpower Space Programmes and the Interests of Third States," in Walter Stutzle, Bhupendra Jasani and Regina Cowen, eds. *The ABM Treaty: To Defend or Not to Defend,* (Oxford University Press, 1987), p. 201.

11. Jeffrey Richelson, "Military Intelligence: SPOT is not Enough," *Bulletin of Atomic Scientists,* vol. 45, September 1989, p. 26.

13

Conclusion

Harlan W. Jencks

Transactions

Motivation

Our authors are in general agreement on the basic motivations for Third-World states to acquire missiles and to focus their limited resources on missile development. These motivations are perceived threats from regional neighbors, national prestige, and the potential economic benefits of developing and exporting missiles and missile technology.

Tim McCarthy (India) and Hua Di (China) both show the importance of nationalism in motivating military and industrial self-sufficiency efforts. As K. Subhramanyam eloquently put it, *Agni's* "role as a weapon is the least of its roles. It is a confidence-builder and a symbol of India's assertion of self-reliance not merely in defence but in the broader international political arena as well."[1] Moreover, by becoming self-sufficient in missiles, a Third-World state sees itself defeating perceived interference by the industrialized states in its domestic affairs. Moreover, as McCarthy writes, military-technical capability—especially with missiles and nuclear weapons—demonstrably buys a state a "place at the table" in the international fora that make globally important decisions.

In the Third World, the Missile Technology Control Regime (MTCR), the Nuclear Non-Proliferation Treaty (NPT), and even the International Atomic Energy Agency (IAEA) are widely regarded as neo-imperialist mechanisms which infringe on the sovereignty of developing states; as part of a conspiracy of the rich countries to keep the developing countries poor, weak, underdeveloped, and dependent. MTCR is "directed at international transfers of hardware and technology. Consequently, adherence to the regime entails no formal obligations with respect to indigenous programs."[2] Thus, established missile powers are free to maintain and to increase their technical and military dominance.

Andrew Mack argues that this widespread perception may make the MTCR, and similar "supply-side" arms control measures enforced by negative sanctions, backfire in the long run. "[W]hatever gains may be extracted in the short term from the use of negative economic sanctions against Third World exporters need to be weighed against the long-term implications of the deep resentments such policies generate." Mack suggests that a possible way to avoid this resentment is to apply sanctions against suppliers in the industrialized world rather than against Third World buyers.[3] Unfortunately, our country studies demonstrate how hard it is to ascertain the ultimate suppliers' identities and intentions.

Military assistance programs and non-missile sales can backfire as well —indirectly contributing to regional threat perceptions that motivate missile proliferation. For example, "the US promise to provide Pakistan with some form of airborne early-warning system [would] if kept, considerably improve Pakistan's air defenses and thus increase the incentive for India to place greater emphasis on missiles."[4]

It is not entirely clear just how important monetary profit is as an incentive for missile proliferation. In general, Janne Nolan is probably correct in writing that "the relatively modest impact on supplier revenues and profits from ceding missile sales could be demonstrated with reasonable precision," though there have been significant exceptions, at least in the short term. For example, China's sale of DF-3 missiles to Saudi Arabia for an estimated $2.5–3.5 billion was certainly a major addition to China's foreign exchange revenues. However, even PRC leaders subsequently may have decided to curtail missile sales. Beijing stated it would abide by MTCR guidelines in the February 1992, though news reports a year later have cast some doubt upon Chinese assurances.[5] Writing elsewhere, Hua Di has made the case that foreign trade is so important to the PRC that it cannot afford to let a few billion dollars' worth of arms sales upset overall foreign trade—for example, by provoking loss of Most-Favored Nation trading status with the United States.[6] China's days as a major missile proliferator *may* be over because of PRC success in non-military export trade.[7]

Peter Hayes shows that North Korea has little of value to sell except weapons, and desperately needs foreign exchange to buy critical imports, particularly oil and food. The contrast between the Chinese and North Korean cases illustrates that negative sanctions, especially economic sanctions, work only against a country that is (1) engaged in world trade and diplomacy—a government that *cares* about trade and the opinions of others; and (2) is selling missile technology primarily for economic reasons. Absent *either* condition, negative sanctions are unlikely to be very effective.

Pariah states and self-styled "outsiders" like North Korea, Iran, Libya, and Iraq are effectively immune to negative sanctions short of military threat.[8]

A further complication is that a country's armed forces may be the main (or sole) arms exporter; and may depend upon exports as the primary (or sole) source of hard currency to finance military R&D. Our authors document this situation in Argentina, China, Pakistan, and elsewhere. A frequent result is that diplomatic representations to a country's foreign ministry may be pointless, since it has no control over arms export behavior and may not even know about it. According to Hua Di, the PRC Foreign Ministry, at least until recently, has been quite ignorant of arms export matters. This helps explain why governments are often internally divided as to whether, and how much, to adhere to export controls like MTCR. We shall return to this subject below.

Péricles Gasparini Alves (Brazil), McCarthy, and others note that MTCR actually may have stimulated missile technology proliferation by means of domestic development. Absent MTCR restrictions, some Third-World countries would simply buy missiles on the international market, as they do other weapons. Denied that option, some have resorted to domestic development and production. Thus, MTCR may have led to the formation of technology networks among non-MTCR states, and to the proliferation of missile production capacity that would not have existed otherwise.

Networks

Given sufficient political will and moderate resources, it appears that many Third-World governments can acquire operational surface-to-surface missiles (SSMs), and develop at least a limited manufacturing capacity. Sufficient facilities, trained people, and money are already available in the Third World. A common thread running through most of our chapters is the formation of formal consortia and informal networks by aspiring missile states to share technology, talent, and other resources—including contacts in advanced industrialized countries. Examples include Iraq-Egypt-North Korea, China-Brazil, Argentina-Iraq-Egypt, Israel-China, and China-Pakistan-Syria. Taken together, these networks form a global web of contacts, cooperation, trade, financing, and criminal activity which facilitates missile proliferation.

Missile technology "networking" can be risky. Some of these networks have involved strange bedfellows indeed, and have resulted in technology flows along unpredictable paths. Markets may be stolen by a consortium partner, or by a supplier connected to it. It appears that in almost all cases however, proliferating states are much more interested in short-term military and technical gains than in long-term markets. How else can we explain North Korea assisting Iraq and Iran to develop their own missile programs, China assisting Iran's missile industry, etc.? Networks can also channel dangerous technology to one's enemies. Missile technology from China may have flowed through Israel to Taiwan, for example. Hua describes how Israeli guidance technology transferred to China during the mid-1980s reportedly was applied to the DF-3 missiles China sold to Saudi Arabia. Those missiles now threaten Israel.

As Scott Tollefson (Argentina) writes, moreover, these networks tend to be politically fragile. If the partner providing the money or a critical technology withdraws, the project will collapse, or be seriously retarded.

Illegal and Black Market Transactions

Even where all parts of a government are sincerely adhering to MTCR, missile technology exporting persons and organizations—including government-owned industrial enterprises—may simply be beyond control. In the past decade there have been examples of the latter in Germany, China, and Italy.

Even where MTCR is fully enforced, Third-World missile-developing states can use illegal methods to get technologies. One important way to do this is to make illegal deals with private individuals or firms. The connivance of private firms such as CONSEN and IFAT in Switzerland, PDG in Germany, and Berta Consult in Austria was crucial to several Middle Eastern missile programs. The reevaluation of such deals after the 1991 Gulf War probably motivated Austria and Switzerland to adhere to MTCR, in 1991 and 1992, respectively (see Appendix A).

In addition to making illegal deals, it is also possible to divert legal shipments to illegal purposes once they are beyond the control of national authorities. Beyond that, there is theft, espionage, intimidation, and various other illegal methods. Mark Kagan (Iraq) and Joseph Bermudez (Egypt and Iran) show the importance of such methods.

Transactions: Conclusions

Technology transfers have become much more important than simple missile sales; they actually produce new missile producers. In particular, PRC and DPRK technology exports pose greater long-term dangers than the sale of missiles.[9] Iran and Iraq have become missile producers with Chinese and North Korean help; Egypt is now manufacturing short-range rockets with Chinese technology; and so forth. Aaron Karp writes that in late 1992, only North Korea still exported entire ballistic missiles.

Capabilities: Pattern Recognition

Our studies demonstrate that proliferating Third-World states must develop certain crucial technologies, and that development often takes similar paths. Learning to identify such patterns is vital to non-proliferation enforcement efforts. Our authors suggest certain patterns: Rogue banking institutions such as the Bank of Credit and Commerce International (BCCI) and the Banca Nazionale del Lavoro are likely to be involved, as are shadowy holding companies such as IFAT and CONSEN. However, we should not assume that in the future they will necessarily look like BCCI or IFAT. Rather, it is the very nature of such organizations to be created, used, and then discarded or mutated.

The same is true of technological development. I believe Karp overstates the case in saying that "the nature of missile technology itself...dictates a narrow path of development with few options for its acquisition. This made it possible to make sense of national programs almost as quickly as they were identified." Too strong an assumption about a "narrow path of development" can lead to the classic intelligence analyst's pitfall of "mirror imaging." Countries developing ballistic missiles in the 1980s and 1990s have not followed the same pathways that Germany, the Soviet Union and the United States followed in the 1940s, 1950s, and 1960s. It is true that the same general classes of problems must be solved—propulsion, guidance, reentry, fusing, etc.—but they do not have to be solved in the same old ways.[10]

On the contrary, there are important advantages to being a latecomer to the field of missile development. A latecomer can take advantage of now well-established technologies which were not available—were not even dreamed of—when the Germans, Russians and the Americans were developing their first long-range missiles. New technologies like high-energy solid fuels, solid-state electronics, computerized control systems, and fiber optics are important examples. It is worth remembering how limited and primitive German telemetry was when they developed the V-2 at Peenemünde during World War II. They would fire a rocket, film its flight, and then try to figure out what had happened, based on little more than film, the dictated observations of engineers watching through telescopes, and perhaps inspection of the wreckage.[11] Telemetry technology has come a long way since then. Not only are radar and photography vastly improved, but such technologies as low-light television, infrared, and lasers are now widely available.

The availability of established modern technologies has made it possible for newcomers to the rocketry field to advance much faster, skipping some stages altogether. Therefore it is not a good idea to be watching for the same development sequences. The Russians and the Americans had to develop high-temperature materials, such as carbon-carbon, which newcomers to the field now merely have to steal. Several of our authors have pointed out carbon-carbon smuggling as a fairly common feature of Third World missile programs.

All rockets were solid-fueled (mainly by gunpowder) for some five centuries. In the 1930s, the Germans and others undertook liquid-fueled rocket development out of their conviction that solid fuels would not have sufficient energy content to lift heavy loads.[12] All the early American and Soviet space launch vehicles were modified liquid-fueled military rockets. Yet, as Gerald Steinberg writes, the first Israeli satellite was launched by a modified *Jericho II*, which has solid fuel. Israel took advantage of being a latecomer to skip big liquid-fueled engines.

Even modest contemporary computers make it possible to avoid much bench and flight testing by means of modeling and simulation. David Kay, formerly of the UN Special Commission on Iraq (UNSCOM), recently pointed out that more computing power is available in today's ordinary lap-top computers than was available in the biggest mainframes extant in the 1950s and early 1960s when most of today's nuclear weapons and big ICBMs were being designed.[13]

It follows that the lists of controlled items and technologies maintained by MTCR states need to be based on what Third-World proliferators actually need for missile and nuclear developments—not what the United States and the Soviet Union needed decades ago. Today's proliferator is engaged in a significantly different enterprise.

One fairly certain marker of a developing missile program is large-scale civil engineering projects. In every case covered in this book, large construction projects, generally in out-of-the-way places, have been a feature of long-range missile projects. However, "national technical means" such as reconnaissance satellites cannot be relied upon to identify the *purposes* of installations. In the 1990s, a rocket project may not look the way one looked in the 1940s and 1950s, or even in the 1970s. Again, technologies have advanced significantly, so newcomers will not necessarily build installations that look the same. Construction of fairly extensive installations, however, is a pattern to watch for.

Missile proliferators are not necessarily interested in advanced technologies. They are willing to use "primitive" technologies which are "good enough." Blueprints for the German V-2 rocket are readily available (e.g., at the Imperial War Museum in London). The SCUD is not much more than a V-2, but is good enough for a Third-World state that wants to terrorize or deter its neighbors. The Smithsonian Institution offers some 500 reels of microfilm containing detailed plans for the American *Jupiter* IRBM—roughly contemporary with the the first SCUD.[14] Several marvelous examples of "good-enough technology" were discovered by a team of *Aviation Week and Space Technology* writers during a visit to China in 1987. The most striking example of "primitive" technology was the use of oak as a heat shield material for reentry vehicles. This is striking in view of the millions of dollars spent in the West and the Soviet bloc over several decades on sophisticated ablative shielding materials. Chinese engineers told their visitors that, although they had done research on such high-tech materials, they simply found that, for the reentry vehicles they had been using, a thick layer of oak seemed to work just as well to char and dissipate the heat of reentry.[15]

An absolute necessity for a missile program is managerial skill. In fact, David Kay believes it is the single most important resource requirement. In every case study in this book, a few top-notch managers—Ghazala and El-Gohary in Egypt; Salim Mehmud and Abdul Qadeer Khan in Pakistan; Safa al-Habubi and "the two Amers" in Iraq; Qian Xuesen in China; Kapur, Kalam, and Arunachalam in India—have pulled together the resources to assemble the "military," "civilian" and "dual-use" components to make a rocket. According to Kay, the second most important people for developing a Third-World rocket (or nuclear weapon) are engineers and technicians—the problem solvers and the doers. Significantly, "rocket scientists" and theoretical physicists are *not* particularly important. They were central to the German, Soviet, and American programs, and continue to be vital to anyone building a sophisticated state-of-the-art missile. To a developing country building a "good-enough" weapon system, however, they are of secondary importance. With the partial exceptions of Israel and China, the states in this book generally have not been interested in state-of-the-art rocketry.

Most of the established technologies which latecomers can use are readily available. The Iraqi nuclear and missile programs pulled together information that was available from every database , computer network, and university graduate program in the Western world and the Soviet bloc. Technology leaks across borders with ever-increasing ease, as a result of the revolution in electronic communications. Today, espionage can be conducted with a personal computer and a modem. The "cloak and dagger" spy to some degree can be replaced by a computer hacker sitting in a safe comfortable office in his homeland.[16]

The research cut-off for the papers in this book varied, but was no later than December 1992 in any case. Accordingly, the breakup of the Soviet Union did not affect the developments covered by our authors, although it is is likely to become increasingly important. Dismantling and destroying Soviet rockets and nuclear weapons, under various arms control and reduction agreements, will be time-consuming and expensive at best. Meanwhile, crime and corruption are rife in the former Soviet republics. The most widely publicized danger is that world-class scientists will be hired by proliferating states. However, top scientists are few, easily watched, and easily bought off by their own (or MTCR) governments. Moreover, as noted above, they are somewhat irrelevant. The truly grave danger is that engineers, technicians, and machinists will be hired away. The Russian Ministry of Security has already prevented two groups of missile "scientists and engineers" (18 of them in December 1992; 32 more in February 1993) from going to work in North Korea. "Despite these successes, Security Ministry officials say they have little idea of how many Russian scientists and engineers have actually gone to North Korea."[17] Perhaps the most dangerous people of all are the thousands of faceless Russian, Ukrainian, and Kazakh security guards, shivering in the cold while they worry about their hungry families. It may be a matter of only a few rubles to bribe them to give up whatever it is they are supposed to be protecting.

A pattern we should certainly watch for is the large-scale hiring of engineers and technicians, but they need not come from the former Soviet Union or even from industrialized states. The Gulf War of 1991, for example, presumably rendered jobless, at least temporarily, technicians and engineers from Iraq. As Kagan points out, they may be available to work elsewhere. Nevertheless, the studies in this book indicate that expatriate engineers and technical personnel, while they may be important, are only part of the story. We should not underestimate the capacity of foreign-trained citizens, not only to be technicians and engineers, but also to be the managers. In all the cases in this book, the individuals *managing* the missile programs have been citizens of the countries in question.

Developing rockets is one thing; developing accuracy is another.[18] Karp writes, "[O]n balance, conventionally armed [current] missiles are mostly political weapons, but their military effect cannot be disregarded." He shows the very limited effect of conventionally armed missiles in war so far. But what if new techniques become available to make ballistic missiles with high-explosive warheads really accurate? Technology such as laser designators, infrared and radar homing, and various kinds of target beacons might be developed. Also, what is the future of missile defense technologies? Again, we cannot assume a straight-line development of current technologies based on past experience. Primitive offensive missiles in the Third World do not mean that Third-World states will neglect missile defense technologies. The Chinese are known to be working on the latter, as is Israel with the *Arrow* project.

Nuclear warheads are widely perceived as an alternative to accuracy. "Long-range missiles generally must carry weapons of mass destruction to be reasonably certain of hitting targets."[19] So missile and nuclear weapons programs tend to be synergistic, and to be indicators of each other. "Most of the regional powers with ballistic missile development programs also rank high on most lists of potential nuclear proliferators."

Cruise missiles may soon offer another alternative to the inaccuracy of ballistic missiles. In the next few years it may become possible to modify existing naval anti-ship cruise missiles to seek out land targets. Hitherto, that was vastly more difficult than seeking a ship on the ocean's surface, because it depended on sophisticated digital mapping, terrain recognition, and terrain-following technologies. In recent years, however, small Global-Positioning Satellite (GPS) terminals have become commercially available. "Off-the -shelf" GPS terminals with accuracies of 30 meters offer much better accuracy than the CEP of any version of the SCUD.[20] The bad news is that cruise missile technology is "easier to master and more readily available" than ballistic missile technology.[21] Conceivably, many of the the numerous states with Soviet STYX, Chinese SILKWORM, US *Harpoon*, or French *Exocet* anti-ship cruise missiles may be able to convert them to relatively accurate land-attack cruise missiles. The good news is that possession of an accurate cruise missile might make nuclear warheads seem less necessary to a Third World regime, just as they seem to be doing for the United States.

Norms

The Legitimacy of MTCR

MTCR has provoked friction among various states, although that can be said about any number of generally praiseworthy international regimes. Cameron Binkley (Pakistan) notes that MTCR has unquestionably worked to the advantage of states outside MTCR which have managed to become suppliers—notably North Korea and (at least until recently) China. Moreover, Mack has argued that if proliferation continues, potential suppliers will increase; making it still harder to restrict supply. That in turn could increase the economic incentives for MTCR member states to quit.[22]

On the other hand, Karp points out that MTCR did not motivate the first cases of missile technology networking. Rather, "pooling of technology among missile proliferators" began as a reaction to the expense and complexity of the technology itself.

Hua and Steinberg both make the familiar argument that since it is warheads, not delivery systems, that cause the grave damage in warfare, it should be warheads rather than delivery systems that are subject to international controls. Hua asks the reasonable question, raised earlier by Uzi Rubin, as to why missiles are under an international control regime while high-performance aircraft are not.[23]

Kagan offers some convincing answers. He points out first that while aircraft are also delivery systems, they have major disadvantages vis à vis missiles. First, pilots need lots of training, skill, and courage to bomb accurately, whereas "missile accuracy [is] a technical problem to be solved with time, money, and technology." Second, defenses against aircraft are much more likely to work than current or prospective anti-ballistic missile (ABM) defenses. Third, the loss of a missile to defenses or to malfunction is more *economically* acceptable than the loss of a much more expensive aircraft and its human pilot. A fourth reason that missiles are more dangerous is that the infrastructure to operate a modern air force is far more complex, expensive, and easily detected than for a missile force. A-4 and F-5 fighter-bombers of the 1970s cost US$4-8 million each, whereas today's F-16, F/A-18, or *Tornado* fighter-bombers cost US$22-40 million apiece. To that, add several million dollars a year in training costs per squadron—"compared to the almost trivial cost of maintaining a ballistic missile battalion."[24] Moreover, training missile crews takes a good deal less time than pilot training. The entire logistical complex required by modern aircraft— everything from airfield maintenance to the myriad spare parts and supplies—is vastly more complex and expensive than for missiles.

Fifth, Third-World states can achieve self-sufficiency in manufacturing surface-to-surface missiles. By contrast, only a diminishing number of even the world's established aviation industries (France, Sweden, USA; possibly Italy, Japan, Russia, and UK) remain capable of designing and manufacturing—let alone financing—"domestic" state-of-the-art warplanes. Multinational projects like the NATO "Eurofighter 2000," Panavia *Tornado*, and Japanese-American FS-X are increasingly common. The Israeli *Lavi* and the Indian LCA both failed badly in the 1980s. Since the jet age began, Taiwan's still unproven *Ching-kuo* Indigenous Defense Fighter is the closest any newly-industrialized country has come to domestically producing a state-of-the-art combat aircraft.

Finally, missiles—especially domestically manufactured ones—are more dangerous than aircraft because of perception. Missiles may encourage a government to act aggressively, feeling that it is significantly less vulnerable and more potent than its prospective enemies.

Perhaps the Gulf War of 1991 provided the most eloquent answers to the question "Why single out missiles for control?" Iraq's expensive and much-touted air force was an embarrassing failure, neutralized with apparent ease in the first hours of the air war. By contrast, the Iraqi SCUD force was effective—politically and militarily—out of all proportion to Bagdad's investment. Coalition air forces, under mounting political pressure, devoted an ever-increasing percentage of their sorties to stopping the SCUD attacks. Destroying them was simple enough, but *finding* them—even with the vast panoply of American and NATO reconnaissance and surveillance systems—was never completed. To this day, even with UNSCOM on the ground, we do not know how many ballistic missiles or launchers Saddam Husayn had then, or has now.

Uzi Rubin has argued that "smart" stand-off air-to-surface missiles (ASMs) give an airborne attacker the best of both worlds, combining an airplane's flexibility and responsiveness with a missile's relative immunity to air defenses.[25] His point is well taken. The reasonable conclusion, however, is that ASM technologies also ought to be subject to MTCR—which some are—and that SSM development should be prevented not only for its inherent danger, but also because it is a technical precursor to ASM development.

Hua's, Rubin's, and Steinberg's position rightly emphasizes another important point: Warheads and reentry vehicles are the only major components of military missiles which are unique. Everything else may just as well be part of a peaceful space-launch vehicle. It follows that the tightest controls ought to focus on terminal guidance; penetration aids; heat shields and heat sinks; and warhead fusing, safing, arming and firing technologies.

Attitudes toward the MTCR seem to be evolving in a favorable direction and MTCR itself seems to be gaining a certain degree of international legitimacy. As Karp points out, today only North Korea still overtly exports entire ballistic missile systems which are beyond MTCR thresholds. Even those countries which have been outspokenly opposed to MTCR have acknowledged at least that it might be a good idea under some circumstances, or have tacitly acknowledged a widespread sentiment favoring MTCR. McCarthy notes that India seems to be implicitly observing MTCR export curbs. Hayes reports an extreme example: In April 1992 North Korean Deputy Prime Minister and Foreign Minister Kim Yong Nam told American visitors that Pyongyang might be willing to associate itself with MTCR at some point in the future. While this seems unlikely, the fact that the statement was made indicates that even North Korea recognizes the Regime's legitimacy.

The *Condor II* case frequently is cited as the MTCR's greatest success, but the situation was unique. Its very success points to the difficulties of making MTCR work widely and effectively. True, American pressure helped motivate Argentina to comply with MTCR and to civilianize its rocketry program. However, President Alfonsín's *modus vivendi* with Argentina's only plausible foreign threats—the UK, Chile, and Brazil—made civilianization of the program possible. This illustrates a point made by several of our authors: Most countries that want operational missile forces want them to meet plausible security threats. As Binkley writes, MTCR does nothing to directly assuage security concerns. Ultimately, it will only succeed if accompanied by efforts at conflict resolution, confidence building, and/or security guarantees.

The overwhelmingly important factors in the demise of *Condor II* had nothing to do with MTCR at all. The *Condor II* program was abandoned and the entire rocketry program was civilianized owing to the fall of Argentina's military government. That, in turn, was a result of the Falklands/Malvinas War of 1982 which discredited the military government and all its works. *Indeed, civil-military relations is at least an implicit theme in every country study in this book.*

Moreover, Tollefson characterizes the *Condor II* program as a "political, economic, and technological enclave" in Argentina. It was politically independent from government control, economically separate from the overall Argentine economy, and technologically unrelated to any other Argentine scientific or technical endeavors. Until recently, at least, a somewhat similar "enclave" seems to have existed in Pakistan. In both countries, for a while, the military succeeded in keeping missile and nuclear weapons programs secret from their own governments. It was much easier for the Menom government to kill the Argentine military missile program because it was an "enclave." Terminating it did little damage to the civilian economy or to civilian scientific and technical programs. The political will to kill the program and deprive the military of it was strong under the civilian government, as was the motivation to exert tighter political control in an area where the military had been a law unto itself. Unfortunately, all this had little to do with the inherent effectiveness of MTCR. In fact, notwithstanding all the above factors, the MTCR is widely resented by soldiers and civilians alike in Argentina (and Brazil), where it is regarded as a tool of the United States rather than an international regime.

Globally, implementation of MTCR guidelines by its members may have become somewhat more rigorous in the aftermath of the Persian Gulf War of 1991, but that remains to be seen. It also remains to be seen how stringently China, Russia, and a potential new supplier—Ukraine—will observe the guidelines. There also is the "grandfathering" problem: Should existing deals be cancelled or allowed to run their course? Two important cases at issue, as this book goes to press, are reported Chinese sales of technology and missiles to Syria (the M-9) and Pakistan (the M-11).

In 1992, China and Russia announced they would comply with MTCR, but have not formally acceded to it. In 1992 the Russian government adopted domestic controls of exports which are similar in many respects to the MTCR guidelines. In February 1992, Beijing provided a written adherence commitment to the U.S. Government, but has made no such commitment to other member governments (see Appendix A). Actually, this makes Chinese and Russian *obligations* little different from those of the formal signatories, since MTCR lacks organizational mechanisms. The MTCR is neither a treaty nor even a formal international agreement. According to Richard Speier, one of the US government's leading experts who was one of the shapers of the MTCR, "It is rather a set of identical policies announced by...governments, to be implemented in parallel." It is administered by adhering governments on a decentralized basis. It has no bureaucracy or enforcement mechanism of its own, beyond political pressure and international opinion. "International opposition will force governments undertaking [missile programs] to sacrifice other objectives that depend on international goodwill."[26] As noted earlier, however, the dangerous pariahs are the governments least interested in "international goodwill."

According to Speier, "the seven original adhering nations felt strongly that the MTCR should not create a new international bureaucracy."[27] The only MTCR "organization" is its "Secretariat," which the French government operates voluntarily. Its only apparent function is to organize the occasional meetings of the MTCR Policy Group and Technical Working Group (see Appendix B). It prepares—but never publishes—the minutes of these meetings. It will not even divulge how many personnel are in the "Secretariat."[28]

The MTCR is only as effective as the political will and domestic implementing mechanisms enacted and enforced by individual governments. Currently, India's formal export laws are wide open and "non-discriminatory;" restrictive and responsible controls are imposed through "case-by-case" informal political review. Sensative exports are controlled because they are few. However, McCarthy writes, "With increased private production of sensitive items, 'informal' controls may be overwhelmed—it will be nearly impossible for each sensitive item to be approved or disapproved by the Cabinet. Export controls will then be left to 'formal' export control authorities..." which are extremely permissive.

Gasparini's detailed description of Brazilian laws, regulations, procedures, and licensing illuminates the effort involved in setting up a formal system, as well as some of the problems of that approach. Under current regulations, only the President and the military have any voice in Brazilian arms export decisions, and may be the only ones to even know about a proposed transaction. For a variety of reasons, regulations might be ignored. Hence, the demand for Congressional involvement in the Brazilian system.

Once enacted, regulations and procedures must be enforced. Even with more decision makers and openness, enforcement failure may stem from simple inattention or from conflicting organizational agendas. While a foreign ministry may be sincere about MTCR, other parts of the same government—particularly foreign trade, military, and/or scientific bureaucracies—may work actively against it. Our authors have documented cases of this in countries as diverse as China and the United States.[29] In his study of Iraq, Kagan describes such cases in several MTCR charter member states.

MTCR and similar "supply-side" measures probably cannot prevent a given state from developing a missile capability if it can tap into the existing networks of Third-World missile states. But it does significantly slow the process and make it much more expensive. As Kagan writes, covert acquisition, almost by definition, is expensive. While some would argue that any delay is a good thing, others argue that MTCR simply burdens the Third World—increasing the cost of national defense.

Because "supply-side" measures do not address the national security threats that often prompt missile programs, Findlay and Mack suggest "demand-side" measures. There is no reason in principle, they write, why the major industrial powers cannot cooperate in "joint diplomatic efforts, beyond the MTCR, to curb missile proliferation." Such efforts should go beyond "supply-side" controls and start to encourage confidence and security building measures.[30]

Janne Nolan probably deserves the last word on the nature and effectiveness of MTCR:

> In the current international political environment, an effort to broaden the MTCR into an international treaty seems quixotic, at best. It would founder on objections by developing countries about its discriminatory nature, and on the difficulties of making the case that ballistic missiles are worthy of universal controls even though other delivery vehicles, including non-ballistic missiles and aircraft, are not. To the degree that the MTCR has been successful, in fact, its success has derived from the regime's modest and consensual nature, and from the fact that it was negotiated out of the glare of the international spotlight. [page 291]

Space Programs

The missile proliferation dilemma is exacerbated by the universally acknowledged right of states to peacefully develop and exploit space technology. Although some reentry vehicles and warhead technologies are uniquely military, missile and space technologies overlap considerably. Even "peaceful" space activities can be exploited to intimidate one's enemies. In 1981, for example, a single Chinese rocket orbited three satellites. The next day, a communist newspaper in Hong Kong pointed out (in case anyone had overlooked it) that this meant China was on the way to developing a multiple independently targeted re-entry vehicle (MIRV).[31] It is probably impossible to maintain *technical* divisions between military and non-military rocketry, even in countries where a bureaucratic boundary is maintained between the military and space programs (e.g., India and the US). In China, the US, the former USSR, and almost everywhere else, the military has been deeply involved in national space programs. Japan is perhaps the only significant exception. Good examples of how national space programs can be kept organizationally peaceful and civilian are Argentina since 1991 and Japan. Another organizational means is to internationalize space activities, as has been done by the European Space Agency.

The MTCR's "drafters were careful to focus its controls on large missiles and rockets but to permit continued international cooperation in the peaceful uses of space (that is, satellites and the information they handle, as opposed to launch vehicles)...." Nevertheless, the MTCR "makes no exceptions for so-called peaceful vehicles,"[32] and the regime has hampered some peaceful space efforts. Gasparini shows it especially clearly in the Brazilian case. With some justification, Brazilians, Chinese, and others suspect MTCR of being used by Americans and Western Europeans to freeze them out of commercial space activities.

Conclusion

This concluding essay has tended to represent the missile technology proliferation glass as half empty whereas, in Chapter I, Aaron Karp represents it as half full. Karp emphasizes the inherent difficulty of the technology itself; and that, thus far, most Third World missile proliferation has involved copying and modifying the Soviet SCUD, which is a relatively primitive rocket. I have emphasized that the SCUD is good enough for a Third-World state that wants to terrorize or deter its neighbors, and that its technology is already widely disseminated though Third World international suppliers' networks. Only a few of our studies depict the proliferation of missile technology that is a generation or more beyond the SCUD—possibly India; certainly Israel and the PRC.

It seems to me that Karp and I are both right. The SCUD genie is probably out of the bottle, but there are distinct limits to how much the SCUD can be modified and improved. Better guidance systems, smaller warheads, and more stages can do only so much. Internationally, it may well be possible to hold the line at the next level of technology, provided all the current MTCR members, plus (at least) China, India, Israel, Russia, and Ukraine adhere to the regime's provisions. In terms of the sophistication of their missiles, none of these is really a "Third World" state at all. China likes to style itself as a "Third World" country, and surely is in many respects, but it is part of the "First World" of rocketry. According to Hua Di, "To enhance the [M-9's] accuracy and penetration capability, a miniature propulsion system is applied on the warhead to adjust its terminal velocity and reentry attitude and to change its flight trajectory and range." If that is true, the Chinese "M-family" missiles pose the most immediate threat of technology proliferation beyond the SCUD to a vastly more sophisticated and dangerous weapon system.

As Janne Nolan intimates in the above quotation, the most promising way ahead for MTCR is probably to widen its membership, rather than attempt to broaden either its formal status or technological scope. At the same time, further missile disarmament initiatives among the major powers, such as the Strategic Arms Reduction Treaties (START I and START II); and the inclusion of China, France and the UK in "START III" talks would at least move toward meeting the objection of India, Argentina, *et al.* that

MTCR embodies a strategic double standard. That perception would at least be alleviated as additional classes of the major powers' missiles followed INF weapons into museums and scrap heaps. As several of our authors suggest, missile disarmament could be facilitated by converting military missiles into space launchers, and by offering space launch services at nominal fees to states without big rockets of their own.

While missile proliferation is surely more dangerous than attack aircraft proliferation, Hua and Steinberg are quite right to raise the latter as part of the global arms proliferation problem. Non-proliferation efforts need to advance on a broad technological front—nuclear, biological, and chemical weapons; attack aircraft; and missiles—because each sort of non-proliferation is somewhat dependent on others. Different systems are seen as militarily compensating for a lack of others: One reason Israel resisted acceding to MTCR was that there are no controls on Arab attack aircraft. Conversely, Libya, Iraq, Egypt, Syria, and Jordan refused to sign the Chemical Warfare Convention (CWC) of January 1993 because Israel has not signed the NPT.

If there is a single pre-eminent non-proliferation issue, it is nuclear weapons. The notion that chemical weapons provide a "poor man's weapon of mass destruction" has been fairly convincingly disabused,[33] and the BWC and CWC provide real hope of a global ban on biological and chemical weaponry. Without a precision that the SCUD design simply cannot achieve, the military utility of ballistic missiles will remain questionable in the absence of nuclear warheads. As that fact becomes more widely appreciated, the utility of missiles as terror weapons may also diminish somewhat; which in turn could render long-range missile development less worth the effort and expense. Thus, nuclear non-proliferation is more important than ever. For more data and studies on that subject, the reader is referred to other publications of MIIS's Program in Nonproliferation Studies.[34]

Notes

1. Quoted by Andrew Mack, in "Beyond MTCR: Additional Responses to the Missile Proliferation Problem," in Trevor Findlay, ed. *Chemical Weapons and Missile Proliferation: With Implications for the Asia/Pacific Region*. Lynne Rienner, 1991, p. 126.

2. Richard H. Speier, "The Missile Technology Control Regime," in Trevor Findlay, ed. *Chemical Weapons and Missile Proliferation: With Implications for the Asia/ Pacific Region*. Lynne Rienner, 1991, p. 117.

3. Andrew Mack, "Beyond MTCR," p. 127.

4. Andrew Mack, "Missile Proliferation in the Asia/Pacific Region," in Trevor Findlay, ed. *Chemical Weapons and Missile Proliferation: With Implications for the Asia/ Pacific Region*. Lynne Rienner, 1991, p. 43.

5. Leonard S. Spector, "China's Nuclear Factor," *Christian Science Monitor*, 11 June 1993, p. 18.

6. On 28 May 1993, in extending MFN for one year, President Clinton did not make missile proliferation a criterian for renewal, although he implied a strong connection of MFN to the M-11 issue: "We have made our concerns on the M-11 issue known to the Chinese on numerous occasions. They understand the serious consequences of missile transfers under U.S. sanctions law. If we determine that China has, in fact, transferred M-11 missiles or related equipment in violation of its commitments, my Administration will not hesitate to act." *Statement by the President On Most Favored Nation Status for China,* (28 May, 1993) Transmitted: 93-05-29 17:38:23 EDT.

7. Hua Di, "China's Arms Proliferation in Perspective: Prospects for Change Due to Economic Reforms," in W. Thomas Wander and Eric H. Arnett, eds. *The Proliferation of Advanced Weaponry: Technology, Motivations, and Responses*. American Association for the Advancement of Science, 1992, pp. 123–134.

8. Andrew Mack makes a similar argument in "Beyond MTCR," p. 126.

9. For documentation of this in the PRC case, see Timothy V. McCarthy. *A Chronology of PRC Missile Trade and Developments.* Monterey, California: International Missile Proliferation Project, Monterey Institute of International Studies, February 1992.

10. Two recent, excellent studies on this subject are: *Short-Range Ballistic Missiles (SRBM) Infrastructure Requirements for Third World Countries.* Arnold Engineering Development Center, Arnold AFB, TN: Air Force Systems Command, September 1991; and Steven M. Flank, "Reconstructing Rockets: The Politics of Developing Military Technology in Brazil, India, and Israel," Ph.D Dissertation, MIT, June 1993.

11. Walter Dornberger, *V-2: The Nazi Rocket Weapon.* Ballantine Books, 1954, chapter 13.

12. Walter Dornberger, *V-2.* p. 26.

13. David Kay, Symposium at the International Missile Proliferation Project, Monterey Institute of International Studies, 9 February 1993.

14. Happily, the Smithsonian data omits details on heat-shielding and guidance. Peter Zimmerman, "Bronze Metal Technology: A Successful Route to Nuclear and Missile Proliferation," *Orbis,* Winter 1994, forthcoming.

15. Craig Covault, "Chinese Facility Combines Capabilities to Produce Long March Boosters, ICBMs," *Aviation Week and Space Technology,* 27 July 1987, pp. 52-53.

16. David Kay, Symposium.

17. "Dangerous Work," *Far Eastern Economic Review,* 13 May 1993, p. 9.

18. Donald MacKenzie. *Inventing Accuracy: A Historical Sociology of Nuclear Missile Guidance.* MIT Press, 1990.

19. Both quotations in this paragraph are from Aaron Karp, "The Impact of Ballistic Missile Proliferation in the Asia/Pacific Region," in Trevor Findlay, ed. *Chemical Weapons and Missile Proliferation: With Implications for the Asia/Pacific Region.* Lynne Rienner, 1991, pp. 54–55.

20. Andrew Mack, "Missile Proliferation in the Asia/Pacific Region," pp. 45–46.

21. W. Seth Carus, "Missile Proliferation in the Third World," Hearings, US Senate Armed Services Committee Subcommittee on Defense Industry and Technology, US Government Printing Office, 21 May 1989, pp. 6ff., quoted by Andrew Mack, "Missile Proliferation in the Asia/Pacific Region," p. 45.

22. Andrew Mack, "Beyond MTCR," p. 124.

23. Uzi Rubin, "Iraq and the Ballistic Missile Scare" *The Bulletin of the Atomic Scientists*, October 1990, pp. 11–13; and Uzi Rubin, "How Much Does Missile Proliferation Matter?" *Orbis*, Winter 1991, pp. 29–39.

24. Aaron Karp, "The Impact of Ballistic Missile Proliferation," p. 60.

25. Uzi Rubin, "Iraq and the Ballistic Missile Scare" p. 13.

26. Richard H. Speier, "The Missile Technology Control Regime,"pp. 115–116, and 119.

27. Richard H. Speier, "The Missile Technology Control Regime," p. 116.

28. I am grateful to Deborah Ozga of the International Missile Proliferation Project at the Monterey Institute of International Studies for this information. Private discussion, 26 May 1993.

29. See Edward J. Laurance, "Political Implications of Illegal Arms Exports from the United States," *Political Science Quarterly*, 107, no. 3 (Fall 1992), 501–533.

30. Trevor Findlay and Andrew Mack, "Multiple Responses to an Evolving Problem," in Trevor Findlay, ed. *Chemical Weapons and Missile Proliferation: With Implications for the Asia/Pacific Region*. Lynne Rienner, 1991, pp. 137–138.

31. *Ta Kung Pao*, 21 September 1981, p. 1

32. Richard H. Speier, "The Missile Technology Control Regime," p. 117.

33. See especially the three chapters by Peter Dunn, Charles C. Flowrree, and Julian Perry Robinson in Part One of Trevor Findlay, ed. *Chemical Weapons and Missile Proliferation: With Implications for the Asia/Pacific Region*. Lynne Rienner, 1991, pp. 3-35.

34. See William C. Potter, ed. *International Nuclear Trade and Nonproliferation: The Challenge of the Emerging Suppliers*. Lexington Books, 1990.

Appendix A: MTCR Member Countries*
(as of April 1993)

A. Original Members (1987)

1. Canada
2. Federal Republic of Germany
3. France
4. Italy
5. Japan
6. United Kingdom
7. United States

B. Acceding Members (Formal)

8. Spain .... (12/89)
9. Belgium .... (04/25/90)
10. Luxembourg .... (04/25/90)
11. Netherlands .... (05/22/90)
12. Australia .... (07/90)
13. Denmark .... (11/15/90)
14. Norway .... (01/01/91)
15. New Zealand .... (01/29/91)
16. Austria .... (03/91)
17. Sweden .... (09/05/91)
18. Finland .... (11/04/91)
19. Portugal .... (before 07/92)
20. Switzerland .... (02/17/92)
21. Ireland .... (07/02/92)
22. Greece .... (before 07/92)
23. Iceland .... (02/23/93)
24. Argentina .... (03/11/93, but membership not finalized)
25. Hungary .... (03/11/93, but membership not finalized)

*Data prepared by Deborah Ozga (International Missile Proliferation Project at the Monterey Institute of International Studies); May 1993.

C. "Adherents"

Soviet Union ....(06/90 agrees to adhere; ceases to exist 31/12/91)
Israel ....(01/01/92 becomes official adherent and applies for membership)
China (PRC) ....(02/01/92 provides an adherence commitment in writing to the U.S. Government; not recognized by other members)
Russia ....(01/92 President Yeltsin verbally announces Russia will adhere to MTCR)
Brazil ....(02/92 expresses interest in participation)
Romania ....(1993 applies for membership)

Appendix B: MTCR Meetings*

A. Policy Group

1. 8–9 September 1988, Rome, Italy.
2. 5–6 December 1989, London, England
3. 18–20 July 1990, Ottawa, Canada.
4. 19–20 March 1991, Tokyo, Japan.
5. 1 November 1991, Washington, DC, USA.
6. 29 June–2 July 1992, Oslo, Norway.
7. 8–11 March 1993, Canberra, Australia.
8. End of 1993 (scheduled), Interlaken, Switzerland.

B. Technical Working Group

1. January 1991, Federal Republic of Germany.
2. 18 March 1991, Federal Republic of Germany.
3. May 1991, Paris, France.
4. Early 1992, Rome, Italy.

C. Special

1. 1987–1989?, European meeting for non-European MTCR participants.
2. 1992?, Warsaw, Poland, for newly democratized Eastern European states.

*Data prepared by Deborah Ozga (International Missile Proliferation Project at the Monterey Institute of International Studies); May 1993.

Appendix C: Glossary and List of Acronyms

AAM .... Air-to-Air Missile
ABD .... Arab British Dynamics Company (Egypt)
ABM .... Anti-Ballistic Missile
ACME .... Arms Control in the Middle East negotiations
ADA .... Air Defense Artillery
AOI .... Arab Organization for Industrialization (Egypt)
APD .... Arab Projects and Developments (Lebanon)
ARDE .... Armament Research and Development Laboratory (India)
ASAT .... Anti-Satellite
ASIANDEX .... Asian Defense Exhibition, 1986 and 1988 (PRC)
ASLV .... Augmented Satellite Launch Vehicle (India)
ASM .... Air-to-Surface Missile
ASTROS .... Artillery Saturation Rocket System (Brazil)
ATBM .... Anti-Tactical Ballistic Missile
AV-LMU .... Universal Multiple Launcher (Brazil)
AVIBRAS .... AVIBRAS Indústria Aeroespacial S.A.(Brazil)
BAe .... British Aerospace Ltd. (UK)
BALCO .... Bharat Aluminum Company (India)
BCCI .... Bank of Credit and Commerce International
BDL .... Bharat Dynamics Ltd. (India)
BEL .... Bharat Electronics, Ltd. (India)
Berta Consult .... Consulting and management firm (Austria)
BM .... Ballistic Missile
BMD .... Ballistic Missile Defense
BME .... Ballistic Missile Egypt Co.
BWC .... Biological Warfare Convention
BWYIC .... Beijing Wan Yuan Industry Corporation (PRC)
CACEX .... Carteira de Comércio do Banco do Brasil (Brazil)
CBERS .... China-Brazil Earth Resource Satellite
CDN .... Conselho de Defesa Nacional (Brazil)
CEP .... Circular Error Probable (the standard for measuring the accuracy of a ballistic missile: the radius of a circle within which 50 percent of warheads will strike)

CGWIC .... China Great Wall Industry Corporation (PRC)
CIA .... Central Intelligence Agency (USA)
CII .... Certificado Internacional de Importação (Brazil)
CINCPAC .... Commander-in-Chief, Pacific (USA)
CIS .... Commonwealth of Independent States
CMC .... Central Military Commission (PRC)
CNAE .... Comision Nacional de Actividades Espaciales (Argentina)
CNES .... Centre National d'Etudes Spatiales (France)
CNIE .... National Commission for Space Research (Argentina)
CoCom .... Coordinating Committee for Multilateral Export Controls
CONSEN S.A.M. .... Contracting group (Transtecno, Delta Consult, et al.) (Monaco and Switzerland)
Consultco .... Engineering company (Austria)
COPUOS .... UN Committee on the Peaceful Uses of Outer Space
COSTIND .... Commission on Science, Technology, and Industry for National Defense (PRC)
CPI .... Comissão Permanente Interministerial (Brazil)
CPMIEC .... China Precision Machinery Import-Export Corporation (PRC)
crore .... Unit of 10 million (India)
CTA .... Centro Técnico Aeroespacial (Brazil)
CVE .... Certificado de Verificação de Entrega (Brazil)
CWC .... Chemical Warfare Convention
Cyanox .... Anti-oxidant compound
DAT .... Code name for construction of *Condor II* facilities (Argentina)
DCE .... Departamento de Comércio Exterior (Brazil)
Delta Consult .... Subsidiary of CONSEN(Austria)
Delta System .... Subsidiary of CONSEN(Austria)
DIO .... Defense Industries Organization (Iran)
DOS .... Code name for construction of *Condor II* facilities (Egypt)
DOT .... Code name for construction of *Condor II* facilities (Iraq)
DPRK .... Democratic People's Republic of Korea
DRDL .... Defense Research and Development Laboratory (India)
DRDO .... Defence Research and Development Organization (India)
EMBRAER .... Empresa Brasileira de Aeronautica S.A. (Brazil)
ENGESA .... Engenheiros Especializados S.A. (Brazil)
Esca .... Engenharia de Sistemas de Controle de Automação (Brazil)
FAE .... Fuel-Air Explosive
FBIS .... Foreign Broadcast Information Service
FOG-MPM .... Fiber Optic Guided Multiple Purpose Missile (Brazil)
GCC .... Gulf Cooperation Council
GHz .... Gigahertz, Gigacycles, One billion cycles per second
GPS .... Global-Positioning Satellite
GSQR .... General Staff Qualitative Requirement (India)
HAL .... Hindustan Aeronautics, Ltd. (India)
HE .... High-Explosive

HOP ....Hugo de Oliveira Piva Company (Brazil)
IAE ....Instituto de Atividades Espaciais (Brazilian Air Force)
IAEA ....International Atomic Energy Agency
IAI ....Israeli Aircraft Industry
ICBM...........................Intercontinental Ballistic Missile
IDF ....Israel Defense Forces
IFAT Corp., Ltd. ....Financial management firm (Switzerland)
IGMDP ....Integrated Guided Missile Development Program (India)
IIAE ....Instituto de Investigaciónes Aeronáuticas y Espaciales (Argentina)
IMBEL.........................Indústria de Material Bélico do Brasil (Brazil)
IMI ....Israeli Missile Industy
IMP ....International Missile Proliferation Project of PNS
INF ....Intermediate Nuclear Forces
INSAT ....Communications satellite (USA)
INVAP ....Applied Research Institute (Argentina)
IPI ....Imposto sobre Produtos Industrializados (Brazil)
IRBM ....Intermediate Range Ballistic Missile
IRGC ....Islamic Revolution Guard Corps (Iran)
IRS ....Internal Revenue Service (USA)
ISA ....Israeli Space Agency
ISC Technologies .....International Signal & Control Technologies, U.S. subsidiary of Ferranti International
ISRO ....Indian Space Research Organization
ISTRAC ....ISRO Telemetry, Tracking and Command Network (India)
ITA ....Instituto Technológico da Aeronautica (Brazil)
ITR..............................Interim Test Range, Baliapal (India)
JATO ....Jet-Assisted Take-Off
JPRS ....*Joint Publications Research Service*
KRIA ....Korea Research Institute of Aerospace (ROK)
LANDSAT ....Unclassified photo-imagery satellite (USA)
LLMT ....Low Level Missile Target Drone
MAN ....Industrial firm (Federal Republic of Germany)
MBB ....Messerschmitt-Boelkow-Blohm (Federal Republic of Germany)
MECB ....Missão Espacial Completa Brasileira (Brazil)
MHz ....Megahertz, megacycles, one million cycles per second
MI5 ....British counter-intelligence agency
MIMI ....Ministry of Industry and Military Industrialization (Iraq)
MIRV ....Multiple Independently Targeted Re-entry Vehicle
MLRS ....Multiple-Launch Rocket System
MOD ....Ministry of Defense
MOST.........................Ministry of Science and Technology (ROK)
MRBM ....Medium-Range Ballistic Missile
MRL ....Multiple Rocket Launcher
MSI ....Ministry of Space Industry (PRC)
MTCR ....Missile Technology Control Regime

NASA .... National Aeronautics and Space Administration (USA)
NATO .... North Atlantic Treaty Organization
NBC .... Nuclear, Biological, and Chemical Weapons/Warfare
NOCIL .... National Organic Chemical Industries Limited (India)
NORINCO .... China North Industries Corporation (PRC)
NPT .... Nuclear Non-Proliferation Treaty
ORBITA .... ORBITA Sistemas Aeroespaciais S.A. (Brazil)
OTRAG .... Orbital Transport und Raketien AG (Federal Republic of Germany)
P-5 .... The five permanent members of the UN Security Council (China, France, UK, USA, and USSR/Russia)
Parcom .... Participações e Consultoria (Brazil)
PDG .... Industrial firm (Germany)
PLA .... People's Liberation Army (PRC)
PLO .... Palestine Liberation Organization
PNEMEM .... Politica Nacional de Exportação de Material de Emprego Militar (Brazil)
PNS .... Program in Nonproliferation Studies, Monterey Institute of International Studies
PRC .... People's Republic of China
PSLV .... Polar Satellite Launch Vehicle (India)
PSU .... Public Sector Undertaking (India)
PTA .... Pilotless Target Aircraft
R&D .... Research and Development
R-105 .... Regulamento para a Fiscalização de Produtos Controlados (Brazil)
Rafael .... National Weapons Development Authority (Israel)
RCI .... Research Centre, Immarat (India)
ROK .... Republic of Korea
ROKAADCOM .... Republic of Korea Army Air Defense Command
RPV .... Remotely-Piloted Vehicle
SAC .... Strategic Air Command (USA)
SAC-B .... Satellite Argentino Cientifico (Argentina)
SAE .... Secretaria de Assuntos Estratégicos da Presidência da República (Brazil)
Sagem .... Industrial firm (France)
SAM .... Surface-to-Air Missile
SDI .... Strategic Defense Initiative (USA)
SHAR .... Shriharikota test range (India)
SIBAT .... Ministry of Defense agency responsible for exporting arms and technology (Israel)
SIPRI .... Stockholm International Peace Research Institute (Sweden)
SLBM .... Submarine-Launched Ballistic Missile
SLV .... Satellite/Space Launch Vehicle
SNIA-BpD .... A subsidiary of the Fiat Corporation (Italy)
SNPE-CE .... Societe Nationale des Poudrers et Explosifs - Division Chimie Expansion (France)

SOTI ....State Organization for Technical Industries (Iraq)
SPL ....Solid State Physics Laboratory (India)
SPOT ....Commercial photo-imagery satellite (France)
SRBM ....Short-Range Ballistic Missile
SSM ....Surface-to-Surface Missile
START ....Strategic Arms Limitation Treaty/Talks
SUPARCO ....Space and Upper Atmosphere Research Commission (Pakistan)
Ta'as ....Israeli Military Industries
TDG ....Technology and Development Group (Iraq)
Technion ....Israeli Institute of Technology, Haifa
Teco ....Technical Corps for Special Projects (Iraq)
TEL ....Transporter-Erector-Launcher
TERLS ....Thumba Equatorial Rocket Launch Station (India)
UNSC ....United Nations Security Council
UNSCOM ....United Nations Special Commission on Iraq
VLS ....Veículo Lançador de Satélites (Brazil)
VSSC ....Vikram Sarabhai Space Center (India)

About the Book

The proliferation of nuclear weapons captures headlines and raises fear within the public, but the Byzantine world of the international missile trade is a much more established and widespread threat to peace and stability. In this informative book, the full extent and interconnections of missile technology networks are laid out for the first time as fourteen experts from six countries present analytical discussions about missile proliferation in the Third World. In detailed histories of eleven national missile programs, the authors identify individuals, organizations, and their international connections. Ironically, all of the missile programs are linked not only with each other but also with the programs of NATO and former Warsaw Pact states. Even the Israeli missile program is linked—through China, Western Europe, and the United States—with those of its enemies.

The chapters follow a common format. Each author examines missile technology transactions and capabilities, structures of trade (including legal provisions, if any), and the norms influencing each country's dealings in the international arena. The result is a clear, comprehensive, and sobering account of the complex network of missile proliferation.

Index

Other Publications of the MIIS Program for Nonproliferation Studies

Edward Laurance. *The International Arms Trade*. Lexington Books, 1992.
William C. Potter. *Nuclear Profiles of the Soviet Successor States*. Monterey Institute of International Studies, 1993.
Gary Gardener. *Nuclear Nonproliferation: A Primer*. Lynne Rienner Publishers, 1993.

For Product Safety Concerns and Information please contact our EU representative GPSR@taylorandfrancis.com
Taylor & Francis Verlag GmbH, Kaufingerstraße 24, 80331 München, Germany

www.ingramcontent.com/pod-product-compliance
Lightning Source LLC
LaVergne TN
LVHW011110300926
849160LV00008B/335
* 9 7 8 0 3 6 7 3 0 8 6 4 3 *